Community Youth Development

Programs, Policies, and Practices

This book is dedicated to youth, who are our present and our future,
who make a difference now and who will make a difference in the future.
May their undaunted enthusiasm for life continue to brighten
our homes, neighborhoods, communities, and world.

Community Youth Development

Programs, Policies, and Practices

Editors

Francisco A. Villarruel
Michigan State University

Daniel F. Perkins
Pennsylvania State University

Lynne M. Borden
University of Arizona

Joanne G. Keith
Michigan State University

SAGE Publications
International Educational and Professional Publisher
Thousand Oaks ▪ London ▪ New Delhi

For information:

Sage Publications, Inc.
2455 Teller Road
Thousand Oaks, California 91320
E-mail: order@sagepub.com

Sage Publications Ltd.
6 Bonhill Street
London EC2A 4PU
United Kingdom

Sage Publications India Pvt. Ltd.
B-42, Panchsheel Enclave
Post Box 4109
New Delhi 110 017 India

Printed in the United States of America

Library of Congress Cataloging-in-Publication Data

Community youth development: Programs, policies, and practices / edited by Francisco A. Villarruel . . . [et al.].
    p. cm.
Includes bibliographical references and index.
ISBN 0-7619-2786-7 (hbd.) — ISBN 0-7619-2787-5 (pbk.)
    1. Youth-Services for-United States.
2. Social work with youth-United States.
I. Villarruel, Francisco.
HV1431 .C6573 2003
362.7´0973—dc21

2002153222

This book is printed on acid-free paper.

03 04 05 06 10 9 8 7 6 5 4 3 2 1

Acquisitions Editor:	Jim Brace-Thompson
Editorial Assistant:	Karen Ehrmann
Production Editor:	Melanie Birdsall
Copy Editor:	Karen Brunson
Typesetter:	C&M Digitals (P) Ltd.
Indexer:	Sylvia Coates
Proofreader:	Ruth Saavedra
Cover Designer:	Janet Foulger

Contents

Preface

For many, the new millennium has been viewed as an opportunity for a new beginning. For others, there has been concern about the status quo and whether the new millennium will truly lead to systemic and structural changes that will ultimately enhance the well-being of our communities and our youth. Today's scholars, practitioners, and policymakers continue to wrestle with the question of what can be done to strengthen and enhance developmental outcomes for our youth in the face of the past decade's realities and nightmares, a period marked by school shootings, increases in the media's negative portrayal of youth, and a public perception that youth were simply engaged in more violence than in any other period of our nation's history.

The issue of promoting developmental opportunities for our nation's youth is not new. Richard M. Lerner, for example, in his volume entitled *America's Youth in Crisis* (1995), outlines many of the issues that confront our communities and calls for responses from all community residents, not just from concerned parents or youth professionals. James Garbarino offers numerous ideas in two different books, *Raising Children in a Socially Toxic Environment* (1995) and *Lost Boys* (1999), arguing that consistent and reliable positive anchors (institutions and people) are necessary "protectors" and "supporters" for youth. Peter Benson, too, in his volume entitled *All Kids Are Our Kids* (1997), asserts that the developmental assets needed by youth can best be supported when boundaries between individuals and institutions are minimized. Finally, Karen Pittman, one of our nation's most highly regarded youth advocates, has argued repeatedly that communities and institutions must provide opportunities for youth to develop the six Cs (i.e., competence, connection, confidence, character, caring and compassion, and contribution). In short, these examples reflect the notion that youth development does not and should not occur in isolated contexts. Rather, it should be embedded within the multiple ecologies in which youth, their peers, and their families interact and live.

Although youth development is not a new area of interest for professionals, what is new is the focus on positive approaches and outcomes. Stated somewhat differently and as briefly noted above, the focus of positive youth development moves from a problem-reduction, deficit-oriented approach to initiatives that build individual capacities; rather than focusing just on risk, there has been a shift to including strengthening protective factors, building competencies, increasing thriving behaviors, and reducing risks.

Paralleling this shift among professionals has been a similar response from communities in general. Parents as well as other community residents and professionals (e.g., teachers, faith communities, professionals in youth development) are asking similar questions pertaining to young people: "What does it take to create a community that will promote the positive opportunities that can promote the optimal development of all young people?" and "Can professionals and communities successfully intervene with high-risk youth and minimize their engagement in further risk behaviors?" In short, there is an increasing recognition that programs in isolation do not contribute to the well-being of youth as do community-wide initiatives characterized by the goal of making *communities* better places for all youth to live and grow. Many such efforts are ongoing in communities across the nation. America's Promise, with leadership by Founding Chairman General Colin L. Powell, is one of the best known of these national and statewide efforts.

Given the growing acceptance of this community-wide approach, practitioners, public policy professionals, the public, and researchers are trying desperately to understand what it takes to create environments that promote the positive and healthy development of all youth. Communities are attempting to redesign themselves to be places that promote the general well-being and positive behavior of all young people while, at the same time, trying to prevent negative behavior. Although communities have begun to see the importance of addressing positive youth development, many communities have a limited understanding of the mobilization required to create an environment that truly promotes positive youth development in all young people. In particular, communities and youth professionals lack an adequate understanding of what their actual actions and institutional programs must be to successfully develop a landscape that provides optimal opportunities for healthy youth development.

The goal of this volume, then, is threefold: First, it attempts to provide some solid information, practical tools, and selected references to practitioners, advocates, policy professionals, and researchers working in the area of community youth development. Second, it is intended to facilitate an understanding that sustained programs and policies must be embedded within communities as opposed to becoming program-specific initiatives. Finally, this volume seeks to examine and present how either individual or contextual factors can and should be considered when embracing a community youth developmental approach. Chapters in this volume not only synthesize current information in accessible language for practitioners and policy professionals but also provide ideas for the types of programs that need to be developed and researched in order to help inform the future.

In summary, by examining several critical aspects related to the community youth development framework, focusing on the needs of multiple audiences, programs, and policies, each chapter contributes to an overall understanding of the how and why of community youth development. This book attempts to mobilize readers to adopt a culture that fosters the positive development of youth through a community youth development approach.

Acknowledgments

Numerous people and institutions must be thanked for their assistance in the preparation of this volume. The four editors came together from different paths and opportunities, fueled by a common passion and commitment to the well-being of youth. We are grateful to our colleagues who willingly and enthusiastically contributed to the conceptualization and submissions to this volume.

We also acknowledge the support and encouragement of Richard M. Lerner, whose leadership and vision have been inspirational. Richard, a friend, mentor, and colleague, has demonstrated unwavering commitment and enthusiasm to the community youth development approach. Dale Blyth, another of our friends and supporters, is also worthy of recognition. The opportunities he has provided us, individually and collectively, have benefited us both personally and professionally. His commitment and leadership within the field of community youth development has contributed to the continued movement toward integration of research, practice, and policy. This continued integration will provide a much-needed foundation in the field.

Support for the work on this volume has come from multiple sources at three land grant universities: Michigan State University (MSU), Pennsylvania State University, and the University of Arizona (UA). We wish to acknowledge the three universities' Agricultural Experiment Stations and Extension Services related to children, youth, and families for encouragement of our development of the book. Jan Bokemeier at the MSU Agricultural Experiment Station provided leadership, support, and opportunities for authors to meet so we could develop a regional research initiative. Support also came from the Pennsylvania Agricultural Experiment Station and from the Arizona Agricultural Experiment Station.

Anne Soderman, a colleague and former department chair at MSU, provided wonderful administrative guidance and encouragement, as did Soyeon Shim, Chair of the School of Family Consumer Sciences at UA, and Blannie Bowen, Chair of the Department of Agricultural and Extension Education at Penn State. Sarra Baraily, Editorial Assistant, demonstrated her skills and remained enthusiastic and willing to contribute to the many creative (but sometimes tedious) tasks involved.

Finally, and most important, we are grateful to our children, teens and adults—Amalia, Brighid, Julie, Kayla, Kiera, Kyle, Peter, Rob, and Staci—who have blessed us with memories, inspiration, and a dedication to this work. We also acknowledge and express our gratitude and love to our spouses—Gail, Tammy, and Bob—who have provided us with space, time, support, motivation, and hope in our work.

1

Community Youth Development

Partnership Creating a Positive World

Daniel F. Perkins, Lynne M. Borden,
Joanne G. Keith, Tianna L. Hoppe-Rooney,
and Francisco A. Villarruel

U.S. citizens have been startled into the realization that their communities are all vulnerable to violence, regardless of whether they are rural, suburban, or urban. The violent acts of young people toward their peers have repeatedly shocked the nation (e.g., the tragic events in Eugene, Oregon; Littleton, Colorado; and Jonesboro, Arkansas). Given this frightening new understanding, across the country communities are trying desperately to understand what it takes to create environments that promote the positive and healthy development of all youth. Communities are attempting to redesign themselves to be places that promote both positive behavior in youth and the general well-being of all young people while simultaneously preventing negative behavior. Although communities have begun to see the importance of addressing what we will call "positive youth development," many communities have a limited understanding of the community mobilization required to create an environment that truly promotes positive youth development in all young people. In particular, communities lack an adequate understanding of what their actual actions and institutional programs must be to successfully develop a community landscape that provides optimal opportunities for healthy youth development. For example, a recent community-wide evaluation of a youth violence collaborative assessment determined that the entire county had adopted a philosophy of "positive youth development" for working with youth and that an "asset-based approach in all future programs" would be used. However, when specifically asked, these community leaders estimated that only about 5% of all programs were actually asset-based. Moreover, their definition of "asset-based approach" was neither consistent nor clear across, or even within, youth-serving professionals and the organizations that they served.

There are several possible explanations for this community's inability to apply a positive youth development framework to its community efforts. Historically, communities have used research and program efforts that focused on deficit models rather than opportunities for positive youth development. These programs and policies have typically focused on the elimination of problems associated with various risk conditions and behaviors. Generally, such efforts have focused on one particular behavior such as drinking, using drugs, or academic failure. Moreover, these efforts have typically targeted young people who were already experiencing some form of difficulty in their daily lives (e.g., juvenile diversion and substance abuse problems). If successful, these programs and policies may prevent young people from further engagement in the same risk behavior or engagement in other risk behaviors (e.g., sexual experimentation and school failure). However, such intervention and prevention programs do not necessarily prepare young people to meet the challenges and demands that they face now or will face in the future. Effectively preparing young people to meet challenges requires providing them with the foundation to make decisions that will promote their own positive development. Thus, programs and policies need to provide a foundation that promotes an individual's growth and development by *engaging* young people in skill-enhancing opportunities. Scholars assert that, if we, as a nation, are to overcome the war against conditions that place youth at risk for unhealthy and negative developmental outcomes, models of positive youth development (e.g., asset models) must be the focus of community efforts (e.g., Benson, 1997; Bogenschneider, 1998; Lerner, 1995, 2002; Lerner, Fisher, & Weinberg, 2000; Lerner & Perkins, 1999). Communities must initially develop community-wide efforts that promote positive youth development for all young people, providing them with the opportunities to develop positive relationships, skills, competencies, and attitudes that will assist them in making positive choices for their lives.

A phrase that captures the movement toward positive youth development in the 1990s was "Problem free is not fully prepared" (Pittman, 1992). Logically, the next question we must ask is, "Fully prepared for what?" Of course, we want our youth to enjoy life and develop their skills and competences to become well-rounded, productive citizens as adults. But what about the present, when they are still youth? Clearly, positive youth development is not enough. Besides being "fully prepared," youth need to be engaged by adults as partners in their own development and in the development of their communities. Coined by the National Network for Youth (Hughes & Curnan, 2000), community youth development integrates the positive youth development framework and provides a context of this engagement. Or as Pittman (2000b) states, "Fully prepared isn't fully participating." Community youth development moves foci from problem-free, fully prepared, to engaged partners.

The purpose of this volume is to examine several critical aspects related to the community youth development framework, focusing on the needs of multiple audiences, programs, and policies. Each chapter, therefore, provides a detailed scientific overview of a specific topic, followed by strategies and recommendations for practitioners, researchers, and policy advocates. These strategies and recommendations are derived from a framework of community youth development.

❖ HISTORY OF COMMUNITY YOUTH DEVELOPMENT

Community youth development has evolved from the ongoing studies of adolescent development. Specifically, research into the issue of resiliency has been important in laying the foundation for the model of community youth development. The research surrounding risk and resiliency was pioneered by scholars such as Rutter, Werner, Garmezy, and Garbarino (Garbarino, 1992, 1995; Garmezy, 1991, 1993; Rutter, 1985, 1987, 1993; Rutter, Maughan, Mortimore, & Ouston, 1979; Werner, 1990, 1992; Werner & Smith, 1982, 1992). These scholars, collectively, have provided the foundation from which the concept of community youth development has evolved.

Resiliency has been defined as the ability of individuals to withstand the stressors of life and the challenges to their healthy development (Masten, 2001; Rutter, 1985, 1987; Werner & Smith, 1982, 1992). In other words, resiliency may be defined as the ability of individuals to do well despite facing overwhelming odds in their lives (Bogenschneider, 1998). Research on resiliency has provided strong evidence of protective factors, or specific variables and processes involved in safeguarding and promoting successful development. These protective factors have the dual effect of decreasing the likelihood of negative consequences from exposure to risk and increasing the likelihood of positive outcomes (Jessor, Turbin, & Costa, 1998; Masten & Coatsworth, 1998). This research identifies protective factors that are responsible for resiliency while also identifying other factors that increase the risk of failure (i.e., risk factors) (Bernard, 1991; Dryfoos, 1990; Garmezy, 1985; Jessor, 1993; Jessor et al., 1998; Lavery, Siegel, Cousins, & Rubovits, 1993; Luster & McAdoo, 1994; Luster & Small, 1994; Luthar, 1991; Masten, 2001; Rutter, 1985, 1987, 1989; Werner, 1990; Werner & Smith, 1982, 1992).

For example, in their longitudinal study of a cohort of children from the island of Kauai, Werner & Smith (1982, 1992) describe three types of protective factors that emerge from analyses of the developmental course of high-risk children from infancy to adulthood. These three categories of protective factors are as follows:

1. Dispositional attributes of the individual, such as physical activity level and high social ability, average or higher intelligence, competence in communication skills (language and reading), and internal locus of control

2. Affectional ties in the family that provide emotional support in times of stress, whether from a parent, sibling, spouse, or mate

3. External support systems, whether in school, at work, or at church, that reward the individual's competencies and determination and provide a belief system by which to live.

Masten and Garmezy (1985) derived similar conclusions. In their review of research, they found three broad sets of variables that operated as protective factors: (1) personality features such as self-esteem, (2) family cohesion and an absence of discord, and (3) the availability of external support systems that both encourage and reinforce an individual's coping efforts.

The results of this longitudinal study and other resiliency studies have provided critical information to the field of youth development. By identifying characteristics that act as buffers for young people against great adversity, researchers and practitioners gained important information for designing and implementing programming for youth development. Researchers and practitioners alike have begun a movement that uses the research on resiliency to focus on positive youth development (Pittman, 1992; Pittman & Cahill, 1992; Pittman & Wright, 1991; Pittman & Zeldin, 1994). Moreover, other applied scholars such as Benson, Blyth, and Lerner (Benson, 1990, 1997; Benson, Leffert, Scales, & Blyth, 1998; Blyth & Leffert, 1995; Blyth & Roehlkepartain, 1993; Lerner, 1995, 2002) have solidified the positive framework by identifying critical elements that youth need to be successful, contributing members of society. Finally, the work of practitioners at the National Network for Youth (Hughes & Curnan, 2000) and the International Youth Foundation (Pittman, 2000a; Pittman & Ferber, 2001) have advanced the field of youth development by integrating positive youth development and community development.

Furthering community youth development means promoting factors that provide *all* youth with the critical elements needed for successful development and engagement in their communities, regardless of their level of risk. So while resiliency focuses on youth that are at high risk or in adverse situations, community youth development focuses on what all youth need to thrive and become engaged partners in their own development and in their communities. Simply put, community youth development involves creating opportunities for young people to increase their ability to succeed.

❖ DEFINING COMMUNITY YOUTH DEVELOPMENT

As with positive youth development, a community youth development orientation involves a shift away from concentrating on problems toward concentrating on strengths, competencies, and engagement in self-development and community development. Therefore, community youth development is defined as purposely creating environments that provide constructive, affirmative, and encouraging relationships that are sustained over time with adults and peers, while concurrently providing an array of opportunities that enable youth to build their competencies and become engaged as partners in their own development as well as the development of their communities.

Youth development, either positive or negative, occurs as youth interact with all levels of their surroundings, including the other people in their environment such as family, peers, other adults, and members of their communities. The importance of different levels of the youth ecology and the systems within those levels has been defined and studied by several scholars (Bogenschneider, 1998; Bronfenbrenner, 1979, 1986; Lerner, 1995; Luster & Small, 1994). Drawing on that research, a community youth development framework shifts the focus from the individual to the interaction of the individual with the multiple levels of his or her environment. Therefore, fostering community youth development requires positive supports, opportunities for skill and competency development, and partnerships with youth at multiple levels of young people's ecology and within the systems that comprise that ecology. These partnerships are youth's efforts with adults to be producers of their own development and shapers of their communities. The definition of community youth development is further explained in Box 1.1.

Box 1.1 Community Youth Development: A Definition in Four Parts

Community youth development is an integration of youth development and community development. The first three parts of the definition below deal with youth development. These three parts are taken directly from Hamilton's "Youth Development: A Definition in Three Parts" (as cited in Lerner, 2002, p. 329-330).

  1. *A natural process*: The growing capacity of a young person to understand and act upon the environment. Youth

development (synonymous in this sense with child and adolescent development) is the natural unfolding of the potential inherent in the human organism in relation to the challenges and supports of the physical and social environment. People can actively shape their own development through their choices and interpretations. Development lasts as long as life, but youth development enables individuals to lead a healthy, satisfying, productive life, as youth and later as adults, because they gain the competence to earn a living, to engage in civic activities, to nurture others, and to participate in social relations and cultural activities. "The Five Cs" are a useful summary of the goals of youth development: caring/compassion, competence, character, connection, and confidence. The process of development may be divided into age-related stages (infancy, childhood, adolescence, and smaller divisions of these stages) and into domains (notably physical cognitive, social, emotional, and moral).

2. *A philosophy or approach*: Active support for the growing capacity of young people by individuals, organizations, and institutions, especially at the community level. The youth development approach is rooted in commitment to enabling all young people to achieve their potential. It is characterized by a positive, asset-building orientation, building on strengths rather than categorizing youth according to their deficits. However, it recognizes the need to identify and respond to specific problems faced by some youth (e.g., substance abuse, involvement in violence, and premature parenthood). The most important manifestation of youth development as a philosophy or approach is the goal of making communities better places for young people to grow up. Youth participation is essential to the achievement of that goal.

3. *Programs and organizations*: A planned set of activities that foster young people's growing capacity. Youth development programs are inclusive; participation is

not limited to those identified as at risk or in need.
They give young people the chance to make decisions
about their own participation and about the program's
operation, and to assume responsible roles. They
engage young people in constructive and challenging
activities that build their competence and foster supportive relationships with peers and with adults. They
are developmentally appropriate and endure over
time, which requires them to be adaptable enough to
change as participants' needs change. Youth development is done with and by youth. Something that is
done to or for youth is not youth development, even
though it may be necessary and valuable. Youth development organizations exist specifically for the purpose
of promoting youth development. Some other organizations operate youth development programs but have
other functions as well. Programs to prevent or treat
specific problems stand in contrast to youth development programs; however, problem-oriented programs
may incorporate youth development principles by
acknowledging participants' strengths and the wider
range of issues they must cope with by giving participants a strong voice in the choice to participate and in
the operation of the program.

4. *Partnerships for the community*: Collaboration and teamwork define the relationships between adults and
   youth on behalf of their communities. Of course, youth
   participation is required in every step of the programming process (e.g., planning, implementation, and
   evaluation), but just as important is youth participation
   in their community. Youth are fully invested in their
   community and are empowered as full partners to
   provide direction, insight, energy, and efforts around
   problem solving for the community. Youth are full
   contributors to their community and are called upon
   to employ the skills and competencies that they are
   developing. Indeed, youth have a right and a civic
   responsibility to participate and contribute to their

communities. Youth participation is viewed as essential to youth and to the thriving of communities and institutions. Youth participation involves learning and work that is woven throughout the community, not just in specific projects (Pittman, 2000). If engaged as partners, youth can be powerful change agents for the betterment of their community. Thus the engagement in the community represents the fourth leg of this stool known as community youth development. Pittman (2000, p. 35-36) summarizes this point in the following quote: "We will have to work carefully in this country to identify or create the public ideas that undergird a sustained effort to bring all young people into civic, social, and economic arenas of their communities as lifelong learners, workers, and change agents. We must recognize that this public idea, like any stable platform, must have at least three legs: one leg in policy, one in public opinion and values, and a third in organizational practice. We could argue for the importance of a fourth leg in youth culture, for this idea must resonate with young people, tap into their resources, and unleash their potential."

Therefore, community youth development means providing youth with the opportunities to acquire a broad range of competencies and a full complement of *positive* connections to self, others, and the larger community (Pittman, 1992; Pittman & Zeldin, 1994; Takanishi, 1993). Moreover, creating communities that promote community youth development means engaging youth as partners in the process of positive youth development, that is, providing young people with sustained positive relationships with adults, and opportunities for new skill development and mastery.

The intervention and prevention perspective of community youth development can be further explained by the analogy of a medical model. Intervention is defined as discontinuing or stopping an already exhibited problem behavior, as when an individual goes to the doctor for medicine to stop a disease from progressing. Prevention, on the other hand, means taking advance measures to keep something (e.g., youth participation in problem behaviors) from happening. To use the medical model once more, prevention would mean going to the doctor for a flu shot to build one's immune system as protection against catching the flu. Community youth development is a step beyond prevention. It is a process by which young people's developmental needs are met, their engagement in problem behaviors is prevented, and (most important) they are empowered to build the competencies and skills necessary to become healthy contributing citizens now and as adults. In terms of the medical example, the individual takes an active role in his/her health by getting an immune shot, strengthening the body through physically appropriate exercise and dietary actions, and shaping the environment to provide support for that endeavor.

❖ BUILDING BLOCKS

With the shift from resiliency to positive youth development, scholars have moved from identifying protective factors in adverse situations to identifying both individual and environmental characteristics that promote and enhance youth development toward becoming successful adults. These characteristics comprise the building blocks of positive youth development. They are referred to by researchers and practitioners as developmental assets (Benson 1990, 1997; Benson et al., 1998; Blyth & Roehlkepartain, 1993), life skills (Hendricks, 1996), and protective factors (Hawkins, Catalano, & Miller, 1992; Masten, 2001). In keeping with current terminology, we employ the Search Institute's term "developmental assets" to refer to the building blocks of positive youth development.

Developmental assets can be external factors in the young person's environment, such as positive relationships in families, friendship groups, schools, and the community. They may also be internal factors that reflect the teenager's personal competencies, values, and attitudes. Just as there are nutritional building blocks in the food pyramid that are necessary for healthy physical development, assets are the necessary building blocks in the positive youth development framework (D. A. Blyth, personal communication, October, 1999). For example, just as one needs to eat calcium-rich foods to have strong bones, youth need opportunities for skill development to gain a sense of self-efficacy. One also needs to eat vegetables for the iron necessary to build red blood cells that fight infections, and likewise youth need caring adults for emotional support in the normal struggle to develop their identity.

Assets are not the outcomes of positive youth development. Rather, they are elements of the developmental process through which young people are able to be contributing members of their communities now and are also launched on a positive trajectory toward becoming productive citizens in adulthood. The relationship between assets and risk behaviors, as well as healthy and positive outcomes, has been clearly documented in research. The more assets youth possess and have available to them, the less likely they are to engage in risky behaviors and the more likely they are to engage in healthy and positive behaviors (Benson, 1997; Benson et al., 1998; Jessor, Van Den Bos, Vanderryn, Costa, & Turbin, 1995; Leffert et al., 1998; Perkins, Haas, & Keith, 1997; Scales, Benson, Leffert, & Blyth, 2000; Scales & Leffert, 1998). In order for youth to reach their full potential, assets must be available to them throughout their formative years and not just at specific points in their development. Therefore, the various contexts that comprise the young person's world (e.g., family, school, neighborhood, and youth programs) all need to incorporate developmental assets. For example, schools may want to target specific assets that they can directly impact, such as bettering school environment or providing opportunities for community service through service-learning. Youth development professionals may want to examine their programs' characteristics to assess whether these specifically target certain assets. This does not mean that youth development professionals should not try to reduce risk. Rather, they need to develop programs that have a dual focus of asset building and risk reduction (Bogenschneider, 1998; Perkins, Borden, & Villarruel, 2001). Moving from positive youth development to community youth development is about engaging youth as partners in the development of external assets and in providing opportunities for skill and competency development.

❖ COMMUNITY YOUTH DEVELOPMENT

National leaders of youth programs, government officials, and policy-makers are all seeking direction to address the needs of young people and foster youth citizenship in their local and national communities. We believe that community youth development provides a framework for the direction they seek. This framework is formed by being intentional about creating and sustaining environments for socialization and learning that surround youth with external developmental assets and also foster internal assets. Indeed, young people who have grown up in communities that promote their positive development have a better understanding of their own values, often become lifelong learners, are actively engaged in their communities, and are more likely to promote the positive well-being of other young people (Benson, 1997; Blyth & Leffert, 1995; McLaughlin, 2000). The goals of community youth development involve what Lerner (2002) has identified as the "five Cs." These include (1) competence in the academic, social, emotional, and vocational arenas; (2) confidence in who one is becoming (identity); (3) connection to self and others; (4) character that comes from positive values, integrity, and a strong sense of morals; and (5) caring and compassion. However, from a community youth development framework there is a sixth C as highlighted by Pittman (2000a), that of contribution. By contributing to their families, neighborhoods, and communities, and through participating in youth programs, youth are afforded practical opportunities to make use of the other five Cs.

Practitioners, researchers, and policy advocates in partnership with youth have a critical role in providing direction to the community youth development framework. From a practitioner's point of view, employing a community youth development framework means including youth as *partners* in program planning or community mobilization efforts to create environments that both link youth with adults in positive *relationships* and provide new opportunities for youth to develop *skills*. In addition, practitioners continually draw from research that provides pertinent information for program design and provides feedback to researchers and policy advocates in terms of needs. From a researcher's point of view, utilizing a community youth development framework means focusing on specific identified assets, linking them to real outcomes, and creating a feedback loop with youth, practitioners, and policy advocates. In addition, community youth development also means conducting scientific inquiry into youth programs as a context for development (Larson, 2000).

In some cases, positive youth development programs have been a springboard for launching community youth development efforts. For example, the results of a recent study that identified the strengths or assets of a group of 4-H youth provided critical information that created changes in programming (Perkins & Butterfield, 1999). A county 4-H agent provided training to adult leaders in specific assets and relationship-building skills, and the results of this study and the training changed the behaviors of the 4-H leaders toward the young people. These youth professionals reported being more focused on developing a positive relationship between themselves and the youth through increased focus on youth as partners. They also reported focusing on the promotion of youth development by engaging the young people in the decision-making process. Moreover, the researcher received feedback from the adult leaders and county agents requesting additional information that would help them understand which components of the adult-youth relationship were critical for fostering positive youth development. Although this paragraph presents an example of positive youth development, it does not present an example of community youth development. In this example, the youth were partners in the problem-solving process, but a community youth development approach would have gone still further and engaged the youth in the interpretation of the results and the development of solutions. We reiterate what Pittman (1992; 2000a, 2000b) has stated, "Problem free is not fully prepared" and "Fully prepared is not fully engaged."

Employing community youth development from policy advocates' perspective is about directing their efforts toward educating policymakers, providing researchers with directions on how to communicate their findings, and advocating proven programs. Moreover, they are called on to engage youth as partners in the process of advocacy. This book lays the groundwork for such individuals to embrace community youth development and take appropriate action.

❖ OUTLINE OF THIS BOOK

This book begins an important journey that assesses multiple ecological components that influence the development of young people. The chapters are divided into three parts: issues related to individuals, the intersection between programs and youth, and the intersection between youth professionals, communities, and youth.

Part I: Individual Issues

Part I examines the relationship between community youth development and working with culturally diverse groups. All too often, programs and research do not consider the role that cultural diversity may play in the development of youth. It is often assumed that simple modifications of programs and research can be generalized to address the developmental pathways of nonwhite minority groups. Yet, as the authors of this section note, the foundation of community youth development for ethnic and racial minorities must be based on contextual and cultural dimensions of development. What is most critical to recognize here is that, in many African American communities, the tenets of community youth development exist at both a formal and informal level. Thus, how practitioners seek to build these links is not only a central issue, but more important, how they choose to expand these is also an issue for consideration.

Rodriguez, Morrobel, and Villarruel, in an effort to summarize information on community youth development issues for Latino youth, conducted a review of selected journals to discern what research has involved Latino youth and to critique findings of this previous research that has engaged (or failed to engage) Latino youth as part of their samples. From there, they discuss issues that should be incorporated into research to help establish a culturally relevant framework for understanding dimensions of community youth development. Finally, ideas that practitioners should consider in working with Latino youth are offered, including adult competencies and programmatic dimensions.

Cheshire and Kawamoto take an ecological perspective in viewing the needs of American Indian youth for developing high self-esteem and maintaining a balanced sense of belonging both in the contexts of the larger societal context and their cultural community. These authors identify the importance of extended family as a critical component to programming and intervention aimed at American Indian youth. In an attempt to highlight the complexity and multilayered aspects of these young people's lives, the barriers they face are recognized, including racism, oppression, isolation, and conflicting messages. A sampling of successful, culturally sensitive programs and role models are identified to demonstrate the strides being made to assist in balancing rather than compromising ethnic differences.

Roffman, Suárez-Orozco, and Rhodes address strengths and, in particular, the multiple challenges that immigrant families and adolescents face in their transition to a new environment. The unique experiences of three major sending regions (Latin America, Asia, and the Caribbean) are identified in detail. The authors propose the inclusion of supportive nonparental adults, specifically mentors, as outlets for easing the transition, reducing stress through caring, and providing adult guidance and supervision while parents are unable to do so. Various roles and objectives for the mentoring adult are identified using the strengths-based model of positive youth development. Multiple examples of youth development programs across the United States are provided as a means of expanding on the vast possibilities and potential components of a mentoring, community-based program. Finally, specific recommendations are proposed, aimed at mentoring and community youth programs regarding specific considerations and training issues that should be addressed when working with an immigrant population.

The significance of examining gender issues and a gender focus in youth programming is presented by Denner and Griffin. The authors argue against polarization that results in pitting boys against girls, because it is not productive to argue about who needs more resources and attention. Rather, they engage the reader to consider variations within the sexes, and that the meaning attached to gender depends on the meaning that influential adults place on it. Youth workers are to be aware of the meaning that masculine and feminine gender role expectations will play in their program. These call for increased participation in opportunities that traditionally do not attract only members of one sex, along with exposure to male and female leaders in these activities to help deconstruct gender roles that limit participation.

The impact of sexuality and sexual identity is also a core developmental foundation that needs to be considered when developing programs that are embedded in a positive developmental framework. Russell and Andrews consider the role youth development can play in fostering healthy adolescent sexuality development, with specific attention to the challenges that youth development efforts face when attending to adolescent sexuality, as well as opportunities presented by recent research findings to support innovative outreach and education. They end their chapter with some action steps that youth development professionals can take in the process of developing and implementing youth development programs for adolescent sexual health.

Finally, Onaga, Carolan, Maddalena, and Villarruel identify two realities facing the families of youth with developmental disabilities. The first is the education system, which supports the inclusion of an assets approach, and the second is living arrangements and governmental agencies that do not see through a strengths-based lens. The inconsistency of these two realities is outlined as a challenge for youth professionals. The authors also identify numerous other roles and tasks that an effective adult working with this population should be prepared to face. Through the Michigan Transition Initiative, a 5-year qualitative and evaluative study, two case stories are highlighted to demonstrate how the principles of positive youth development and an assets-based approach can be incorporated into the work with youth who are developmentally disabled and their families. Family, neighborhood, work, school, individual resources, and lessons learned are areas explored through the telling of the two individuals' stories.

Taken together, the chapters in Part I provide critical insight related to identity issues and the impact that these have on approaches to enhancing the well-being of youth. In other words, these chapters underscore the fact that issues of ethnic and racial identity, as well as sexual orientation and gender, are critical factors that communities should take into consideration when trying to respond to the developmental needs of today's youth.

Part II: The Intersection of Youth and Community Programs

Part II of this volume examines the macrolevel issues that must be taken into consideration when developing programs, applied research, and policies in a community youth development framework. All too often, programs focus solely on individual outcomes, without attempting to create bridges between individuals and the contexts in which they live. Caldwell and Baldwin investigate the leisure context and its importance to community youth development. These authors offer a convincing argument that leisure education and community-based youth leisure programs are not only essential but also a critical dimension of individual growth and development. Caldwell and Baldwin extend their discussion by describing some practical considerations that youth professionals and communities should consider in providing community-based recreation and leisure programs.

In her chapter on workforce development programs, Ferrari provides further insight about the importance of creating bridges between micro- and macrolevel outcomes. Specifically, she divides her chapter into three sections: (1) design considerations (audience, role of adults, and experiential learning model), (2) content (delivery, skills, and activities), and (3) training. In addition, this chapter highlights the importance of youth developmental stages as well as contextual considerations when initiating workforce preparation programs for youth.

Brown, DeJesus, Maxwell, and Schiraldi extend the ideas presented by Ferrari when they examine the current juvenile justice system and its sway toward punishment over rehabilitation for today's youth. This chapter's content was born out of a study that looked at 15 exemplary juvenile offender programs. The authors share a list of commonalities that successful delinquency programs demonstrate, and, more important, offer insight about how workforce development programs, embedded in a community context, can facilitate a new life path for adjudicated youth.

A common struggle identified between youth and communities across generations has been the issue of common or community values. In the next chapter, Pace reviews the moral development theory and explains effective character education initiatives and the multiple components of those initiatives. Pace suggests practical strategies for incorporating a community youth development approach to character development. Moreover, she presents a discussion of the role that youth development professionals, researchers, program evaluators, and policymakers must assume in defining and implementing community-based character education initiatives.

Flanagan and Van Horn present a slightly different perspective on community-youth related issues. This chapter explores how nonformal youth groups can be used as a means of fostering civic participation and establishing community and individual assets. The authors argue that participation in nonformal community youth development programs is an underutilized practice of citizenship. Moreover, they advocate for innovating community youth development as a next step in revitalizing civic participation in youth leading into adulthood.

The final chapter in Part II takes a comprehensive look at the opportunity and barriers to including youth as participants in community organizations as decision makers and active leaders through the idea of youth governance. Huber, Frommeyer, Weisenbach, and Sazama provide several case examples of programs in communities that have successfully incorporated youth as key participants, to illustrate what needs to be done in an organization to assess and prepare for youth involvement. In short, this chapter provides important insight about how community-youth development programs can be implemented and sustained.

In sum, the chapters in this section examine the employment of a community youth development framework in various contexts. They provide concrete examples of engaging youth as full partners in programs and also frame a direction for future research and policies.

Part III: Youth Professionals, Communities, and Youth

The third and final section of this volume examines the programmatic issues that need to be well thought out by youth professionals. In the first chapter of Part III, through a concise review of the literature, Perkins and Borden focus on out-of-school-time youth programming and summarize what these programs offer participants in terms of development of life and social skills, competencies, and opportunities. Special note is given to program quality as a key factor to meaningful outcomes for youth. Along with offering four steps to creating effective youth development programs, Perkins and Borden construct a comprehensive list of characteristics identified by various researchers as important considerations when initiating or implementing a youth-focused program in a community context.

In the next chapter, which focuses on adult competencies, Huebner examines the central role of "competence" in the framework of positive youth development. The definition of competence is reviewed, along with the relevant research findings on specific competence domains. In short, Huebner demystifies the complex concept of competence by moving into specific domains related to developmental tasks. She provides examples and research outcomes in each of six areas (civic and social, cultural, physical health, emotional health, intellectual, and employability). She also points out that the competence domains are related to developmental tasks and are context specific. She concludes with recommendations on how communities can create environments that support the development of competence in young people.

Yohalem offers some critical insight into the roles related to the knowledge, skills, characteristics and beliefs that competent youth development professionals should possess. The chapter is aimed at youth development professionals as well as the youth-serving agencies that hire them. A number of recommendations are offered for community agencies, including more attention to addressing training, recruitment, compensation, and turnover. Yohalem also presents a call for certification or endorsement for adults working with youth.

Walker's chapter explores concepts for systematic opportunities and comprehensive community-wide supports designed to strengthen the professional development and competence of community-based youth workers. She draws this information from extensive work with practitioners as well as from academic, administrative, funding, and intermediary perspectives. Specifically, she asserts that involving youth in community organizations and efforts promotes positive youth development by focusing on the adult mentors needed along the way for success. Data from interviews conducted by the author are used to guide the chapter discussion. Specific topics such as youth worker preparation (education and training), support (success, recognition, accountability), advocacy, influence, and common language are explored. More important, this chapter provides insight related to how adults themselves benefit from engaging youth in their common efforts.

The chapters in this section provide an overview of key programming issues that must be considered during the design of youth development programs. They identify key principles such as the role of adults in enhancing a program's ability to foster the positive development of young people.

❖ SUMMARY

From all these chapters, it is clear that the community youth development efforts must not only be systematic if they are to impact the well being of youth, but that they must also be grounded in both a contextual and future (outcome) oriented perspective. Moreover, a theoretical underpinning of the chapters in this volume is that of engagement—the notion not only that adult youth professionals and communities themselves must be involved in the lives of youth, but that youth themselves are more likely to prosper when they are engaged with adults and communities. This reciprocal relationship, based in part on the notion of assets, underscores the notion that there is no quick fix to developing healthy youth. As the field of youth development expands, more concentrated research, practice, and policy development must occur if we are truly dedicated to supporting individual and youth development for *all* youth.

The chapters of this book are woven together by the common theme of action with and on behalf of youth. That action is about creating contexts that foster community youth development. An African proverb sums it up nicely: "He who does not cultivate his field will die of hunger." The message is simple, that the progression of the world is dependent on the cultivation of our youth so that they are problem free, fully prepared, and fully engaged in their own lives and the communities in which they live.

❖ REFERENCES

Benson, P. L. (1990). *The troubled journey: A portrait of 6th-12th grade youth.* Minneapolis, MN: Search Institute.

Benson, P. L. (1997). *All kids are our kids: What communities must do to raise caring and responsible children and adolescents.* San Francisco: Jossey-Bass.

Benson, P. L., Leffert, N., Scales, P. C., & Blyth, D. A. (1998). Beyond the "village" rhetoric: Creating healthy communities for children and adolescents. *Applied Developmental Science, 2(3),* 138-159.

Bernard, B. (1991). *Fostering resiliency in kids: Protective factors in the family, school, and community.* Portland, OR: Northwest Regional Educational Laboratory, Western Regional Center for Drug-Free Schools and Communities, Far West Laboratory.

Blyth, D. A., & Leffert, N. (1995). Communities as contexts for adolescent development. *Journal of Adolescent Research, 10,* 64-87.

Blyth, D. A., & Roehlkepartain, E. C. (1993). *Healthy communities, healthy youth.* Minneapolis, MN: Search Institute.

Bogenschneider, K. (1998). What youth need to succeed: The roots of resiliency. In K. Bogenschneider and J. Olson (Eds.), *Building resiliency and reducing risk: What youth need from families and communities to succeed* (Wisconsin Family Impact Seminars Briefing Report). Madison, WI: Center for Excellence in Family Studies.

Bronfenbrenner, U. (1979). *The ecology of human development: Experiments by nature and design.* Cambridge, MA: Harvard University Press.

Bronfenbrenner, U. (1986). Ecology of the family as a context for human development: Research perspectives. *Developmental Psychology, 22,* 723-742.

Dryfoos, J. G. (1990). *Adolescents at risk: Prevalence and prevention.* New York: Oxford University Press.

Garbarino, J. (1992). *Children in danger.* San Francisco: Jossey-Bass.

Garbarino, J. (1995). *Raising children in a socially toxic environment.* San Francisco: Jossey-Bass.

Garmezy, N. (1985). Stress-resistant children: The search for protective factors. In J. E. Stevenson (Ed.), Recent research in developmental psychopathology. *Journal of Child Psychology and Psychiatry Book Supplement, 4,* 213-233.

Garmezy, N. (1991). Resilience and vulnerability to adverse developmental outcomes associated with poverty. *American Behavioral Scientist, 34*, 416-430.

Garmezy, N. (1993). Children in poverty: Resilience despite risk. *Psychiatry, 56*, 127-136.

Hawkins, J. D., Catalano, R. F., & Miller, J. Y. (1992). Risk and protective factors for alcohol and other drug problems in adolescence and early adulthood: Implications for substance abuse prevention. *Psychological Bulletin, 112*, 64-105.

Hendricks, P. A. (1996). *Developing youth curriculum, using the Targeting Life Skills Model* (a publication of Iowa State University Extension [4H-137A]). Ames: Iowa State University.

Hughes, D. M., & Curnan, S. P. (2000). Community youth development: A framework for action. *Community Youth Development Journal, 1*, 7-11.

Jessor, R. (1993). Successful adolescent development among youth in high-risk settings. *American Psychologist, 48*, 117-126.

Jessor, R., Turbin, M. S., & Costa, F. M. (1998). Risk and protection in successful outcomes among disadvantaged adolescents. *Applied Developmental Science, 2*, 194-208.

Jessor, R., Van Den Bos, J., Vanderryn, J., Costa, F. M., & Turbin, M. (1995). Protective factors in adolescent problem behavior: Moderator effects and developmental change. *Developmental Psychology, 31*, 923-933.

Larson, R. W. (2000). Toward a psychology of positive youth development. *American Psychologist, 55*, 170-183.

Lavery, B., Siegel, A. W., Cousins, J. H., & Rubovits, D. S. (1993). Adolescent risk-taking: An analysis of problem behaviors in problem children. *Journal of Experimental Child Psychology, 55*, 277-294.

Leffert, N., Benson, P., Scales, P., Sharma, A., Drake, D., & Blyth, D. (1998). Developmental assets: Measurement and prediction of risk behaviors among adolescents. *Applied Developmental Science, 2*, 209-230.

Lerner, R. M. (1995). *America's youth in crisis: Challenges and options for programs and policies.* Thousand Oaks, CA: Sage.

Lerner, R. M. (2002). *Adolescence: Development, diversity, context, and application.* Upper Saddle River, NJ: Prentice Hall.

Lerner, R. M., Fisher, C. B., & Weinberg, R. A. (2000). Toward a science for and of the people: Promoting civil society through the application of developmental science. *Child Development, 71*, 11-20.

Lerner, R. M., & Perkins, D. F. (1999). Issues in studying social interactions in, and promoting the positive development of, adolescents. In R. M. Lerner & D. F. Perkins (Eds.), *Social interactions in adolescence and promoting positive societal contributions of youth.* New York: Garland.

Luster, T., & McAdoo, H. P. (1994). Factors related to the achievement and adjustment of young African American children. *Child Development, 65*, 1080-1094.

Luster, T., & Small, S. A. (1994). Factors associated with sexual risk-taking behaviors among adolescents. *Journal of Marriage and the Family, 56,* 622-632.

Luthar, S. S. (1991). Vulnerability and resiliency: A study of high risk adolescents. *Child Development, 62,* 600-616.

Masten, A. S. (2001). Ordinary magic: Resilience processes in development. *American Psychologist, 56,* 227-238.

Masten, A. S., & Coatsworth, J. D. (1998). The development of competence in favorable and unfavorable environments: Lessons from research on successful children. *American Psychologist, 53,* 205-220.

Masten, A. S., & Garmezy, N. (1985). Risk vulnerability and protective factors in developmental psychopathology. In B. B. Lahey & A. E. Kazdin (Eds.), *Advances in clinical child psychology* (Vol. 8, pp. 1-52). New York: Plenum Press.

McLaughlin, M. (2000). *Community counts: How youth organizations matter for youth development.* Washington, DC: Public Education Network. Retrieved September 25, 2002, from www.publiceducation.org/cgi-bin/downloadmanager/publications/p72.asp

Perkins, D. F., Borden, L. M., & Villarruel, F. A. (2001). Community youth development: A partnership for change. *School Community Journal, 11*(2).

Perkins, D. F., & Butterfield, J. R. (1999). Building an asset-based program for 4-H. *Journal of Extension, 37,* 1-10.

Perkins, D. F., Haas, B., & Keith, J. G. (1997). An integration of positive youth development within the runaway youth and homeless shelter system. *New Designs for Youth Development, 13,* 36-41.

Pittman, K. J. (1992). *Defining the fourth R: Promoting youth development.* Washington, DC: Center for Youth Development and Policy Research.

Pittman, K. J. (2000a). Balancing the equation: Communities supporting youth, youth supporting communities. *Community Youth Development Journal, 1,* 33-36.

Pittman, K. J. (2000b, March). Grantmaker strategies for assessing the quality of unevaluated programs and the impact of unevaluated grantmaking. (Speech presented at Evaluation of Youth Programs symposium at the Biennial Meeting of the Society for Research on Adolescence, Chicago)

Pittman, K. J., & Cahill, M. (1992). *Youth and caring.* Washington, DC: Center for Youth Development and Policy Research.

Pittman, K. J., & Ferber, T. (2001). *Finding common ground within the big picture: Toward a common vision, analysis, and accountability for youth.* Takoma Park, MD: Forum for Youth Investment, International Youth Foundation.

Pittman, K. J., & Wright, M. (1991). *Bridging the gap: A rationale for enhancing the role of community organizations in promoting youth development.* Washington, DC: Center for Youth Development and Policy Research.

Pittman, K. J., & Zeldin, S. (1994). From deterrence to development: Shifting the focus of youth programs for African-American Males. In R. B. Mincy (Ed.), *Nurturing young black males: Challenges to agencies, programs, and social policy* (pp. 45-58). Washington, DC: Urban Institute.

Rutter, M. (1985). Resilience in the face of adversity: Protective factors and resistance to psychiatric disorder. *British Journal of Psychiatry, 147*, 598-611.

Rutter, M. (1987). Psychosocial resilience and protective factors. *American Journal of Orthopsychiatry, 57*, 316-331.

Rutter, M. (1989). Pathways from childhood to adult life. *Journal of Child Psychology and Psychiatry, 30*, 23-51.

Rutter, M. (1993). Resilience: Some conceptual considerations. *Journal of Adolescent Health, 14*, 626-631.

Rutter, M., Maughan, N., Mortimore, P., & Ouston, J. (1979). *Fifteen thousand hours: Secondary school and their effects on children.* Cambridge, MA: Harvard University Press.

Scales, P. C., Benson, P. L., Leffert, N., & Blyth, D. A. (2000). Contribution of developmental assets to the prediction of thriving among adolescents. *Applied Developmental Science, 4*, 27-46.

Scales, P., & Leffert, N. (1998). *Developmental assets: A synthesis of the scientific research on adolescent development.* Minneapolis, MN: Search Institute.

Takanishi, R. (1993). The opportunities of adolescence—research, interventions, and policy: Introduction to special issue. *American Psychologist, 48*, 85-87.

Werner, E. E. (1990). Protective factors and individual resilience. In S. J. Meisels & J. P. Shonkoff (Eds.), *Handbook of early childhood intervention* (pp. 97-116). New York: Cambridge University.

Werner, E. E. (1992). The children of Kauai: Resiliency and recovery in adolescence and adulthood. *Journal of Adolescent Health, 13*, 262-268.

Werner, E. E., & Smith, R. S. (1982). *Vulnerable not invincible: A longitudinal study of resilient children and youth.* New York: McGraw-Hill.

Werner, E. E., & Smith, R. S. (1992). *Overcoming the odds: High risk children from birth to adulthood.* Ithaca, NY: Cornell University.

Part I

Individual Issues

2

The African American Child and Positive Youth Development

A Journey from Support to Sufficiency

Edna Olive

We must recapture and care about our lost children and help them gain the confidence, self-esteem, values, and real-world opportunities—education and jobs—that they need to be strong future guardians of the black community's heritage. And tell them to take the initiative in creating their own opportunity. They can't wait around for other people to discover them or to do them a favor.

—Marian Wright Edelman (1987, p. 134)

These words from a speech delivered by Marian Wright Edelman depict the lofty goal facing professionals who endeavor to address the positive development of African American youth. The formation and implementation of effective programs serving youth comprise a complex issue, particularly when focused on the challenges of the African American youth and his or her community. The obstacles facing the young African American are numerous and have been well documented (Black & Krishnakumar, 1998; Burton, Allison, & Odeidallah, 1995; Coleman & Cunningham, 1996; Davis, 1999; Illback, 1994; Jarrett, 1998; Kennedy, 1997; McLoyd, 1998; Taylor, 1995; Welsing, 1991). The literature is replete with research that connects the current status of the African American youth with many labels, including several frequently used classifications: at-risk, high-risk, disadvantaged, and troubled (Burt, Resnick, & Matheson, 1992; Davis, 1999; Garbarino, 1999; Illback, 1994; Masten & Coatsworth, 1998; McLoyd, 1998).

However, the issue of addressing the complexities of community youth development for African American youth has not been well documented. Although descriptions of programs or services that can be provided to these youth and their families exist, a scarcity exists in research efforts that describe the creation of environments that concurrently engage youth in (a) positive skill/competency development and practice, (b) supportive adult and peer relationships, (c) identification and prevention of self-defeating behaviors, (d) active connection with self as an individual and as a member of a larger whole, and (e) meaningful partnerships with adults and peers that facilitate self-development and community development. As it relates to African American youth, however, the question still remains, "How do we comprehensively address the issue of assisting African American youth in the movement from recipients of extrinsic support services to young adults who are intrinsically self-aware, self-sufficient, well developed, and contributing members of their communities?"

In moving toward an answer to this question, the contents of this chapter address the issue of community youth development as related to African American youth and specifically endeavor to discuss the following concerns:

1. What contributing factors to youth development are prominent in the culture of the African American youth?

2. How do these factors affect the development of the African American youth?

3. What recommendations can be offered to professionals seeking to implement effective community youth development practices for African American youth?

As stated in the introduction of this volume, community youth development efforts recognize the need for programming and practices that present *all* youth with opportunities to develop to their fullest potential. To do so, we must acknowledge that the necessary elements for success logically vary among culturally diverse groups. Rather than engage in superficial adaptation of community programs and practices that may currently exist, community youth development calls for the consideration and development of programs that embrace the individuality and diversity of our many communities. This chapter provides a context for the examination of the African American youth and community to build a foundation for addressing the unique needs of these young people.

❖ PROMINENT FACTORS IN AFRICAN AMERICAN YOUTH DEVELOPMENT

The development of any youth is partially, if not largely, dependent on the interplay between existing factors that play a significant role in the life of the youth, including family/home, school, community, societal norms, socioeconomic status, and physical environment (Benson, 1997; Benson, Leffert, Scales, & Blyth, 1998; Catalano, Berglund, Ryan, Lonczak, & Hawkins, 1999; Illback, 1994). However, in examining the development of African American youth, there are unique issues that must be considered in understanding the challenges and the developmental journeys of these youth. A recognition and knowledge of these issues is crucial to the effectiveness of community youth development efforts, because it is clear that programming that embraces the uniqueness of those it serves is more likely to be successful.

Research providing evidence that African American youth develop in ways separate and distinct from other social and racial groups must be considered by community youth development efforts (Walker & White, 1998; Welsing, 1991). In terms of distinctive differences in development, we must recognize that youth of African American descent begin their identity formation as a minority, as something other than the majority. The nature of formation as a minority is a challenge to the development of a positive self-image and a functional self-awareness (Moshman, 1999; Spencer, 1999; Tatum, 1999; Welsing, 1991).

Another related concern of development for African American youth is the assumption that this process is largely linear, orderly, and forward moving (Jarrett, 1998). Yet due to the transient nature of the lives of many African American youth and their families, development for these youth is often indirect, chaotic, and disorderly. Moreover, a dramatic difference exists in the cultural values of many African American youth regarding the importance or unimportance of major societal institutions (Benson, 1997; Davis, 1999; Edelman, 1999; Welsing, 1991). For example, many African American youth do not believe that academic achievement is a direct indicator of the likelihood of adult success. This influences their development by shaping their behavior and perceptions, because they are inculcated with the notion that institutions created by and for the majority have no direct bearing on their lives. Community youth development recognizes that the recruitment of youth as partners in their own development is essential to its work, and the unique perspective of all youth it seeks to engage must be thoroughly analyzed and understood.

The presence of particular factors prominent in the development of African American youth bear specific mention in examining the necessity for and how-to of community youth development efforts that include these youth. In examining the factors that play a critical role in the life of African American youth, Coleman and Cunningham (1996) identify the following four factors as critical to development: family, support systems such as extended family and community supports, spirituality, and resistance. Black and Krishnakumar (1998) indicate that the factors of availability of economic resources (or the lack thereof), social and physical environment, families and communities, schools and education, and the social/ecological context in which youth live are vital factors in the development of African American youth. Similarly, Jarrett's (1998) study of African American youth yielded several themes that were identified as key factors affecting youth development. These included community/neighborhood, family, significant peers and adults, gender, and economic/social class. In this chapter, six prominent factors that influence African American youth will be briefly discussed as each of these emerged throughout the child and youth development literature. These factors are family influence, community/neighborhood influence, socioeconomic status, spirituality, culture, and education.

❖ SIX PROMINENT FACTORS IN AFRICAN AMERICAN YOUTH DEVELOPMENT

The fact that family, community/neighborhood, socioeconomic status, spirituality, culture, and education all influence youth development is not exclusive to the study of the African American youth. However, these factors influence their development in a distinctive manner and degree.

The Factor of Family Influence

The family of the African American youth has been a topic of extensive study and research (Farrell, 1999; Franklin, 1997; Jarrett, 1998). Specifically, the African American family has been analyzed from three angles: construction, disorganization, and destruction (Farrell, 1999; Franklin, 1997; Welsing, 1991). The construction of this family is often viewed as compromised, given the disproportionate number of fatherless or female-headed families among African Americans as compared to families of other races (Benson, 1997; Prothrow-Stith, 1991). The familial construction has been found to have an influence on the identity formation of the African American male youth as he searches for a positive role model in his immediate environment (Franklin, 1997; Garbarino, 1999; Prothrow-Stith, 1991).

The disorganization of the African American family is linked to the difficulties experienced by many African American youth who find themselves in the center of multiple concurrent transitions, including movement between rural and urban settings, numerous moves between environments and living quarters, and constant rearrangement of the familial structure as relatives and/or friends are injected and extracted from the nuclear family. African American youth may experience familial disorganization when all members of the family are present, because their roles and responsibilities are ambiguous. In these situations, routines and rituals for family interactions are seldom established or adhered to. As a result, it is not uncommon, particularly for the older African American youth, to be relatively isolated and overly responsible for the upbringing of self and any siblings.

The destruction of the African American family has been linked to many variables, including the absence of the male figure due to death, incarceration, or abandonment; the high percentage of young African American children and youth who experience the early death of their parents due to drugs, AIDS, alcoholism, and/or other health-related issues; and parental abandonment, abuse, and neglect of many children, which often results in relative, foster care, or adoptive placements.

In the examination of familial impact on the African American youth, research also indicates that the family can have the sole positive impact on the youth if the presence is both strong and consistent, regardless of its singularity or relation. In other words, the familial impact may be exceptionally strong in the life of an African American youth regardless of whether the source is a single mother, single father, grandmother, aunt, or other close relative.

The Factor of Community/Neighborhood Influence

Jarrett (1998) states the following regarding the influence of communities and neighborhoods on child development: "Development is influenced by the setting in which it occurs. Neighborhoods (and communities), by virtue of their economic, institutional, and social resources, shape opportunities for the families and children who live there" (p. 3).

Neighborhoods and communities provide the backdrop for the activities and interactions of children and youth. As related to many African American youth, the neighborhood represents the scarcity of economic, social, and institutional resources for youth who live in high-risk or at-risk situations. The neighborhood and community also represent the setting for the formation of significant relationships. For many African American youth, significant relationships are sought outside the home and are found throughout the community. Substitutes for fathers, mothers, siblings, significant others, and true kinship are found in the community. African American youth who are gang involved describe the initial period of their exposure to gangs as a search for belongingness (Garbarino, 1999; Prothrow-Stith, 1991).

Many African American youth are taught their social lessons on the streets of their deprived neighborhoods and communities. Perhaps most significantly, they are taught those lessons in accordance with the beliefs and values held by others occupying those streets of scarcity. Additionally, those African American youth who do not seek lessons specifically from those occupying their neighborhoods and communities continue to be influenced by their living environments, because the neighborhood provides a belief system of acceptable and unacceptable behaviors.

Benson and colleagues (1998) describe communities as environments that can provide opportunities for socialization. Although socialization occurs primarily in the context of family, families do not and cannot exist in isolation from community. Consequently, communities and neighborhoods have great influence on families and thus youth by providing both positive and negative experiences for youth. Communities and neighborhoods can range from severely dangerous to plentiful with regard to economic and social resources. However, the existence or absence of poverty as an isolated variable does not *solely* define the positive or negative impact of the community on the development of youth (Jarrett, 1998).

The Factor of Socioeconomic Status

Recent data indicate that over half of African American youth are living below the poverty line (Davis, 1999; McLoyd, 1998). This solitary fact influences the development of African American youth in ways that are both debilitating and defeating. Research indicates that children and youth living in poverty are more susceptible to depression, low self-worth, behavioral problems, and posttraumatic stress symptoms (McLoyd, 1998; Wilson, 1996; Wiltfang & Scarbecz, 1990). Due to such conditions, many African American youth are preoccupied with acquiring the basics of daily living. Their caretakers are preoccupied with survival issues. The positive social, moral, and behavioral development of these children and youth is greatly compromised and in some cases, nonexistent, as the focus must remain on survival from day to day. The child living in poverty is subject to an increased number of stressors and is exposed to life-threatening situations at a greater rate than peers living above the poverty threshold (Black & Krishnakumar, 1998; Dryfoos, 1998; Garbarino, 1999; Illback, 1994; Jarrett, 1998; McLoyd, 1998).

Socioeconomic status also plays a significant role in the development of African American youth because the world at large continues to bombard children with the idea that the more one has materially, the better or more important one is. Edelman (1999) states it this way:

[We] face the same challenges today to help children define who they are and what to value in a culture that assigns worth more by extrinsic than intrinsic measures; by material rather than spiritual values; by money rather than morality; by greed rather than goodness; by consumerism rather than conscience. (p. xiv)

The focus is often placed on African American youth who live in poverty and the detrimental effects of such living, but socioeconomic status also plays a role in development. African American children and youth of middle- to high-class parents find themselves surrounded by more things, which are not adequate substitutes for the comfort, connection, and direction needed by all youth. Children living in poverty are not well prepared for the dilemmas of development, whereas children living in wealth run the risk of being as ill-prepared. Economic status greatly influences the development of youth; however, its impact is largely dependent on the additional supports available to African American youth to assist them in reaching and moving through developmental milestones.

The Impact of Spirituality

Spirituality has historically played a great role in the development of the African American youth (Coleman & Cunningham, 1996). Beliefs and values regarding the importance of spirituality were passed through the many generations of African American families and were thought of as sacred. As related to the development of socialization, for many African American youth the presence of religious/spiritual beliefs and practices in the home provides opportunity for routine, consistency, and conviction to guiding principles. For African American youth who are experiencing adversity, spiritual beliefs may also provide the source of perseverance and faith necessary to move through their challenges (Breggin, 2000; Coleman & Cunningham, 1996). Although numerous formal settings for spiritual worship have experienced the same difficulties as other social institutions, for many of today's youth, participation in organized activities that develop spirituality (such as attending church) represent one of the few remaining rituals offering protection, guidance, and support.

Research also indicates that children and youth, particularly those of color, are constantly questioning the presence of the spiritual realm in their lives (Coles, 1990, 1995a, 1995b; Dowd, 1997; Larson, 1996, 1999). In terms of the impact of spirituality on the developing youth, Coles (1990) writes that a child's life is comprised of "many mansions—including a spiritual life that grows, changes, responds constantly to the other lives that, in their sum, make up the individual we call by a name and know by a story that is all his, all hers" (p. 308).

The Impact of Culture

The development of the African American youth is greatly impacted by his or her knowledge about and ability to embrace the culture of the race. It is important for all youth to know and connect with their cultural roots, but the African American youth must often do so in the face of great controversy. Many African American youth are told that being smart, articulate, well-dressed, and stable are the behaviors of white people, or that they are trying to "act white" by demonstrating such behaviors (Tatum, 1999). This is particularly confusing for today's youth, who are bombarded with negative messages from the media regarding what it is to "act black."

For the African American youth, the impact of cultural awareness is critical to emotional development and self-empowerment. Welsing (1991) describes the "destroyed sense of self, the negative self-image and self concept" of youth as one of several results of the disconnection to cultural roots and self-awareness. She reports that, as African American children learn to disrespect themselves through negative images and stereotypes presented by the media of the majority, the ability to respect others is critically damaged. Edelman (1995) indicates that the failure of African American adults to teach our children and youth the lesson about their heritage is partially responsible for the lack of strength and cultural pride among African American youth.

Regardless of the cause for the lack of cultural awareness and appreciation among African American youth, it is clear that the impact of culture—on them and their perceptions of themselves as belonging to a specific culture and heritage—has far-reaching consequences related to social, mental, behavioral, and emotional development.

The Impact of Education

The effects of education on the development of the African American youth are varied. For many of these youth, education is devalued by the home, community, and significant others in their lives (Prothrow-Stith, 1991; Tatum, 1999; Welsing, 1991). As mentioned earlier, a level of distrust and disbelief exists among some African American children and youth regarding the necessity of formal education and the values they teach. As these children become further disconnected from institutions of learning, the gap widens between different classes of African Americans (the "haves" and "have-nots").

For far too many of them, there is no understanding of an existing relationship between what is learned in these institutions and what the goals or aspirations of the individual may be. In these cases, education simply represents another requirement being forced on the youth by parents, adults, and existing laws. The potential positive impact of education is minimized, because these are the children who habitually fail, do not attend school regularly, or eventually drop out altogether.

Inversely, for some African American youth and their families, education represents the only valid path to a particular lifestyle and desired status. In speaking with persons of African American descent, Coleman and Cunningham (1996) discovered that schools and education often provided the motivation for inner-city youth to move through their challenges and become successful and self-sufficient adults. The importance and value placed on education among African Americans can also be seen in the patterns of sports figures and celebrities who did not finish either high school or college but who returned to complete their studies. This behavior indicates that the institution of education continues to be of great importance to some African Americans, regardless of its necessity to provide material wealth and gain. Obviously, for these youth, education heavily influenced their development because it represented a goal, or an end result, to be strived for and obtained. In these cases, educational settings can become the practice field for many opportunities and life lessons that can be generalized into successful adulthood.

In facilitating the development of such a belief among African American youth, the challenging task for youth workers is to illustrate a direct connection between education and functional, successful adult living. To accomplish this, programming for African American youth must be purposeful in its efforts to create a meaningful relationship between education and quality of daily living for the youth. In other words, education becomes meaningful when youth can directly observe and experience the benefits of remaining engaged in the institution of formal education.

Community youth development workers must constantly engage in the analysis of contributing factors to the development of the population whom they serve. It is no secret that a large percentage of African American youth are facing crises that critically affect their development. Due to the "siege mentality" described by Davis (1999) as the conscious destruction of the psyche of the African American youth, many of the traditions and establishments that supported these youth are deteriorating or have completely disappeared. In examining the abovementioned factors as they relate to African American youth, it is essential that those working with these children and youth be mindful of the ways in which these variables enhance or subdue the developmental efforts of these young people.

❖ RECOMMENDATIONS FOR WORKING WITH AFRICAN AMERICAN YOUTH

Consider the following statistics reported by the Children's Defense Fund (2002): Every day in America for African American children 24 babies die, 514 babies are born into poverty, 1,065 children are arrested, 76 children are arrested for violent crimes, 999 public school students are corporally punished, 5,542 public school students are suspended, 617 high school students drop out, 1 person under 25 dies from HIV infection, 6 children and youth under 20 die from firearms, 1 youth under 20 commits suicide, and 4 children and youth under 20 are homicide victims. Many questions arise after reading and feeling the full impact of such a list. The questions include these: How do those of us who endeavor to work with African American youth battle against these odds and help children become their own saviors? What are the variables we must keep in mind when working with these children and youth that may be different from working with other children and youth? What are the practices that must be implemented to maximize opportunities for effective service delivery to African American youth? In an effort to address these questions and the critical question asked earlier in this chapter—"How do we comprehensively address the issue of assisting African American youth in their movement from being recipients of extrinsic support services to young adults who are intrinsically self-aware, self-sufficient, well developed, and contributing members of their communities?"—the following recommendations are made to those developing programs for and working with African American youth and children.

Understand, recognize, and appreciate the differences of African American children. Many of us endeavoring to help African American youth would contend that we must see beyond the color of their skin, believing that this viewpoint will make African American children and youth more comfortable. Instead, the mental assimilation and homogenization of African American youth is often used as a mechanism to make ourselves more comfortable. Refusing to acknowledge the uniqueness of an individual contributes to the depravation and degradation of that individual. We must intentionally acknowledge the importance of African Americans in the human race and in the smaller context of our daily work and lives. At other times than the month of February, those of us working with this population have the responsibility of highlighting the unique and special character of African Americans as a race and of the individuals who contributed to the betterment of our society.

Be aware of the life circumstances of the children and youth who are being served. Too many African American children experience daily life circumstances that would render most of us nonfunctional in the everyday tasks of living and learning. Many service models fail these children and youth because they are delivered in ignorance of the environment in which the youth lives and functions. Consequently, unrealistic expectations are placed on the youth, resulting in frustration and anger for both the youth and adult.

David was a young African American adolescent male who attended a therapeutic day treatment facility for educational and clinical services. During a period of David's attendance, he and his father were forced to sleep in their car with their belongings. Each morning, as David came to the facility, he would jog around the building and talk loudly. Those who were not aware of David's situation found themselves constantly frustrated and aggravated by a behavior that was viewed as intrusive and disruptive. Those who knew of his circumstances made allowances for his behaviors and, in addition to helping his father find appropriate housing, worked with him to develop coping mechanisms for functional living in spite of his situation. Youth workers must view themselves as facilitators of change by empowering youth to be creators of their own destinies.

In an effort to communicate our concern and care for children and youth, we often allow ourselves to view these children and youth as victims, and thus we allow them to view themselves as victims, also. We see them as victims of poverty, victims of familial dysfunction, victims of health issues, victims of poor self-esteem, and victims of the hardships of life. Furthermore, many of us believe that our role as youth workers and advocates includes that of savior. This is particularly true for professionals working with African American youth, as many of us allow sympathy for these youth, as opposed to empathy, to guide our work.

African American youth must be reminded that their destinies have not been predetermined by a cultural history that includes slavery, segregation, and oppression. Rather, they must understand that their cultural history is also comprised of individuals who created their own destinies in the face of slavery, segregation, and oppression. We must assist African American youth in becoming architects of sprawling futures as opposed to acceptors of limited existences.

Youth workers have convinced themselves that we have the power and the know-how to save children and youth when, in reality, the only ones who have such authority and power are the children or youth themselves. If we believe that *we* are responsible for saving the life of a child or youth and carry out our work based on this belief, we are robbing the individual of the opportunity to develop the skills, competencies, and attitudes that foster self-responsibility. Our work must include practices which will maximize success once our youth have moved beyond our reach.

Lickona (1991) reminds us that, whereas respect is the "restraining side of morality" that prevents us from harming the environment, others, and ourselves, responsibility is the "active side of morality." The teaching of responsibility requires that youth workers instill the importance of taking care of self and others, meeting our obligations, contributing to our communities, and working to contribute to the betterment of our world. Simply stated, for youth to learn responsibility, they must have responsibilities. Effective community youth development efforts will provide real-life opportunities for African American youth to exercise positive influence over their own lives while being guided and encouraged by adults in the development of responsibility and self-discipline. Fostering responsibility also dictates that adults communicate clear, consistent, and realistic expectations for youth behavior. Once these expectations have been communicated, the youth worker must demand the demonstration of responsible behavior, not in ways that create hostility and conflict between adults and youth, but in ways that convey belief that the youth is capable of being responsible for his or her life. As specifically related to African American youth, cultural and societal influences often communicate and encourage the avoidance of responsibility, leading many youth to begin internalization of the victim or helpless mentality. Community youth development workers must be willing and prepared to counter the development of such beliefs and to challenge behaviors that demonstrate irresponsibility. While simultaneously encouraging youth to take full ownership of their lives, we must discourage youth activities that excuse them from taking full responsibility for their feelings, thoughts, and behaviors.

Provide multicultural experiences for African American youth. Many times, youth development work is done in isolation from others who are of a different race and culture in an effort to protect the psyches of these youth. For example, it has been said by some African American professionals that white youth workers cannot effectively work with youths of color. If this attitude is perpetuated for African American children, we are simply manifesting the behavior of those who are oppressive.

When I discussed the issue of race relations and racism with an African American youth, she said that one of the program components that she found helpful was the variety of cultures and races she was able to interact with among the youth and adults. When asked why she found this helpful, she responded, "Working with other kinds of people lets me know that there are people who truly want to help me, other than African American people. When I receive their help, it reminds me that I should be helping everyone, too, not just other black kids or adults." In creating an environment that is multiracial, we remind African American students that each of us has an important role to play in contributing to the development and betterment of our world and that one race's role is not more significant than another's.

Provide opportunities to interact with positive African American adults. The African American youth often experiences a lack of positive and active role models in everyday living. Although role models often take the shape of television stars and millionaire athletes, these individuals do not play a significant role in the daily interactions and challenges of African American youth. Consequently, it is critical that African American youth have the opportunity to identify with those in their immediate environment who can provide them with support, guidance, and care.

One of the most powerful instances of the importance of cultural role models that I have witnessed occurred during several years of work in an educational facility for African American troubled youth. Many of these youth were unaccustomed to the presence of so many African American men who were well educated, well dressed, articulate, gentle, and caring. The nature of the relationships between these professional men and the youth was transforming. It was evident that the youth were learning that men are able to engage in expressive and passionate relationships with one another. The young men began to learn to seek the guidance and companionship of the male youth workers in ways that were appropriate and amiable instead of through aggressive and disruptive acts.

Involve African American youth as equal partners in the development and delivery of programs. Many programs that purport to provide opportunities for youth to be an integral part of their own development are merely paying lip service to a concept of human development. When individuals have been integrally involved in the development and implementation of a particular process or decision, the likelihood of ownership increases. The challenge in working with African American youth on equal partnering relates to history. Many times, youth have been promised that their input is valuable, only to learn that the majority rules. When working with children and youth, we must actively recruit them as our partners in the development and implementation of programming that addresses their needs. As we enlist them as our partners, we must demonstrate that their contributions are invaluable to the ongoing success of the program.

Adhere to the practices of strength-based paradigms. Strength-based paradigms are important to working with African American youth due to the abundance of deficit-based programming that exists and has been traditionally delivered to these youth. Strengths-based programming requires a specific method of communicating and interacting with youth. Most important, it provides the conceptual framework that dictates the nature of programs and their implementation. Traditional program models of youth development have focused on the identification and remediation of weaknesses rather than emphasizing strengths and how these can be used for the purposes of goal attainment. Strengths-based programming provides the opportunity for youth to develop the critical self-awareness, self-respect, and self-empowerment necessary for successful adult living.

Involve community stakeholders in the development and implementation of youth programs. Although many community programs deliver services to youth without the involvement of stakeholders, successful programs addressing youth development cannot exist in isolation from their communities and neighborhoods, just as youth do not live in ways that are exclusive to the influence of their communities, neighborhoods, and families. Because so many of our community, neighborhood, and familial connections have been broken, by choice and by necessity, programming is often seen as an entity outside the larger macrocosm of a youth's existence. Consequently, programming for African American youth may continue to be viewed as separate and apart from daily living. Programs that aspire to develop the total person must address the young person's ecology. Programming that understands and implements the integrative and inclusive approach to service delivery will make every effort to involve youth, youth's families, communities, and all those interested in the well-being of youth.

Know thyself. Knowledge of self is the centerpiece for successful work with any youth. No one working with youth can effectively do so if his or her intimate knowledge of self is faulty, based on self-deception, or is seen as unimportant to working with youth. This knowledge is particularly pertinent for those working with African American youth, because of the core issues surrounding these youth and their development. Those of the same race may find themselves mirrored in the faces of youth with whom they work and must be able to separate any personal challenges from the challenges of the young persons sitting before them. Those of a different cultural or ethic background may find their values, beliefs, and attitudes challenged by this work and the complexity of the issues that this population brings. Regardless of ethnic or cultural background, working with youth requires a diligence on the part of the youth worker to remain on constant watch and in constant contact with the self.

Furthermore, because the work of community youth development involves the youth in a process of self-exploration and self-awareness, knowing oneself is paramount in the ability to guide another through such an expedition. Jersild (1955) summarizes this point well in the following words:

> The [adult's] understanding and acceptance of himself is the most important requirement in any effort he makes to help students to know themselves and to gain healthy attitudes of self-acceptance. A teacher's understanding of others can be only as deep as the wisdom he possesses when he looks inward upon himself. To gain

in knowledge of self, one must have the courage to seek it and the humility to accept what one may find. (pp. 3, 83)

❖ CONCLUSION

The work of the community youth development movement faces a mammoth task. In a society where we are still largely encouraged to disengage from others and do whatever is necessary to obtain what we want, community youth development asks that youth workers, advocates, and professionals do the opposite. This work asks us to embrace youth in a more complete and authentic manner. Furthermore, community youth development asks us to recognize children and youth as active participants in the creation of their life stories as opposed to passive recipients of our knowledge and care.

In addition to the difficulties inherent in working with today's youth, our efforts with African American youth are further complicated by a set of complex variables, some of which have been discussed here. These youth remind us of the work we have yet to do and perhaps of the work we have not done at all. Community youth development asks us to embrace African American youth in ways that not only celebrate their differences but also ensure their status as valued members of the whole.

In her 1999 book, *Lanterns,* Marian Wright Edelman poignantly describes the gravity of the charge for those of us who choose this work, as she remembers the challenges facing those who chose to contribute to her development:

> They had to affirm and help us children internalize our sanctity as children of God, as valued members of family, of the Black community, of the American community, and of the entire human community, while simultaneously preparing us to understand, survive in, and challenge the prevailing values of a nation with a history of slavery, that did not value or affirm us as equal citizens or practice the self-evident belief that "all men are created equal" as its founding fathers professed. (p. xiv)

Although community youth professionals who chose to work with African American youth may discover that the mammoth task is both complex and demanding, if we are to serve these youth in ways that ensure their standing as the self-sufficient equal citizens Edelman describes, we will also discover that the task is both inspirational and necessary to the ongoing development of our children, and ultimately, our society.

❖ REFERENCES

Benson, P. L. (1997). *All kids are our kids: What communities must do to raise caring and responsible children and adolescents.* San Francisco: Jossey-Bass.

Benson, P. L., Leffert, N., Scales, P. C., & Blyth, D. A. (1998). Beyond the "village" rhetoric: Creating healthy communities for children and adolescents. *Applied Developmental Science, 2*(3), 138-159.

Black, M. M., & Krishnakumar, A. (1998). Children in low-income, urban settings: Interventions to promote mental health and well-being. *American Psychologist, 53,* 635-646.

Breggin, P. R. (2000). *Reclaiming our children: A healing solution for a nation in crisis.* Cambridge, MA: Perseus.

Burt, M. R., Resnick, G., & Matheson, N. (1992). *Comprehensive service integration programs for at-risk youth.* Washington, DC: Urban Institute.

Burton, L. M., Allison, K. W., & Odeidallah, D. (1995). Social context and adolescence: Perspectives on development among inner-city African American teens. In L. J. Crockett & A. C. Crouter (Eds.), *Pathways through adolescence: Individual development in relation to social contexts.* Mahwah, NJ: Lawrence Erlbaum.

Catalano, R. F., Berglund, M. L., Ryan, J. A. M., Lonczak, H. S., & Hawkins, J. D. (1999). *Positive youth development in the United States: Research findings on evaluations of positive youth development programs.* Washington, DC: U.S. Department of Health and Human Services.

Children's Defense Fund. (2002). *Every day in America.* Washington, DC: Children's Defense Fund. Retrieved September 19, 2002, from www.childrensdefense.org/everyday.htm

Coleman, G., & Cunningham, P. (1996). *African American stories of triumph over adversity: Joy cometh in the morning.* Westport, CT: Bergin & Garvey.

Coles, R. (1990). *The spiritual life of children.* New York: Houghton Mifflin.

Coles, R. (1995a). The profile of spirituality of at-risk youth. In T. Everson (Ed.), *The on-going journey: Awakening spiritual life in at-risk youth* (pp. 7-35). Omaha, NE: Boys Town Press.

Coles, R. (1995b). Some thoughts on religious and spiritual education with vulnerable youth. In T. Everson (Ed.), *The on-going journey: Awakening spiritual life in at-risk youth* (pp. 376-361). Omaha, NE: Boys Town Press.

Davis, N. J. (1999). *Youth crisis: Growing up in the high-risk society.* Westport, CT: Praeger.

Dowd, T. (1997). Spirituality in at-risk youth. *Reclaiming Children and Youth, 5,* 210-212.

Dryfoos, J. G. (1998). *Safe passage: Making it through adolescence in a risky society.* New York: Oxford University Press.

Edelman, M. W. (1987, September 26). *An Agenda for Empowerment* (speech delivered at the Congressional Black Caucus Awards Dinner, Washington, DC).

Edelman, M. W. (1995). *Guide my feet: Prayers and meditations for our children.* New York: HarperCollins.

Edelman, M. W. (1999). *Lanterns: A memoir of mentors.* New York: HarperCollins.

Farrell, B. G. (1999). *Family: The making of an idea, an institution, and a controversy in American culture.* Boulder, CO: Westview Press.

Franklin, D. L. (1997). *Ensuring inequality: The structural transformation of the African American family.* New York: Oxford University Press.

Garbarino, J. (1999). *Lost boys: Why our sons turn violent and how we can save them.* New York: Random House.

Illback, R. J. (1994). Poverty and the crisis in children's services: The need for services integration. *Journal of Clinical Child Psychology, 23,* 413-424.

Jarrett, R. L. (1998). African American children, families, and neighborhoods: Qualitative contributions to understanding developmental pathways. *Personality and Social Psychology Review, 2,* 2-16.

Jersild, A. T. (1955). *When teachers face themselves.* New York: Teachers College, Columbia University.

Kennedy, E. (1997). Male African Americans, single parent homes, and educational plans: Implications for educators and policymakers. *Journal of Education for Students Placed at Risk, 3,* 229-250.

Larson, S. (1996). Meeting needs of youthful offenders through the spiritual dimension. *Reclaiming Children and Youth, 5,* 167-172.

Larson, S. (1999). *At risk: Bringing hope to hurting teenagers.* Loveland, CO: Group.

Lickona, T. (1991). *Educating for character: How our schools can teach respect and responsibility.* New York: Bantam Books.

Masten, A. S., & Coatsworth, J. D. (1998). The development of competence in favorable and unfavorable environments: Lessons from research on successful children. *American Psychologist, 53,* 205-220.

McLoyd, V. C. (1998). Socioeconomic disadvantage and child development. *American Psychologist, 53,* 185-204.

Moshman, D. (1999). *Adolescent psychological development: Rationality, morality, and identity.* Mahwah, NJ: Lawrence Erlbaum.

Prothrow-Stith, D. (1991). *Deadly consequences.* New York: HarperCollins.

Spencer, M. B. (1999). Social and cultural influences on school adjustment: The application of an identity-focused cultural ecological perspective. *Educational Psychologist, 34(1),* 43-57.

Tatum, B. D. (1999). *Why are all the black kids sitting together in the cafeteria? And other conversations about race.* New York: Basic Books.

Taylor, R. L. (1995). *African American youth: Their social and economic status in the United States.* Westport, CT: Praeger.

Walker, J., & White, L. (1998, Winter). Caring adults support the healthy development of youth. *The Center,* 14-19.

Welsing, F. C. (1991). *The Isis papers: The keys to the colors.* Chicago: Third World Press.

Wilson, W. J. (1996). *When work disappears: The world of the new urban poor.* New York: Knopf.

Wiltfang, G., & Scarbecz, M. (1990). Social class and adolescents' self-esteem: Another look. *Social Psychology Quarterly, 53,* 174-183.

3

Research Realities and a Vision of Success for Latino Youth Development

Michael C. Rodriguez, Diana Morrobel, and Francisco A. Villarruel

For the first time in the history of the United States of America, there are more youth of Latino origin than any other ethnic or racial group, excluding non-Latino whites (U.S. Census Bureau, 2000a).[1] This momentous event has great implications for the social, economic, educational, and political future of the United States, yet it has gone largely unnoticed.

Thirty-five percent of Latinos residing in the United States are 18 years of age or younger. In comparison, the percentage of youth among non-Latino whites and African Americans is 24% and 31%, respectively. The number of Latino youth may even be greater than recently reported. It is estimated that at least 3 million people were not counted in the last census, many of whom are believed to be undocumented immigrants from Latin America, including many adolescents and children (Ramos, 2002).

The Latino community in the United States, described as one that is young and growing in numbers, is largely invisible (Montero-Sieburth & Villarruel, 2000). Although Latinos constitute 12.5% of the population of the United States, they are severely underrepresented in positions of power. For example, there is no Latino governor, senator, or Supreme Court justice, and Latinos hold only 4% of the seats in Congress (Ramos, 2002). This lack of representation is not exclusive to political arenas.

Despite overwhelming evidence indicating the significant increase of Latino youth throughout the United States, there is a dearth of research that focuses on this growing population. Latinos are noticeably absent from the literature that is often used to guide further research, program development, and policymaking. There is a dire need for researchers, practitioners, and policymakers to place greater attention on understanding the issues and factors that influence Latinos and foster positive development among the fastest-growing population of youth.

In this chapter, we provide an overview of the status of the research literature, identify some of the unique factors that influence Latino youth and merit further investigation, present recent reviews of model youth programs, and propose a vision of success for youth development researchers, programmers, and policymakers. Finally, we close with implications for research, policy, and practice.

❖ WHAT WE KNOW ABOUT LATINO YOUTH

In 1990, an estimated 22.4 million Latinos resided in the 50 United States and the District of Columbia, constituting 9% of the total population. In 2000, there were an estimated 35.3 million Latino residents, an increase of 58%, constituting 12.5% of the total population (U.S. Census Bureau, 2002). U.S. Census Bureau (2000b, 2000c) population projections estimate that by 2010, Latinos will constitute nearly 15% of the total population, and 17% by 2020. The numbers among youth are even more striking. In 2000, approximately 15% of all youth ages 5 to 18 and 14% of those between 10 and 20 were of Latino origin. The proportion of youth of Latino origin in the 10 to 20 age group is projected to be 20% by 2010. Projections are based on middle (rather than low or high) rates of fertility, life expectancy, and net migration.

Progress in the United States is often measured by economic and educational attainment. The presence and progress of Latinos in the nation's schools is an alarming situation. Nationwide, the Latino dropout rate has consistently been over 30% and for some Latino communities is over 40% (Fashola & Slavin, 2001). The U.S. Census Bureau (2000d), in its report on the 2000 educational attainment of people 25 years old and over, estimated that nearly 43% of Latinos have less than a high school diploma, whereas only 12% of the non-Latino white population are in this group. Similarly, 10% of Latinos 25 years old and over have 4-year college degrees or advanced degrees, but 22% of non-Latino whites are in this group. In addition, Latino youth are overrepresented among those who are economically disadvantaged. Recent immigrants who work at unskilled jobs with few possibilities for upward mobility constitute a significant portion of Latinos in the United States (McLoyd, 1998). Despite statistics that indicate a bleak outlook for Latinos, there are Latinos who succeed and thrive. Much can be learned from investigating normal and positive youth development; however, attention on Latino youth is lacking.

Latino Youth Research

The amount of research that has been conducted with Latino youth is not only sparse but also must be interpreted cautiously. In a review of research published in youth development journals, Rodriguez and Morrobel (2002) noted a serious lack of content addressing Latino youth issues. The paucity of research is parallel to what Graham (1992) and McLoyd (1998) have noted for African Americans. However, what is striking in the review of research conducted by Rodriguez and Morrobel is that those studies that did include Latino youth often failed to report the results for the Latino subjects separately, even in cases where hundreds of subjects were available.

Rodriguez and Morrobel (2002) reviewed the contents of six adolescent-focused journals (6 years of issues, from 1996 through 2001), including *Adolescence, Journal of Adolescent Research, Journal of Early Adolescence, Journal of Research on Adolescence, Journal of Youth and Adolescence,* and *Youth and Society.* They noted that, out of 1,141 journal articles, 86% were empirical (others included literature reviews and essays). Of the empirical literature, 30.6% reportedly included Latino subjects, 6.7% reported data on Latino subjects, and 3.0% studied

Latino subjects exclusively. If we were to rely on the mainstream youth development literature, we must conclude that we know little about Latino youth because developmental researchers fail to focus their work on them or fail to report results for them when included in research efforts.

It is evident from this review that Latino youth are not a priority among the interests of youth development researchers. However, researchers who do investigate issues regarding Latino youth adopt a wide range of theoretical perspectives. Based on their review, Rodriguez and Morrobel (2002) noted that the majority of the research during these 6 years had been primarily exploratory. No unifying developmental theory or perspective has been applied to the study of Latino youth.

With respect to positive youth development, Rodriguez and Morrobel (2002) further analyzed the content of articles by coding the focus of the empirical-based manuscripts. Using the asset-deficit development framework developed by the Search Institute (Benson, 1993; Scales, 1996), there was again a paucity of information that could be used by policymakers or youth programmers. In the 66 of 984 empirical articles that reported results for Latino subjects, the vast majority were deficit oriented, including issues related to sexual activity and pregnancy (42% of the 66 articles), depression and suicide (17%), negative peer pressure and deviant peers (17%), drug use (17%), and alcohol use (13%), including many more with less frequency. Among the assets employed were family support (15%), parental communication (11%), the presence of other adult resources and families having clear rules or consequences (6% each), and several others with less frequency.

Included in the review were manuscripts published in the *Hispanic Journal of Behavioral Sciences* and the *Latino Studies Journal*. Between the two Latino-focused journals reviewed during the same period, 23% of the 261 articles focused on developmental issues and were fairly balanced in terms of asset and deficit orientations. Of the 59 development-based articles, 40 were either mixed or neutral in terms of an asset or deficit orientation, whereas 12 were deficit oriented and 7 were asset oriented. The deficit-oriented articles focused on alcohol and drug use, sexual activity, depression and suicidal behavior, dropouts, sexual abuse, and trouble with law enforcement. Assets employed in these studies included family support, optimism about one's future, motivation to do well in school, and parent communication.

In summary, there is a dire need for research that can help to discern normative and healthy development processes for Latino youth. As already noted, the foundation of this research is tentative at best. Although 984 articles were published in six mainstream journals, only 66 reported results for Latino youth, less than half (30) of which focused exclusively on Latino youth. Whether the scarcity of research is viewed as poor scholarship or neglect, the field suffers substantially because of the lack of focus on Latino youth. The promotion of developmental research on Latino youth cannot be relegated to Latino-focused journals.

The Importance of Latino Youth Research

The gross underrepresentation of Latino youth in the current research literature is only part of the problem. Not only are Latinos noticeably absent from the current literature, but also a significant amount of what has been published further clouds our understanding of Latino youth and promotes damaging stereotypes. As noted earlier in this chapter, the current literature is plagued with conceptualizations and investigations that are based on a deficit model. Some issues facing Latino youth have been well documented: low educational attainment, lack of employment opportunities, poverty, teen pregnancy, poor health status, and limited health care (Padilla, 1995; Perez, 1992; Romo & Falbo, 1996). However, the factors that influence Latinos to thrive and succeed are yet to be explored and understood. We may know how many Latinos graduate at various levels of education or how many are in any given income bracket, but we are no closer to knowing Latino youth because of it, or knowing what might be done to enhance their well-being. Unfortunately, any effort that falls short of building on the unique contributions of Latino youth and families, in essence, can and perhaps will lead to the continued failure and underachievement of Latino youth and communities throughout the United States.

The tendency to focus on and describe at length the problems and deficits that characterize Latino youth is strong. The drive to focus on the negative aspects is based on our assumption that barriers must be overcome to achieve successful youth development. This has led to an unfortunate orientation toward intervention and prevention presuming that, unless external action is taken, Latino youth will succumb to negative, harmful, or life-threatening behaviors and conditions. Latino youth are often viewed as lacking skills and abilities to manage their environment and succeed. Focusing exclusively on negative outcomes fails to capture how culturally and contextually specific strengths can be built on to increase the number of youth who can thrive in an environment laden with poverty of ideal conditions.

The challenges to positive healthy development among Latino youth have traditionally been overlooked or altogether ignored by scholars and our nation in general (Montero-Sieburth & Villarruel, 2000; Perkins, Luster, Villarruel, & Small, 1998). Yet, the need to invest in this area of scholarship has not gone unnoticed. Prominent adolescent scholars (e.g., Lerner, 1995), educators (Darder, Torres, & Gutierrez, 1997; Suárez-Orozco & Suárez-Orozco, 2001; Valencia, 1991), and demographers (Chapa & Valencia, 1993; Hernandez, Siles, & Rochin, 2001) have noted the lack of research focused on Latino youth in the United States. They have also called attention to the need for this scholarship if policy, programs, and practices are to be established in a culturally and contextually relevant manner, and more important, if our nation is truly interested in promoting the positive and healthy development of Latino youth.

Previous researchers have left tremendous gaps in culturally relevant and sensitive research, and such gaps underscore the need for a change in the theoretical paradigms that serve as the foundation of rationale that guide and inform programmatic interventions. The failure to conduct research that documents the unique and normative developmental milestones in racially and ethnically diverse communities such as Latinos will only exacerbate the information needs of future communities and ethnic diversities.

Rodriguez and Morrobel (2002) argued that youth development research has ignored Latino youth, failed to report results for Latino youth when included, and concentrated on deficit models while failing to employ theory-based frameworks. The limiting nature of deficit-oriented models and research is not a new critique (Feldman & Elliott, 1990). A more productive orientation is one that focuses initially on Latino youth development as the primary strategy to promote positive development and long-term outcomes. Young people engage and invest in their development as a continuous process. "Throughout this process, young people seek ways to meet their basic physical and social needs and to build the competencies and connections they perceive as necessary for survival and success" (Pittman, 1992, p. 14).

This call for a new paradigmatic emphasis on Latino youth development is not unparalleled in the developmental sciences. As Stanfield (1993) noted, researchers and professional societies face a unique, albeit necessary, challenge. Not only must we reflect on the policy ramifications and the cultural inappropriateness of past research and current methodological approaches, but also we must establish discourse and develop new methodologies that are not ideologically determined or culturally biased reproductions of previously generated knowledge. McLoyd (1998), for example, asserted that culturally relevant conceptual frameworks are a basic necessity of the developmental sciences. Moreover, McLoyd argued that if we are to expand our knowledge of normative development across racial, ethnic, and socioeconomic groups, we must expand our understanding of what constitutes normative development.

Others (e.g., Fisher, Jackson, & Villarruel, 1997; Graham, 1992) have challenged future researchers not only to include more ethnic minorities in their research but also to develop a grounded theory of the developmental contextual issues related to their development as opposed to continuing the perspective of using nonminority groups as a normative comparative group.

We must reexamine, perhaps more critically, previously conducted research to assess its adequacy for the development of programs and policies, and more important, for its relative contribution to the existing knowledge base of ethnically and racially diverse individuals, families, and communities. One means of accomplishing this objective, Stanfield (1993) suggested, is to expand our knowledge of resiliency among ethnic minority youth in the United States and to subsequently translate this information so that it can be used in programmatic efforts as well as to inform and develop relevant policies that support the positive development of youth.

❖ A FEW RELEVANT FACTORS

Following the many recommendations presented earlier, we have identified several key factors that affect Latino youth and may contribute to positive developmental outcomes. These factors include Latino variants of adolescence, language, gender roles, religion, family, and ethnic identity.

Adolescence

The period of adolescence is typically defined to include youth between the ages of 10 and 20. Due to the lack of meaningful biological markers to note the end of this stage of life, social factors such as joining the workforce and becoming married have been traditionally used in industrialized societies to define entry into adulthood (Elliot & Feldman, 1990). Adapting this framework, Latino adolescents (especially those of lower socioeconomic status) may experience fewer years in the adolescent period due to early entry into the workforce and marriage.

Adolescence is marked by physical, social, and cognitive development. Physical changes often result in social changes by putting adolescents into new social roles. An individual's ability to think, reason, and make decisions also changes dramatically through adolescence. Unfortunately, much of our understanding of these transitions has been based on developmental research from non-Latino youth. Although there is no clear a priori theoretical expectation that many of these transitional stages differ for Latino youth, there is little to no evidence that they are similar for youth of different racial or ethnic backgrounds.

Adolescents face a variety of developmental challenges. Latino adolescents, because of their unique environmental contexts and ethnic minority status, face an additional set of challenges, the effects of which are relatively unknown. A common experience among Latino youth is discrimination. The additional stressors brought on through discriminatory acts are largely ignored in the research. Some researchers have suggested that Latino youth face at least three times as much institutional distress and more than twice as much educational distress because of the impact of discrimination (Fisher, Wallace, & Fenton, 2000). Discriminatory experiences described in the research included being hassled by store personnel, receiving poor service in restaurants, being treated as though they were not too smart, having more expected of them than of others, and being assumed to have poor English skills.

Language

Approximately half of the 35 million Latinos living in the United States prefer to speak Spanish. Thirty-seven percent of Latinos residing in the United States do not speak English well or at all, and 15% describe themselves as bilingual (Ramos, 2002). There are a number of indigenous languages, "Spanglish" words, and colloquialisms that are specific to certain Latin American subgroups and may not be understood by all Latinos (Ramos, 2002). Therefore, the language or expressions used by adolescents may vary depending on the age group, social class, geographic location, and ethnicity. In addition, Latinos have different levels of English and Spanish fluency and language preference that can influence youth development, an important consideration for researchers and practitioners.

Youth development is influenced by language through the communication of beliefs, values, cultural norms, and strategies for managing internal and external cues. Language is often conceptualized as static; however, we define it as a dynamic construct that may vary among individuals and within Latino communities.

Language is a complex factor that must be taken into account when working with Latino youth. Often, we assume that for programs to be culturally appropriate, relevant, or effective with Latinos, they must be in Spanish. This is no longer true. Latinos can be described as consisting of myriad individuals and families from diverse economic, educational, racial, ethnic, and linguistic backgrounds, including those who are monolingual English speakers and have been so for many generations. Although Spanish language programs may actually be an incentive for some youth to participate in programs, they also may serve as a deterrent for others. For some Latinos, maintenance of traditional Latino familial values and cultural practices has remained a way of life, but Spanish language use has decreased.

English language fluency among Latino adolescents may enhance their ability to aptly manage or negotiate various systems, including school, peers and other social networks, and community settings. Latino youth who are monolingual Spanish speakers will most likely face different or an increased number of challenges when compared to those who are monolingual English speakers or are bilingual. In light of the heterogeneity that exists among Latinos, it is no longer appropriate or useful to rely on surnames alone or ethnic heritage as an indicator of linguistic ability. To understand the complexity of youth development among Latino youths, researchers and practitioners must carefully consider how they address issues of language so that their practices are inclusive and address the linguistic needs of Latinos.

Gender Roles

Gender roles in traditional Latino families are still fairly distinct compared to the dominant culture in the United States. *Machismo* and *marianismo* shape gender role socialization and include a complex set of attitudes, behaviors, values, and beliefs. Machismo incorporates characteristics for males such as being courageous, trustworthy, responsible, authoritarian, and providing fully for one's family (Alvarez, Bean, & Williams, 1981). Latino males are also traditionally encouraged to be sexually active beginning in adolescence.

These characteristics vary widely from marianismo, which stresses for young women the value of virginity and chastity, as well as spiritual strength and obedience to males (Baca Zinn, 1982; Falicov, 1982). Marianismo is based on many of the qualities of the Virgin Mary in the Catholic faith.

Both males and females are socialized to abide by these gender roles from a young age, but they become increasingly prominent during the adolescent years. However, the validity of these stereotypical descriptions of gender roles (machismo and marianismo) in Latino communities has been challenged repeatedly (Casas, Wagenheim, Banchero, & Mendoza-Romero, 1995; Valentine & Mosley, 2000). These stereotypes do not consider social class, acculturation, regional differences, generational status, and simple issues such as rural versus urban life, level of education, and the presence of extended family (Vasquez, 1999).

Vasquez (1999) has suggested another, more positively oriented version of gender roles, in which

women most frequently take care of the household and family affairs and, in many places in the United States, are the brokers between the family and the community. Men bear the responsibility for financial support, make major decisions (often in consultation with their spouses), and provide a sense of security and stability to the family. (p. 180)

Even this description varies as a function of urban versus rural living, which is affected by employment options and economic goals of both men and women.

Religion

Gender roles and lifestyle choices of many Latinos are greatly influenced by religion. A nationwide study on Hispanic religion and politics was conducted recently as part of the Hispanic Churches in American Public Life Project (Parks, 2001). The researchers found a slight shift in religious affiliation, with 70% of the nation's Latinos reported to be Roman Catholic and 22% Protestant (up from 18% since 1990). Researchers also reported a U-shaped curve to the church attendance of Latinos around the country, in which attendance dropped off in second-generation Latinos compared to those in the first generation but increased in the third.

Others have estimated that nearly 90% of the Spanish-speaking world (internationally) is Roman Catholic (Clutter & Nieto, 2000). Religion plays a significant role in the daily living activities of Latinos around the world. "The church influences family life and community affairs, giving spiritual meaning to Hispanic culture" (Clutter & Nieto, 2000, para. 7). Attitudes toward family, gender, and community-based responsibilities are shaped by religion (Stevens-Arroyo & Diaz-Stevens, 1994). The significant role religion plays in the lives of Latinos has been studied extensively and continues to be the target of intense research, including researchers at the Brooklyn College Center for Research of Religion in Society and Culture at the City University of New York, and the Inter-University Program for Latino Research, a 16-member consortium headquartered at the University of Notre Dame.

Family

The role of the family is one of the least-understood and most-underestimated factors in Latino youth development. Common theories of youth development hold the task of gaining independence from parents as a key hallmark of adolescent development. Autonomy and increased emotional and social distance from parents and family is seen as a common stage of maturation (Cole & Cole, 1993; Comstock, 1994; Elliot & Feldman, 1990). Elliot and Feldman (1990) also argued that, in the United States, "adolescence is characterized by marked age segregation and little regular interaction with adults" (p. 3). These characterizations and outcomes of youth development stages may not be true of Latino youth.

In a study on new immigrant Puerto Rican youth and delinquency and crime, family appeared to be a significant factor that played a different role for Puerto Rican youth than for white non-Latino youth. With white youth, peers played the role of primary predictor for delinquent behavior; among Puerto Rican youth, family played as large a role as peers (Rodriguez, 1996). The prominence of the family in the lives of youth and the retention of traditional and cultural identity were significant deterrents to involvement in crime. There is other evidence demonstrating the negative impact on behavior of Latino youth facing changes in family composition and deteriorating family functioning (Vega, 1995).

In addition, many of the youth development researchers reporting results for Latino youth included sexual activity as a variable in their studies. There is evidence that the emotional environment in families is an important factor in adolescent sexuality (Huerta-Franco & Malacara, 1999). In a review of the literature, Driscoll, Biggs, Brindis, & Yankah (2001) noted several issues that were prominent in the area of Latino reproductive health, including socioeconomic status, national origin, peers, acculturation, and family involvement. Overall, they stressed the lack of information in each area as a limiting factor in our understanding of the critical issues.

Fathers may also function in a more significant role in strengthening Latino families than in white families. In a national survey of families and households, Latino fathers outperformed white fathers regarding behavioral (engaging in various activities) and cognitive (restrictions regarding television and time outside home) interactions with their teens, whereas Latino fathers approached fathering with a strong belief in the value of family (Toth & Xu, 1999). Latino fathers appear to reinforce the value of family closeness and respect for parents more than do white fathers.

Montero-Sieburth and Batt (2001) argued that many Latino students are caught in a social and cultural "tug of war between the assimilative efforts of schools against the resistance sought by their families" (p. 359). However, this pattern may not be characteristic of new Latino immigrants, who expend more effort to retain their ethnic identities, resisting assimilation. As an aside, assimilation (or acculturation) is an area that is largely confounded with many other characteristics of Latino youth, and some have suggested that what may look like assimilation may simply be differential development (Valentine & Mosley, 2000). The unique interactions of acculturation, family, and other aspects of youth development are not well understood and have typically focused on elements of dysfunction. Models that integrate aspects of adaptation, which some researchers have begun to investigate, are greatly needed (Vega, 1995). The role of families as a protective buffer against the impact of social ills must be closely evaluated.

Ethnic Identity

A key developmental marker of adolescence is identity development. Swanson, Spencer, and Petersen (1998) argued that environmental contexts are critical in identity development processes, whether from an ecological, psychological, or phenomenological perspective. The unique ecology of Latino youth provides a set of environmental contexts that require attention when considering identity development and the concomitant development of ethnic identity.

Ethnic identity is one area of adolescent development that has received significant attention and has been viewed as an aspect of personal identity (Phinney, 1989; Phinney & Alipuria, 1990). The majority of work in this area has focused on African Americans (e.g., Kerwin, Ponterotto, Jackson & Harris, 1993; Phinney, 1990); fewer studies have involved Latino youth (e.g., Bautista del Demanico, Crawford, & De Wolfe, 1994; Phinney, 1990; Phinney, Cantu, & Kurtz, 1997). Moreover, the theoretical work in this area far outweighs empirical work (e.g., Knight, Bernal, Garza, Cota, & Ocampo, 1993; Kerwin et al., 1993; Marshall, 1995; Phinney, 1990; Phinney & Chavira, 1992; Stevenson, 1994).

Although the models of ethnic identity have generally been based on Erikson's (1968) theory of ego identity formation and Marcia's (1966) empirical work on the stages of ego development, important insight related to Latino youth development can be noted. In general, ethnic identity formation is conceptualized as a series of stages an individual passes through over time, from a cultural identity to a highly diffused identity that develops in concert with dominant cultural views (Phinney, 1991). Three significant findings are central to our discussion. First, ethnic identity research supports a developmental process of ethnic identity formation (Phinney, 1989, 1992; Phinney & Chavira, 1992). Second, Latino ethnic identity is highly influenced by interpersonal relationships and other external factors such as family, extended family, and members of the community, rather than by internal factors (Marin & Marin, 1991; Zayas & Solari, 1994). Both of these findings support the need for additional research in this domain, and this important fact remains: The knowledge base on child development has generally come from studies of middle-class white families based on Euro-American values and standards of behavior (Zayas, 1994; Zayas & Solari, 1994).

Variations in the level of different forms of ethnic identity have been found between monoracial and multiracial Latino adolescents. Spencer, Icard, Harachi, Catalano, and Oxford (2000) examined affirmation of ethnicity (identification) and the level of activity youth engage in to learn more about their ethnicity (exploration), finding differences in the level of identification but not in the level of exploration. Among Mexican youth, family social class did not appear to be related to level of ethnic identity, but factors such as parental maintenance of culture, native language proficiency, and in-group peer interactions were important determinants (Phinney, Nava, & Huang, 2001). In addition, ethnic identity appears to play a significant role in the development of self-esteem among Latino adolescents (Carlson, Uppal, & Prosser, 2000).

Formation of ethnic identity in Latino adolescents is a complex process, complicated by building relationships in mainstream culture while participating in families with various levels of traditions and acculturation. Suarez (1993) reported that the bicultural environment has led to identity crises for some Cuban American youth. However, some youth are able to develop integrative ethnic identities in multicultural settings, where they develop the capacity to handle themselves in various settings, negotiate the demands of each situation, and maintain pride in their various roles. Guanipa-Ho and Guanipa (1998) developed these ideas in a review of identity formation and ethnicity in which they employed a definition of identity that included issues related to internalizing and self-selecting characteristics (such as values and beliefs) that define one's sense of self, including experiences inside and outside the family.

Guanipa-Ho and Guanipa (1998) also cited the work of Rosenthal and Feldman (1992), who argued that evidence exists regarding the interaction of contextual and developmental factors in the ethnic identify formation of adolescents, including such forces as the family. Families provide the primary experiences of ethnic group membership for youth, and the degree to which parents are involved in the ethnic community relates directly to the stability of an adolescent's ethnic identity. There is also evidence suggesting a relationship between the stability of ethnic identity and behavior. Phinney (1993) argued that adolescents with positive ethnic identities more effectively handle negative stereotypes and prejudice instead of internalizing negative self-perceptions. She also reported that positive ethnic identity contributes to positive psychological adjustment.

Taken together, these findings reinforce the notion that the limited scientific foundation of Latino adolescent development may be skewed so that Latinos appear to be less successful developmentally because there is no theoretical foundation from which we can understand Latino youth development, and in this case, the development of their ethnic identity.

❖ MODEL PROGRAMS

The connections between research and practice are not strong, in large part because of the lack of empirical research involving Latino youth and, in the existing limited research, the absence of theory. Much of what we know of Latino youth programming is anecdotal and relatively untested. Latino youth workers have told us repeatedly, "We know what works and what doesn't work with our kids; we just don't have the framework to describe it or the evidence to prove it."

The literature on model programs for youth development has been summarized in at least four recent reports. The American Youth Policy Forum released two volumes of abridged program evaluations (James, 1997, 1999). Roth, Brooks-Gunn, Murray, and Fester (1998) reviewed youth development program evaluations with an eye toward promoting healthy adolescents. We briefly comment here on their attention to programs that serve Latino youth. Finally, Slavin and Calderon (2001) edited a text that addressed effective educational programs for Latino students. We also comment briefly on their contributions.

James (1997) reviewed evaluation reports of 49 youth-serving programs including extended learning, community service learning and mentoring, and postsecondary access and retention programs. Of the 49 programs evaluated, 37 reportedly included Latino youth among those served (10 did not report the makeup of program clients). However, none of the programs were reported to be focused on Latino youth or to have culturally relevant components targeting Latino youth.

Ten programs that targeted minority youth were evaluated. Of those, few included key programmatic components regarding culture and cultural awareness, including the Job Corps, Big Brother Big Sisters, and the federally funded TRIO programs, including Upward Bound.

Although most of the evaluations reviewed were based on programs that served diverse communities of youth including Latinos, none of them focused on Latino youth or contained culturally relevant program components specifically for Latino youth. The few programs that focused on minority youth were similarly described without noting any culturally relevant factors contributing to their success with Latino youth. This did not exclude the possibility that these programs did in fact contain components designed for Latino youth despite their lack of inclusion in the review.

James (1999) also reviewed an additional 64 program evaluations of 46 youth-serving programs, in an attempt to be more comprehensive and to broaden the scope of the first review. Programs were divided into three general areas, including education and career development, building strong communities, and special programs of interest.

Of the program evaluations reviewed, only two were focused on Latino youth, and both were English development programs, including *Español Aumentativo* in Houston, Texas, and Santa Ana Unified School District in California. At least five of the programs were not reported to include Latino youth in their populations; however, none of the other programs included culturally relevant characteristics in their descriptions of key program components or factors contributing to their success.

Roth et al. (1998) reviewed 15 youth-serving program evaluations from a set of over 60 programs that focused on promoting healthy adolescents. The 15 selected met certain criteria regarding methodological rigor and included only those that served youth that were not clearly problematic (excluding programs focused on pregnancy, dropouts, or adjudicated youth).

Roth and colleagues (1998) provided a basic definition of youth development programs as those that "provide opportunities and support to help youth gain the competencies and knowledge they need to meet the increasing challenges they will face as they mature" (p. 423). As a basis for understanding outcomes, they used a definition for successful youth development based on the Carnegie Council on Adolescent Development, which suggested that successful youth are (a) intellectually reflective, (b) bound for a lifetime of meaningful work, (c) good citizens, (d) caring and ethical, and (e) healthy. They found that positive outcomes for youth development resulted from incorporation of aspects of youth development, caring adult-adolescent relationships, and longer-term programmatic efforts. They made no mention of the role of culture or ethnicity throughout their review.

In their text on effective programs for Latino students, Slavin and Calderon (2001) organized a series of chapters by various authors with the common assumption that "Latino students can succeed at the highest levels if they are given the quality of instruction they deserve, and a shared belief that reform of schools serving many Latino students is both possible and essential" (p. ix). The chapters presented case studies, data, and examples of school-based efforts to help Latino students succeed in elementary and secondary schools. The programs discussed included language development (English, Spanish, and bilingual language development), dropout prevention, and college attendance programs; several chapters focused on literacy and reading programs. The final two chapters presented factors that place Latino youth at risk for failure and a review of educational models that have been used to explain academic achievement.

The evidence from youth program literature regarding Latino youth development is severely limited, focusing almost exclusively on language and literacy development. About those programs that do serve Latino youth in the context of diverse communities, we know little of what makes them successful for Latino youth, if in fact they are successful with Latino youth.

❖ A VISION OF SUCCESS

A vision of success is a notion of strategic planning that stems from the private and corporate sector, which has been applied to public and nonprofit sectors as well. The importance of a vision of success has been widely recognized. When possible, it should be based on consensus among key stakeholders, which in our context includes service providers, policymakers, researchers, and youth and their families. The vision of success serves as a source of inspiration and can mobilize and direct energy. It should be challenging enough to spur action, yet not impossible to achieve so as to demoralize individuals (Bryson, 1988).

A vision of success for Latino youth development must be developed. What we propose here is a draft statement. This statement must be reviewed, evaluated, discussed, and strengthened. Although broad-based consensus may never be achieved, we should not let our philosophical or theoretical orientations distract us from this simple notion: Successful Latino youth development is attainable for all. Most professional organizations have developed statements of ethics and responsible, professional conduct. The vision of success is one step beyond such statements. It provides a guide and outcome to strive for, a common ground or focal point. It should not limit our work but should motivate continued groundbreaking efforts. It recognizes that there is a common goal, however that goal is achieved, and that this goal deserves concerted broad-based attention.

Our Vision

Our mission, as researchers and youth advocates, is to promote the positive development of Latino youth in all arenas, including research, policymaking, and program design, implementation, and evaluation. Our basic philosophy is focused on positive youth development as the primary means of achieving success for all youth. Problems faced by many teens, particularly Latino teens, derive from an imbalance of assets and deficits throughout all developmental stages. The critical issue for us is the identification of relevant assets for Latino youth. This imbalance leads to unsuccessful development and personally, socially, and physically maladjusted young adults. The basic goal is to foster developmentally appropriate environments that embrace the culturally unique strengths of Latino youth in ways that enhance their ability to take advantage of the assets they have.

As Pittman (1992) suggested, when youth can effectively build the competencies and connections they perceive as necessary for success (and in some cases, survival), risk factors can be overcome. Ironically, the concept of community youth development is something that has been inherent within and across Latino communities long before it became part of our current ideological framework. Suffice it to say, academia has failed to understand the significance of this phenomena for Latino youth, whereas grassroots organizations have made this a pillar of their efforts—but often they too fail to disseminate information on the relative importance of creating connections for youth within and across their communities.

Strategies to achieve the goal of successful Latino youth development must be undertaken collectively through more direct communication between researchers, policymakers, youth service providers, parents, and youth themselves. Initial strategies must include greater effort to include culturally appropriate frameworks for the study of Latino youth development. This presumes the inclusion of Latino subjects in developmental investigations and the reporting of results for Latino subjects. Policymakers should continue to inform their policymaking with relevant evidence and should seek that evidence vigilantly— providing funds to do so where the evidence is absent. Youth service providers, educators, and parents should continue to learn about developmental issues facing Latino youth and structure developmentally appropriate and culturally sensitive environments that allow Latino youth to identify and take advantage of their assets and strengths. Youth service organizations and programs must begin to adopt developmental strategies to secure positive development— successful development is our strongest tool to overcome and move beyond the limiting nature of deficit-oriented services.

Youth development researchers, policymakers, and youth service providers must be held to high standards of performance. Our reviews of the developmental research and the evaluation literature on youth development programs are indications of the neglect in the field toward Latino youth. Continued monitoring of the developmental research and more concerted efforts to evaluate Latino-focused youth development programs should help keep these issues salient. Salience, however, is not enough to promote change. Accountability for our own work and the inclusive and diverse nature of the research investigations undertaken, policies designed, and programs implemented must become a core ethical standard. Our work must be congruent with the world in which we live. To continue to ignore the fastest-growing segment of the population is an ethical offense and practical disaster. Youth service workers, educators, and policymakers are not released from their responsibility because of the lack of empirical research on Latino youth development. Ethical standards for policy and program design, implementation, and evaluation must be maintained, even in the face of an empirical research drought.

❖ IMPLICATIONS FOR RESEARCH, POLICY, AND PRACTICE

Implications for researchers and youth programmers, and through their efforts, policymakers, are imbedded throughout the discussions in each chapter in this volume. The focus here has been largely a critique of recent research on Latino youth development, including a brief look at what some see as effective youth programs, and our call for a vision of success—a mission statement for researchers, policy-makers, and programmers. To bring this chapter to a close, we offer two areas of thought for future work, including a few comments on research methodology and a note on the development of research protocols and programming materials.

Research Methodology

As may be evident from our earlier review of the literature, our preference is for theory-based or theory-directed research. Although we certainly recognize the need and role for exploratory research, it is time to move ahead. The troubling step is the identification of relevant conceptual frameworks or theories that are culturally or contextually appropriate. However, unless we start with theory, the development of theory itself is limited. "When theory reflects the reality of the populations under study, and when reality, in turn, contributes to the development of theory, cross-culturally relevant data can emerge to guide policy and practice" (Baca Zinn, 1995, p. 200).

Cross-cultural methodologies have been plagued by a lack of grounding and understanding of contextual, structural, and cultural factors relevant to the individual groups under study; they attempt to meet multiple cultural concerns simultaneously, which leads to a lack of clarity of such factors for each culture under study. The critical issues in such a grounding include

measurement of social inequality indicators, namely, the repeated confounding of race, ethnicity, culture, and socioeconomic status; the use of instruments that have limited applicability to the Latino experience and the lack of collaboration and partnerships with community-based agencies, organizations, and providers. (Baca Zinn, 1995, p. 199)

From the categorization of Latinos as one homogeneous ethnic group to the use of cross-cultural research design, the problems that plague current literature are numerous. Ethnic groups are defined as "distinct American groups that have a common culture, heritage, and place of origin outside of Europe" (Phinney & Landin, 1998, p. 90).

The term "Latino" is used to refer to individuals from Mexico, Central and South America, the Spanish-speaking Caribbean (Cuba, Dominican Republic, and Puerto Rico), or other Spanish culture or origin. The assumption that Latinos form a homogeneous ethnic group is erroneous. Latinos can trace their ancestry to myriad cultures from Africa, Europe, Asia, and indigenous tribes. The use of such classification ignores the heterogeneity of each cultural subgroup and minimizes the importance of subgroup differences. This classification forces researchers to assume a homogeneity that does not exist, rendering cross-cultural comparisons inadequate.

Cross-cultural studies have limited capacity to increase our understanding of Latino youth. Although recent investigations have attempted to refrain from comparing minority groups to a white sample, most researchers continue to rely on this methodology. A cross-cultural or between-group design (even among Latino subgroups) poses serious problems to valid interpretations of data and can lead to damaging applications of erroneous findings. As noted by Phinney and Landin (1998) "It is impossible to select a sample of one ethnic group that will precisely match a sample from another group" (p. 97). It is argued that even within a particular ethnic group, such a task may be impossible. There are significant differences in race, socioeconomic class, language, immigration patterns (voluntary vs. involuntary), and educational attainment that must be considered in all aspects of research design.

The differences addressed here, and many others, can profoundly affect and define the social context of an individual and consequently affect his or her development. Failure to account for or clearly assess and explore such factors can be detrimental. For example, it has been documented that Latinos have less educational attainment than whites (Fashola & Slavin, 2001). But perhaps such poor educational attainment is due to poverty experienced by Latino youth. Poverty is often measured by income and not by qualitative measures that assess the experience and social context in which the poverty is experienced. Latinos and whites who live below the poverty line are not necessarily similar. Their contexts may be qualitatively different. However, current methodology does not allow researchers to explore such a possibility.

Another relevant difference is the effect of skin color between and within groups. Few researchers have documented the impact of skin color on the psychological and social development of Latinos. Discrimination and racism also exist within Latino subgroups. Latinos whose skin color is of a darker hue may encounter more discrimination than those of a lighter hue because they are overtly different from the white majority. Lighter skin color is associated with more positive attributes and is deemed more desirable. The experiences of Latinos may be qualitatively different because of their skin color.

The psychosocial characteristics of Latinos may also differ in significant and relevant ways. Employing commonly used measures for assessing ethnic identity, self-esteem, emotional autonomy, and familial ethnic socialization, Umana-Taylor and Fine (2001) tested 1,176 adolescents living in the United States who were Columbian, Guatemalan, Honduran, Mexican, Nicaraguan, Puerto Rican, and Salvadoran. Although reliability (internal consistency) estimates varied across nationalities, it was difficult to assess the meaning of these differences because score variability information was not presented (score reliability varies directly as a function of score variability). Correlations among scores for ethnic identity, self-esteem, and family ethnic socialization (indicators of concurrent validity) also varied significantly across nationalities. The authors argued that nationality, immigrant history, and generational status are relevant variations among Latino subgroups that affect the consistency and meaningfulness of important psychological and social measures. Erkut, Szalacha, García-Coll, and Alarcón (2000) also argued that Latino subgroups must be studied separately in their investigation of self-esteem patterns.

Various recommendations have been made by researchers to address some of the inadequacies of past research. Cooper, Jackson, Azmitia, and Lopez (1998) suggested three strategies in their review of research with ethnic minority youth. Ecocultural models that employ multidimensional aspects of culture; ethnicity; and family, goals, and communication may uncover socially constructed meanings in communities. Parallel research designs could study multiple cultural communities and employ insider perspectives to measure community concepts and processes from relevant orientations. Finally, collaboration among stakeholders can strengthen links between researchers, youth, families, and institutions while coordinating goals, needs, and perspectives among stakeholders to enhance trust and improve research endeavors. Such strategies are rarely seen in current research.

Trust and understanding may provide the basis for successful research in Latino youth development. As an example, consider how we recruit Latino youth to participate in research or after-school programs. Because schools are frequently the primary site for recruitment of youth, professionals should understand that a large segment of the Latino youth population is left untapped when other settings are not considered. At times, youth that are in most need of programming are those that are not in the school system. This is especially important when working under a community youth development perspective, because this framework stresses the importance of building on strengths of all youth in a community context. Youth in the workforce or outside school environments may have valuable insights and experiences to offer those involved in research or programming efforts.

Recruitment alternatives include such places as neighborhood grocery stores, restaurants, churches, community ethnic events, and places that youth are known to work. Community outreach efforts can also be particularly effective, including the recruitment of youth from locations such as parks, bus stops, and even while riding public transportation.

Finally, ethnic group designations in developmental research are particularly complex, as Gjerde and Onishi (2000) pointed out: "Students of ethnicity need to realize that their object does not exist independently of their description of it" (p. 296). Use of global ethnic group categories fails to capture potentially meaningful within-group differences. In sum, cross-cultural research has led to conclusions that have strengthened stereotypes and discriminatory practices. Unless we account for and adequately explore these variables, we will continue to fail to understand Latino youth.

Research Protocols and Programming Materials

Language differences in research as well as in the field of service delivery and programming typically have been addressed through translation of protocols and materials. Special consideration must be paid to ensure that protocols and materials are appropriate for both monolingual (English/Spanish) and bilingual individuals. Linguistic equivalence as well as the conceptual equivalence of protocols and materials must be addressed. Several methods have been developed for the translation of materials.

One of the most commonly used methods of developing non-English versions of materials and procedures is direct translation. Under this method, protocols, questionnaires, and the like are translated from the source language to the target language. Although this method is often used in programs and research, it has been criticized as inappropriate for achieving equivalence in meaning (Brislin, 1970; Olmedo, 1981).

Caution in relying on direct translation is warranted. Materials that were created originally in English may include constructs that do not exist or are defined differently in Spanish. Some materials may not adhere to cultural norms that dictate how certain topics or issues are appropriately presented in a particular setting. Failure to account for these issues often results in material that is difficult to understand, culturally insensitive, or insulting, and may ultimately confuse and mislead the reader, which may render the results or information gathered invalid.

Another method for creating bilingual measures and materials has been the use of a combination of back translation and decentering. When using the back-translation method in creating new versions of materials (for example, from English to Spanish), one person (or a team of translators) translates from English to Spanish and a different person (or team) translates the Spanish version back to English. Decentering, used to deal with inconsistencies between resulting translations, is a process of revising language usage and removing any peculiarities of language to achieve greater equivalence. The combination of back translation with decentering is an improvement because of its iterative nature, increasing the opportunities to detect and correct nonequivalence (Erkut, Alarcón, García-Coll, Tropp, & Vázquez García, 1999). However, there are still concerns over the validity of the results (Bontempo, 1993; Olmedo 1981).

Erkut, Alarcón, and colleagues (1999), agreeing with Bontempo's (1993) argument that measurement equivalence cannot be achieved simply by creating materials in one language and using some process of translation, developed a dual-focus approach method. They implemented this method in a longitudinal study of Puerto Rican adolescents growing up on the mainland (Erkut, Szalacha, Alarcón, & García-Coll, 1999). A team of people with expertise in the issues studied and in the culture involved was employed. The researchers argued that most of the team members should be bilingual/bicultural and should include members indigenous to both cultures. The process included joint definition of research questions, construct operationalization, joint generation and critique of items, and evaluation of resulting psychometric properties.

The dual-focus approach offers an advantage over translation-based methods, particularly from a positive youth development perspective, because it uses the strengths not only of bilingual collaborators but also of monolingual collaborators from both cultures. The inclusion of Latino youth in this process is an additional benefit for youth development researchers and program developers and secures greater internal validity. The youth can be viewed as co-collaborators in this process, drawing on their expertise, ideas, and energy. Using a community youth development framework in both research and applied settings includes adults working together with youth in a way that both employs and develops their strengths.

Toward a Contextual Approach to Working With Latino Youth

Fulfillment appears to be a more common goal among youth around the world than the negative experiences that lead to or come from the turmoil typically found during the adolescent years. In fact, the turmoil we attribute so saliently to adolescence may not be a characteristic found in all adolescents. Csikszentmihalyi and Schmidt (1998) argued that "healthy growth requires that the individual be fully functioning and involved with meaningful challenges" (p. 14). They also suggested that almost anything adults can do to challenge and involve youth in meaningful ways is bound to help promote healthy development. Csikszentmihalyi and Schmidt described a set of obstacles to fulfillment, including physical restrictions, absence of responsibility, problems related to sex and intimacy, lack of adult role models, real or sensed powerlessness, and lack of control. Herein lies another set of research questions regarding the role of such obstacles in the lives of Latino youth, given the unique set of characteristics of development presented earlier.

Meaningful and challenging activities must be situational, integrated with the environment and ecology of Latino youth in their own communities. This goal argues against any potential universal approach to working with Latino youth. Given unique and diverse experiences in Latino communities around the country, youth service providers must approach each youth in his or her own environment.

We now have a set of factors that can inform the provision of services so that the goal of positive development may be enhanced and optimized. Our goal of developing a vision of success is intended to more closely align two aspects of our work: what we know and what we do. Unfortunately, what we know rarely informs what we do. With respect to Latino youth development in a theoretical or academic context, we know very little. With respect to Latino youth in a more general sense, we know a lot, particularly from youth service providers. With a commitment to our work, our professions, and our youth, we can fulfill the goals of our vision of success to secure more successful positive youth development in all Latino communities.

❖ NOTE

1. The racial classification used by the U.S. Census Bureau generally adheres to the guidelines in Federal Statistical Directive No. 15, issued by the Office of Management and Budget, which provides standards on race and Hispanic origin categories for statistical reporting to be used by all federal agencies. The category "Hispanic" includes persons of Mexican, Puerto Rican, Cuban, Central or South American, or other Spanish culture or origin, regardless of race. In this chapter, we elected to use the term Latino to reflect the linguistic and regional diversity of those it characterizes.

❖ REFERENCES

Alvarez, D., Bean, E. D., & Williams, D. (1981). The Mexican American family. In C. H. Mindel & R. W. Habenstein (Eds.), *Ethnic families in America: Patterns and variations* (pp. 269-292). New York: Elsevier North Holland.

Baca Zinn, M. (1982). Familism among Chicanos: A theoretical review. *Humboldt Journal of Social Relations, 10,* 224-238.

Baca Zinn, M. (1995). Social science theorizing for Latino families in the age of diversity. In R. E. Zambrana (Ed.), *Understanding Latino families: Scholarship, policy and practice* (pp. 177-189). Thousand Oaks, CA: Sage.

Bautista del Demanico, Y., Crawford, I., & De Wolfe, A. S. (1994). Ethnic identity and self-concept in Mexican-American adolescents: Is bicultural identity related to stress or better adjustment? *Child & Youth Care Forum, 23,* 197-206.

Benson, P. L. (1993). *The troubled journey: A portrait of 6th-12th grade youth.* Minneapolis, MN: Search Institute.

Bontempo, R. (1993). Translation fidelity of psychological scales: An item-response theory analysis of an individualism-collectivism scale. *Journal of Cross-Cultural Psychology, 24*(2), 149-166.

Brislin, R. W. (1970). Back-translation for cross-cultural research. *Journal of Cross-Cultural Psychology, 1*(3), 185-216.

Bryson, J. (1988). *Strategic planning for public and nonprofit organizations.* San Francisco: Jossey-Bass.

Carlson, C., Uppal, S., & Prosser, E. C. (2000). Ethnic differences in process contributing to the self-esteem of early adolescent girls. *Journal of Early Adolescence, 20*(1), 44-67.

Casas, J. M., Wagenheim, B. R., Banchero, R., & Mendoza-Romero, J. (1995). Hispanic masculinity: Myth or psychological schema meriting clinical consideration. In A. M. Padilla (Ed.), *Hispanic psychology: Critical issues in theory and research.* Thousand Oaks, CA: Sage.

Chapa, J., & Valencia, R. R. (1993). Latino population growth, demographic characteristics, and educational stagnation: An examination of recent trends. *Hispanic Journal of Behavioral Sciences, 15*(2), 165-187.

Clutter, A. W., & Nieto, R. D. (2000). *Understanding the Hispanic culture* (Ohio State University Fact Sheet, HYG-5237-00). Retrieved September 19, 2002, from http://ohioline.osu.edu/hyg-fact/5000/5237.html

Cole, M., & Cole, S. R. (1993). *The development of children* (2nd ed.). New York: Scientific American Books.

Comstock, J. (1994). Parent-adolescent conflicts: A developmental approach. *Western Journal of Communication, 58*(4), 263-82.

Cooper, C. R., Jackson, J. F., Azmitia, M., & Lopez, E. M. (1998). Multiple selves, multiple worlds: Three useful strategies for research with ethnic minority youth on identity, relationships, and opportunity structures. In V. C. McLoyd and L. Steinberg (Eds.), *Studying minority adolescents: Conceptual, methodological, and theoretical issues* (pp. 111-125). Mahwah, NJ: Lawrence Erlbaum.

Csikszentmihalyi, M., & Schmidt, J. A. (1998). Stress and resilience in adolescence: An evolutionary perspective. In K. Borman and B. Schneider (Eds.), *The adolescent years: Social influences and educational challenges* (pp. 1-17). Chicago: University of Chicago Press.

Darder, A., Torres, R. D., & Gutierrez, H. (1997). *Latinos and education: A critical reader.* New York: Routledge.

Driscoll, A. K., Biggs, M. A., Brindis, C. D., & Yankah, E. (2001). Adolescent Latino reproductive health: A review of the literature. *Hispanic Journal of Behavioral Sciences, 23*(3), 255-326.

Elliot, G. R., & Feldman, S. S. (1990). Capturing the adolescent experience. In S. S. Feldman and G. R. Elliot (Eds.), *At the threshold: The developing adolescent* (pp. 1-13). Cambridge, MA: Harvard University Press.

Erikson, E. H. (1968). *Identity, youth, and crisis.* New York: W. W. Norton.

Erkut, S., Alarcón, O., García-Coll, C., Tropp, L. R., & Vázquez García, H. A. (1999). The dual-focus approach to creating bilingual measures. *Journal of Cross-Cultural Psychology, 30* (2), 206-218.

Erkut, S., Szalacha, L. A., Alarcón, O., & García-Coll, C. (1999). Stereotyped perceptions of adolescents' health risk behaviors. *Cultural Diversity and Ethnic Minority Psychology, 5*(4), 340-349.

Erkut, S., Szalacha, L. A., García-Coll, C., & Alarcón, O. (2000). Puerto Rican early adolescents' self-esteem patterns [Electronic version]. *Journal of Research on Adolescence, 10*(3), 339-364.

Falicov, C. J. (1982). Mexican families. In M. McGoldrick, J. K. Pearce, & J. Giordano (Eds.), *Ethnicity and family therapy* (pp. 134-163). New York: Guilford Press.

Fashola, O. S., & Slavin, R. E. (2001). Effective dropout prevention and college attendance programs for Latino students. In R. E. Slavin & M. Calderon (Eds.), *Effective programs for Latino students* (pp. 67-100). Mahwah, NJ: Lawrence Erlbaum.

Feldman, S. S., & Elliott, G. R. (1990). Progress and promise of research on adolescence. In S. S. Feldman and G. R. Elliot (Eds.), *At the threshold: The developing adolescent* (pp. 479-505). Cambridge, MA: Harvard University Press.

Fisher, C. B., Jackson, J. J., & Villarruel, F. A. (1997). The study of ethnic minority children and youth in the United States. In R. M. Lerner (Ed.), *Theoretical models of human development* (pp. 1145-1207). New York: Wiley.

Fisher, C. B., Wallace, S. A., & Fenton, R. E. (2000). Discrimination distress during adolescence. *Journal of Youth and Adolescence, 29*(6), 679-695.

Gjerde, P. F., & Onishi, M. (2000). In search of theory: The study of "ethnic groups" in developmental psychology [Electronic version]. *Journal of Research on Adolescence, 10*(3), 289-298.

Graham, S. (1992). "Most of the subjects were white and middle class": Trends in published research on African Americans in selected APA journals, 1970-1989. *American Psychologist, 47*, 629-639.

Guanipa-Ho, C., & Guanipa, J. A. (1998). *Ethnic identity and adolescence.* Retrieved September 29, 2002, from http://edweb.sdsu.edu/people/CGuanipa/ethnic.htm

Hernandez, R., Siles, M., & Rochin, R. I. (2001). *Latino youth: Converting challenges to opportunities* (JSRI Working Paper No. 50). East Lansing, MI: Julian Samora Research Institute.

Huerta-Franco, R., & Malacara, J. M. (1999). Factors associated with the sexual experience of underprivileged Mexican adolescents. *Adolescence, 34*(134), 389-401.

James, D. W. (Ed.). (1997). *Some things do make a difference for youth: A compendium of evaluations of youth programs and practices.* Washington, DC: American Youth Policy Forum.

James, D. W. (Ed) (1999). *More things that do make a difference for youth: A compendium of evaluations of youth programs and practices* (Vol. 2). Washington, DC: American Youth Policy Forum.

Kerwin, C., Ponterotto, J. G., Jackson, B. L., & Harris, A. (1993). Racial identity in biracial children: A qualitative investigation. *Journal of Counseling Psychology, 40*(2), 221-231.

Knight, G. P., Bernal, M. E., Garza, C. A., Cota, M. K., & Ocampo, K. A. (1993). Family socialization and the ethnic identity of Mexican-American children. *Journal of Cross-Cultural Psychology, 24*(1), 99-114.

Lerner, R. M. (1995). The place of learning within the human development system: A developmental contextual perspective. *Human Development, 38*(6), 361-366.

Marcia, J. E. (1966). Development and validation of ego-identity status. *Journal of Personality and Social Psychology, 3*(5), 551-558.

Marin, G., & Marin, B. (1991). *Research with Hispanic populations.* Newbury Park, CA: Sage.

Marshall, S. (1995). Ethnic socialization of African American children: Implications for parenting, identity development, and academic achievement. *Journal of Youth and Adolescence, 24*(4), 377-396.

McLoyd, V. C. (1998). Changing demographics in the American population: Implications for research on minority children and adolescents. In V. C. McLoyd & L. Steinberg (Eds.), *Studying minority adolescents: Conceptual, methodological, and theoretical issues* (pp. 3-28). Mahwah, NJ: Lawrence Erlbaum.

Montero-Sieburth, M., & Batt, M. C. (2001). An overview of the educational models used to explain the academic achievement of Latino students: Implications for research and policies into the new millennium. In R. E. Slavin & M. Calderon (Eds.), *Effective programs for Latino students* (pp. 331-368). Mahwah, NJ: Lawrence Erlbaum.

Montero-Sieburth, M., & Villarruel, F. A. (Eds.). (2000). *Making invisible Latino adolescents visible: A critical approach for building upon Latino diversity.* New York: Falmer Press.

Olmedo, E. L. (1981). Testing linguistic minorities. *American Psychologist, 36*(10), 1078-1085.

Padilla, A. M. (1995). *Hispanic psychology: Critical issues and theory.* Thousand Oaks, CA: Sage.

Parks, T. (2001, May 28). *Landmark study examines Hispanic religion & politics.* Retrieved September 19, 2002, from www.baptiststandard.com/2001/5_28/print/study.html

Perez, S. M. (1992). Community-based efforts and youth development policy: An effective partnership for Latino youth. In National Governors' Association (Ed.), *Investing in youth: A compilation of recommended policies and practices* (pp. 11-12). Washington, DC: National Governors' Association.

Perkins, D. F., Luster, T., Villarruel, F. A., & Small, S. (1998). An ecological, risk-factor examination of African American and Latino adolescent sexual activity. *Journal of Marriage and the Family, 60*(3), 660-673.

Phinney, J. S. (1989). Stages of ethnic identity development in minority group adolescents. *Journal of Early Adolescents, 9*(1), 34-49.

Phinney, J. S. (1990). Ethnic identity in adolescents and adults: Review of research. *Psychological Bulletin, 108*(3), 499-514.

Phinney, J. S. (1991). Ethnic identity and self-esteem: A review and integration. *Hispanic Journal of Behavioral Sciences, 13*(2), 193-208.

Phinney, J. S. (1992). The multigroup ethnic identity measure: A new scale for use with diverse groups. *Journal of Adolescent Research, 7*(2), 156-176.

Phinney, J. S. (1993). A three-stage model of ethnic identity development in adolescence. In M. E. Bernal & G. P. Knight (Eds.), *Ethnic identity: Formation and transmission among Hispanics and other minorities*. New York: State University of New York Press.

Phinney, J. S., & Alipuria, L. (1990). Ethnic identity in college students from four ethnic groups. *Journal of Adolescence, 13*, 171-183.

Phinney, J. S., Cantu, C. L., & Kurtz, D. A. (1997). Ethnic and American identity as predictors of self-esteem among African American, Latino, and White adolescents. *Journal of Youth and Adolescence, 26*, 165-185.

Phinney, J. S., & Chavira, V. (1992). Ethnic identity and self-esteem: An exploratory longitudinal study. *Journal of Adolescence, 15*, 271-281.

Phinney, J. S., & Landin, J. (1998). Research paradigms for studying ethnic minority families within and across groups. In V. C. McLoyd & L. Steinberg (Eds.), *Studying minority adolescents: Conceptual, methodological, and theoretical issues* (pp. 89-109). Mahwah, NJ: Lawrence Erlbaum.

Phinney, J. S., Nava, M., & Huang, D. (2001). The role of language, parents, and peers in ethnic identity among adolescents in immigrant families. *Journal of Youth and Adolescence, 30*(2), 135-153.

Pittman, K. (1992). From deterrence to development: Toward a national youth policy. In National Governors' Association (Ed.), *Investing in youth: A compilation of recommended policies and practices* (pp. 13-14). Washington, DC: National Governors' Association.

Ramos, J. (2002). *The other face of America: Chronicles of the immigrants shaping our future*. New York: HarperCollins.

Rodriguez, M. C., & Morrobel, D. (2002, April). *Latino youth development: A vision of success in a period of empirical drought*. Paper presented at the annual meeting of the American Educational Research Association, New Orleans, LA.

Rodriguez, O. (1996, May). *The new immigrant Hispanic population: An integrated approach to preventing delinquency and crime*. Retrieved September 19, 2002, from www.ncjrs.org/txtfiles/hispop.txt

Romo, H. D., & Falbo, T. (1996). *Latino high school graduation*. Austin: University of Texas Press.

Rosenthal, D. A., & Feldman, S. S. (1992). The nature and stability of ethnic identity in Chinese youth: Effects of length of residence in two cultural contexts. *Journal of Cross-Cultural Psychology, 23*(2), 214-227.

Roth, J., Brooks-Gunn, J., Murray, L., & Fester, W. (1998). Promoting healthy adolescents: Synthesis of youth development program evaluations. *Journal of Research on Adolescence, 8*(4), 423-459.

Scales, P. C. (1996). A responsive ecology for positive young adolescent development. *Clearing House, 69*(4), 226-230.

Slavin, R. E., & Calderon, M. (Eds.). (2001). *Effective programs for Latino students.* Mahwah, NJ: Lawrence Erlbaum.

Spencer, M. S., Icard, L. D., Harachi, T. W., Catalano, R. F., & Oxford, M. (2000). Ethnic identity among monoracial and multiracial early adolescents. *Journal of Early Adolescence, 20*(4), 365-387.

Stanfield, J. H. (1993). Epistemological considerations. In J. H. Stanfield II & R. M. Dennis (Eds.), *Race and ethnicity in research methods* (pp. 16-36). Newbury Park, CA: Sage.

Stevens-Arroyo, A. M., & Diaz-Stevens, A. M. (Eds.). (1994). *An enduring flame: Studies on Latino popular religiosity.* New York: Bildner Center for Western Hemisphere Studies, City University of New York.

Stevenson, H. C. (1994). Validation of the scale of racial socialization for African American adolescents: Steps toward multidimensionality. *Journal of Black Psychology, 20,* 445-468.

Suarez, Z. E. (1993). Cuban Americans. In H. P. McAdoo (Ed.), *Family ethnicity: Strength in diversity* (pp. 164-176). Newbury Park, CA: Sage.

Suárez-Orozco, C., & Suárez-Orozco, M. (2001). *Children of immigration.* Cambridge, MA: Harvard University Press.

Swanson, D. P., Spencer, M. B., & Petersen, A. (1998). Identity formation in adolescence. In K. Borman and B. Schneider (Eds.), *The adolescent years: Social influences and educational challenges* (pp. 18-41). Chicago: University of Chicago Press.

Toth, J. F., Jr., & Xu, X. (1999). Ethnic and cultural diversity in fathers' involvement: A racial/ethnic comparison of African Americans, Hispanic, and White fathers. *Youth and Society, 31*(1), 76-99.

Umana-Taylor, A. J., & Fine, M. A. (2001). Methodological implications of grouping Latino adolescents into one collective ethnic group. *Hispanic Journal of Behavioral Sciences, 23*(4), 347-362.

U.S. Census Bureau. (2000a, January 13). *Projections of resident population by age, sex, race, and Hispanic origin: 1999-2100* (NP-D1-A). Retrieved September 29, 2002, from www.census.gov/population/projections/nation/detail/d1999_00.pdf

U.S. Census Bureau. (2000b, January 13). *Projections of resident population by age, sex, race, and Hispanic origin: 1999-2100* (NP-D1-A). Retrieved September 29, 2002, from www.census.gov/population/projections/nation/detail/d2001_10.pdf

U.S. Census Bureau. (2000c, January 13). *Projections of resident population by age, sex, race, and Hispanic origin: 1999-2100* (NP-D1-A). Retrieved September

29, 2002, from www.census.gov/population/projections/nation/detail/ d2011_20.pdf

U.S. Census Bureau (2000d, March). *Educational attainment of people 25 years and over, by nativity and period of entry, age, sex, race, and Hispanic origin.* Retrieved September 29, 2002, from www.census.gov/population/ socdemo/education/p20-536/tab10.pdf

U.S. Census Bureau. (2002, May 9). *USA statistics in brief, a supplement to the statistical abstract of the United States.* Retrieved September 29, 2002, from www.census.gov/statab/www/poppart.html

Valencia, R. R. (1991). Conclusions: Towards Chicano school success. In R. R. Valencia, (Ed.), *Chicano school failure and success: Research and policy agendas for the 1990s* (pp. 321-325). London: Falmer Press.

Valentine, S., & Mosley, G. (2000). Acculturation and sex-role attitudes among Mexican Americans: A longitudinal analysis. *Hispanic Journal of Behavioral Sciences, 22*(1), 104-113.

Vasquez, P. (1999). Culture: The pervasive context. In J. D. Koss-Chioino & L. A. Vargas (Eds.), *Working with Latino youth: Culture, development, and context.* San Francisco: Jossey-Bass.

Vega, W. A. (1995). The study of Latino families. In R. E. Zambrana (Ed.), *Understanding Latino families: Scholarship, policy and practice* (pp. 3-17). Thousand Oaks, CA: Sage.

Zayas, L. H. (1994). Hispanic family ecology and early childhood socialization: Health care implications. *Family Systems Medicine, 12,* 315-325.

Zayas, L. H., & Solari, F. (1994). Early childhood socialization in Hispanic families: Context, culture, and practice implications. *Professional Psychology: Research and Practice, 25*(3), 200-206.

4

Positive Youth Development in Urban American Indian Adolescents

Tamara C. Cheshire and Walter T. Kawamoto

U rban American Indian adolescents face a wide variety of challenges in terms of positive youth development in mainstream society. In fact, mainstream society can learn a thing or two from the resiliency strategies American Indian families and communities have used in promoting positive youth development in adolescents.

❖ BACKGROUND

To understand positive youth development from an American Indian experience, it is crucial to recognize the composition of family in that culture. Only a few articles have attempted to discuss the intricacies of the American Indian family and its resiliency. Red Horse (1980) explained that the family is the foundation in American Indian society; the American Indian family is characteristically a system of extended kin who "form a network over several households" (p. 462). Because many Indian families continue this cultural tradition of relying on the extended family, researchers, policymakers, and youth professionals must realize that the extended family is a valid family system and that the role of the extended family fosters "interdependence, not independence or autonomy" (Red Horse, 1980, p. 462). Indeed, this extended family system has survived despite U.S. policies that have, in part, attempted to dismantle the cultural-familial value system of American Indian families (Harjo, 1999; Kawamoto & Cheshire, 1999). The fact that this extended family system has survived provides testimony to the resiliency of indigenous values that contribute to positive youth development in American Indian adolescents.

In the extended family system, there is a sense of mutual obligation in family development. Collateral relationships exist in which involvement, approval, and self-worth are featured (Red Horse, 1980). Individuals are expected to fulfill cultural obligations to family members. Some obligations may include giving other family members money when they need it or taking care of a niece or nephew for an extended period of time. Collateral relationships are based on obligations of individual family members that create a system of family support that is maintained and secure. Being a responsible individual and performing necessary functions in a collateral relationship, where one is involved with other family members, brings with it approval and self-worth.

One example that illustrates the collateral relationship, mutual obligations in family development, involvement, approval, and self-worth, is the giveaway. A giveaway is an event that usually happens at a pow-wow (an Indian community celebration). Although the specifics may be different from one region to the next, a giveaway is generally held to mark a special occasion (birth, death, marriage, any rite of passage or memorials) (Whitehorse, 1988). The giveaway promotes a community recognition of a rite of passage for a specific member of a certain family who is associated with the community.

One type of giveaway is held to recognize the "coming out" or transition to adulthood for young women. At the time of adolescence, many girls have their first menses. To mark this rite of passage, a giveaway may be planned by the girl's family, who begin by discussing the importance of this occasion with the adolescent. Family members work together to prepare for the giveaway by making items or saving money to contribute. At the pow-wow, a friend of the family will speak for the young woman and call forth family and friends to receive items, while discussing the role these people have played in the adolescent's life and encouraging them to continue to fulfill their roles. It would be inappropriate and boastful for the girl to speak for herself (Whitehorse, 1988). After items have been given out, the adolescent and family participate in an honor dance in which the community dances behind them in support of the youth, after shaking hands and sometimes offering money to the family (Whitehorse, 1988). Thus, the family supports the youth becoming a full member of the community as a young adult, the youth acknowledges the support of blood and fictive kin, and the community expresses literally and symbolically their support for the youth and her family. When it comes time for one of her sisters or female cousins to have a coming out, the adolescent will fulfill her new role by supporting the next in line in that ceremony as she was supported by her family, maintaining the interdependent system. For the family to continue functioning, everyone must fulfill their individual and group roles.

Cross (1998) continued his emphasis on extended family by linking it to a relational worldview. The relational worldview, or the cyclical worldview, is rooted in tribal cultures. This view focuses on "the balance and harmony in relationships among multiple variables, including metaphysical forces. . . . Every event is in relation to all other events regardless of time, space or physical existence" (Cross, 1998, p. 147). Harmony and balance are conducive to good health. This relational worldview is conducive to positive youth development in American Indian adolescents in that the view itself promotes harmony and balance. Hope and working toward a goal of balance are two factors included in the cyclical worldview that is rooted in many tribal cultures. Brendtro, Brokenleg, and Van Bockern (1990) focused on harmony and balance in their discussion of the Circle of Courage. The Circle of Courage incorporates traditional American Indian child-rearing philosophies that provide an alternative way of thinking about positive youth development. This focus of child-rearing and positive youth development lies in the "education and empowerment of children" (Brendtro et al., 1990, p. 35) and relates to the primary goal of fostering self-esteem and self-worth in child-rearing practices.

Through Bronfenbrenner's ecological theory (Bretherton, 1993), we can see the urban American Indian family placed in its own subcultural system. The next system emanating from the urban Indian family is the urban Indian community, which serves to reinforce traditions and values including the interdependence of the family and the family's interdependence with the community. The urban American Indian family and community are placed in a larger sphere called the dominant society. Here, the family and community face institutionalized oppression. Each environment has its own specific issues, but they all relate to and affect each other. One emphasis from Bronfenbrenner was that to study members of a subculture, one must participate in that subculture (Bretherton, 1993). This was a call to all practitioners to get involved in the local ethnic communities and discover what those communities have to offer in terms of preexisting systems that promote positive youth development.

❖ ISSUES

Although the preponderance of research has not focused on issues of positive youth development, a review of work on American Indian adolescents provides insight into some of the key issues on which youth professionals and researchers need to focus their attention.

As discussed earlier, a positive aspect of the American Indian family and community is the relational worldview (Cross, 1998). Because the relational worldview is in direct opposition to the linear worldview of mainstream society, it is often valued less. The linear worldview focuses on the individual and isolates the adolescent from his or her family, thereby promoting individualism and causing more harm than good in interdependent American Indian families. Within this larger social framework of independence and capitalism lies a hierarchy and oppression. American Indian families deal with oppression that originates from and is sustained by society. Overt oppression, the extreme being physical violence and attempts to annihilate the target group (Sherover-Marcuse, n.d.), has been and continues to be experienced by American Indians in the United States (Green, 1992). Covert oppression (subtle aspects of discrimination) takes place and is inherent in the various institutions of society from the private to the public sector (Green, 1992).

Racism impacts urban American Indian youth on many levels. Because of stereotypes, American Indian youth are initially seen as troublemakers or deviant. According to Brendtro and colleagues (1990), negative expectations can produce failure and futility in youth. Policymakers and professionals may be promoting a self-fulfilling prophecy for Indian youth without ever realizing it. Although it is not often discussed, internalized oppression rests on doubts of self-worth that are instilled through the education system, the media, and society, undoing years of positive youth development and reinforcement in the American Indian home and community. This internalized oppression can lead to destructive behavior toward the self and aggressive inter-actions within and outside the group or community (Gunn Allen, 1992). This internalized oppressive behavior is taught by the larger society. Marginalization also aids the process of internalized oppres-sion, in that Indian people are encouraged to believe the fabricated image of the stereotypic Indian, which replaces the actual being. When existence is defined by the oppressor, self-identity, self-respect, and self-worth are lost.

Besides the loss of identity, self-respect, and self-worth in American Indian youth, the feeling of isolation is the next most impor-tant factor. American Indian youth who are living in foster homes and/or being adopted into non-Indian families are at high risk of being isolated and committing suicide (Johnson & Tomren, 1999). These youth experience stress from acculturation and are isolated from family, community, and culture. According to Johnson and Tomren (1999), among American Indian youth ages 15-19, suicide is the second leading cause of death. This rate is almost three times higher than the national average. In addition, "American Indian children placed in non-Indian homes for adoptive or foster care suffer a rate of 70 suicides per 100,000, six times higher than that of other youth in the United States" (Johnson & Tomren, 1999, p. 287). Thousands of American Indian adoptees remain at risk in non-Indian homes (Berlin, 1987), despite attempts to place them with Indian families in response to the Indian Child Welfare Act.

Urban American Indian youth may feel that they do not belong anywhere. They may feel "too Indian" to belong and be accepted by their non-Indian foster or adopted parents or "not enough Indian" or "too assimilated" to belong and be accepted by their family of origin or Indian community. This isolation can manifest in low self-esteem as well as depression. Other than suicide, additional high risk behaviors are likely, such as gang involvement, substance abuse (Herring, 1994) and high dropout rates in school (Wood & Clay, 1996).

Many do not consider that the nation's schools reinforce the oppression of American Indian youth. Children become aware at an early age about racism and their social standing from school, the media, books, and so on (Levine, 1967). This perception either becomes the motivator or the deterrent to academic achievement (Wood & Clay, 1996). The oppression experienced by Indian children in school is a serious deterrent to retention. We must also take into account that the education system is based on the independence of the individual within a larger community, not interdependence.

When dealing with American Indian youth, the emphasis should not be on the individual but on the extended family and the individual's interdependence within that framework. For instance, teachers may see an urban American Indian adolescent failing in classes. There are two ways of dealing with this:

1. Stereotype the adolescent and expect that the youth will continue to do poorly in school and blame it on the youth's individual inability to perform and maintain average grades, which will lead to the youth's continued poor performance and eventual suspension.

2. Realize that the adolescent is experiencing systemic oppression inherent in the school and society and attempt to motivate the youth by getting to know him or her, the culture, and the family. Realize that the adolescent may need a different type of motivation, interdependent versus independent. Pair the youth with others to work as a team. Professionals can reach out and stop the isolation that occurs with the cycle of oppression.

Currently there is a revitalization movement happening among all tribes. American Indian youth in schools know that if they graduate from both high school and college, they will be more likely to help their tribes survive in the 21st century. The idea here is that the focus on the individual in education has changed to the focus on the tribe or community and how one's individual education can make a difference for the tribe.

Issues facing American Indian youth can be overcome with the help of the extended family, the Indian community, and with important changes in the outside society.

❖ COMMUNITY

Reservation and urban American Indian communities have been forming organizations for decades to address numerous issues, including
the needs of their youth. Some of these organizations were formed to
serve critical life-and-death concerns. One such organization is the Ain
Dah Yung (Our House) Center in St. Paul, Minnesota, established in
1985. This American Indian youth shelter has numerous services for
the homeless, runaways, and survivors of abuse and neglect
("American Indian youth shelter," 1999). Another is Juel Fairbanks
Chemical Dependency Services, also in St. Paul, established in 1975.
Originally serving only American Indian men, this residential and out-
patient treatment center has opened its services to chemically dependent youth of all ethnicities (DeRockbraine, 1998).

Many other programs address issues such as education and personal development through a strengthening of cultural ties. These programs share a few key elements. First, programs interested in
education and Indian culture are often indistinguishable. The mission
statement of the Capitol Area Indian Resources (CAIR) of Sacramento,
California, states that it "was formed in 1985 to provide academic assistance and culturally related activities for American Indian youth" (La
Marr, 1998, p. 2). CAIR uses culture and education to enhance each
other by such activities as training tutors in culturally specific learning
styles and helping Indian elders to understand how to stand up for
their culture in the school setting. Similarly, the Spokane Medicine
Wheel Academy—the focal point of the Spokane, Washington, Title IX
Indian Education Program—uses traditional customs and ceremonies
for the intended goal of increasing retention and graduation rates
(Howell, 1997). Among this program's efforts to support educational
goals is a series of efforts to feature Indian cultural issues as subjects of
study. Educational goals and self-esteem through Indian culture go
hand in hand.

Another element many of these programs share is an expectation
that family, of one kind or another, will be a major component of their
activities. For CAIR, parents of participating students are required to
attend a parent orientation workshop before services are provided.
This workshop was enacted for parents to learn about their opportunities and responsibilities as parents in the CAIR tutoring program (La
Marr, 1998). At the Spokane Medicine Wheel Academy, fictive kin in
the form of Indian elders from the Spokane community are called on to

participate in academy activities so that urban youth who may not have blood relatives in Spokane can still feel a sense of family and continuity with their ancestors (Howell, 1997). Successful Indian education programs value the critical role of family in the development of skills and Indian identity in children.

Some of the best success stories involving community efforts to address urban American Indian youth issues have been in conjunction with reservation communities and have been pan-Indian in scope. An example of this dynamic is "Navajo Nights," hosted by Lorie Lee. Lee, a radio personality in Window Rock, Arizona, is helping to bring a new era of Indian sounds and music to the nation. Her program on the Navajo Nation's 50,000-watt AM station (KTNN 660 AM) features talent from across the country such as Haida, an American Indian hip-hop artist; Casper, a Hopi reggae band; and Indigenous, an American Indian blues band. The Tuesday night program reaches youth in 13 western states and was selected the number one station in the United States by E! Online (Norrell, 1998). Another respected young entertainer, Litefoot, recently organized the largest-ever gathering of American Indian youth at the Wind River Reservation in central Wyoming (Little Eagle, 1998). This gathering to recognize the wealth of energy, talent, and opportunity inherent in American Indian youth and to help them see ways in which they can walk in two worlds was certainly a family affair. The motivation for this event was prompted when Litefoot's niece died, along with five other youth, in a senseless car accident. Litefoot decided to help the community heal after the loss of these youth; so he asked his adopted mother if he could have a gathering on her 40 acres of land located on the Wind River Reservation (Friday, 1998). Such pan-Indian initiatives by young role models show the vital role of integrating urban and reservation concerns with homegrown solutions. American Indian children must have successful Indian role models (Farris & Farris, 1976). Role models can be found in the extended family and the community. The task before other youth service professionals is to facilitate similar initiatives and support them, not to impose solutions from the outside.

One of the most comprehensive accounts of American Indian youth was a survey of more than 1,000 high school and college age youth from reservation and urban populations by the Solidarity Foundation (Ewan, 1997). Although there are many interesting results from this study, a few are of particular interest in the context of education, families, and community organizations. Youth raised on reservations were reported as only slightly less likely to be the first of their families to attend college (Ewan, 1997), suggesting that education concerns are just as serious in one setting as another. When asked what would help keep youth in school, youth responded by suggesting counseling, increased self-esteem, and parental involvement (Ewan, 1997). Finally, a comparison with older American Indians showed that young people are finding it easier to feel comfortable with their Native identity while also being a part of contemporary society. This is especially evident when one notes that the vast majority identified with their own Indian nations (96%), whereas many of those same respondents identified Martin Luther King Jr. (76%) as their number one role model (Ewan, 1997). This means that community organizations must consider the very complex, multilayered needs and interests of today's American Indian youth.

❖ SOCIETY

For programs to work for American Indians, we must first acknowledge that oppression exists and know that it is inherent in the systems and institutions we deal with daily. Education about American Indian families is part of the solution. To educate about Indian families, we must understand them from an internal perspective. External factors can and do affect American Indian youth and whether positive youth development is reinforced or chipped away by systemic oppression in the dominant society.

❖ CONCLUSION

Human service professionals should develop training and programs that recognize the importance of the extended family or the urban Indian community in American Indian culture. There is a need to "know that family and culture are inseparably linked to individual mental health, in that sense of selfhood is derived from an historic culture as transmitted through family systems" (Red Horse, 1980, p. 462). By taking into consideration the cultural context, we can use coping and healing mechanisms that are already in the American Indian family system or introduce strategies that will work in the family system instead of working against it to create even more discord.

Because cultural identity is strongly linked to high self-esteem (Johnson & Tomren, 1999), Indian youth must have the connection to extended family who practice traditions and transfer cultural values from one generation to the next. Involvement in the urban Indian community also plays an integral role in reinforcing cultural identity and supporting self-esteem in Indian youth. Thus, identification with and strong involvement in American Indian culture, community, and family can lead to positive youth development, a protective factor against the risks adolescents face daily.

❖ REFERENCES

American Indian youth shelter to celebrate fifteen years of service. (1999, January 29). *The Ojibwe News, 11*(16), 4.

Berlin, I. N. (1987). Suicide among American Indian adolescents: An overview. *Suicide and Life-Threatening Behavior, 17*(3), 218-232.

Brendtro, L., Brokenleg, M., & Van Bockern, S. (1990). *Reclaiming youth at risk: Our hope for the future.* Bloomington, IN: National Educational Service.

Bretherton, I. (1993). Theoretical contributions from developmental psychology. In P. Boss, W. Doherty, R. LaRossa, W. Shumm, and S. Steinmetz (Eds.), *Sourcebook of family theories and methods: A contextual approach* (pp. 286-297). New York: Plenum.

Cross, T. (1998). Understanding family resiliency from a relational world view. In H. McCubbin, E. Thompson, A. Thompson, and J. Fromber (Eds.), *Resiliency in Native American and immigrant families* (pp. 143-157). Thousand Oaks, CA: Sage.

DeRockbraine, T. D. (1998, December 31). Celebrating 25 years of sobriety. *The Circle, 19*(12), 6-7.

Ewan, A. (1997, December 31). Generation X in Indian country: A Native American Indian Youth Survey. *Native Americas, XIV*(4), 24-29.

Farris, E. E., & Farris, L. S. (1976). Indian children: The struggle for survival. *Social Work, 21,* 386-389.

Friday, B. (1998, July 30). Red Nations gathering: Recognizing the wealth found in Native youth. *Wind River News, 21*(31), 1-3.

Green, R. (1992). *Women in American Indian society.* New York: Chelsea House.

Gunn Allen, P. (1992). Angry women are building: Issues and struggles facing American Indian women today. In M. L. Andersen & P. Hill Collins (Eds.), *Race, class and gender: An anthology* (pp. 42-46). Belmont, CA: Wadsworth.

Harjo, S. S. (1999). The American Indian experience. In H. McAdoo (Ed.), *Family ethnicity: Strength in diversity* (2nd ed., pp. 63-71). Thousand Oaks, CA: Sage.

Herring, R. D. (1994, July/August). Substance use among Native American Indian youth: A selected review of causality. *Journal of Counseling & Development, 72*(6), 576.

Howell, R. (1997, January 27). Spokane Medicine Wheel Academy enriched with traditional teachings. *Indian Country Today,* p. B1.

Johnson, T., & Tomren, H. (1999). Helplessness, hopelessness, and despair: Identifying the precursors to Indian youth suicide. *American Indian Culture and Research Journal, 23*(3), 287-301.

Kawamoto, W. T., & Cheshire, T. C. (1999). Contemporary issues in the urban American Indian family. In H. McAdoo (Ed.), *Family ethnicity: Strength in diversity* (2nd ed., pp. 94-104). Thousand Oaks, CA: Sage.

La Marr, C. (1998). *Capitol Area Indian Resources, Inc., Tutor Training Guide/Manual.* (Available from Capitol Area Indian Resources, Inc., 2701 Cottage Way, Suite 9, Sacramento, CA 95825)

Levine, R. A. (1967). *Dreams and needs: Achievement motivation in Nigeria.* Chicago: University of Chicago Press.

Little Eagle, A. (1998, July 27). Litefoot: Empowering the youth. *Indian Country Today,* p. C6.

Norrell, B. (1998, June 29). Barbara Walters of Indian Rock. *Indian Country Today,* p. C1.

Red Horse, J. G. (1980). Family structure and value orientation in American Indians. *Social Casework: The Journal of Contemporary Social Work, 61,* 462-467.

Sherover-Marcuse, R. (n.d.). Unlearning Racism Workshop handout. Unpublished.

Whitehorse, D. (1988). *POW-WOW: The contemporary Pan-Indian celebration* (San Diego State University Publications in American Indian Studies No. 5). San Diego, CA: San Diego State University.

Wood, P. B., & Clay, W. C. (1996, September). Perceived structural barriers and academic performance among American Indian high school students. *Youth & Society, 28*(1), 40-60.

5

Facilitating Positive Development in Immigrant Youth

*The Role of Mentors
and Community Organizations*

*Jennifer G. Roffman, Carola
Suárez-Orozco, and Jean E. Rhodes*

Today, one in five children in the United States is a child of immigrants; by 2040, it is projected that one in three will be the child of an immigrant (Rong & Preissle, 1998). These youth bring with them remarkable strengths—strong family ties, a deep-seated belief in education, and optimism about the future. However, their journey presents a number of challenges. Many are settling in highly segregated neighborhoods of deep poverty (Orfield & Yun, 1999). Immigrant parents often must work long hours, leaving their children relatively unsupervised. The family system is placed under stress by the social and cultural dislocations inherent in migration (Sluzki 1979; Suárez-Orozco & Suárez-Orozco, 2001). Immigrant parents, many of whom have limited English skills, often find it difficult to monitor their children's academic progress, keep track of their children's after-school activities, and understand their children's experiences (Cooper, Denner, & Lopez, 1999; Phelan, Davidson, & Yu, 1993; Suárez-Orozco & Suárez-Orozco, 2001). As a result, many immigrant youth are vulnerable to emotional difficulties as well as the lure of the street.

Immigrants come from a variety of circumstances and contexts. Some come for economic reasons, whereas others are fleeing political, religious, or ethnic persecution. Nearly 80% of present-day immigrants to the United States come from Latin America, Asia, and the Afro-Caribbean basin (Rumbaut, 1997). Latino immigrants from Central and South America make up the largest group, and the bulk of the research on immigration and the challenges facing immigrant youth has focused on this group. Immigrants from Asia, especially the countries of Southeast Asia, constitute the second-largest group, comprising almost 30% of the foreign-born population of the United States. Caribbean immigrants make up the third-largest group, comprising just over 10% of the U.S. foreign-born population (U.S. Census Bureau, 1997). Naturally, youth from each of these three regions of origin face different types of challenges, further complicated by the fact that there is as much variation within each group as between them. Nonetheless, members of all three groups share the stress associated with migration to a new country, as well as often-intense discrimination and related challenges to achieving high levels of education and employment as they and their families become settled in the United States.

This chapter examines issues associated with immigration that may affect the development of immigrant youth from all three groups. A treatment of each specific group of origin's experience is beyond its scope. Furthermore, although the chapter necessarily deals with the experiences of parents as well as youth, our primary focus is issues affecting the development of the children of immigration. These issues influence both first- and second-generation youth who share the experience of growing up with immigrant parents.[1]

For immigrant youth, mentors and nonparental adults in community agencies may prove to be invaluable for optimal development. Volunteer mentors and community youth workers can support children and adolescents growing up in challenging environments by providing structure and supervision during out-of-school hours. They can be a source of explicit information about the rules of engagement in the new society. They may also serve as a valuable source of emotional support, acting as attachment figures in a new context where youth are often socially isolated. The guidance provided by volunteer mentors or adult staff members at community youth organizations represents an important resource to foster the healthy development of immigrant children.

As noted in the introduction to this volume, such external support systems can be essential to families and to youth development (Perkins & Borden, 2003, this volume). Research on nonparental adult support figures interacting with youth through volunteer mentoring programs, community sports programs, or neighborhood activity centers indicates that these relationships can contribute to positive outcomes for youth by improving academic performance, behavior, socioemotional development, and family relationships (Freedman, 1993; McLaughlin, Irby, & Langman, 1994; Rhodes, Grossman, & Resch, 2000; Tierney, Grossman, & Resch, 1995). In the present chapter, we examine the contributions made by mentors and community youth workers to the lives of immigrant children and adolescents. We do this by first exploring several different sorts of challenges faced by many immigrant youth, which make their experiences with mentors and community youth workers particularly salient to their development. We then examine the processes involved in mentoring and in participating in community youth programs that have the potential to positively influence youth development. Finally, we discuss implications for policy concerning mentoring, community youth programs, and the healthy development of immigrant adolescents.

❖ STRESS RELATED TO EXCLUSION

Immigrants typically face a number of institutional barriers to acceptance and inclusion in the culture and the economy of the nation. In recent years, widespread concern about the influx of new immigrants has led to several anti-immigrant initiatives designed to prevent immigrants from receiving benefits or public services (Suárez-Orozco, 1998). These practices generate a pattern of intense exclusion and segregation among large numbers of immigrants and the larger society in several contexts, including the workforce (Smith, Tarallo, & Kagiwada, 1991; Waldinger & Bozogmehr, 1996), schools (Orfield, Chew, et al., 1999;

Waters, 1997), and housing (Bankston & Zhou, 1997a; Suárez-Orozco, 1998). The result is a dramatic growth in the numbers of recent immigrant families struggling in segregated communities with inadequate services, substandard schools or insufficient bilingual education services, and limited access to employment (Orfield & Yun, 1999; Silka & Tip, 1994; Tienda, 1995), even though many of these immigrants are highly educated and skilled (Rumbaut, 1997).

These problems are compounded by the hostile reception often given to poor immigrant youth, which includes intolerance for their native languages and skin colors (García-Coll & Magnuson, 1997). Fear of the cultural dilution of the country's institutions and values feeds an anti-immigrant ethos that includes intolerance of immigrants who do not speak the language of the new setting and who "look different" from the dominant majority (Espenshade & Belanger, 1998). The negative attributes projected onto these immigrants include expectations of sloth, irresponsibility, low intelligence, and even danger. This negative social mirror reflected by other young people, teachers, school administrators, and the media is eventually internalized by immigrant youth (Camino, 1994; Katz, 1999; Suárez-Orozco & Suárez-Orozco, 2001).

Immigrants from many countries, including those in the Caribbean, Southeast Asia, and Latin America, have parents who may have grown up as part of the ethnic majority and are therefore unprepared to help their children deal with being marginalized as part of a minority group (Waters, 1997). The psychological effects of internalizing the negative perceptions of the majority culture, especially when associated with the combined effects of poverty and prejudice, can be devastating (Adams, 1990; Suárez-Orozco & Suárez-Orozco, 2001).

❖ STRESS RELATED TO POVERTY

Many immigrant youth suffer from the challenges associated with urban (as well as rural) poverty. Of course, immigrants to the United States come from many different circumstances. Some are among the elite of their countries, often leaving home to escape political turmoil. Others are solidly middle-class, mobilized either by better economic opportunities or by ethnic, religious, or political persecution. Many come from situations of relative poverty (though it is important to note that the very poorest, lacking the resources, do not emigrate). Others may not come from poverty but will suffer (at least an initial) economic decline on emigrating. New arrivals typically settle first in highly segregated areas of deep poverty (Orfield & Yun, 1999), either in urban contexts or in rural farming communities.

Poverty has long been recognized as a significant risk factor for children (Luthar, 1999; Weissbourd, 1996). Children raised in circumstances of socioeconomic deprivation are vulnerable to an array of psychiatric distress including difficulties concentrating and sleeping, anxiety, and depression as well as a heightened propensity for delinquency and violence (Luthar, 1999). Those living in poverty often experience greater major life events stress as well as the stress of daily hassles (Luthar, 1999). Poverty frequently coexists with a variety of other risk factors that augment the risks of poverty alone, such as single parenthood, residence in neighborhoods plagued with violence, gang activity, and drug trade as well as school environments that are segregated, overcrowded, and poorly funded (Luthar, 1999). However, research has demonstrated that these circumstances can be significantly attenuated by parental supervision in the context of a warm parent-child relationship as well as by the social support provided by extended kin, interested teachers, involved community members, and mentors (Luthar 1999; Rutter, 1900; Weissbourd 1996; Zhou, Adefuin, Chung, & Roach, 2000).

❖ SEPARATIONS AND CULTURAL DISLOCATIONS

In addition to the trauma associated with growing up in an atmosphere of pervasive poverty and racism, there are several challenges unique to the immigrant experience that affect the nuclear family unit and the development of youth. Migrations often result in family members being separated from one another for extended periods as individuals are brought across borders separately. In a study of 400 immigrant youth from five regions, it was found that 80% had been separated from their parents for between several months and several years (Suárez-Orozco & Suárez-Orozco, 2001).[2] Children may be sent to live with relatives in the United States, or parents may emigrate ahead of their children to establish a home before the arrival of the entire family. Extended family systems in both countries are usually involved in these migrations and may provide interim care and support for youth whose parents are not available. However, these transitions can be unsettling and disturbing, because youth grow up without their parents, and become attached to extended family members from whom they must later separate to move back with their parents (Suárez-Orozco, 2001; Suárez-Orozco & Suárez-Orozco, 2001).

Psychologist Pauline Boss (1999) richly describes the experience of "ambiguous loss" that may be engendered when a loved one is *physically absent but psychologically present* (as with those missing in action or in immigrant separations). She also describes the circumstances of ambiguous loss where loved ones are *physically present but psychologically absent* (as with Alzheimer victims or depressed individuals). Boss (1999) argues that the experience of ambiguous loss can have serious emotional and psychological implications for youth. The fluctuation between hope and hopelessness may ultimately result in a deadening of emotion and stagnation of emotional development.

In addition to the extended family separations, immigrant children may suffer from two other forms of ambiguous loss. Immigrant parents may be psychologically unavailable to their children as they suffer from depression and other emotional symptoms brought on by the stress associated with migration (Athey & Ahern, 1991; Suárez-Orozco, 2001). Furthermore, parents may work long hours at multiple jobs, causing them to be apart from their children before and after school hours and on weekends. Under these circumstances, immigrant youth may develop into hyperresponsible youth who care for themselves and their younger siblings (Valenzuela, 1999). Conversely, the lack of structure and adult responsiveness makes them susceptible to the lure of alternative family structures such as gangs (Vigil, 1988).

Unsupervised out-of-school time is dangerous for youth, because it is during these after-school hours when most youth delinquency occurs (Carnegie Council on Adolescent Development, 1994; Grossman & Garry, 1997; see Perkins & Borden, 2003, this volume). Although extended family networks (when they are available) can sometimes serve to provide necessary monitoring and after-school support, immigrant families often find themselves unable to monitor their children's behavior and provide the guidance their children need to navigate the waters between childhood and adulthood. Family separations resulting from migration may leave families with fewer adult members to provide supervision. Furthermore, immigrant parents as well as other adult family members often work at more than one job or may be assigned less desirable afternoon and evening shifts. Unsupervised, youth may increasingly turn away from adults in their family to their peers.

The children's more rapid acculturation can lead to a disconnection between the generations (Sluzki, 1979; Suárez-Orozco & Suárez-Orozco, 2001). Children may learn English more quickly than their parents, simultaneously losing fluency in their native languages, resulting in a diminishing effectiveness of communication between parents and children and an interruption in the traditional balance of power and authority in the family because children must act as interpreters for their parents (Silka & Tip, 1994; Suárez-Orozco & Suárez-Orozco, 2001). Children's increasing familiarity with American cultural norms and adolescents' interest in American music, movies, and other cultural artifacts may alienate parents from their experiences, just as parents' adherence to the language and culture of the country of origin may embarrass adolescents. These changes may result in a mutual disappointment and disconnection between parents and children. In addition, youth and adolescents attending middle school and high school may be approaching a level of formal education that surpasses that achieved by their parents, rendering parents less able to help with schoolwork and perhaps even more uncomfortable with monitoring their children's academic progress. These developments contribute to a premature individuation of children and adolescents from their parents, in a world that demands more difficult choices than they may be capable of making without adult guidance.

❖ IDENTITY FORMATION

Psychologists agree that the central developmental task of adolescence is the formation of an integrated identity or sense of self (Erikson, 1980). During this stage, adolescents advance cognitively, developing skills that will allow them to formulate a more complex understanding of themselves and their relationships with others (Selman et al., 1992). They use these new skills to renegotiate their parental relationships to cultivate relationships with peers and other nonfamily individuals from whom they will learn about beliefs and values that differ from those with which they were raised (Hamilton & Darling, 1989). Through the lenses provided by each new relationship, an adolescent begins to make sense of his or her place in the world and to formulate an identity. This task is challenging and often painful, as adolescents simultaneously need independence from their parents and increasing amounts of nurturing and guidance (Allen, Aber, & Leadbeater, 1990).

For immigrant adolescents, the stresses associated with developing a sense of identity are accompanied and aggravated by the challenges of existing and growing up in disparate cultures. Camino (1994) identifies the dual "liminalities," or ways of being caught between two realities that exist for immigrant and refugee youth. As adolescents, these young people are negotiating the stages and tasks of childhood and adulthood. As immigrants, they navigate between the identity of their culture of origin and the identity associated with growing up in the United States. The difficulty experienced by youth in traversing between these identities, none of which fully explains their experiences, can be isolating. The implications of the prejudice often experienced by immigrants make the process even more difficult, as youth must attempt to reconcile two cultures that may be in opposition to one another (García-Coll & Magnuson, 1997; Waters, 1997). Pressure is exerted on immigrant youth by the majority culture, the peer culture, the schools, and the media to acculturate completely into an American way of life.

This process of acculturation and forging a positive ethnic identity is a challenge for all youth navigating between two or more cultures. For immigrant youth of color, the process is complicated by the context of racial tension and discrimination they encounter in this society. They must negotiate the terrains of their immigrant culture, the minority culture, as well as mainstream American culture. For these adolescents, the old message of acculturation and assimilation conflicts with the reality that, for them, being American may mean being perceived as a member of a disparaged minority group. For example, when Caribbean youth describe their experiences after coming to the United States, many explain that the prejudices they face as nonwhite, non-English-speaking immigrants are less severe than those they encounter when they are perceived by members of the majority as being African American. By assimilation into the underclass, they suffer the very real risk of being marginalized in ways that may be even more devastating than those associated with an immigrant identity (Waters, 1996).

The local context that the youth encounters will play a significant role in this process. If an immigrant youth finds herself living in an inner-city area, she may interact largely with other immigrants and native-born peers of color. The models, choices, and opportunities in this case relate to a very different trajectory than if the adolescent lives in a predominantly white suburb (Portes & Zhou, 1993). A growing body of literature indicates that the pressure to assimilate to the majority culture is strong and may be associated with several negative outcomes, including risk-taking behaviors (such as substance abuse and unprotected sex), academic disengagement, and delinquency (Bankston & Zhou, 1995a; Bankston & Zhou, 1997b; Chen, Unger, Cruz, & Johnson, 1999; Ogbu, 1978). Counterintuitively, acculturation seems to be associated with declining health and poorer academic performance among immigrants (Hernandez & Charney, 1998). Although exposure to English improves performance on standardized test scores, grades, time spent doing homework, educational aspirations, and the importance of family decreases with the amount of time spent in the United States (Rumbaut, 1997; Steinberg, 1996).

In some cases, immigrant youth embrace total assimilation and complete identification with American culture. Other immigrant youth develop an adversarial stance toward the mainstream culture, not unlike their poor inner-city peers who hold little hope for the future (Ogbu, 1978). These children construct identities around rejecting—after having been rejected by—the institutions of the dominant culture (Suárez-Orozco & Suárez-Orozco, 1995; Ogbu, 1978).

Yet other youth forge a bicultural (or multicultural) identity. A growing body of literature suggests that crafting an identity incorporating elements of both cultures may be the most adaptive strategy for immigrant youth (Bankston & Zhou, 1995b; Camino, 1994; Suárez-Orozco & Suárez-Orozco, 2001). These youth must creatively fuse aspects of both cultures—the parental tradition and the new culture—in a process of transculturation. They achieve bicultural and bilingual competencies that become an integral part of their sense of self. The culturally constructed social structures and the authority of their immigrant parents and elders are seen as legitimate, whereas learning standard English and doing well in school are viewed as competencies that do not compromise their sense of who they are. Youth who successfully develop bicultural identities easily communicate and make friends with their own ethnic groups as well as with students and teachers from other backgrounds. However, the development of a bicultural identity is challenging. Since so much of the process of adolescents' identity development depends on the definition of self through relationships with others, immigrant youth must experience relationships with older peers or adults who have successfully integrated two cultures into one identity, and who support this endeavor in members of the next generation. In addition, they must face the frustration and disappointment that their parents may experience as they perceive their children developing cultural identities that they do not completely share.

It is important to note that most immigrant parents have made tremendous sacrifices for the sake of their children's future well-being, often including the decision to emigrate to the United States and the need for each parent to work more than one full-time job. Physical and psychological separations between parents and children often result from these concerned parents' belief that their sacrifices will enable their adolescent offspring to obtain quality education and be well prepared for successful careers in the future. These forms of disconnection between immigrant youth and their parents, as well as the stressors associated with poverty and discrimination, add to the already challenging period of adolescence and its tasks of identity formation. One way in which immigrant youth can be supported as they confront these challenges involves the formation of relationships with caring, nonparental adults from youth-serving programs, school, or elsewhere in the community. Mentors and youth workers can complement the efforts of immigrant parents, helping to guide adolescents through difficult transitions. Some of the ways in which this is accomplished are discussed in the section that follows.

❖ CONTRIBUTIONS OF MENTORS AND COMMUNITY ORGANIZATIONS

With negative stereotypes of immigrants more plentiful than positive bicultural role models, immigrant youth are challenged as they attempt to formulate healthy, bicultural adult identities. The support of nonparental adults, through either volunteer mentoring programs or community youth-serving agencies, can prove invaluable in minimizing the risks associated with the stresses of acculturation as well as in facilitating the identity formation process. Mentors and supportive youth workers can complement the efforts of parents to guide immigrant youth through adolescence. These individuals may be immigrants or descendants of immigrants and therefore able to relate to the experiences of immigrant youth and serve as positive bicultural role models. They may also be adults from the majority culture who display a sensitivity to specific issues facing immigrants, a willingness to engage in mutual learning with youth from backgrounds that differ from their own, and the ability to act as cultural interpreters. In either case, rather than supplanting the role of parents who have somehow failed to live up to their responsibilities, nonparental adults should instead be seen as supporting parents' efforts, as the entire family attempts the difficult task of adapting to life in a new and often hostile country.

There are many examples of programs and individuals working in immigrant communities that foster healthy youth development. These may take the form of volunteer mentoring programs, which provide youth with intensive one-on-one relationships with caring adults, or community-based youth organizations, which provide structured activities and settings in which to interact with peers while under the supervision of adult staff. These organizations represent an important form of social capital at work in immigrant communities, as they represent "the investment that individuals create through involvement in social relationships" (Furstenberg & Hughes, 1995, p. 581). Several theorists, beginning with Coleman (1988), have indicated that the presence of resources—in a family, a school or agency, a neighborhood, or even an entire society—engenders positive interactions between individuals and contributes to positive outcomes (Furstenberg & Hughes, 1995; Stevenson, 1998). Youth-serving organizations and individuals, much like ethnic-owned businesses and family networks, enrich immigrant communities and foster healthy development among its youth through the support they provide to parents and families (Nevarez-La Torre, 1997). The key element of both types of programs, from the perspective of meeting the developmental needs of immigrant youth, is the potential for forming caring, meaningful relationships with adults.

Mentoring

Volunteer mentoring programs have gained considerable attention in recent years. An estimated 5 million American youth are involved in school- and community-based volunteer mentoring programs, ranging from the prototypic Big Brothers Big Sisters program to other, less structured organizations. Many of these mentoring programs represent a recent development in youth-service interventions, with nearly half of the active mentoring programs in the United States having been established between 1994 and 1999 and only 18% having been in operation for more than 15 years (Rhodes, 2002).

Although there is wide variation among the services provided by mentoring programs, mentoring is generally defined as a one-on-one relationship between an older, more experienced adult and an unrelated, younger protégé. In these relationships, an adult provides guidance and encouragement aimed at developing the competence and character of the protégé. Over time, a special bond of mutual respect, affection, and loyalty may develop that facilitates the protégé's transition into adulthood (Hamilton & Darling, 1989; Rhodes, 2002). As evaluations of mentoring programs begin to be conducted and published, successful mentoring relationships appear to be those that involve greater amounts of contact and involvement between the mentor and the protégé, as well as a positive orientation toward youth ability and potential on the part of the mentor. Long-lasting, successful matches between volunteer mentors and youth in the Big Brothers Big Sisters program, for example, tend to involve mentors who approach the relationship with respect for the adolescent's interests, abilities, and needs, involving him or her at all stages of decision making in the relationship (Morrow & Styles, 1995; Tierney et al., 1995).

Youth in successful mentoring relationships have been found to benefit in terms of improved academics, healthier family and peer relationships, and reduced incidences of substance abuse and aggressive behavior (Grossman & Tierney, 1998; Rhodes, 2002). The mechanisms by which mentoring has an impact on youth development, however, are less well understood. It is likely that several important factors come into play, relating to the attitude and efforts of the mentor as well as the background and temperament of the youth in question and the encouragement of the youth's parents, family members, and teachers. Although mentoring relationships are quite varied, they usually share the basic element of an emotional connection between the mentor and the protégé, which enables the protégé to trust the mentor's advice, value the mentor's opinion and guidance, and feel valued and cared for by a significant adult in meaningful ways (Rhodes, 2002).

These processes have special implications for immigrant youth. During the course of migration, loved ones are often separated from one another and significant attachments are ruptured. Mentoring relationships can give immigrant youth an opportunity to be involved in reparative relationships engendering new significant attachments. Since immigrant adolescents' parents and other adult relatives may be unavailable due to long work hours or emotional distress, the guidance and affection of a mentor may help to fill the void created by parental absence. The mentor, as an adult who has been in the United States longer than the protégé, can also provide information about and exposure to American cultural and educational institutions, and help as the adolescent negotiates developmental transitions. If the mentor is of the same ethnic background as the protégé, he or she can interpret the rules of engagement of the new culture to parents and thus help to attenuate cultural rigidities. Furthermore, bicultural mentors can serve as role models in the challenging process of developing a bicultural identity, exemplifying the ways in which elements of the ethnic identity can be preserved and celebrated even as features of the more mainstream culture of the United States are incorporated into young people's lives. Many of the youth who are served by mentoring programs are immigrants or the children of immigrants, and many community programs that provide human services to specific segments of the immigrant population include mentoring for youth as one of their services.

Although numerous benefits are associated with mentoring for the development of immigrant youth, mentoring may not be ideally suited to the needs of some immigrant adolescents. First, an intense one-on-one relationship with another adult may represent a source of discomfort for some immigrant parents, who may feel threatened by the prospect of a nonrelative adult usurping parental authority or be mistrustful of the intentions of a nonfamilial adult who will be learning intimate family information through his or her relationship with a child (Suárez-Orozco & Suárez-Orozco, 2001). Second, many of the volunteers who come into adolescents' lives are from different ethnic and socioeconomic backgrounds than the youth they are mentoring. In the Big Brothers Big Sisters mentoring program, for example, the waiting lists for minority youth requiring a mentor of the same race can be much longer than for those willing to be paired with mentors from the majority culture (Rhodes, Reddy, Grossman, & Lee, in press). Although same-race mentoring matches have not been clearly shown to be superior to cross-race matches (Rhodes et al., in press), these differences can have implications for immigrant youth, who may face language barriers if matched with a mentor who only speaks English and who may not receive needed support in the formation of a bicultural identity from a mentor who identifies too closely with the mainstream culture. Third, mentoring relationships are not suitable for all youth. Adolescents who are experiencing psychological, emotional, or behavioral distress may have difficulty engaging in a mentoring relationship, and older youth, as compared with younger children, may be more peer-oriented and less amenable to becoming invested in a relationship that requires spending significant amounts of time alone with an adult (Rhodes, 2002).

Finally, not all mentoring relationships are successful; an estimated half of all matches dissolve after only a few months (Freedman, 1993; Styles & Morrow, 1992). These premature terminations may occur if a child's emotional needs are too great, if a mentor is not able to spend enough time with the protégé to build the necessary trust and mutual respect, or if for some other reason the two individuals do not forge a strong connection. When this occurs, the resulting feelings of rejection and loss of another adult support figure can be devastating for the adolescent (Grossman & Rhodes, 2002), exacerbating feelings of loss and rejection engendered by previously ruptured attachments. This type of loss may be particularly destructive for an immigrant adolescent who has likely already experienced the loss of family members and cherished adults during the difficult process of migration (Suárez-Orozco & Suárez-Orozco, 2001). For these reasons, immigrant youth are often well served when they form mentoring relationships with nonparental adults encountered in programs oriented on activities, thereby eliminating some of the pressures involved in more intensive mentoring programs.

Community-Based Youth Development Programs

Many aspects of a successful mentoring relationship can also be found in the bonds that form between youth and staff members at community programs. Community youth workers encounter immigrant youth through their involvement in a variety of programs. Some of these organizations have long histories and are chapters of national agencies, such as the YMCA-YWCA or the Boys and Girls Clubs of America. Some are funded by municipal grants designed to provide after-school or summer activities in parks, schools, or other public spaces. Still others are smaller, localized programs designed to meet the needs of a particular segment of the population by providing tutoring, career guidance, or other targeted services.

Regardless of the size or scope of these programs, many of those that are most successful at engaging youth and providing them with adult guidance, supervision, and support are oriented on a youth development philosophy (Roth, Brooks-Gunn, Murray, & Foster, 1998; Larson, 2000; see Perkins & Borden, 2003, this volume). In contrast with the deficit philosophy of many programs designed to prevent negative outcomes among youth, a youth development program emphasizes the positive attributes and strengths that children and adolescents possess, and it attempts to provide the support and encouragement needed for youth to achieve their goals and reach their potential. The youth development philosophy is embraced by many of the larger, national youth-serving agencies, but it has been adopted to differing degrees in smaller programs. Many of the programs that have been designed to target Latino and Caribbean youth, for example, are oriented on more of a deficit approach, seeking to prevent the onset of risky behaviors and negative outcomes such as adolescent pregnancy, substance use, or academic failure (Zhou et al., 2000). On the other hand, many of the programs that target Asian youth are of a more proactive nature, focusing on the development of academic skills and the provision of information regarding college admissions (Zhou et al., 2000).[3] In community agencies oriented on a youth development approach, adult volunteers and staff members typically espouse many of the qualities enumerated by Yohalem (2003, this volume) in her description of effective youth workers, as well as many of the qualities of successful volunteer mentors. These include an understanding of the adolescent's family dynamics and an ability to work with both youth and parents; the ability to create safe, collaborative spaces for learning and exploration in which youth take ownership and responsibility for their activities; a belief in youth potential; and an enthusiasm for and commitment to youth work (Baker, Pollack, & Kohn, 1995; Camino, 1994; Heath, 1994; McLaughlin et al., 1994; Morrow & Styles, 1995; Scales, 1990).

Community organizations working with immigrant youth provide a broad array of services within the framework of youth development. The programs described below exemplify this spectrum.

Combining Mentoring and the Arts. Bajucol is a community organization that provides Colombian youth living in the Boston area with an opportunity to embrace their roots, culture, and folklore. Under the guidance of Colombian adults, a group of 25 youth meet twice weekly to practice Colombian folkloric dance, culminating in an annual performance to an audience of 1,000. Their practices and the elaborate preparations for their performances provide a focus in the lives of these youth. They develop a sense of connectedness with both adults and peers while focusing on an activity that fosters their ethnic pride. In addition, their mentors act as explicit guides to pathways of success and advocate with schools on behalf of the youth they serve.

Schools that serve both immigrant parents and children. Five years ago in New York, the Children's Aid Society inaugurated a "full-service" school. Based in Washington Heights, an area with a large immigrant community, this school provides before- and after-school care for children. To make parents feel welcome, they hold classes in English as a second language. Most staff are bilingual and bicultural, generating a warm sense of community for parents and students. Adults and youth work together toward achieving a variety of goals.

Using the Arts to Cope With the Realities of Immigrant Life. Urban Improv is a Boston area group that uses music, improvisational acting, and movement in its work with urban youth. The program was developed to help youth cope with the harsh realities of growing up in inner-city areas, and adults meet with youth weekly. Talented community educators develop vignettes that recreate difficult situations that urban youth often encounter in schools and communities. At a critical moment, the action is "freeze-framed," and youngsters are invited to enact solutions. Such themes as self-esteem, peer pressure, culture shock, and tensions between old-world parents and new-world realities are explored. In a supportive atmosphere of safety, children strategize solutions to common problems. Thereafter, rich group discussions take place in which youth exchange ideas and experiences. Recently, in connection with two teachers of English as a second language, Urban Improv has begun two new, successful groups consisting entirely of immigrant youth.

Intergenerational Community Problem Solving. Haitian Teens Confront AIDS (HTCA) is a peer education and leadership program based in Cambridge, Massachusetts. HTCA was initiated to respond to the need for HIV/AIDS-prevention education among Haitian youth and to provide them with the tools to confront the discrimination and racism at the heart of stereotypes concerning Haitians and AIDS. The program brings Haitian youth together with adult educators, artists, and activists in weekly 6-hour meetings for training in the epidemiology and transmission of HIV/AIDS, in group discussion and performing arts skills, and to strategize about outreach approaches. The program uses skits, plays, music, and videos created by HTCA youth to conduct educational sessions at schools, at church-based parent and youth group meetings, and in the local Haitian media. These sessions engage young people and adults in cross-generational dialogues about such themes as the transmission patterns of HIV among youth, the shame that keeps AIDS a hidden disease in the community, communication issues between parents and teenagers, differences in Haitian and U.S. cultural values, discrimination against people with AIDS, and the role that racial discrimination, homophobia, and gender inequalities play in increasing young adults' risks for the disease. Since 1989, over 200 Haitian teenagers have graduated from the program, and many have returned as adult advisors in HTCA and other community programs. Parents have become active members of the organization and advocate along with their children for HIV/AIDS prevention and compassion for people with AIDS. Through cross-generational dialogues and peer-led activities, HTCA has helped to change the view of HIV/AIDS in the Haitian community from a shameful, hidden disease to a problem that the community can mobilize to solve (Nicoleau, 2000).

Combining Mentoring and Academic Guidance. Puente in California has been acting as a bridge for Latino youth in making the transition from middle school to high school and then from high school to college. This highly successful program emphasizes several critical components. Fundamentally, an adult mentor is responsible for introducing to students academic opportunities that may not have been envisioned. Explicit and intensive instruction in the steps necessary to enter the college system is provided, as well as ways in which youth can be successful once they have entered the system. Students are also provided with instruction in writing and literature. Last, they are assigned a peer partner who acts as guide in the initial transition (Gandara, 1998).

At the most basic level, participation in a community youth program such as one of those described above translates into out-of-school time that is not spent unsupervised, in isolation, or on the streets with peers. These programs are often seen by participants as havens from the pressures of the streets or as second homes—places where youth feel comfortable expressing themselves and letting down their guard (Hirsch et al., 2000; Villarruel & Lerner, 1994). The existence of a setting in which youth can congregate, socialize, and participate in recreational activities during their out-of-school hours represents an important third option as they react to lack of supervision while parents are at work or are emotionally unavailable. Instead of having youth stay home to care for younger siblings or seek an alternate family structure in peer groups or street gangs, families can choose for their adolescents to attend a community center or club. This option allows youth to feel supervised by caring adults while preserving their freedom to choose activities and interact with peers, an autonomy that becomes more and more important as youth grow older (Beck, 1999; Bryant, 1989). Parents can feel that their children are in a safe setting, without feeling threatened by the intensity of a one-on-one relationship with a volunteer mentor.

As is true with many volunteer mentors, the adults who work in community programs are often equipped to provide tutoring, educational guidance, advice about the college application process, and job search assistance, information that may be inaccessible to immigrant youth who attend schools with few guidance counselors and whose parents have not navigated the academic system in the United States. Youth programs such as Puente may provide a welcome alternative to the environment in many schools serving disadvantaged communities, where immigrant youth may not feel comfortable or welcome. This is often the case among low-income Latino immigrants, who report feeling discriminated against by their teachers, are placed disproportionately into lower-track and special-needs classes, and cite a sense of rejection by the school as a main reason for dropping out (García, Wilkinson, & Ortiz, 1995; Katz, 1999). Staff members at community youth-serving agencies often report that they believe an important part of their role is the reversal of inner-city schools' and teachers' negative impact on the educational trajectories and academic achievement of minority youth (McLaughlin et al., 1994).

In addition to providing safety and offering the opportunity for tutoring and other forms of direct academic enrichment, many community youth workers can serve as role models for youth embroiled in the difficult process of identity development in a bicultural context. This aspect of Bajucol, the Children's Aid Society, and Urban Improv contributes in important ways to these programs' success. In addition, in the drop-in program described by Camino (1994), staff members (not all of whom were Latino but most of whom spoke Spanish) were able to create an atmosphere in an after-school context where Latino refugee youth felt comfortable exploring the intersections between the parts of their identities that were Latino and the parts that were developing as they grew up in the United States. With supportive staff to guide them (both through role modeling and through creating a norm of self-expression, joint ownership, and the communal responsibility and fictive kinship associated with their Latino background), youth found ways to fuse both parts of their identities, expressing each at different times and for different purposes. Similarly, Cooper and colleagues (1999) expressed the difficulties inherent in Mexican immigrant children's transitions from elementary to middle school, describing ways in which community program staff can serve as "culture brokers" for youth. These culture brokers act as intermediary figures, able to bridge the often-considerable gaps between the norms in children's homes and those at school. Support from figures such as these youth workers increases the chances of academic success among Latino youth entering middle school and encountering numerous challenges to their newly forming bicultural identities.

Some researchers have characterized community youth centers as performing a bridging function, discussing the link these programs provide between two disparate cultures, that of the inner city and that of the mainstream population. All of the programs described above play this role for the families they serve. In addition, Heath (1994) characterized a youth program as a border zone between the streets and the mainstream culture. McLaughlin and colleagues (1994) described the adults working in the "urban sanctuaries" they evaluated as providing bridges between the inner city and the outside world of mainstream employment. Schinke, Orlandi, and Cole (1992), in an evaluation of Boys and Girls Clubs located in housing projects, found that the presence of a Boys or Girls Club was associated with lower drug and delinquency problems and more effective communication patterns among residents, police, housing authority management personnel, and community groups.

An 18-year-old Colombian youth expressed how a community organization working with Colombian immigrant youth helped him navigate his adolescence shortly after migrating:

> Before I began participating in Bajucol, . . . I was not active. I spent most of my time in my apartment, watching TV and not doing much. I suspect I would still be like that without the group. . . . A good friend of mine had been involved in the group and she told me about it. At the beginning, I had a wait-and-see attitude. I did not know how to dance; I had no idea about folk dancing. Slowly, it grabbed me. . . .
>
> For our group, the folkloric dance is the most important thing. We practice a great deal—we do it to represent . . . Colombia's positive traditions. Colombia is going through a difficult time. There are many stereotypes about our land. Our purpose is to put

forward the other side of Columbia—the happiness, the beauty, the traditions. . . . because we are far away from our land. . . .

We are like a family. We have known each other for 5 years by now. The friendship goes to the heart of the dancing. My family supports my work with the group because my work with the group helps my family. . . .

Now what I do is teach others how to dance. I am giving back to the group what the group gave to me. . . . When we come here we are all alone and the group gives us support. We do it for each other and we do it for our country. (Andres, program participant, personal communication, June 18, 2001)

By focusing on the potential of youth and operating in a respectful and informal manner, staff at community-based youth programs such as those described above seem to fill many gaps that exist for low-income minority individuals and their children. The benefits of belonging to a caring organization that can perform such a bridging function are particularly salient for many immigrant youth, whose most challenging tasks involve the reconciliation of multiple cultures and value systems against a backdrop often characterized by hostility. Through the provision of activities, instruction, and/or supervised time to interact with peers, these programs provide an opportunity for youth who might not have access to mentoring programs, or for whom the intensity of a one-on-one mentoring relationship might not be appropriate, to form supportive relationships with caring adults. These relationships, whether they occur with a mentor or a community youth worker, can help immigrant youth build skills, adapt to a new culture, and develop healthy bicultural identities in ways that are not always accessible to parents or peers. When successful, these relationships help immigrant youth and their families overcome some of the barriers associated with poverty and discrimination that prevent full participation in the new country's economic and cultural life.

❖ IN CONCLUSION

Immigrant youth growing up in the United States face many challenges. The normal tasks of adolescence, involving the development of identity, are exacerbated by the effects of poverty and discrimination and by parents' frequent absence and inability to provide guidance in dealing with the complexities of growing up in transcultural contexts. The support of a mentor or community youth worker can prove invaluable to many immigrant youth and their families dealing with these issues. Nonparental adults can ease the difficult transitions that immigrant youth face in several ways. They can reduce stress by forming a caring, supportive relationship with youth, by providing adult guidance and supervision when parents are unable to do so, and by serving as lenses through which to see the possibility of a healthy, transcultural adult identity. Of course, mentors and youth workers cannot be seen as the entire solution to the complex constellation of challenges encountered by immigrant families. However, their efforts can provide much-needed support to adolescents and, in turn, their families, contributing to healthy development.

Understanding the issues that affect immigrant youth development can inform the design of mentoring and community youth service programs seeking to make a difference in these populations. Some adolescents' experiences may leave them better suited for participation in a mentoring program. Such youth may be hesitant to approach adults in group settings or have family histories and situations that give rise to the need for more intensive one-on-one relationships. Other youth, by virtue of their developmental needs and family preferences, may be more effectively served by a community youth program. Attention should be devoted to exploring the effects of adolescents' psychological, emotional, and behavioral well-being as well as any age-related preferences for spending time so that each youth can be referred to the type of program that may prove most meaningful for him or her.

In terms of mentoring programs, training for volunteer mentors and staff should be expanded to include elements of cultural sensitivity, particularly relating to the specific immigrant groups that have settled in a given community. There are great potential benefits of pairing an immigrant adolescent with a mentor of the same ethnic background, especially considering the guidance and role modeling that can be provided by such a mentor as an adolescent explores identity issues in multiple cultural contexts. Consequently, recruitment of volunteer mentors in communities with immigrant populations should target adults who are immigrants themselves or the descendants of immigrants. Careful screening of potential volunteers is a part of all reputable mentoring programs, but a particular understanding of the negative repercussions of a prematurely terminated mentoring relationship for immigrant adolescents should be included in the screening and training process (Rhodes, 2002).

Mentors and community youth service workers should be aware of the complicated parent-child dynamics at work in immigrant families. Immigrant parents tend to bring with them strong cultural values of respect for elders and of familial interdependence. These cultural models are deeply challenged by the American cultural value of independence, by the interruptions of power and authority that occur when youth serve as language and cultural interpreters for their parents, and by the separations inherent in immigration. (Suárez-Orozco & Suárez-Orozco, 2001). Programs in immigrant populations should be even more focused than usual on gaining parental trust, with the goal of serving the entire family and not just the adolescent participant. Because a community youth program may be better positioned to provide these types of services to entire families than a volunteer mentoring program, attention and resources should be directed toward these types of initiatives being developed in immigrant communities.

Finally, in addition to volunteer mentoring and community youth service agencies, there are many natural mentoring resources in immigrant communities, including coaches, school personnel, church officials, neighbors, and extended family members. Members of the extended family often serve as resources to both immigrant adolescents and their parents as they confront the many challenges facing them. Other resources may be encountered by youth in a particular setting or context. Churches, for example, are frequent sponsors of mentoring, tutoring, and other small-scale human service programs in immigrant communities, and their efforts should be publicized and supported. Schools are the settings in which adolescents spend the most time, but they are frequently described as hostile, violent, and negative environments in which immigrant adolescents feel unsafe and marginalized by mainstream peers and by teachers and administrators (Katz, 1999). A more complete understanding of the issues facing immigrant youth, and the many strengths that they and their families bring with them to the tasks of development and adjustment, can contribute to the generation of positive environments as well as effective utilization of volunteer mentors and community youth workers as valuable resources in the lives of immigrant adolescents.

❖ NOTES

1. For detailed exploration of the different issues faced by first- and second-generation youth, please see Suárez-Orozco and Suárez-Orozco (2001).

2. The Harvard Immigration Project (directed by Carola Suárez-Orozco with Marcelo Suárez-Orozco) is following longitudinally 400 immigrant children (ages 9 to 14 at the beginning of the study) coming from five major regions (China, Central America, the Dominican Republic, Haiti, and Mexico) to the Boston and San Francisco areas for 5 years. This is an interdisciplinary project using a variety of methods including structured student and parent interviews, ethnographic observations, projective and objective measures, reviews of school records, and teacher questionnaires and interviews. The project was made possible with funding provided by the National Science Foundation, the W. T. Grant Foundation, and the Spencer Foundation.

3. This distinction reflects the erroneous bias of by the majority culture toward perceiving all Latino youth as high risk, and Asian youth as the "model minority," destined to achieve academically (Matute-Bianchi, 1986; Ogbu, 1978). In reality, although Latinos do suffer from dropout rates twice as high as those of black youth and four times as high as those of white youth (National Center for Education Statistics, 1999), Asian immigrant youth do not perform well in school uniformly across subgroups; their achievement is related to economic factors and levels of acculturation. In cases where Asian immigrant youth do outperform their white American-born peers, these accomplishments may take an emotional toll (Bankston & Zhou, 1997; Suárez-Orozco & Suárez-Orozco, 2001; Toupin & Son, 1991). To promote achievement among youth from various ethnic groups, programs that focus on youth strengths and potential rather than concentrating on preventing specific negative outcomes have been found to be more successful (Roth et al., 1998).

❖ REFERENCES

Adams, P. L. (1990). Prejudice and exclusion as social trauma. In J. D. Noshpitz & R. D. Coddington (Eds.), *Stressors and adjustment disorders.* New York: Wiley.

Allen, J. P., Aber, J. L, & Leadbeater, B. J. (1990). Adolescent problem behaviors: The influence of attachment and autonomy. *Psychiatric Clinics of North America, 13,* 455-467.

Athey, J. L., & Ahern, J. L. (1991). *Refugee children: Theory, research, and services.* Baltimore, MD: Johns Hopkins University Press.

Baker, K., Pollack, M., & Kohn, I. (1995). Violence prevention through informal socialization: An evaluation of the South Baltimore Youth Center. *Studies on Crime and Crime Prevention, 4*(1), 61-85.

Bankston, C. L., & Zhou, M. (1995a). Effects of minority-language literacy on the academic achievement of Vietnamese youth in New Orleans. *Sociology of Education, 68*(1), 1-17.

Bankston, C. L., & Zhou, M. (1995b). Religious participation, ethnic identification, and adaptation of Vietnamese adolescents in an immigrant community. *Sociological Quarterly, 36*(3), 523-534.

Bankston, C. L., & Zhou, M. (1997a). The social adjustment of Vietnamese American adolescents: Evidence for a segmented-assimilation approach. *Social Science Quarterly, 78*(2), 508-523.

Bankston, C. L., & Zhou, M. (1997b). Valedictorians and delinquents: The bifurcation of Vietnamese American youth. *Deviant Behavior, 18*(4), 343-364.

Beck, E. L. (1999). Prevention and intervention programming: Lessons from an after-school program. *Urban Review, 31*(1), 107-124.

Boss, P. (1999). *Ambiguous loss: Learning to live with unresolved grief.* Cambridge, MA: Harvard University Press.

Bryant, B. K. (1989). The need for support in relation to the need for autonomy. In D. Belle (Ed.), *Children's social networks and social supports,* 332-351. New York: Wiley.

Camino, L. A. (1994). Refugee adolescents and their changing identities. In L. A. Camino & R. M. Krulfeld (Eds.), *Reconstructing lives, recapturing meaning: Refugee identity, gender, and culture change,* 29-56. Amsterdam: Gordon & Breach.

Carnegie Council on Adolescent Development. (1994). *A matter of time: Risk and opportunity in the out-of-school hours.* New York: Carnegie Corporation of New York.

Chen, X., Unger, J. B., Cruz, T. B., & Johnson, C. A. (1999). Smoking patterns of Asian-American youth in California and their relationship with acculturation. *Journal of Adolescent Health, 24*(5), 321-328.

Coleman, J. S. (1988). Social capital in the creation of human capital. *American Journal of Sociology, 94,* S95-S120.

Cooper, C. R., Denner, J., & Lopez, E. M. (1999). Cultural brokers: Helping Latino children on pathways toward success. *The Future of Children, 9*(2), 51-57.

Erikson, E. (1980). *Identity and the life cycle.* New York: W. W. Norton.

Espenshade, T., & Belanger, M. (1998). Immigration and Public Opinion. In M. Suárez-Orozco (Ed.), *Crossings: Mexican immigration in interdisciplinary perspective.* Cambridge, MA: David Rockefeller Center for Latin American Studies and Harvard University Press.

Freedman, M. (1993). *The kindness of strangers: Adult mentors, urban youth, and the new volunteerism.* San Francisco: Jossey-Bass.

Furstenberg, F., & Hughes, M. E. (1995). Social capital and successful development among at-risk youth. *Journal of Marriage and the Family, 57*(3), 580-592.

Gandara, P. (1998). Final report on the evaluation of High School Puente. (Executive Summary to the Carnegie Corporation of New York).

García, S. B., Wilkinson, C. Y., & Ortiz, A. A. (1995). Enhancing achievement for language minority students: Classroom, school, and family contexts. *Education and Urban Society, 27*(4), 441-462.

García-Coll, C., & Magnuson, K. (1997). The psychological experience of immigration: A developmental perspective. In A. Booth, A. C. Crouter, & N. Landale (Eds.), *Immigration and the family: Research and policy on U.S. immigrants* (pp. 91-131). Mahwah, NJ: Lawrence Erlbaum.

Grossman, J. B., & Garry, E. M. (1997). *Mentoring: A proven delinquency prevention strategy.* Washington, DC: Office of Juvenile Justice Prevention.

Grossman, J. B., & Rhodes, J. E. (2002). The test of time: Predictors and effects of duration in youth mentoring relationships. *American Journal of Community Psychology, 30,* 199-206.

Grossman, J. B., & Tierney, J. P. (1998). Does mentoring work? An impact study of the Big Brothers/Big Sisters program. *Evaluation Review, 22,* 403-426.

Hamilton, S., & Darling, N. (1989). Mentors in adolescents' lives. In K. Hurrelman (Ed.), *The social world of adolescents: International perspectives.* Berlin: Walter de Gruyter.

Heath, S. B. (1994). The project of learning from the inner-city youth perspective. *New Directions for Child Development, 63,* 25-34.

Hernandez, D., & Charney, E. (1998). *From generation to generation: The health and well-being of children of immigrant families.* Washington, DC: National Academy Press.

Hirsch, B. J., Roffman, J. G., Deutsch, N. L., Flynn, C., Loder, T. L., & Pagano, M. E. (2000). Inner-city youth development programs: Strengthening programs for adolescent girls. *Journal of Early Adolescence, 20*(2), 210-230.

Katz, S. R. (1999). Teaching in tensions: Latino immigrant youth, their teachers and the structures of schooling. *Teachers College Record, 100*(4), 809-840.

Larson, R. W. (2000). Toward a psychology of positive youth development. *American Psychologist, 55*(1), 170-183.

Luthar, S. S. (1999). *Poverty and children's adjustment.* Thousand Oaks, CA: Sage.

Matute-Bianchi, M. E. (1986, November). Ethnic identities and patterns of school success and failure among Mexican-descent and Japanese-American students in a California high school: An ethnographic analysis. *American Journal of Education,* 233-255.

McLaughlin, M., Irby, M., & Langman, J. (1994). *Urban sanctuaries: Neighborhood organizations in the lives and futures of inner-city youth.* San Francisco: Jossey-Bass.

Morrow, K. V., & Styles, M. B. (1995). *Building relationships with youth in program settings: A study of Big Brothers/Big Sisters.* Philadelphia: Public/Private Ventures.

National Center for Education Statistics. (1999). *Digest of Education Statistics, 1999,* Table 108. Washington, DC: U.S. Department of Education.

Nevarez-La Torre, A. A. (1997). Influencing Latino education: Church-based community programs. *Education and Urban Society, 30*(1), 58-74.

Nicoleau, G. (2000). Pitimi san gado—Haitian teens confront AIDS: Crafting cross-generational leadership in a Haitian-American community in a time of disease and discrimination. Ed.D. diss. Cambridge, MA: Harvard Graduate School of Education.

Ogbu, J. (1978). *Minority education and caste: The American system in cross-cultural perspective.* New York: Academic Press.

Orfield, G., Chew, L., Green, R. L., Liddell, H., Ramirez, J. D., & Stephens, G. (1999). *Progress made, challenges remaining in San Francisco school desegregation.* San Francisco: Report of the Consent Decree Advisory Committee to the Federal District Court.

Orfield, G., & Yun, J. T. (1999). *Resegregation in American schools.* Cambridge, MA: Civil Rights Project, Harvard University.

Perkins, D. F., & Borden, L. M. (2003). Key elements of community youth development programs. In F. A. Villarruel, D. F. Perkins, L. M. Borden, & J. G. Keith (Eds.), *Community Youth development: Programs, policies, and practices.* Thousand Oaks, CA: Sage.

Phelan, P., Davidson, A. L., & Yu, H. C. (1993). Students' multiple worlds: Navigating the borders of family, peer, and school cultures. In P. Phelan & A. L. Davidson (Eds.), *Cultural diversity: Implications for education* (pp. 52-88). New York: Teachers College Press.

Portes, A., & Zhou, M. (1993). The new second generation: Segmented assimilation and its variants. *Annals of the American Academy of Political & Social Science, 530,* 74-96.

Rhodes, J. E. (2002). *Stand by me: The risks and rewards of mentoring today's youth.* Cambridge, MA: Harvard University Press.

Rhodes, J. E., Grossman, J. B., & Resch, N. L. (2000, November/December). Agents of change: Pathways through which mentoring relationships influence adolescents' academic adjustment. *Child Development, 71*(6), 1662-1671.

Rhodes, J. E., Reddy, R., Grossman, J. B., & Lee, J. M. (in press). Volunteer mentoring relationships with minority youth: An analysis of same race vs. cross-race matches. *Journal of Applied Social Psychology.*

Rong, X. L., & Preissle, J. (1998). *Educating immigrant students: What we need to know to meet the challenges.* Thousand Oaks, CA: Corwin.

Roth, J., Brooks-Gunn, J., Murray, L., & Foster, W. (1998). Promoting healthy adolescents: Synthesis of youth development program evaluations. *Journal of Research on Adolescence, 8*(4), 423-459.

Rumbaut, R. G. (1997). Ties that bind: Immigration and immigrant families in the United States. In A. Booth, A. C. Crouter, & N. Landale (Eds.), *Immigration and the family: Research and policy on U.S. immigrants* (pp. 3-46). Mahwah, NJ: Lawrence Erlbaum.

Rutter, M. (1990). Psychosocial resilience and protective mechanisms. In J. Rolf, A. S. Masten, D. Cicchetti, K. H. Nuechterlein, & S. Weintraub (Eds.), *Risk and protective factors in the development of psychopathology* (pp. 181-214). New York: Cambridge University Press.

Scales, P. (1990). Developing capable young people: An alternative strategy for prevention programs. *Journal of Early Adolescence, 10*(4), 420-438.

Schinke, S. P., Orlandi, M. A., & Cole, K. C. (1992). Boys and Girls Clubs in public housing developments: Prevention services for youth at risk. *Journal of Community Psychology, OSAP Special Issue,* 118-128.

Selman, R. L., Schultz, L. H., Nakkula, M., Barr, D., Watts, C., & Richmond, J. B. (1992). Friendship and fighting: A developmental approach to the study of risk and prevention of violence. *Development and Psychopathology, 4,* 529-558.

Silka, L., & Tip, J. (1994). Empowering the silent ranks: The Southeast Asian experience. *American Journal of Community Psychology, 22*(4), 497-529.

Sluzki, C. (1979). Migration and family conflict. *Family Process, 18(4),* 379-390.

Smith, M. P., Tarallo, B., & Kagiwada, G. (1991). Colouring California: New Asian immigrant households, social networks, and the local state. *International Journal of Urban and Regional Research, 15*(2), 250-268.

Steinberg, L. (1996). *Beyond the classroom.* New York: Simon and Schuster.

Stevenson, H. C. (1998). Raising safe villages: Cultural-ecological factors that influence the emotional adjustment of adolescents. *Journal of Black Psychology, 24*(1), 44-59.

Styles, M. B., & Morrow, K. V. (1992). *Understanding how youth and elders form relationships: A study of four Linking Lifetimes programs* (research report). Philadelphia: Public/Private Ventures.

Suárez-Orozco, C. (2001). Immigration stress and refugee trauma: Psychocultural factors in the adaptation of adolescent girls. In M. Agosin, (Ed.), *Women, gender, and human rights: A global perspective.* New Brunswick, NJ: Rutgers University Press.

Suárez-Orozco, C., & Suárez-Orozco, M. (1995). *Transformations: Migration, family life, and achievement motivation among Latino adolescents.* Palo Alto, CA: Stanford University Press.

Suárez-Orozco, C., & Suárez-Orozco, M. (2001). *Children of immigration.* Cambridge, MA: Harvard University Press.

Suárez-Orozco, M. (1998). *Crossings: Mexican immigration in interdisciplinary perspectives.* Cambridge, MA: David Rockefeller Center for Latin American Studies and Harvard University Press.

Tienda, M. (1995). Latinos and the American pie: Can Latinos achieve economic parity? *Hispanic Journal of Behavioral Sciences, 17*(4), 403-429.

Tierney, J., Grossman, J., & Resch, N. (1995). *Making a difference: An impact study of Big Brothers/Big Sisters.* Philadelphia: Public/Private Ventures.

Toupin, E. S. W. A., & Son, L. (1991). Preliminary findings on Asian Americans: "The model minority" in a small private East Coast college. *Journal of Cross-Cultural Psychology, 22*(3), 403-417.

U.S. Census Bureau. (1997, March). Current population survey. Washington, DC: Author.

Valenzuela, A. (1999). Gender roles and settlement activities among children and their immigrant families. *American Behavioral Scientist, 42*(4), 720-742.

Vigil, D. (1988). *Barrio gangs: Street life and identity in Southern California*. Austin: University of Texas Press.

Villarruel, F. A., & Lerner, R. M. (1994). *Promoting community-based programs for socialization and learning*. San Francisco: Jossey-Bass.

Waldinger, R., & Bozogmehr, M. (1996). *Ethnic Los Angeles*. New York: Russell Sage Foundation.

Waters, M. C. (1996). The intersection of gender, race, and ethnicity in identity development of Caribbean American teens. In B. Leadbeater & N. Way (Eds.), *Urban girls: Resisting stereotypes, creating identities* (pp. 65-84). New York: New York University Press.

Waters, M. C. (1997). Immigrant families at risk: Factors that undermine chances for success. In A. Booth, A. C. Crouter, & N. Landale (Eds.), *Immigration and the family: Research and policy on U.S. immigrants* (pp. 79-87). Mahwah, NJ: Lawrence Erlbaum.

Weissbourd, R. (1996). *The vulnerable child*. Reading, MA: Perseus.

Yohalem, N. (2003). Adults who make a difference: Identifying the skills and characteristics of successful youth workers. In F. A. Villarruel, D. F. Perkins, L. M. Borden, & J. G. Keith (Eds.), *Community youth development: Programs, policies, and practices*. Thousand Oaks, CA: Sage.

Zhou, M., Adefuin, J. A., Chung, A., & Roach, R. (2000). How community matters for immigrant children: Structural supports and constraints for inner-city neighborhoods. Presented at the Annual Meeting of the Population Association of America, Los Angeles, California, March 23-25, 2000.

6

The Role of Gender in Enhancing Program Strategies for Healthy Youth Development

Jill Denner and Amy Griffin

Youth workers confront an array of challenges when trying to develop and implement programs that are intended to promote competencies, skills, and opportunities for youth. As noted in this volume, these challenges include how programming can respond to developmental stages, socioeconomic classes, ethnicity, race, gender, and context. This chapter examines research on the role of gender in healthy youth development. Gender is one of the key factors that guide youth decisions about who they will be and what they will do. Therefore, the primary goal of this chapter is to show the importance of including a gender "lens" to develop and implement more effective youth development programs. The following four questions will be addressed:

1. What does research say about the role of gender in healthy development?

2. Which assets or protective factors are gender specific?

3. What existing programming strategies are responsive to gender?

4. Given the information from the above questions, how can programs be tailored to meet the gender-specific needs required for healthy youth development?

❖ WHAT DOES RESEARCH SAY ABOUT THE ROLE OF GENDER IN HEALTHY DEVELOPMENT?

Social scientists typically think of gender as a somewhat fluid part of identity and different from "sex," which is linked to physical characteristics. According to Kimmel (2000) "Sex refers to the biological apparatus, the male and the female—our chromosomal, chemical, anatomical organization. Gender refers to the meanings that are attached to those differences within a culture" (p. 2-3). In other words, people who are physically male or female can have a combination of masculine (e.g., independent, assertive) and feminine (e.g., nurturing, passive) characteristics. Many studies suggest that there is greater variation in behaviors *within* than *across* sex groups (Campbell & Storo, 1994; Kimmel, 2000; Thorne, 1993).

Our review of research on gender reveals gaps in what is known about the role of gender in youth development. Therefore, this review will not cover all aspects of youth development. What we have compiled is intended to complement the needs of youth workers as they consider program planning and modification for youth.

How Youth Negotiate Gender Identities

One of the primary tasks of adolescence is the development of a personal identity. Expectations about how males and females should behave play an influential role in identity development. During adolescence, gender identity develops along with physical, cognitive, and social changes. Hill and Lynch (1983) suggest that gender role expectations intensify during adolescence, resulting in more profound differences in boys' and girls' attitudes, behaviors, and psychology. Some research supports this finding, saying the intensification of gender roles occurs in the second year of junior high (Alfieri, Ruble, & Higgins, 1996). However, other research challenges this theory in part, finding that boys endorse more rigid masculine roles, whereas girls become more flexible in how they define femininity (Galambos, Almeida, & Petersen, 1990; Katz & Ksansnak, 1994). Rather than a linear process of boys embracing masculine roles and girls embracing feminine roles, some researchers believe that the meaning of being a man or a woman varies across social class and culture (Fordham, 1993; Maccoby, 1990; and see other chapters in this volume).

How can youth workers make sense of these varied findings? Despite the variation across culture and social class and within sex, gender role expectations do play an influential role in youth self-concept, beliefs, and behaviors. It is important that youth workers be aware of their own gender role expectations and how they convey these expectations in their words and behaviors to youth. It is also critical for youth workers to know the community's gender role expectations, because violating them can result in social rejection for both females and males (Brown, 1993; Espin, 1997; Pleck, 1981). Youth workers can use observations of their own programs to see if patterns emerge in how girls versus boys respond to adolescence. To provide examples of what patterns to look for, we review studies of gender expectations for male and female adolescents and the ways that youth respond to these expectations that either help or hinder their healthy development.

Boys

Research suggests that boys face narrow definitions of what it means to become a man. Although these expectations vary by race/ethnicity, social class, urban versus rural setting, and age, males typically experience pressure to prove that they are neither feminine nor homosexual. For example, in children's textbooks, male characters are portrayed as aggressive, argumentative, and competitive (Evans & Davies, 2000). As boys grow older, a positive sense of masculinity is associated with success in sports (Davison, 2000; Stein & Hoffman, 1978). In the absence of positive role models, becoming a man may involve appearing cool, bad, or behaving violently (Heath & McLaughlin, 1993). Many view this bad-boy image as acceptable and even inevitable. For example, Moffitt (1993) claims, "for many boys, delinquency is not only normative but is also 'adjustive' in that it serves as a developmental function by expressing autonomy" (as cited in Compas, Hinden, & Gerhardt, 1995). The expectation of being a bad boy can sometimes start as early as elementary school. When asked what was the worst thing about being a boy, the majority of fifth- to eighth-grade students described pressure to be strong, getting blamed for troubles at school, and getting picked on by peers (Mee, 1995).

In addition to the narrow definitions about what it means to be a man, research suggests that males lack the intimate relational supports that females their age enjoy. Boys tend to have large groups of friends with whom they engage in activities, whereas girls tend to have more intimate friendships (Brown, 1990). Teenage boys from minority groups in urban settings describe mistrust, betrayal, and loss in their peer relationships and report being victims of frequent experiences of racism, discrimination, and harassment in their communities and schools (Way, 2001). Some suggest that a fear of being perceived as gay keeps males from sustaining intimate friendships with male peers, beginning in adolescence (Raymond, 1994).

Youth development programs can offer male adolescents support for a wider set of expectations about what it takes to become a man. It is important to encourage boys who do not do well in traditionally masculine activities to explore other skills. In addition, youth programs can help fill the gap in the relational needs of boys by offering activities to help boys build supportive and positive relationships with their peers. Program staff can provide adult role models to show ways to be a man outside rigidly defined masculine roles and can provide support when youth face discrimination and peer pressure.

Girls

Girls also face a set of clearly defined gender expectations as they approach adolescence. European American families with traditional gender role attitudes grant less autonomy and decision making to girls than to boys (Bumpus, Crouter, & McHale, 2001). African American families living in high crime neighborhoods afford less mobility outside the home to adolescent girls than boys (Jarrett, 1998). Similarly, in traditional Mexican families, expectations for girls include family commitment, respect for authority, and limitations on girls' mobility (De Len, 1996; Negy & Woods, 1992; Solis, 1995). Girls are confronted with contradictory expectations to maintain relationships and to be autonomous, to be nice but not dull, and to be both sexy and innocent (Basow & Rubin, 1999; Girl Scouts of the USA, 2000; Hudson, 1984;

Hurtado, 1997). As they decode these messages, many learn that if they stray outside the bounds of proscribed gender roles, they will be physically attacked or ostracized (Madriz, 1997).

Girls say that the worst thing about being female is the monthly menstrual cycle, not being taken seriously, and rules about physical appearance (Denner & Dunbar, 2002). Girls can easily cite advantages to being a boy, including having more freedom to leave the house (Denner & Dunbar, 2002; Mee, 1995). Not surprisingly, research suggests that girls who embrace more masculine or androgynous characteristics also report more self-confidence, self-esteem, and participation in some sports (Guillet, Sarrasin, & Fontayne, 2000; Johnson & McCoy, 2000; Wulff & Steitz, 1999). Girls who are not overprotected and who are encouraged to take positive risks with ample support are most resilient against the conditions of poverty (Werner & Smith, 1992). Youth workers can be mindful about providing opportunities for girls to exercise these positive risks by creating a supportive environment for them to explore. They can help youth value their feminine characteristics while supporting them to challenge gender roles that limit their opportunities for success or lower their self-esteem.

These different expectations for boys and girls result in sex differences in beliefs about ability, school achievement, and expectations for the future. For example, girls are not encouraged to take math, science, or technology classes as frequently as boys (American Association of University Women [AAUW], 1998). Sex typing limits girls' sense of possible future selves (Curry, Trew, Turner, & Hunter, 1994; Gottfredson, 1996). In addition, one study found that when they think of their future, girls report greater fear about relationships, whereas boys report greater fear about occupation, general failure, and inferiority (Knox, Funk, Elliott, & Bush, 2000). As described in a later section of this chapter, youth workers can encourage girls to pursue nontraditional careers by providing them with mentors and experiences of success in a range of academic fields.

Research can help us to recognize and promote some of the strategies girls use in response to limiting gender role expectations. As girls reach adolescence, many choose silence and negate their own knowledge and needs to minimize conflict in their relationships (Brown & Gilligan, 1992). This is particularly true for girls who identify more with traditional European American middle-class values about femininity, such as pleasing others and being physically attractive (Harter, Waters, & Whitesell, 1997; Tolman, 1999). Girls may also use silence to maintain power or to protect themselves in relationships (MacPherson & Fine, 1995; Pastor, McCormick, & Fine, 1996; Thompson, 1995). Some European American white girls resist a simple definition of femininity by shifting identities and making fun of beauty ideals (Brown, 1998). African American girls may negotiate gender role expectations in their schools by speaking out, conforming to academic expectations, and moving across different cultural or peer groups (Cohen & Blanc, 1996; Fordham, 1988). These studies suggest that girls actively resist, question, and embrace gender roles, and do not simply become more passive to maintain relationships.

Youth program staff must make sure that they do not perpetuate gender role stereotypes attempting to limit girls' autonomy, career options, or decision making. It is important to recognize how girls question gender roles and not simply to silence them in an attempt to keep the peace. Male and female staff can be positive role models by challenging traditional gender roles in their own behaviors. All staff should take seriously the concerns and comments that youth make about their abilities, and should convey high expectations for both girls and boys. Given the problematic nature of some of the strategies some youth use to negotiate limiting gender role expectations (e.g., tactics such as violence or silencing the self), youth workers must help them identify strategies that contribute to healthy development. The research suggests that the best way to support youth on these issues is to allow for a range of acceptable behaviors for females and males.

Physical Development

Research documents a host of physical, emotional, and social changes during adolescence for both boys and girls. The extent to which these present as risk factors for each sex depends on many factors, including the timing and the social context in which they occur. It is important that youth workers are aware of the challenges and that how youth respond to these challenges varies across sex.

The most noticeable sex differences are physical changes. Girls begin to develop on average two years before boys, and their changes are more visible, resulting in weight gain that is inconsistent with the type of female body society prefers (Brooks-Gunn & Reiter, 1990). Studies suggest that body image is a greater concern for girls due to the importance our society places on appearance for females. Girls show a decline in well-being following the first menstrual period, and boys show a small but temporary decline following voice change (Benjet & Hernandez-Guzman, 2001).

The effect of physical development depends on the timing and meaning of those changes in the child's family, school, and community. Adults' own anxiety about sexual maturation can result in treating youth differently if they mature relatively early or late compared to their peers. This treatment may vary across sex. For example, as physical changes occur, girls are interrupted more than boys, whereas boys assert themselves more than girls in interactions with parents (Hill, 1988). Youth workers should remain open to discussion about physical changes without making comments about visible changes that youth are already sensitive about. They should provide safe places for girls and boys to talk separately about the changes taking place in their bodies. They should pay particular attention to girls who mature early relative to their peers and to boys who mature late, and help them accept the timing of their changes as normal. They can do this by noticing how these youth are being treated by their peers, observing their reactions, and talking to them about how it affects them.

❖ WHICH ASSETS OR PROTECTIVE FACTORS ARE GENDER SPECIFIC?

Studies of "resilient" youth, those who succeed despite adversity, have contributed to our understanding of normal, healthy development. Across many studies, the factors that help youth succeed include individual characteristics such as self-esteem, having a positive connection with the community, and supportive and caring relationships with adults (Garmezy, 1993; Masten, 2001; Werner & Smith, 1992). We focus on the importance of considering gender when developing strategies to support three key aspects of youth development: (1) self-esteem, (2) community connection, and (3) relational support.

Self-Esteem

Many believe that adolescent boys have higher self-esteem than girls, but research tells a more complex story. An extensive review of studies found that gender differences are greatest between 15 and 18 years (Kling, Hyde, Showers, & Buswell, 1999). Overall, boys have a slightly more positive regard for themselves, primarily in areas related to physical appearance and math, but girls are stronger in some domains related to relationships. Another review of the research finds that boys have higher self-esteem, but only in the areas of school, job, and physical appearance (Scales & Leffert, 1999, p. 199). Some research suggests that self-esteem varies across race/ethnicity, with African American girls the least likely to experience a decline in self-esteem at adolescence (AAUW, 1996; Simmons & Blyth, 1987).

Different qualities are associated with self-esteem in boys and girls. Boys acquire prestige through sports, grades, and intelligence, whereas the qualities valued in girls are physical appearance, social success, and school achievement (Suitor & Reavis, 1995). Boys who endorse more masculine traits have higher self-esteem, and both sexes can identify more positive aspects of being a boy than of being a girl (Lamke, 1982; Massad, 1981; Mee, 1995). These and other studies (Block & Robins, 1993; Stein, Newcomb, & Bentler, 1992) suggest that youth have higher self-esteem when their behavior is consistent with their community's gender role expectations. On the other hand, studies also suggest that youth who endorse both male and female characteristics (are more androgynous) report higher levels of self-esteem with peers and in school (Rose & Montemayor, 1994).

Youth program staff can use different strategies to foster self-esteem in boys and girls. For example, activities such as sports can have a positive impact on identity development (Shaw, Kleiber, & Caldwell, 1995) and help girls overcome negative feelings about their physical appearance. Youth workers should take the concerns girls have about their relationships seriously and recognize that relationship problems can have a serious impact on girls' self-esteem. They must encourage girls to speak their minds, and they should not overprotect or limit girls' freedom more than that of boys. Although research suggests that a more androgynous gender role is related to higher self-esteem, there is limited research on how participation in nontraditional activities will promote androgyny or raise self-esteem.

It is important not to assume that boys consistently have higher levels of self-esteem in all aspects of their lives. Activities for boys should help them negotiate relationships so they can avoid conflict and express their feelings in ways that are direct and nonviolent. Programs should offer ways to build esteem for boys who do not enjoy competitive sports by building on their interests and skills. Finally, youth workers should help both boys and girls to value feminine characteristics such as listening and caring for others.

Community Connection

Community connections for youth can include access to resources, opportunities to participate in activities, and opportunities to have a voice in decisions that address community needs. Connections with caring adults or older youth who are positive role models in the community can result in increased access to education, work, and activities. These connections play an important role in youth decisions to participate in programs (McLaughlin, Irby, & Langman, 1994). In a study of 15 programs, both boys and girls stated that their primary reason for participating was to have fun (Gambone & Arbreton, 1997). However, girls were more likely to say that they came for relationships with friends or adults or because they learned a lot, whereas boys were more likely to report attending because they liked the activities or felt safe there.

Some research suggests that girls feel more connected to their schools and communities than boys. For example, girls have more positive attitudes toward service in their community. They are more likely than males to express concern and responsibility for the well-being of others and are more prosocial than boys in general (Beutal & Marini, 1995; Miller, 1994; Scales & Leffert, 1999; Stukas, Switzer, Dew, Goycoolea, & Simmons, 1999). Adolescent girls are more likely than boys to demonstrate helping behaviors, affirm diversity, and to report school success (Scales, Benson, Leffert, & Blyth, 2000). Some studies suggest that girls are more motivated to do well in school, that they value school more, and that they are more engaged and interested in school than boys (Scales & Leffert, 1999).

These differences in how boys and girls engage with the school and community may be due in part to differences in how they are treated. Although sex differences in parental monitoring allow boys more access to community resources, girls appear to have stronger, more intimate connections with people in and outside their families (Lytton & Romney, 1991). In a group of African American 6th to 10th graders, girls experienced higher levels of support for youth development, more opportunities to be a resource in both school and nonschool settings, and a more positive feeling and sense of belonging in school settings (Kahne et al., 2001).

Due to the different ways that society treats girls and boys, strategies for helping them connect with their communities might also look different. To illustrate, boys are less likely to cite relationships as part of their motivation to attend programs, suggesting that youth workers should consider how they form connections with boys. In addition, because helping others is often consistent with girls' definition of what it means to be female, youth workers can help boys to see the role of community helper as a positive aspect of masculinity. In this way, youth programs can play an important role in building boys' sense of connection with and responsibility for the community.

Relational Support

As stated earlier, girls may be more likely to receive more consistent, positive support from adults. Across adolescence, girls report the presence of a greater number of positive adult role models (Benson, Leffert, Scales, & Blyth, 1998). However, these relationships may look different for boys and girls. For example, teachers are more likely to give boys detailed directions on how to do a task but to help girls by doing the task for them (Sadker & Sadker, 1994). In one youth program, African American and Hispanic girls were more likely to cite adult staff as a reason they participated, even though boys report greater benefit from those relationships (Roffman, Pagano, & Hirsch, 2001). To enhance adult relationships with girls, it is important that they not be overprotected (Werner & Smith, 1992). Girls need to be guided but not rescued, and boys need access to a greater number of positive male role models.

Both boys and girls need social support from a variety of people, but they differ in how they use that support during adolescence. Boys appear to be more influenced than girls by support from the community and are motivated by personal affirmations, such as recognition of their competence in school and athletics (Scales & Leffert, 1999). On the other hand, girls respond more to support from one-on-one relationships (Entwisle, Alexander, & Olson, 1994; Scales & Leffert, 1999; Werner, 1993) and use support to make decisions about career choices, relationships, and other life-changing decisions. For example, girls' motivation for school achievement and academic self-concept is influenced by parent and teacher support, which is not a contributing factor for boys (Cotterell, 1992; Scales & Leffert, 1999).

Friendships also play a different role for boys and girls. Indeed, girls perceive their friendships to be more rewarding and fulfilling than do boys. For example, one study found that girls rated their friendships higher in admiration, affection, companionship, helping each other, intimacy, nurturance, reliable alliance, and satisfaction when compared to boys across all stages of adolescence (Clark-Lempers, Lempers, & Ho, 1991). Moreover, girls perceive their friendships to be closer and more supportive than boys do (Way & Chen, 2000). In fact, boys' perceived support from friends can be negatively related to self-concept and educational plans (Cotterell, 1992). For example, in early adolescence, boys who reported lower resistance to peer pressure were more likely to miss class and do worse in math, whereas resistance to peer pressure was unrelated to girls' math grades (Santor, Messervey, & Kusumakar, 2000). The emphasis among girls on relationships and social networks has led some to suggest that girls seek safe places where they can be themselves, resist social expectations, and receive support (Pastor et al., 1996).

Why boys and girls experience relational support so differently is not clear, but it is likely that they are offered different kinds of support by the adults in their lives. Youth workers must recognize that boys are not always able to ask for the support they need. In fact, boys are more likely than girls to lack the consistent support that helps them negotiate difficult challenges and personal growth and would benefit greatly from ongoing relationships with youth workers. Girls, on the other hand, need support that helps them achieve in a range of activities. Youth workers must be careful to balance support with independence and not overprotect girls.

In summary, although there may be greater variation within than across sex, we have highlighted the research that shows differences in the factors that help girls and boys succeed. In the rest of this chapter, we review existing programming strategies that take gender into account and provide recommendations for how programs can most constructively be responsive to sex differences.

❖ WHAT PROGRAMMING STRATEGIES ARE RESPONSIVE TO GENDER?

Many youth development programs take gender into consideration, either by creating single-sex settings or adapting activities to sex-specific risks or strengths. In this section, we review these strategies and discuss how program activities affect participation for boys and girls.

The earliest youth development programs were offered in single-sex settings (e.g., Boy Scouts and Girl Scouts) and based on the belief that boys and girls need to be prepared for different roles. As times changed, programs like the Boys and Girls Clubs began to accept girls into full membership (Folaron & Watkins, 1998), and many have debated the benefits and limitations to providing program activities in single-sex settings. Research suggests that coed settings put early-maturing girls at greater risk for involvement with delinquent peers and delinquent behavior and late-maturing girls at risk for school failure (Caspi & Moffitt, 1991). However, a report by the American Association of University Women (1998) suggests that coed settings can provide equal supports as long as certain qualities are present such as individual attention, equitable teaching practices, and a focused curriculum.

Although many single-sex programs offer activities consistent with gender role stereotypes, some programs are designed to help girls overcome inequities and build self-esteem in nontraditional areas. For example, a recent wave of programming is designed to increase female participation in math, science, and technology by offering role models and opportunities for girls to work together (e.g., Girls Inc.'s Operation SMART). Other programs help girls to think critically about how the media influences their self-esteem, body image, and career choices (e.g., Girls Inc.'s Friendly PEERsuasion; see Weiss & Nicholson, 1998). And still others create a forum for young women to define the issues that affect their lives and outline solutions for change (Haag, 2000). Single-sex programs for boys tend to focus on helping them become strong, independent, and responsible rather than helping them over-come barriers to nontraditional careers. For example, it is still hard to imagine a program that would help boys pursue a career as a secretary or in sewing.

Although most settings currently welcome girls and boys, many attract more of one sex or the other, and boys and girls spend their time out of school differently. For example, boys are more likely to partici-pate in clubs focused on computers and computer games (Van Roosmalen & Krahn, 1996; AAUW, 2000). Sports programs are also more popular with boys, whereas girls are more likely to participate in a wider range of activities and clubs, including performing arts and service activities (Eccles & Barber, 1999; Halpern, Barker, & Mollard, 2000; Scales & Leffert, 1999). Girls are more likely than boys to spend their leisure time helping others do their chores (Van Roosmalen & Krahn, 1996). It is important to note that participation does not vary simply because girls and boys enjoy different activities, but that gender role expectations dictate what girls and boys spend their time doing. For example, boys are often discouraged from participating in dance and other female-identified activities. And girls often say that they want to play sports, but that family obligations, as well as verbal and physical harassment, have kept them away from sports activities (Halpern et al., 2000).

Clearly, adults have responded to these different trends in participation by offering different kinds of programs to boys and to girls. Based on a survey of youth development workers, programs serving a higher percentage of females stated fewer program goals and were less likely to focus on the prevention of violence and juvenile delinquency and more likely to focus on adult mentoring and leadership training (Roth, 2000). Studies suggest that the different opportunities afforded girls and boys have an impact on the skills and knowledge they acquire (Zarbatany, Hartmann, & Rankin, 1990). Boys report taking on more leadership opportunities in after-school programs than girls (Gambone & Arbreton, 1997). Adults reward students whose communication styles are consistent with their gender role expectations, resulting in limited opportunities for African American girls who are seen as too "loud" (Fordham, 1993) and boys whose behavior is seen as threatening (McIntyre & Tong, 1998).

In summary, some programming strategies were developed in response to known differences in the needs and interests of boys and girls. Some of the programs offered to girls aim to undermine restrictive gender role expectations, and there is a need for more programs that do this with boys. For example, boys who work on computers can teach that skill to senior citizens in their communities. In addition, coed programs that resist gender role stereotypes can build strengths for both boys and girls by encouraging them to participate in a range of activities. Similar to the "bicultural" identity used by well-adapted ethnic minority youth (Cooper, Jackson, Azmitia, Lopez, & Dunbar, 1995; Hurtado, 1997; Negy & Woods, 1992; Phelan, Davidson, & Yu, 1991; Taylor, 1996; Vega, Khoury, Zimmerman, Gil, & Warheit, 1995; Zhou & Bankston, 1994), a "bigender" identity will help youth experience success despite narrow gender role expectations.

In the next section, we discuss how youth workers can respond to the different needs, strengths, and interests of each sex without perpetuating limited definitions of what are acceptable activities for boys and girls.

❖ RECOMMENDATIONS FOR CONSIDERING
     GENDER IN YOUTH DEVELOPMENT PROGRAMS

It is said that "successful interventions do not simply build skills, they promote a sense of efficacy, support, and self-worth, and they prevent future adversities," (Sandler, 2001, p. 48). The research reviewed above suggests that all youth need similar kinds of support and opportunities to succeed, but that narrow gender role expectations have resulted in different opportunities and treatments for boys and girls. Based on this research, below are recommendations for ways that youth workers can respond to this inequity by tailoring their practices to support boys and to support girls.

Programming Strategies That Support Boys

Researchers and youth workers are less clear about what healthy youth development looks like for boys than for girls. Although boys who endorse more masculine behaviors have higher self-esteem, they also are more likely to engage in risk behaviors (Courtenay, 2000; Eccles & Barber, 1999; Isenhart & Silversmith, 1994). Therefore, many advocate expanding adolescent males' conceptions of manhood and appropriate gender roles. Youth workers can do this by helping them reflect on the costs of a traditional masculine role and encouraging a range of acceptable masculinities (Barker, 2000; Connell, 2000; Forrest, 2000). Some find that this can reduce the likelihood of boys' engaging in violent behaviors (Hong, 2000). These suggestions imply that youth workers need to think carefully about the meaning of masculinity for themselves and members of their community and the extent to which restrictive gender roles constrain healthy youth development. Gurian (1999) recommends allowing boys opportunities to make significant contributions in the role of leader as well as follower, to experience a sense of belonging to a group, and to have role models who provide guidance, nurturance, and praise.

Coed programs can help boys to resist harmful gender stereotypes. Some coed settings offer single-sex groups to discuss issues, as well as offering program activities for boys and girls together (Halpern et al., 2000). Staff can make sure that boys and girls have equal access to adults and to opportunities for participation in different kinds of activities (Girls Inc., 1992). If there is a noticeable sex difference, they can ask youth why they do not participate in certain activities. In addition, staff can take advantage of teachable moments where there is disrespect across the sexes to lead discussions with girls and boys about gender relations (Halpern et al., 2000).

Programming Strategies That Support Girls

Many advocates for women and girls emphasize the importance of girls-only programming. In general, expectations for what healthy youth development looks like for girls is more clear than it is for boys. Those who offer single-sex settings want girls to explore a range of roles, experiences, and activities that are usually not available to them (Girls Inc., 1992). Strategies to accomplish this include creating a safe place where physical and emotional safety is assured, with a presence of strong and supportive adult females (Hirsch et al., 2000; Three Guineas Fund, 2001). Creating a safe space is key to girls' physical safety and ability to be themselves and assert their voices (Hirsch et al., 2000; Ms. Foundation for Women, 2000; Pastor et al., 1996). Intergenerational relationships are a natural source of mentoring for girls (Rhodes & Davis, 1986), and celebrating women's accomplishments is another strategy for promoting their positive development (Girls Inc., 1992).

Other recommendations include having adults redefine their sense of leadership to include girls' culture, strengths, challenges, and aspirations, and helping girls to see themselves as agents of change (Denmark, 1999; Ms. Foundation, 2000). Programs can build on existing models of leadership that include building relationships and nurturing others (Lyons, Saltenstall, & Hanmer, 1990), which are more consistent with gendered expectations for girls. Including girls in the planning and implementation of activities is also essential for promoting the strengths and the voices of young women (Hirsch et al., 2000; Ms. Foundation, 2000).

Given the challenges that girls face as their bodies begin to change, program activities that include physical challenges such as sports or rock climbing create a space where appearance is not the primary factor for girls' success. Girls who participate in sports are more likely to report androgynous qualities (Guillet et al., 2000). Sports are also associated with decreased likelihood of stress and depression symptoms, teen motherhood, school dropout, and cigarette smoking

(Shaw et al., 1995; Zill, Nord, & Loomis, 1995). Sports may be especially positive for adolescent girls because they place girls in less traditional female roles. Programs that challenge girls "by choice" and promote courage to take chances and speak their minds promote individual competence while also strengthening relational ties (Stemmermann & Antonellis, 2000). Youth workers should help girls focus on what they can do rather than on what they don't do well (Girls Inc., 1992). Also, when a safe place to try new opportunities is provided, girls can build on their strengths by expanding their understanding of what they know that they can do. The same can be said for boys who are given opportunities to try new roles that they would not have necessarily explored due to gender typing.

What Youth Workers Can Do to Support Gender Equity in All Settings

Youth workers can build a range of strengths in both boys and girls by (a) examining their own beliefs about how males and females should act, (b) becoming aware of how they translate those beliefs into their own actions and interactions, and (c) striving to provide positive messages and encouragement for a broad range of options for all youth. As suggested by Nicholson (1992), "Differences of opinion about the ideal roles of women and men will always result in differences of opinion about what constitutes 'positive youth development' for each sex" (p. 6). Efforts to respond to existing differences in girls and boys without also responding to the causes of those differences risk perpetuating harmful gender stereotypes (AAUW, 1998; Ms. Foundation, 1993).

We cannot underestimate the importance of youth workers' gender role expectations for promoting positive youth development. For example, studies show ways that adult expectations for sex differences in math performance can influence how youth feel about their math abilities (Eccles, Jacobs, & Harold, 1990). Thus, if adults expect boys to have higher self-esteem or expect them to prefer basketball instead of art, they may perpetuate the sex differences rather than simply respond to them. Alternatively, youth workers can attempt to provide and encourage a broader range of options for both female and male youth.

Staff can be role models for the equitable treatment of the sexes. For example, girls should be praised for their skills and successes, not just for their appearance (Girls Inc., 1992). Girls should not be rescued from difficult situations. Instead, staff should help girls develop the skills to navigate their challenges. Boys should be praised for their artwork and for reaching out to others, not just for accomplishments in sports. There should be opportunities for boys to develop positive and supportive friendships. Male and female staff should model a range of career interests and should treat each other with the kind of respect they hope to see in youth.

The following recommendations build on those suggested by Nicholson (1992) for creating equity in youth programming and by Phillips (1998) for promoting healthy development in girls:

- Involve adults who have examined their own beliefs about gender and are trained in delivering services equitably.
- Have high expectations of both girls and boys, and don't rescue girls or expect boys to be superhuman.
- Give youth space to lead, but watch for dominance by one sex; offer different kinds of leadership roles, and vary group size and the amount of structure to override dominant groups (e.g., males, high-income).
- Through role modeling, encourage boys and girls to value and respect girls and women.
- Notice and support youth who behave in ways that challenge traditional gender stereotypes.
- Encourage interactions between boys and girls that are not focused on romance.
- Offer activities that speak to the interests and skills of girls and boys.
- Help youth recognize and challenge the gender stereotypes that perpetuate inequities, including assumptions about careers, involvement in sports, and family responsibility.

❖ THE IMPLICATIONS OF THESE FINDINGS
FOR TWO YOUTH DEVELOPMENT STRATEGIES

We selected two popular youth development strategies to illustrate how research on sex differences can help youth workers adapt their own programming strategies.

Mentoring

Increasing evidence reveals the importance of nonparental adult relationships for youth. Research suggests that mentoring can increase school attendance and academic achievement even when tutoring and school-based activities are not an explicit part of the program (Obeidallah & Earls, 1999; Phillips, 1999). These relationships are most effective when they last six months or longer (Rhodes, Grossman, & Resche, 2000). Most of what is known about mentoring is from Big Brothers Big Sisters, where a previously unknown adult is assigned to support a youth described as needy. However, youth who seek out and experience supportive relationships with adults also experience more positive well-being (Blum, Beuhring, & Rinehart, 2000; Cooper, Denner, & Lopez, 1999; Werner & Smith, 1992).

The focus of the mentoring might vary for girls and boys. Some research suggests that boys prefer mentors who are more experienced and provide support and knowledge, whereas girls prefer supportive relationships with friends they can trust and with whom they can share concerns (Philip & Hendry, 1996; Sullivan, 1996). It may be for this reason that older sisters are more likely to be cited as sources of support than older brothers (Cooper et al., 1995). In fact, a young woman often seeks relationships with people who are already part of her community, such as neighbors, boyfriends' female relatives, and teachers (Rhodes & Davis, 1986). Mentors for girls might concentrate on identity development issues, sports, and math or science competencies, whereas mentors for boys might concentrate efforts on school success, relationships, and prosocial behavior.

Service Learning

Service learning provides opportunities for youth to take on leadership roles in their communities, building on existing strengths, interests, and challenges. However, leadership has different meanings for girls and boys. Leadership for girls may involve less hierarchical, more collaborative decision making (Lyons et al., 1990). Many girls see themselves as change agents, concerned with making the world a better place for themselves and their families (Denner & Dunbar, 2002; McKay, 1998; Ms. Foundation, 2000). This is supported by studies cited above that document girls' higher participation and interest in community service. However, doing service for others may increase the struggle of some adolescent girls to care for others and also care for themselves (Gilligan, 1990).

Switzer, Simmons, Dew, Regalski, & Wang (1995) found key gender differences in the benefits of service learning. The authors noted,

> Although girls did report feeling more like better persons after having participated in the program than did the boys, the results indicate that boys were the main beneficiaries of this program; participating boys exhibited positive changes in self-esteem, depressive affect, involvement, and problem behavior relative to other groups. (p. 445)

Service-learning program staff should be aware of how gender role stereotypes may affect participation in and benefit from this activity. Recommendations for programming for boys would be to tap into their interests to engage them in community service activities. For example, a boy who is good in art can teach classes at a senior center. Since boys express less interest in this activity, it is important to provide them with meaningful roles and projects of interest in which they can see a direct effect from their efforts. It is also important to provide boys with the opportunity to see themselves as relational caregivers, a role that many do not experience. With girls, it is important not to reinforce the stereotype that girls are solely responsible for helping others or that they should enjoy serving others just because they are girls. Although girls also need praise for caregiving, it must be balanced in relation to their other strengths and successes.

❖ CONCLUSION: MINIMIZE THE POLARITY BETWEEN THE SEXES

In this chapter, we emphasize the importance of increasing awareness about gender in youth development programs. Over the last 15 years, we have seen an increase in research on female development. More recently, we have seen a rise in the number of books that focus on the strengths and needs of males as they move from childhood to adulthood. We need to avoid the polarization that results in pitting boys against girls. It is not productive to argue about who needs more resources and attention, particularly because all youth benefit from the same basic developmental supports. Rather, we need to consider variations within sex, with the understanding that the meaning attached to sex depends on the meaning that influential adults place on it.

We also need youth workers to be aware of the meaning associated with masculine and feminine gender roles in their communities, because these expectations will impact their programs. As Heath and McLaughlin (1993, p. 25) suggest, "In inner cities, decisions related to how one plays out gender roles can make the difference between life and death." Opportunities for participation in a range of activities, along with exposure to male and female leaders in these activities, will help deconstruct gender roles that limit participation. Like West and Zimmerman (1987), we believe that youth are actively constructing gender identity and behavior in response to external risks, opportunities, and expectations. Given this dynamic process of development, youth workers are in a uniquely powerful position to help youth explore a range of healthy choices about how to become a man or a woman.

❖ REFERENCES

Alfieri, T., Ruble, D. N., & Higgins, E. T. (1996). Gender stereotypes during adolescence: Developmental changes and the transition to junior high school. *Developmental Psychology, 32*(6), 1129-1137.

American Association of University Women. (1996). *Girls in the middle: Working to succeed in school.* Washington, DC: AAUW Educational Foundation.

American Association of University Women. (1998). *Separated by sex: A critical look at single-sex education for girls.* Washington, DC: AAUW Educational Foundation.

American Association of University Women. (2000). *Tech-savvy: Educating girls in the new computer age.* Washington, DC: AAUW Educational Foundation.

Barker, G. (2000). Gender equitable boys in a gender inequitable world: Reflections from qualitative research and programme development in Rio de Janeiro. *Sexual & Relationship Therapy, 15*(3), 263-282.

Basow, S. A., & Rubin, L. R. (1999). Gender influences on adolescent development. In N. G. Johnson, M. C. Roberts, & J. Worell (Eds.), *Beyond appearance: A new look at adolescent girls* (pp. 25-52). Washington, DC: American Psychological Association.

Benjet, C., & Hernandez-Guzman, L. (2001). Gender differences in psychological well-being of Mexican early adolescents. *Adolescence, 36*(141), 47.

Benson, P. L., Leffert, N., Scales, P. C., & Blyth, D. A. (1998). Beyond the village rhetoric: Creating healthy communities for children and adolescents. *Applied Developmental Science, 2*(3), 138-159.

Beutal, A. M., & Marini, M. M. (1995). Gender and values. *American Sociological Review, 60*(3), 436-448.

Block, J., & Robins, R. (1993). A longitudinal study of consistency and change in self-esteem from early adolescence to early adulthood. *Child Development, 64*, 909-923.

Blum, R. W., Beuhring, T., & Rinehart, P. M. (2000). *Protecting teens: Beyond race, income, and family structure.* (Available from the Center for Adolescent Health, University of Minnesota, 200 Oak Street SE, Suite 260, Minneapolis, MN 55455)

Brooks-Gunn, J., & Reiter, E. P. (1990). The role of pubertal processes. In S. S. Feldman & G. R. Elliott (Eds.), *At the threshold: The developing adolescent* (pp. 16-53). Cambridge, MA: Harvard University Press.

Brown, B. B. (1990). Peer groups and peer cultures. In S. S. Feldman & G. R. Elliott (Eds.), *At the threshold: The developing adolescent* (pp. 171-196). Cambridge, MA: Harvard University Press.

Brown, L. M. (1998). *Raising their voices: The politics of girls' anger.* Cambridge, MA: Harvard University Press.

Brown, L. M., & Gilligan, C. (1992). *Meeting at the crossroads.* New York: Ballantine Books.

Brown, L. S. (1993). New voices, new visions: Toward a lesbian/gay paradigm for psychology. *Psychology of Women Quarterly, 13*, 445-458.

Bumpus, M., Crouter, A. C., & McHale, S. M. (2001). Parental autonomy granting during adolescence: Exploring gender differences in context [Abstract]. *Developmental Psychology, 37*(2), 163-173.

Campbell, P. B., & Storo, J. N. (1994). *Girls are . . . boys are . . .: Myths, stereotypes and gender differences.* Groton, MA: Campbell-Kibler.

Caspi, A., & Moffitt, T. E. (1991). Individual differences are accentuated during periods of social change: The sample case of girls at puberty. *Journal of Personality & Social Psychology, 61*(1), 157-168.

Clark-Lempers, D. S., Lempers, J. D., & Ho, C. (1991). Early, middle, and late adolescents' perceptions of their relationships with significant others. *Journal of Adolescent Research, 6*, 296-315.

Cohen, J., & Blanc, S. (1996). *Girls in the middle: Working to succeed in school.* Washington, DC: American Association of University Women Educational Foundation.

Compas, B. E., Hinden, B. R., & Gerhardt, C. A. (1995). Adolescent development: Pathways and processes of risk and resilience. *Annual Review of Psychology, 46*, 265-293.

Connell, R. W. (2000). *The men and the boys.* Berkeley: University of California Press.

Cooper, C. R., Denner, J., & Lopez, E. M. (1999). Cultural brokers: Helping Latino children on pathways toward success. In M. B. Larner (Ed.), When school is out. *The Future of Children, 9*, 51-57.

Cooper, C. R., Jackson, J. F., Azmitia, M., Lopez, E. M., & Dunbar, N. (1995). Bridging students' multiple worlds: African American and Latino youth in academic outreach programs. In R. F. Macías & R. G. García Ramos (Eds.), *Changing schools for changing students: An anthology of research on language minorities* (pp. 211-234). Santa Barbara: University of California Linguistic Minority Research Institute.

Cotterell, J. L. (1992). The relation of attachments and supports to adolescent well-being and school adjustment. *Journal of Adolescent Research, 7,* 28-42.

Courtenay, W. H. (2000). Constructions of masculinity and their influence on men's well-being: A theory of gender and health. *Social Science & Medicine, 50,* 1385-1401.

Curry, C., Trew, K., Turner, I., & Hunter, J. (1994). The effect of life domains on girls' possible selves. *Adolescence, 29*(113), 133-150.

Davison, K. G. (2000). Boys' bodies in school: Physical education [Abstract]. *Journal of Men's Studies, 8*(2), 255.

De Len, B. (1996). Career development of Hispanic adolescent girls. In B. J. R. Leadbeater & N. Way (Eds.), *Urban girls: Resisting stereotypes, creating identities* (pp. 380-398). New York: New York University Press.

Denner, J., & Dunbar, N. (2002). Negotiating gender roles in adolescence: Mexican American girls' strategies. Manuscript submitted for publication.

Denmark, F. L. (1999). Enhancing the development of adolescent girls. In N. G. Johnson, M. C. Roberts, & J. Worell (Eds.), *Beyond appearance: A new look at adolescent girls* (pp. 377-404). Washington, DC: American Psychological Association.

Eccles, J. S., & Barber, B. L. (1999). Student council, volunteering, basketball, or marching band: What kind of extracurricular involvement matters? *Journal of Adolescent Research, 14*(1), 10-43.

Eccles, J. S., Jacobs, J. E., & Harold, R. D. (1990). Gender role stereotypes, expectancy effects, and parents' socialization of gender differences. *Journal of Social Issues, 46,* 183-201.

Entwisle, D. R., Alexander, K. L., & Olson, L. S. (1994). The gender gap in math: Its possible origins in neighborhood effects. *American Sociological Review, 59*(6), 822-838.

Espin, O. M. (1997). *Latina realities: Essays on healing, migration, and sexuality.* Boulder, CO: Westview.

Evans, L., & Davies, K. (2000). No sissy boys here: A content analysis of the representation of masculinity in elementary school reading textbooks. *Sex Roles, 42*(3-4), 255-270.

Folaron, G., & Watkins, M. (1998). Creating gender equity in a youth-serving agency: A case study of organizational change. *Journal of Child and Youth Care, 12*(13), 46-57.

Fordham, S. (1988). Racelessness as a factor in Black students' school success: Pragmatic strategy or Pyrrhic victory? *Harvard Educational Review, 58*(1), 54-84.

Fordham, S. (1993). "Those loud black girls": (Black) women, silence, and gender "passing" in the academy. *Anthropology and Education Quarterly, 24*(1), 3-32.

Forrest, S. (2000). Big and tough: Boys learning about sexuality and manhood. *Sexual & Relationship Therapy, 15*(3), 247-261.

Galambos, N. L., Almeida, D. M., & Petersen, A. C. (1990). Masculinity, femininity, and sex role attitudes in early adolescence: Exploring gender intensification. *Child Development, 61*(6), 1905-1914.

Gambone, M. A., & Arbreton, A. J. (1997). *Safe havens: The contributions of youth organizations to healthy adolescent development.* Philadelphia: Public/Private Ventures.

Garmezy, N. (1993). Children in poverty: Resilience despite risk. *Psychiatry: Interpersonal & Biological Processes, 56*(1), 127-136.

Gilligan, C. (1990). Teaching Shakespeare's sister. In C. Gilligan, N. Lyons, & T. Hanmer (Eds.), *Making connections: The relational worlds of adolescent girls at Emma Willard School* (pp. 6-29). Cambridge, MA: Harvard University Press.

Girl Scouts of the USA. (2000). *Girls speak out: Teens before their time.* New York: Girl Scouts of the USA.

Girls Inc. (1992). *Past the pink and blue predicament: Freeing the next generation from sex stereotypes.* New York: Author.

Gottfredson, L. S. (1996). Gottfredson's theory of circumspection and compromise. In D. Brown, D. Brooks, and associates (Eds.), *Career choice and development* (3rd ed., pp. 179-232). San Francisco: Jossey-Bass.

Guillet, E., Sarrasin, P., & Fontayne, P. (2000). If it contradicts my gender role, I'll stop. *European Review of Applied Psychology, 50*(4), 417-421.

Gurian, M. (1999). *A fine young man: What parents, mentors and educators can do to shape adolescent boys into exceptional men.* New York: Penguin Putnam.

Haag, P. (2000). *Voices of a generation: Teenage girls report about their lives today.* New York: Marlowe.

Halpern, R., Barker, G., & Mollard, W. (2000). Youth programs as alternative spaces to be: A study of neighborhood youth programs in Chicago's West Town. *Youth & Society, 31*(4), 469-506.

Harter, S., Waters, P. L., & Whitesell, N. R. (1997). Lack of voice as a manifestation of false self-behavior among adolescents: The school setting as a stage upon which the drama of authenticity is enacted. *Educational Psychologist, 32*(3), 153-173.

Heath, S. B., & McLaughlin, M. W. (1993). Casting the self: Frames for identity and dilemmas for policy. In *Identity and Inner-City Youth: Beyond ethnicity and gender.* New York: Teachers College, Columbia University.

Hill, J. P. (1988). Adapting to menarche: Familial control and conflict. In M. R. Gunnar and W. A. Collins (Eds.). *Development during the transition to adolescence.* (pp. 43-77). Hillsdale, NJ: Lawrence Erlbaum.

Hill, J. P., & Lynch, M. E. (1983). The intensification of gender-related role expectations during early adolescence. In J. Brooks-Gunn & A. C. Petersen (Eds.), *Girls at puberty: Biological and psychological perspectives* (pp. 201-230). New York: Plenum.

Hirsch, B. J., Roffman, J. G., Deutsch, N. L., Flynn, C., Loder, T. L., & Pagano, M. E. (2000). Inner-city youth development programs: Strengthening programs for adolescent girls. *Journal of Early Adolescence, 20*(2), 210-230.

Hong, L. (2000). Toward a transformed approach to prevention: Breaking the link between masculinity and violence. *Journal of American College Health, 48*(6), 269-279.

Hudson, B. (1984). Femininity and adolescence. In A. McRobbie & M. Nava (Eds.), *Gender and Generation,* (pp. 31-53). Houndmills, UK: Macmillan.

Hurtado, A. (1997). Understanding multiple group identities: Inserting women into cultural transformations. *Journal of Social Issues, 53,* 299-328.

Isenhart, C. E., & Silversmith, D. J. (1994). The influence of traditional male role on alcohol abuse and the therapeutic process. *Journal of Men's Studies, 3,* 127-135.

Jarrett, R. L. (1998). African American children, families, and neighborhoods: Qualitative contributions to understanding developmental pathways. *Applied Developmental Science, 2*(1), 2-16.

Johnson, W., & McCoy, N. (2000). Self-confidence, self-esteem and assumption of sex role in young men and women. *Perceptual & Motor Skills, 90*(3, Pt. 1), 751-756.

Kahne, J., Nagaoka, J., Brown, A., O'Brien, J., Quinn, T., & Thiede, K. (2001). Assessing after-school programs as contexts for youth development. *Youth & Society, 32,* 421-446.

Katz, P. A., & Ksansnak, K. R. (1994). Developmental aspects of gender role flexibility and traditionality in middle childhood and adolescence. *Developmental Psychology 30*(2), 272-282.

Kimmel, M. S. (2000). *The gendered society.* New York: Oxford University Press.

Kling, K. C., Hyde, J. S., Showers, C. J., & Buswell, B. N. (1999). Gender differences in self-esteem: A meta-analysis. *Psychological Bulletin, 125,* 470-500.

Knox, M., Funk, J., Elliott, R., & Bush, E. G. (2000). Gender differences in adolescents' possible selves. *Youth & Society, 31*(3), 287-309.

Lamke, L. K. (1982). The impact of sex-role orientation on self-esteem in early adolescence. *Child Development, 53*(6), 1530-1535.

Lyons, N. P., Saltenstall, J. F., & Hanmer, T. J. (1990). Competencies and visions: Emma Willard girls talk about being leaders. In C. Gilligan, N. P. Lyons, & T. J. Hanmer (Eds.), *Making connections: The relational worlds of adolescent* girls at Emma Willard School (pp. 183-214). Cambridge, MA: Harvard University Press.

Lytton, H., & Romney, D. M. (1991). In D. Sabo (Ed.), *Understanding Men's Health: A relational and gender sensitive approach* (p. 4). Harvard, MA: Harvard School of Public Health, Center for Population and Development Studies.

Maccoby, E. E. (1990). Gender and relationships: A developmental account. *American Psychologist, 45*(4), 513-520.

MacPherson, P., & Fine, M. (1995). Hungry for an us: Adolescent girls and adult women negotiating territories of race, gender, class and difference. *Feminism and Psychology, 5,* 181-200.

Madriz, E. (1997). *Nothing bad happens to good girls: Fear of crime in women's lives.* Berkeley: University of California Press.

Massad, C. M. (1981). Sex role identity and adjustment during adolescence. *Child Development, 52*(4), 1290-1298.

Masten, A. S. (2001). Ordinary magic: Resilience processes in development. *American Psychologist, 56*(3), 227-238.

McIntyre, T., & Tong, V. (1998). Where the boys are: Do cross-gender misunderstandings of language use and behavior patterns contribute to the overrepresentation of males in programs for students with emotional and behavioral disorders? *Education and Treatment of Children, 21*(3), 321-332.

McKay, S. (1998). The effects of armed conflict on girls and women. *Peace & Conflict: Journal of Peace Psychology, 4*(4), 381-392.

McLaughlin, M. W., Irby, M. A., & Langman, J. (1994). *Urban sanctuaries: Neighborhood organizations in the lives and futures of inner-city youth.* San Francisco: Jossey-Bass.

Mee, C. S. (1995, March). Middle school voices on gender identity. *Women's Educational Equity Act Publishing Center Digest.*

Miller, F. (1994). Gender differences in adolescents' attitudes toward mandatory community service. *Journal of Adolescence, 17,* 381-393.

Ms. Foundation for Women. (1993). *Programmed neglect: Not seen, not heard.* New York: Author.

Ms. Foundation for Women. (2000). *The new girls' movement: Charting the path.* New York: Author, Collaborative Fund for Healthy Girls/Healthy Women.

Negy, C., & Woods, D. J. (1992). The importance of acculturation in understanding research with Hispanic-Americans. *Hispanic Journal of Behavioral Sciences, 14,* 224-247.

Nicholson, H. J. (1992). Gender issues in youth development programs. Washington, DC: Carnegie Council on Adolescent Development.

Obeidallah, D. A., & Earls, F. J. (1999, July). *Adolescent girls: The role of depression in the development of delinquency.* U.S. Department of Justice, Office of Justice Programs, National Institute of Justice. Retrieved September 20, 2002, from www.ncjrs.org/txtfiles1/fs000244.txt

Pastor, J., McCormick, J., & Fine, M. (1996). Makin' homes: An urban girl thing. In B. J. R. Leadbeater & N. Way (Eds.), *Urban girls: Resisting stereotypes, creating identities* (pp. 15-34). New York: New York University Press.

Phelan, P., Davidson, A. L., & Yu, H. C. (1991). Students' multiple worlds: Navigating the borders of family, peers, and school cultures. In P. Phelan & A. L. Davidson (Eds.), *Cultural diversity: Implications for education* (pp. 52-88). New York: Teachers College Press.

Philip, K., & Hendry, L. (1996). Young people and mentoring—towards typology? *Journal of Adolescence, 19,* 189-201.

Phillips, L. (1998). *The girls report: What we know and need to know about growing up female.* New York: The National Council on Research on Women. Retrieved September 20, 2002, from www1.umn.edu/aurora/thegirlsreport.html

Phillips, L. (1999). *Girls report: What we know and need to know about growing up female.* New York: National Council for Research on Women.

Pleck, J. H. (1981). *The myth of masculinity.* Cambridge, MA: MIT Press.

Raymond, D. (1994). Homophobia, identity, and the meanings of desire: Reflections on the cultural constructions of gay and lesbian adolescent sexuality. In J. Irvine (Ed.), *Sexual cultures and the construction of adolescent identities.* Philadelphia: Temple University Press.

Rhodes, J. E., & Davis, A. B. (1986). Supportive ties between nonparent adults and urban adolescent girls. In B. J. R. Leadbeater & N. Way (Eds.), *Urban girls: Resisting stereotypes, creating identities* (pp. 213-225). New York: New York University Press.

Rhodes, J. E., Grossman, J. B., & Resche, N. L. (2000). Agents of change: Pathways through which mentoring relationships influence adolescents' academic adjustment. *Child Development, 71*(6), 1662-1671.

Roffman, J. G., Pagano, M. E., & Hirsch, B. J. (2001). Youth functioning and experiences in inner-city after-school programs among age, gender, and race groups. *Journal of Child and Family Studies, 10*(1), 85-100.

Rose, A. J., & Montemayor, R. (1994). The relationship between gender role orientation and perceived self-competency in male and female adolescents. *Sex Roles, 31*(9-10), 579-595.

Roth, J. (2000, April). *What we know and what we need to know about youth development programs.* Paper presented at Evaluation of Youth Programs symposium at the Biennial Meeting of the Society for Research on Adolescence, Chicago.

Sadker, M., & Sadker, D. (1994). *Failing at fairness: How America's schools cheat girls.* New York: Scribner.

Sandler, I. (2001). Quality and ecology of adversity as common mechanisms of risk and resilience. *American Journal of Community Psychology, 29,* 19-61.

Santor, D. A., Messervey, D., & Kusumakar, V. (2000). Measuring peer pressure, popularity, and conformity in adolescent boys and girls: Predicting school performance, sexual attitudes, and substance abuse. *Journal of Youth & Adolescence, 29*(2), 163-182.

Scales, P. C., Benson, P. L., Leffert, N., & Blyth, D. A. (2000). Contribution of developmental assets to the prediction of thriving among adolescents. *Applied Developmental Science, 4*(1), 27-46.

Scales, P. C., & Leffert, N. (1999). *Developmental assets: A synthesis of the scientific research on adolescent development.* Minneapolis, MN: Search Institute.

Shaw, S. M., Kleiber, D. A., & Caldwell, L. L. (1995). Leisure and identity information in male and female adolescents: A preliminary examination. *Journal of Leisure Research, 27*(3), 245-263.

Simmons, R. G., & Blyth, D. (1987). *Moving into adolescence: The impact of pubertal change and school context.* New York: Aldine De Gruyter.

Solis, J. (1995). The status of Latino children and youth: Challenges and prospects. In R. E. Zambrana (Ed.), *Understanding Latino families: Scholarship, policy, and practice* (pp. 62-81).Thousand Oaks, CA: Sage.

Stein, J. C., Newcomb, M. D., & Bentler, P. M. (1992). The effect of agency and communality on self-esteem: Gender differences in longitudinal data. *Sex Roles, 26,* 465-483.

Stein, P. J., & Hoffman, S. (1978). Sports and male role strain. *Journal of Social Issues, 34,* 136-150.

Stemmerman, J., & Antonellis, J. (2000). Girls on the edge: Rethinking out-of-school programs for adolescent girls. In S. J. Danish & T. P. Gullota (Eds.), *Developing competent youth and strong communities through after-school programming.* Washington, DC: CWLA Press.

Stukas, A. A., Jr., Switzer, G. E., Dew, M. A., Goycoolea, J. M., & Simmons, R. G. (1999). Parental helping models, gender, and service-learning [Abstract]. *Journal of Prevention & Intervention in the Community, 18*(1-2), 5-18.

Suitor, J. J., & Reavis, R. (1995). Football, fast cars, and cheerleading: Adolescent gender norms, 1978-1989. *Adolescence, 30*(118), 265-272.

Sullivan, A. M. (1996). From mentor to muse: recasting the role of women in relationship with urban adolescent girls. In B. J. R. Leadbeater & N. Way (Eds.), *Urban girls: Resisting stereotypes, creating identities* (pp. 226-253). New York: New York University Press.

Switzer, G. E., Simmons, R. G., Dew, M. A., Regalski, J. M., & Wang, C. H. (1995). The effect of a school-based helper program on adolescent self-image, attitudes, and behavior. *Journal of Early Adolescence, 15,* 429-455.

Taylor, J. M. (1996). Cultural stories: Latina and Portuguese daughters and mothers. In B. J. R. Leadbeater & N. Way (Eds.), *Urban girls: Resisting stereotypes, creating identities* (pp. 117-131). New York: New York University Press.

Thompson, S. (1995). *Going all the way: Sex, romance, and pregnancy.* New York: Hill and Wang.

Thorne, B. (1993). *Gender play: Girls and boys in school*. New Brunswick, NJ: Rutgers University Press.

Tolman, D. L. (1999). Female adolescent sexuality in relational context: Beyond sexual decision making. In N. G. Johnson, M. C. Roberts, & J. Worell (Eds.), *Beyond appearance: A new look at adolescent girls* (pp. 227-246). Washington, DC: American Psychological Association.

Three Guineas Fund. (2001). *Improving philanthropy for girls' programs.* San Francisco: Author.

Van Roosmalen, E., & Krahn, H. (1996). Boundaries of youth. *Youth & Society, 28*(1), 3-39.

Vega, W. A., Khoury, E. L., Zimmerman, R. S., Gil, A. G., & Warheit, G. J. (1995). Cultural conflicts and problem behaviors of Latino adolescents in home and school environments. *Journal of Community Psychology, 23*(2), 167-179.

Way, N. (2001). Using feminist research methods to explore boys' relationships. In D. L. Tolman & M. Brydon-Miller (Eds.), *From subjects to subjectivities: A handbook of interpretive and participatory methods* (pp. 111-129). New York: New York University Press.

Way, N., & Chen, L. (2000). Close and general friendships among African American, Latino, and Asian American adolescents from low-income families. *Journal of Adolescent Research, 15*, 274-301.

Weiss, F. L., & Nicholson, H. J. (1998). Friendly PEERsuasion against substance use: The Girls Incorporated model and evaluation. *Drugs & Society, 12*(1-2), 7-22.

Werner, E. E. (1993). Risk, resilience, and recovery: Perspectives from the Kauai Longitudinal Study. *Development & Psychopathology, 5*(4), 503-515.

Werner, E. E., & Smith, R. S. (1992). *Overcoming the odds: High risk children from birth to adulthood*. Ithaca, NY: Cornell University Press.

West, C., & Zimmerman, D. (1987). In D. Sabo (Ed.), *Understanding men's health: A relational and gender sensitive approach* (pp. 2, 5). Harvard, MA: Harvard School of Public Health, Center for Population and Development Studies.

Wulff, M. B., & Steitz, J. A. (1999). A path model of the relationship between career indecision, androgyny, self-efficacy and self-esteem [Abstract]. *Perceptual & Motor Skills, 88*(3, Pt 1), 935-940.

Zarbatany, L., Hartmann, D. P., & Rankin, D. B. (1990). The psychological functions of preadolescent peer activities. *Child Development, 61*(4), 1067-1080

Zhou, M., & Bankston, C. L., III. (1994). Social capital and the adaptation of the second generation: The case of Vietnamese youth in New Orleans. *International Migration Review, 28*, 821-845.

Zill, N., Nord, C. W., & Loomis, L. S. (1995). *Adolescent time use, risky behavior, and outcomes: An analysis of national data*. Rockville, MD: Westat.

7

Adolescent Sexuality and Positive Youth Development

Stephen T. Russell and Nicole Sigler Andrews

*A phenomenon particular to **adolescence that never occurs again** in the life of the individual is **the process of developing sexual maturation**, different from the state of accomplished sexual maturation. Biologically this is a totally new experience. Its significance is due partly to its pervasiveness and partly to the societal expectations surrounding it. It creates in adolescents a great wonderment about themselves and the feeling of having something in common with all human beings. It influences their whole relationship to each other, whether male or female. Entering this part of maturity also stimulates them to newly assess the world.*

—Gisela Konopka (1973, p. 1)

A mong the developmental changes of adolescence, physical maturation and its resulting sexual awareness are perhaps the most distinctive (Katchadourian, 1990; Konopka, 1973). For many if not most youth in Western cultures, these changes are also the most personally compelling, exciting, and sometimes frightening. Although sexuality development is a process that continues across the child and adult life course, adolescence is a particularly unique and critical period for sexuality development due to the physical, emotional, cognitive, and social changes that take place during the teenage years. These changes are fundamental to human development, yet our society is ambivalent about the messages youth receive regarding the development of healthy sexuality. Nowhere is this truer than in the field of youth development. Individuals and communities struggle to address sexuality development during adolescence in appropriate ways. What role should positive youth development play in the sexuality development of young people? In our view, positive youth development is a fundamentally appropriate venue for education, clarification of values, problem solving, and decision making regarding sexuality.

Adolescence is the first time that most people experiment with sexual expression. This not only includes masturbation, petting, oral sex, or heterosexual sexual intercourse (Katchadourian, 1990; Koch, 1993). It is also the period during which most people first learn about the earlier stages of intimacy: having a crush, going on a date, kissing, or holding hands with a boyfriend or girlfriend. Furthermore, adolescence is also the period of life during which most gay, lesbian, bisexual, and transgendered people begin to identify their sexual orientation or gender identity as different from that of most of their peers (Koch, 1993). Although most young people report these experiences during the teenage years, many of these sexual behaviors remain socially proscribed.

The introduction to this volume discusses the positive youth development (PYD) framework and its growth during the 1990s as a framework for youth development. How is this PYD framework relevant to sexuality development? It has been argued that we live in a society that generally views the period of adolescence negatively (Konopka, 1973), and this is particularly true in the case of sexuality. With many youth issues in our culture, the focus is usually on the problems rather than the possibilities. The challenge for youth development professionals is to find the best ways to put the PYD framework into practice in communities. In this chapter, we consider some of the unique challenges that youth development efforts face when addressing healthy adolescent sexuality development.

We consider the role youth development can play in fostering healthy adolescent sexuality development, with specific attention to the challenges that youth development efforts face when attending to adolescent sexuality, as well as opportunities presented by recent research findings to support innovative outreach and education. Finally, we suggest some action steps that youth development professionals can take in the process of developing and implementing positive youth development programs for adolescent sexual health. First, however, we consider the "beacons" to guide our understanding of adolescent sexuality: the meanings attributed to sexuality, its development during adolescence, and the diversity of experiences and desires among young people.

❖ BEACONS: UNDERSTANDING YOUTHFUL SEXUALITY

Sexuality development is a central task of healthy adolescent development. During the late childhood and teenage years, adolescents' bodies change faster than at any other period of life except infancy (Steinberg, 1999). Most adolescents have an awareness that the changes in their bodies are associated with sexuality, yet they often receive mixed messages from parents, peers, or the media about how to integrate their sexual thoughts and feelings into their developing sense of self. As is indicated in the quote that prefaces this chapter, sexuality development encompasses much more than the dramatic physical changes of puberty. As an integral aspect of adolescent maturation, sexuality development includes the emergence of healthy sexuality attitudes and behaviors, as well as a sexual identity. By sexual identity, we not only mean a person's sexual orientation (heterosexual, bisexual, or homosexual) but also the gender identity (a person's feelings about self as masculine or feminine). Furthermore, sexual identity encompasses the self-perception as a sexual being, and how that aspect of self is integrated into personality, values, and behavior.

An important element of positive youth development must be recognition of the breadth of sexual feelings and behaviors that often begin during adolescence. Too often, *adolescent sexuality* is used to mean adolescent sexual activity or behavior. When we hear *adolescent sexuality*, we often think of promiscuity, too-early sexual activity, or teenage pregnancy, rather than the wide range of sexual behaviors that are healthy and developmentally appropriate parts of adolescent exploration and intimacy (such as having a crush, holding hands, or kissing). We use the term *sexuality* in this chapter to refer to the broad range of feelings, behaviors, and attitudes that youth experience as they develop through childhood to young adulthood.

In contemporary society, youth develop sexually at a much earlier age than they become viewed as socially mature and ready to take on the roles of adulthood. Recent research suggests that pubertal maturation occurs at younger ages than was true in the past, at least among girls (Herman-Giddens et al., 1997). In addition, people marry and leave home at increasingly older ages; in fact, more and more young adults now return to the parental home for some period (Settersten, 1998). The result has been a growing gap between the age at which young people become physically and sexually mature and the age at which they become socially mature. For some youth, there is as much as a 15-year period between the time that they are physically mature and the time that they achieve social and financial independence. Certainly, attention to sexual feelings and desires does not simply wait for social maturity to take place. Thus, recent generations are among the first in history to negotiate a significant proportion of young adulthood as sexually mature but with cultural proscriptions against most sexual behavior.

How do youth negotiate this gap between sexual maturity and social maturity?

In the United States, this negotiation has been unquestionably problematic. The United States surpasses all other Western nations in its teenage pregnancy rate; in fact, the U.S. teenage pregnancy rate is almost double that of any other Western country. This difference cannot be explained by abortion rates or by more frequent sexual activity among teens. First, abortion rates are higher in the United States than in other countries. Second, teenagers in Sweden and France, for example, report that they become sexually active at younger ages than youth in the United States, yet their teenage pregnancy rates are markedly lower than in this country (Foster, Greene, & Smith, 1990). Clearly then, adolescents in the United States are acting on their sexual desires. In our view, only two solutions to the problematic outcomes exist: (1) prevent sexual behavior during adolescence, or (2) educate young people about healthy sexual expression. Given the general failure of abstinence-only education efforts to produce lasting behavioral change among youth (Kirby & Coyle, 1997a), it appears that preventing sexual expression is not an effective strategy. However, there is strong evidence that education about sexual health can make a difference in the decisions young people make (Kirby, 1999). In addition, educating young people about healthy sexuality is consistent with developmental approaches that acknowledge and honor youth's developing sexuality (Koch, 1993).

The frightening statistics regarding teenage pregnancy and sexually transmitted diseases place our focus on the problematic outcomes of adolescent sexual activity. However, as described above, a wide range of sexual experience and experimentation occurs during the adolescent years. It is important to value this broad range of experiences in youth's lives as normal and healthy. Although adults may not wish for young teenagers to engage in sexual intercourse, we must keep in mind that sexual development is inevitable, and that a whole range of sexual experiences are healthy and normal. Now more than ever it is important for communities to consider the alternatives and choices young people face regarding sexuality.

The challenge for adolescents and the adults who care about them is to identify their values about what constitutes developmentally appropriate sexual expression. At a fundamental level, healthy sexual expression must be "consensual, nonexploitative, honest, pleasurable, and protected against disease and unintended pregnancy" (National Guidelines Task Force, 1996). In addition, values about sexual expression during adolescence must be consistent with personal, family, and community values about youthful sexuality. Certainly, this is a significant challenge for youth and adults. Without doubt, tension exists between individuals and family members and within communities regarding the appropriate expression of sexuality during the teenage years. Youth are aware of this tension, and it is these conflicts that they negotiate when making decisions about sexual expression. Negotiating competing values about sexuality is one of the most difficult challenges of the adolescent years. Youth need caring adults to guide them through this process.

Issues of sexuality will not be relevant or appropriate for all forms of youth development or in all of the diverse contexts where positive youth development occurs. Nevertheless, we suggest that because sexuality development is central to adolescence, youth development professionals have a responsibility to provide leadership and education for youth in this domain. For many teens with limited access to parents or other adults, youth development programs are a central system of support and education in their lives. For these youth in particular, sexuality must be included as part of their experience of positive youth development.

So, what is the role of positive youth development professionals? Our role, as adults who foster positive youth development, should be to help young people clarify their own sexual identities and values. In this process, we should of course share with them our opinions and values; this is what youth need and want from the adults in their lives. However, we must recognize that what youth need are the tools to make their own decisions. The reality that is hard for many adults to recognize is that each individual youth will be faced with decisions regarding her or his sexuality—decisions that adults cannot control, but that the youth will have to make. It is the role of adults to foster positive youth development by providing young people with education and experiences to assist them in making healthy decisions for themselves.

❖ CHALLENGES: SEXUALITY AND POSITIVE YOUTH DEVELOPMENT

In our culture, taking a positive youth development approach to adolescent sexuality is particularly challenging. We live in a culture that is not comfortable with sexuality or with adolescence, and least comfortable of all with the notion of adolescent sexuality. As we have described above, adolescent sexuality is often seen as a problem, viewed in terms of the possible negative outcomes rather than the developmentally healthy possibilities. We first outline several general social issues that shape attitudes and values about adolescent sexuality. In the context of these characteristics of U.S. society, there are several key barriers to effective youth development addressing sexuality that communities should consider. We outline some of these barriers below.

U.S. Culture and Adolescent Sexuality

Several dimensions of U.S. culture shape social attitudes regarding adolescent sexuality: the mixed messages about sexuality that youth receive, a belief in the noncongruence in sexual values between generations, the lack of recognition of adolescents' ability and opportunity to make their own decisions about sexuality, and tensions concerning sexual values. First, our society gives youth conflicting messages about sexuality. Being sexy is highly valued in our culture, and young people constantly receive sexualized images through entertainment and advertising media. At the same time, teenagers are warned by adults about the many negative things that happen to sexually active teenagers, such as unintended pregnancy or sexually transmitted infections. The mixed messages young people hear about sexuality reflect the mixed emotions and values adults in our society have about sexuality.

Of major concern for many adults is the belief that there is non-congruence between the sexual values of youth and those of their parents or adults in their community (Konopka, 1973). Although it is not true for all contemporary adults, a common perception assumes that peers have more influence on adolescents' values than do parents, and that teen culture accepts and promotes unhealthy adolescent sexual values and behavior. Peers are an important source of influence in the lives of youth, but this influence is more likely to pertain to clothing or music tastes than to fundamental values (Steinberg, 1999). Research continues to affirm that young people are more likely to share common values with their parents than with their peers (Resnick et al., 1997). Nevertheless, this perception creates a context in which adults respond to youth sexuality issues in ways that assume that generational differences are greater than similarities.

An additional general issue shaping the way communities approach adolescent sexuality is that it is difficult for many adults to acknowledge that adolescents want to make their own decisions regarding healthy sexuality, and that they have the ability and the opportunities to do so. Adults often fail to acknowledge that, by middle and certainly late adolescence, teenagers have the cognitive capability to make health-promoting decisions. It seems that many adults assume that, if they can just keep enough control over adolescents, they will protect youth from "bad" decisions. Unfortunately, this view of teenagers is developmentally inappropriate and inconsistent with the positive youth development framework. Except in the most sheltered circumstances, young people will eventually be faced with making their own decisions about their bodies and their sexual behavior. Adults cannot make decisions for youth. Ultimately, young people need education and support from caring adults to make their own healthy decisions.

A final general social issue includes the very real tensions concerning sexual behaviors and values in our society and the difficulties that communities face when attempting to reconcile individual differences in values and opinions. Since the 1960s, Western cultures have experienced significant changes in social attitudes regarding sexuality and gender (Twenge, 1997). Before this period, there was much more societal consensus on these issues. Today, issues of sexuality include the possibility of many more choices than in the past. This is indicated, for example, by increasing rates of nonmarital cohabitation and its view as a legitimate family form during the past 25 years (Graefe & Lichter, 1999), and by the increasing visibility and social acceptance of gay, lesbian, bisexual, and transgendered people (Yang, 1997). These changes have brought with them clearly visible cultural tensions regarding acceptable and sanctioned behavior and values. Even young children may be aware of these tensions and must learn some way to understand and interpret them. The social issues described here shape the environment in which youth grow up and learn about their sexuality. Any positive youth development efforts aimed at promoting healthy sexuality development among adolescents must be aware of these tensions in their communities.

Barriers to Integrating Sexuality in Positive Youth Development

In these contexts, attempts to provide education and support to adolescents about their developing sexuality must recognize both the mixed and inconsistent messages that young people hear regarding sexuality, as well as the lack of consensus about what constitutes healthy adolescent sexuality. In addition, there are multiple community-specific barriers that may arise for programs attempting to provide education or outreach regarding adolescent sexuality:

- Resistance from community groups based on their religious beliefs
- Claims of intrusion in the family among adults who believe that sexuality concerns are only appropriately considered within the family context
- Parenting styles that are authoritarian, in which parents assume the role of making all decisions for their adolescent children
- Denial by some community members that adolescent sexuality concerns are relevant for the youth in their community

- Fear that open discussion and education about sexuality development will result in the unintended effect of prompting adolescents to act on sexual feelings, leading to greater risk of negative sexual health outcomes for youth

Each of these barriers offers unique challenges for youth development efforts that attempt as a part of their focus to address healthy adolescent sexuality development. Some of these barriers are based on fear, some are based on individuals' core values, and others are based on community norms; whatever the basis, these are often very real barriers that pose challenges. Addressing these barriers requires a community-based effort aimed at involving stakeholders from multiple perspectives, including parents or other caregivers of adolescents; community leaders and organizers; and professional educators, institutional administrators, and youth program providers.

❖ OPPORTUNITIES: RECENT RESEARCH

In light of the challenges that exist for positive youth development efforts to address adolescent sexuality development, multiple opportunities and resources are available to aid professionals and communities. Among the leading resources are recently published studies that demonstrate the efficacy of positive youth development efforts in playing a leading role in healthy adolescent sexuality development (Kirby, 1999; Kirby & Coyle, 1997b). We discuss social and political change during the last 20 years that altered the sexuality education available to adolescents in the United States. We then consider recent research on the effectiveness of sexuality education. For the first time, this research provides a firm footing on which positive youth development efforts that address adolescent sexuality can be justified.

Broadly put, sexuality education has been motivated by dual goals: providing adolescents with information regarding their sexual development and healthy sexual behavior while also aiming to delay adolescent sexual activity and/or promote healthy sexual behavior practices (such as effective use of contraception). For many years, however, there have been debates about the degree to which sexuality education in the United States has been successful. Through the 1980s, it was clear that sexuality education had more success in influencing young people's knowledge about sexuality than their attitudes or behavior (Russell, 1998). In the early 1990s, many questioned the efficacy of sexuality education, suggesting that new methods and foci were required to stem the rise in adolescent pregnancy and sexually transmitted infection rates. These concerns became politicized in 1996 with the signing by President Clinton of the Temporary Assistance to Needy Families Act, better known as "welfare reform." This legislation included funding for states to provide education that teaches "abstinence from sexual activity outside marriage as the expected standard for all school age children" and "that a mutually faithful monogamous relationship in the context of marriage is the expected standard of human sexual activity" (Daley & Wong, 1999, p. 7). By the end of the 1900s, the questions asked by many were "Does sexuality education work? If so, do abstinence programs have more success than comprehensive sexuality education programs (those that focus on building a range of knowledge and skills, including information about contraception)?" It is important here to distinguish between educational efforts that focus on abstinence at the exclusion of all other sexuality information (abstinence only) and sexuality education that integrates abstinence messages with a broad range of knowledge and skills (abstinence based).

Even 5 years ago, the answers were uncertain. Today, several general conclusions about contemporary sexuality education can be drawn. First, there is little evidence that sexuality education that focuses exclusively on abstinence is effective in promoting long-term delays in sexual activity or in preventing teen pregnancy (Kirby & Coyle, 1997a). Second, comprehensive sexuality education programs aimed at reducing sexual risk-taking behavior have demonstrated success in helping adolescents postpone sexual activity and delay pregnancy (Kirby, 1999). Third, and most relevant, youth development efforts are among the programs that appear to have the most success for positive sexual health outcomes (postponing sexual activity and reducing the risk for teenage pregnancy and parenthood) (Kirby, 1999; Kirby & Coyle, 1997b).

How does positive youth development affect adolescent sexuality behavior? Kirby and Coyle (1997b) reviewed published evaluations of eight youth development programs, many of which were not intentionally designed to decrease teen pregnancy risk. Among these youth development programs, those that were effective in postponing sexual activity and lowering the risk for teen pregnancy provided opportunities that emphasized education, employment, and life options.

Successful programs also addressed cognitive and social skills, social influence and group norms, and individual values; they set clear goals and communicated clear values about those goals; and they were age, experience, and culture appropriate. Finally, they were ongoing and intense; each involved trained and committed trainers using diverse and experiential methods. In addition to their effect on adolescent sexual health, these programs also often show efficacy in promoting other positive outcomes, such as increasing educational achievement, improving employment histories, and reducing negative outcomes such as substance use and abuse and incarceration (Kirby & Coyle, 1997b). Through attention to the broad range of needs of youth and involvement of young people in meaningful activities that help them chart their futures, positive youth development has been proven as an effective strategy for adolescent sexuality development and health promotion.

❖ ACTION STEPS

How can youth development professionals proceed with providing youth development programs and education about adolescent sexuality? In our view, preparation has to take place at three levels: the individual, the institution, and the community. Attention to these three levels will provide youth development professionals and volunteers with the optimal context for program efforts on adolescent sexuality. We consider each of these areas below.

Personal Readiness for Sexuality in Youth Development

Before turning to institutions and communities for support and guidance on sexuality in youth development efforts, it is important to consider our own individual values and assumptions with regard to adolescent sexuality. There are several important questions that any youth development professional or volunteer should ask:

- How informed am I regarding the facts about sexuality development?
- How comfortable am I communicating about sexuality development, both among youth and among other adults?

- How prepared am I to respond to anxiety in other people and their reaction to sexuality as an integrated part of positive youth development efforts?

Each of these is an important consideration for preparing oneself to begin any youth development effort that includes attention to healthy adolescent sexuality development. Along with assessing personal values and assumptions about adolescent sexuality, we also encourage youth development professionals to consider their own and their communities' goals for positive youth development:

- What are the intended outcomes of the youth development program or effort?
- What are the community's goals for their youth regarding sexuality?
- What is the community's capacity to develop and deliver sexuality-related youth development programs?

As we have noted, there is a wide range of attitudes, values, and behaviors regarding youth sexuality. In fact, values and beliefs about sexuality are often so fundamental that an individual is likely to think of the goal for positive youth development regarding sexuality in terms of those values. One of the reasons that sexuality education and outreach is often accompanied by community tension is that such efforts are based in the fundamental values that individuals hold. Thus, when conflict occurs, it is often intense because the goals people hold are basic to their personal values and experience regarding youthful sexuality. Is the goal to prevent negative outcomes of precocious sexual behavior or to promote healthy adolescent sexual expression? These are different goals that may require different youth development approaches. In assessing one's own goals, it is important also to be aware of different goals and assumptions that others in your institution or community may have about what is appropriate for adolescent sexuality and positive youth development.

Preparing Your Institution

Having determined your own readiness and ability to provide leadership for positive sexuality development support for youth, an assessment of the degree to which your institution is prepared to engage in such outreach is necessary. An important step in assessing an institution's willingness to address youthful sexuality will involve seeking input from stakeholders regarding their perceptions of the community needs and the timeliness of the proposed outreach. At this point, providing institutional and community stakeholders with education about adolescent sexuality development is essential. Education about adolescent sexuality issues is an important first step for establishing the need for outreach in a community and building a foundation of support. If issues concerning teenage sexuality are not viewed as relevant or important in the community, it is unlikely that outreach efforts will be successful.

Other important action steps include reviewing the success of past youth development efforts in the institution. Have sensitive issues been addressed in the past? How did the institution manage those situations, and what lessons have been learned? As part of this process, one should review positive youth development programs currently in use and identify new program options based on their effectiveness in promoting positive development. It is often possible to revise existing and successful programs to include a component on sexuality. In being wise consumers of outreach and education curricula, youth development professionals need to ask who produced the program, where it has been used, and how it has been evaluated to demonstrate its effectiveness.

Building Community Support

One of the first steps in building community support should be to inform community stakeholders (educators, community leaders, parents, and youth) and enlist their support. These key stakeholders will be able to provide knowledge of the community and additional potential supporters—parents, teachers, school administrators, and school board members. To respond to community needs, supportive individuals and institutions may form a collaborative advisory group. This group can assess the community climate and overall level of support for the initiative and can advise on the youth development plan so that it meets the unique needs of the community (Kelly et al., 1988). Building a network of community-based support for any youth development initiative is critical for sustaining the program beyond its initial conception.

A crucial aspect of this process is to recognize the value of youth as resources for public action and education. The positive youth development framework encourages young people to view themselves as active participants in their communities. At the same time, the PYD framework prompts adults to view youth as resources for social action and change. The involvement of youth in the early planning stages of a youth development program that includes addressing adolescent sexuality is very important. They have the unique ability to speak for themselves and describe the challenges that they and their peers face.

Having developed a central support group and established contact with key stakeholders, education about the need for positive youth development regarding adolescent sexuality can begin at the community level. The process of educating a community about the sexuality development concerns of its youth will foster support for the positive youth development efforts, ensuring that the youth development program adequately reflects the needs of the community. Community-based education will also provide decision makers and public officials with advance information and education about potential controversy.

❖ CONCLUSION

During the 1990s, *positive youth development* became a buzzword and began to guide the field of youth development. There has been a movement toward thinking about adolescent issues not from a problem focus but with attention to the resources and strengths young people possess. In this chapter we have argued that sexuality development is a fundamental guiding process of the transition from childhood to young adulthood. Because it is a primary force in young lives, youth require proactive support from parents and adults regarding their healthy sexuality development. We argue that positive youth development is a logical framework from which to address adolescent sexual health and development.

What difference would attention to healthy sexuality development make in positive youth development efforts? In our view, healthy sexuality development has been excluded in traditional youth development frameworks. It has been viewed as either irrelevant or inappropriate for youth development by many professionals and in many communities. In the past, the few programs that have addressed sexuality have had an almost exclusive problem or prevention focus (as in the case of youth development aimed at teenage pregnancy prevention). We argue that attention to healthy sexuality should be a central component of positive youth development. As such, sexuality would become a fully integrated aspect of positive youth development efforts, included in our ongoing programming in citizenship, life skills, and workforce preparation, for example. Although it is not in the scope of this chapter to consider how sexuality issues might be integrated into these and other core youth development program areas, our intention is to suggest that attention to healthy sexuality development will build on and enhance our holistic approaches to positive youth development.

How would youth benefit from a positive youth development approach that integrated healthy sexuality? First, the programs, education, and resources in which young people participate would acknowledge this fundamental dimension of their development. More importantly, sexuality would become a central part of the information, support, and guidance that youth experience in their relationships with caring adults. Adult-youth relationships and partnerships are central to positive youth development; however, sexuality is often the dimension of adolescents' lives for which adult guidance and support is absent. Through attention to healthy sexuality development, positive youth development can provide the adult guidance and support that youth need regarding this important aspect of their lives.

❖ REFERENCES

Daley, D., & Wong, V. C. (1999). *Between the lines: States' implementation of the federal government's Section 510(b) Abstinence Education Program in fiscal year 1998.* New York: Sexuality Information and Education Council of the United States.

Foster, H. W., Greene, L. W., & Smith, M. S. (1990). A model for increasing access: Teenage pregnancy prevention. *Journal of Health Care for Poor and Underserved, 1,* 136-146.

Graefe, D. R., & Lichter, D. T. (1999). Life course transitions of American children: Parental cohabitation, marriage, and single motherhood. *Demography, 36,* 205-217.

Herman-Giddens, M. E., Slora, E. J., Wasserman, R. C., Bourdony, C. J., Bhapkar, M., Koch, G. G., & Hassemeir, C. M. (1997). Secondary sex characteristics and menses in young girls seen in office practice: A study from the Pediatric Research in Office Setting Network. *Pediatrics, 88,* 505-512.

Katchadourian, H. (1990). Sexuality. In S. S. Feldman, & G. R. Elliott (Eds.), *At the threshold: The developing adolescent.* Cambridge: Harvard University Press.

Kelly, J. G., Dassoff, N., Levin, I., Schreckengost, J., Stelzner, S. P, & Altman, B. E. (1988). *A guide to conducting prevention research in the community: First steps.* New York: Haworth Press.

Kirby, D. (1999). Reducing adolescent pregnancy: Approaches that work. *Contemporary Pediatrics, 16,* 83-94.

Kirby, D., & Coyle, K. (1997a). School-based programs to reduce sexual risk-taking behavior. *Children and Youth Services Review, 19,* 415-436.

Kirby, D., & Coyle, K. (1997b). Youth development programs. *Children and Youth Services Review, 19,* 437-454.

Koch, P. B. (1993). Promoting healthy sexual development during early adolescence. In R. M. Lerner (Ed.), *Early adolescence: Perspectives on research, policy, and intervention.* Hillsdale, NJ: Lawrence Erlbaum.

Konopka, G. (1973). Requirements for healthy development of adolescent youth. *Adolescence, 8,* 1-26.

National Guidelines Task Force. (1996). *Guidelines for comprehensive sexuality education* (2nd ed.). New York: Sexuality Information and Education Council of the United States.

Resnick, M. D., Bearman, P. S., Blum, R. W., Bauman, K. E., Harris, K. M., Jones, J., Tabor, J., Beuhring, T., Sieving, R. E., Shew, M., Ireland, M., Bearinger, L. H., & Udry, J. R. (1997). Protecting adolescents from harm: Findings from the National Longitudinal Study on Adolescent Health. *Journal of the American Medical Association, 278*(10), 823-832.

Russell, S. T. (1998). Sex education content and teenage motherhood. *Childhood: A Global Journal of Child Research, 5,* 283-302.

Settersten, R. A., Jr. (1998). A time to leave home and a time never to return? Age constraints on the living arrangements of young adults. *Social Forces, 76,* 1373-1400.

Steinberg, L. (1999). *Adolescence.* Boston: McGraw-Hill.

Twenge, J. M. (1997). Attitudes toward women, 1970-1995: A meta-analysis. *Psychology of Women Quarterly, 21,* 35-51.

Yang, A. (1997). Trends: Attitudes toward homosexuality. *Public Opinion Quarterly, 61,* 477-507.

8

Positive Development for Youth With Disabilities

Lessons Learned From Two Stories of Success

Esther Onaga, Marsha Carolan,
Cathryn Maddalena, and Francisco A. Villarruel

Without a doubt, youth with developmental disabilities face an array of challenges that nondisabled youth do not confront in their daily lives or in their communities. Unfortunately, contemporary youth prevention and intervention approaches have been slow to respond to national efforts to promote positive developmental outcomes, especially for youth with disabilities. Perhaps one reason for this inattention is the fact that youth with developmental disabilities possess an array of risk and environmental factors that increase the likelihood that a less than optimal outcome in their life will occur. This perspective is reinforced in service and educational programs that seek to address the deficits that exist in youth with disabilities rather than to build on their strengths or assets.

An area of concern for both parents and professionals who work with youth with disabilities focuses on life after formal educational opportunities (K-12) have been achieved. In response to this concern, greater attention has been paid to the transition of special education students to the world after formal schooling (Halpern, 1992). Researchers have looked at postschool outcomes such as employment, postsecondary education, and residential independence (Blackorby, 1993; Blackorby & Wagner, 1996) as indicators of success in transition, but these outcomes by themselves do not reveal the conditions and processes that led to them.

In this chapter, two case studies will be presented as a means of highlighting critical factors in promoting positive youth developmental outcomes for youth with disabilities. The vignettes that follow are from data collected during a 5-year evaluation of youth who participated in the Michigan Transition Initiative, a 5-year systemic change project that sought to enhance the school-to-work and school-to-community transitions in the lives of youth with developmental disabilities.

In the introduction to this volume, the editors offer a perspective on which this chapter is written: "What does it take to create a community that will promote the positive development of all young people?" The vignettes and insights offered in this chapter attempt to address this issue for youth with disabilities. However, what is presented here serves only as an introduction to the array of support structures and unique opportunities that can be offered to individuals with disabilities to promote positive and healthy developmental outcomes. It is important to note that caution must be exercised when reading this chapter, as the nature and severity of a handicapping condition are inextricably **linked with the types** of supports and opportunities that a community **makes available for** youth with disabilities. Moreover, the size of the **community (e.g., rural** versus urban) and the prevalence of the disabil**ity in this** community may further restrict the choices available to fami**lies and** individuals with disabilities. Efforts to apply these pillars of **positive** youth development, although recommended, should be judiciously considered for individuals with varying disabilities and the contexts and communities in which these individuals live and work.

❖ FAMILY REALITIES

Medical advances, policy changes (e.g., Education of the Handicapped Act (EHA), Public Law 94-142, the Rehabilitation Act of 1973,

P.L. 03-112), mainstream educational efforts, and the increase in advocacy and support groups for families who have members with disabilities have resulted in two realities for families and communities. The primary legislation that guides school services is an act passed in 1979, the Education of the Handicapped Act (EHA), which is more commonly known through its latest amendments, the Individuals with Disabilities Education Act (IDEA). Related to transition of special education youth, the legislation stipulates that an Individualized Education Program (IEP) will be developed for each child, stating what kinds of special and related services each child will receive. Stipulations dictate that youth receiving special education have the right to receive the related services necessary to benefit from special education instruction.

Of the aforementioned policies, IDEA has a theoretical underpinning in positive youth development. Specifically, these new mandates require that student strengths be listed in the IEP forms and central in their educational programming. Moreover, it is the expectation that parents and teachers, in collaboration with the IEP team, will build on these strengths to build a comprehensive educational plan for students.

In the state of Michigan, parent training groups encourage parents to include students in the development of their individual learning and transition plans to further build on the interests and strengths of students. Although more students have been involved in recent educational plans, it is still far from a normative process. Yet, it should be noted that this has resulted in plans that contribute to lifelong skills of interest to individuals with disabilities, thus facilitating their successful transition to workplace and community living settings.

Policy changes and parent advocacy groups have helped to facilitate better involvement of families and youth with disabilities in educational and transitional planning and choices. Some of this has led to an emphasis on positive youth development as described above. However, a second reality is in the management of living arrangements and the consequent dependency on governmental agencies that are not based on or concerned with a strengths or assets approach. Currently, most individuals with disabilities are living either in their parental homes or in community group homes as opposed to being isolated in remote institutional settings where interaction with family and community was traditionally minimized. As a result, families, in their daily efforts to cope with stressors, are seeking community assistance in the ongoing care of their offspring, which will continue throughout the life span (Hayden & Heller, 1997). Despite deinstitutionalization efforts, the burden of providing services for individuals with disabilities and their families has remained under the purview of a few governmental agencies such as Community Mental Health, the Department of Special Education, and the Department of Rehabilitative Services as opposed to more general community agencies. In addition, families are turning to a variety of mainstream institutions to supplement services. This array of service providers and managers results in inconsistency and variability regarding an emphasis or lack of emphasis on strengths and assets of youth.

Thus a major challenge for youth professionals is in the variability and inconsistency across systems with which they must work: families, communities, and provider institutions. Through the two case studies detailed below, we explore the question, "Is the model of positive youth development being effectively implemented for youth with disabilities?" In our presentation that follows, the answer appears to be both yes and no.

Historically, agencies that serve individuals and families with disabilities tend to work from the perspective of intervention rather than prevention. The ability to program across the life span and across agencies, although desirable, is extremely complex and rare. Moreover, professionals in the area of developmental disabilities are often overwhelmed with caseloads that are not only challenging but also demanding and time intensive. The burden of responsibility has traditionally been thrust on individual professionals to facilitate the systematic changes considered optimal in a youth's life.

Contributing to the challenge of providing for youth with disabilities are the physical, cognitive, emotional, and/or communicative constraints that individuals with disabilities possess. These constraints can readily overshadow a positive youth development focus as the challenges and demands of daily living must be faced first. For example, parents with physically disabled youth must often confront choices such as the purchase of a new wheelchair versus a computer. State and federal guidelines and restrictions force parents and professionals to make such choices; a new wheelchair is thought to facilitate independence, whereas a computer is thought to provide an array of learning opportunities. Although this is only one example of the choices and challenges that must be met in the daily lives of youth with disabilities, it reflects the reality of life for individuals and families with disabled youth. Choices made at any time in the life span can have grave impact on long-term developmental opportunities.

These realities—which include variability among providers, overburdening of individual professionals, constraints of living with disabilities, and daily choices that families and youth must make—contribute to an emphasis on short-term rather than long-term outcomes. As the above example illustrates, often the focus of intervention is on resolving the current crisis rather than focusing on the long-term goals or well-being of the individual.

The remaining sections of this chapter will focus on dimensions of positive youth development embodied in the paradigm presented by the Search Institute (Benson, 1997). Each of the case studies presented below showcase the role of both internal and external assets in the lives of youth with disabilities. The vignettes selected illustrate certain principles of positive youth development as applied to two youth with different handicapping conditions that serve as building blocks for well-being and healthy development. The successful youth highlighted in this chapter had assets that were strong and permeated the interactions and life chances that were made available to these individuals.

❖ AN OVERVIEW OF THE
   MICHIGAN TRANSITION INITIATIVE

The Michigan Transition Initiative was launched in 1994 as a means of addressing the needs of young adolescents with disabilities. Working at the county level, this systemic change initiative sought to develop innovative models that could support the transition of youth with disabilities from school to work and school to community. Participants in this initiative received competitive funds from a federal grant and were required to participate in a multifaceted evaluation. During this project period, the laws guiding transition planning changed from requiring plans for 16-year-olds to requiring them for 14-year-olds. Schools in Michigan were moving toward being part of a collaboration with adult agencies. Local transition councils comprised of adult service professionals, families, students, and school personnel became more commonplace.

In addition to traditional evaluation approaches that were designed to measure the impact of this initiative, qualitative ethnographies were conducted. A sample was sought that represented diversity in participants (i.e., region of the state, type of disability, family context, socioeconomic status, ethnicity, and gender). Initially, 25 students and their families agreed to participate in qualitative interviews in which participants were asked to identify supports and obstacles that they perceived would contribute to a successful transition. Based on these interviews, the authors, in collaboration with key stakeholders in this initiative, selected 8 students and families (of the initial 25) who agreed to participate in a longitudinal piece for the remaining 4 years of the evaluation grant. Students and families who were willing to participate agreed to make themselves available to the authors for several more interviews. They also agreed to identify key individuals and agencies that had made a significant impact in the life of their youth with disabilities. These additional contacts served two specific purposes. The first purpose was to broaden the range of information about the circumstances, obstacles, and opportunities in the lives of families and their youth. The second purpose was to allow the authors an opportunity to observe the identified youth in multiple contexts.

Ky's Story

Ky's unique family structure and support system provide rich information describing the context of his transition years from school to young adulthood. The numerous connections across vocational and recreational sectors of his life provide unique examples of how a youth with challenging beginnings in life is nurtured and supported by a variety of community members.

Family

One of the participants in the longitudinal study was Ky, a young African American male living in an urban community. For the first 18 months of his life, Ky lived with his teenage mother (age 19), who was described as a drug user. The neighbors reported overhearing, on several occasions, Ky screaming and crying and his mother yelling at him at the "top of her lungs."

One neighbor in particular, Joy, observed Ky and noticed that he was not speaking or mobile. She was concerned about the continued frequency of his crying and screaming. Self-described as a person who "likes kids," Joy and her husband offered to care for Ky for a few hours each day. This was proposed as a way to relieve his mother of the stress of caring for him, thus allowing her to address personal and familial needs such as grocery shopping. In retrospect, Joy stated that she and her husband enjoyed caring for Ky, feeling that he responded positively to their interactions with him. He was also described as being an energetic toddler, getting into various types of mischief. In addition to bringing him into their household, they began taking Ky into the community—to the park, the circus, to the mall. Joy stated that the motivation for doing this was twofold. First, they enjoyed being with him, and it appeared that he enjoyed being with them. Perhaps more important, however, was that Ky's mother did not seem to take significant interest in his development.

With time, these brief periods of caring for Ky turned into longer-term care. It was not uncommon for Ky to sleep overnight at their home or to stay with them without seeing his mother for days or weeks. When she did come to visit Ky, it was only for a few hours. This is partially explained by the fact that Ky's mother was enrolled in an alternative education program completing her requirements for high school. His maternal grandparents expressed that they were not interested in providing temporary or long-term care for Ky. Hence, it seemed natural to Joy and her husband to provide temporary care, albeit informally, for whatever period of time they could.

Eventually, they obtained temporary custody. When Ky was about 4, his biomother reengaged with Ky. In addition, she was pregnant with another child, who was not born with any known developmental challenges. In a matter of a few months, however, Ky's mother recognized that she could not tolerate or care for him and released him for adoption to Joy and her husband. Sadly, the adoptive father died from a heart attack shortly after the adoption.

Neighborhood

During his early years, other neighbors besides Joy joined in caring for Ky. One participant reported that although it began with one neighbor, eventually the entire neighborhood took turns caring for him. By the time he was six or seven, Ky knew and was known by the neighborhood. He would go over to play or hang out with others, and they came looking for him, too. And when he got older, he would help with yard work, raking leaves, cutting grass, shoveling snow. Some gave him money; some did this as a way of saying, "You're a part of our family, and we must each do our work."

Several community residents who participated in interviews told of how they often took Ky along with them as they participated in other community events. Athletics, movies, concerts, or simply shopping at the mall—several participants conveyed that engaging Ky in the social aspects of their life was a choice and an aspect of their life that they thoroughly enjoyed.

The importance of neighborhood can be further evidenced in the following excerpt from additional qualitative data that was collected as part of the overall study. One participant noted that as

> Ky grew older, his physical abilities began to develop. Although he was not fully coordinated, he was big. He couldn't run or catch, but he could throw long and hard. One of his proudest accomplishments was Special Olympics. He won lots of medals and always competed, obviously enjoying it. When he started high school, we thought Special Olympics might be a thing of the past. But the truth is that it became the doorway to even more experiences. Someone convinced him to try out for track and field, which he did. And while he wasn't the fastest, he could throw the longest because of his size. He won several events, and as a consequence, several of his nonhandicapped peers befriended him. And they seemed to like having him on the team. They took him to movies with them, and bowling, and to the mall.

Work

A planned dimension of Ky's transition plan was to work in a local store. Apparently, Ky was popular in that environment as well; he eventually developed a close relationship with the manager and some of his coworkers, who invited him to dinner and eventually to join the softball team. Joy reported,

> They even took him on weekend trips to amusement parks. While it always concerned me that he was spending more time with these people, I knew he liked it and that it was probably good for him. And some of these college-age kids have come to the house, assuring me that they would not drink with him around, so I learned to trust and allow this to happen.

Individual Resources

Equally important, Ky was able to participate in athletics at multiple levels: recreation, Special Olympics, and high school track and field with his others of his age. In every interview, in multiple settings, Ky enthusiastically spent time talking about his involvement in sports. For Ky, this involvement led to some unanticipated opportunities. After being recognized at the local bowling alley as a frequent customer and a person with a handicapping condition, the management of the bowling alley invited Ky to clean their parking lot on weekends in return for unlimited bowling. Over time, his skills increased, leading to his being invited to bowl in three different leagues by people who observed him having fun. His 180 average was the highest on at least one team.

Lessons Learned From Ky

Garbarino (1995) and Schorr (1997) offer a compelling argument illustrating the unique function of communities in the lives of youth in the United States. By the same token, Kretzmann and McKnight (1993) assert that healthy communities are those in which the skills, abilities, and talents of local community residents are brought to the forefront to benefit the lives and well-being of everyone. Moreover, Benson (1997) asserts that healthy communities provide an array of developmental supports that are needed by youth to support optimal individual developmental outcomes.

There are several lessons learned in the abbreviated summary of the neighborhood contribution to Ky during his developmental years. First, although scholars such as Benson (1997), Garbarino (1999), and Schorr (1997) have discussed the importance of community in providing an array of structures to support positive youth development, we assert that for youth with disabilities, neighborhoods are more significant.

Moreover, embedding this in the framework of the Search Institute's internal and external assets (Benson, 1997), the aforementioned excerpt from Ky's life history indicates that the neighborhood became more than a residential space. Rather, it became a community in which boundaries and rules were clearly expressed, accepted, and equally acted on by Ky, his family, and his neighbors. It was through these contacts that an investment in Ky's life began to evolve.

As other events in Ky's life revealed, extracurricular opportunities and positive peer role models were integral and important components of his development. These nonfamilial relationships gave Ky an opportunity to experience life with companions of his own age. More important, they resulted in his experiencing parts of life that were typical of adolescents. And although Ky did admit that there was periodic name calling from individuals who did not know him, his friends protected him from the "enemies."

The work environment provided multiple outlets and supports for Ky's personal development. It provided him with additional recreational opportunities, involvement with his peers, and a structured use of his time. Ky ensured that he was regularly scheduled to work at the grocery store. Despite all of the other activities that he had in his life, this was essential to him.

When an opportunity in a new franchise arose, the manager and Ky's job coach and parent discussed a transfer. They decided that the loss of the social network and the supportive environment would not be beneficial for Ky. Instead, they decided to increase his wages in recognition of his effort and to expand his responsibilities to minimize the likelihood of his becoming bored.

Ky was blessed with a caring and supportive adoptive mother and a caring and supportive neighborhood and community. In addition, he possessed or developed temperamental and social abilities that helped to create relationships with those around him, which in turn helped to create social, work, and recreational opportunities. Caregiving, support, and Ky's individual resources combined to provide a context for positive youth development.

Bo's Story

Although Bo's rocky beginnings in the school system created some stressful family life, a strident and visionary mother and a grandmother who believed in him successfully supported Bo into young adulthood. Again, much like Ky, Bo's individual positive attributes sustained him through some difficult times.

Family

A second young man, Bo, participated in the study for 4 years. A Caucasian youth from a rural setting, Bo was 20 years old at the beginning of the study. He was diagnosed at age 2 with attention deficit hyperactivity disorder and oppositional self-destructive behavior. Over the course of his school years, he was given the additional labels of learning disability and emotional impairment. His mother described his early years of life in some challenging terms: "He was hyperactive at age 2. He was putting holes in the walls."

Bo's family comprised his mother and father, his grandmothers and a grandfather, an older sister, and a younger brother. He lost another sister in a tragic accident when she was in her teens. His father worked in the mine in a neighboring town and was unemployed for a period of time during our study. His mother worked for a local human service agency and also owned a retail shop in town. During the course of the study, it was evident that Bo's behavior and actions influenced the relationship with his father and brother in either positive or negative directions. His mother, grandmother, and longtime girlfriend seemed more capable of unconditional positive regard, despite having some expectations of him.

The relationships that were most significant in terms of this chapter were Bo's relationship with his maternal grandmother and his mother. These two women supported Bo throughout his development during his school years to young adulthood. Bo's mother relentlessly sought professional assistance and guidance for herself and her son. She advocated for him with the school, for vocational placement, and during difficulties with local law enforcement. Bo's grandmother, who exhibited a personality similar to her grandson's, recognized that his temper was like hers. Her empathy for his difficulty with school and his quick temper led her to give him her garage and the property surrounding the garage for his use. She thought that he could repair his own car there and also have some space to work on cars for others. This gift had a significant impact on the course of his life, as he was able to develop a little side business of painting and repairing cars.

School

School was a difficult place for Bo. He was not a good reader and did not see the content taught in school as having much relevance for him. Although he had some teachers who were able to accommodate his learning style and needs, his mother had a number of run-ins and struggles with the local school system. She was pleased with some of his teachers and unhappy with others. She observed that being firm yet caring was the best combination for her son:

> Some of the teachers were real good with Bo. Some gave him the slack he needed; others didn't. As much as he said he hated his special education teacher, he really liked her. A lot of times with Bo, you have to read the opposite of what he says. You have to learn it by action more. He was always real good to her. He always thought about bringing her stuff. But he'd come home and say "You know what she did?" and he'd smile when he was telling

you a lie about it. I think she was a good influence because she was pushing him in the right direction.

Challenges were also encountered at the upper levels of administration. Through the mother's advocacy, however, some of the challenges were overcome. She argued against the school's suspending her son, and a place was set up in the school for in-school suspension. Through the state parent training program, she acquired skills for advocating instead of "yelling and screaming to get his attention," which she had learned was ineffective in the long run.

I made a lot of mistakes, and I think every parent makes mistakes; every parent is entitled to mistakes. Then I started support groups and talking with other parents. It took me 5 years to gain respect from school principals, administrators, and teachers. I think part of that is that I didn't only focus on what I wanted for Bo, but I wanted it for everybody.

The mother's efforts led to one of the first community-based employment experiences in car mechanics for the students in the high school. She got a local shop to take Bo on as a work-study student when he was finding high school education to be meaningless. She continues to hold the belief that schools can become meaningful places for students who may become dropouts.

Bo's mother insisted that he participate in his educational plan so, beginning in eighth grade, Bo joined the group for the IEP meeting.

Work

Bo's biggest asset was his love of working. When he was 14, he had the largest paper route in the area and was the highest-paid deliverer. After graduating from high school, Bo worked successfully at several different jobs, ultimately ending up in a well-paid full-time job with a major excavating firm that pays benefits.

The owner of the firm agreed to allow Bo to use the equipment to work on his own home, building on the property that his grandmother gave him. In exchange, he did work on the company trucks. He seemed to thrive in this new job; not only with his boss, but with coworkers as well. His employer spoke fondly of him, recognizing both his strengths and challenges: "For a young kid, he's real sharp, even though he may not be able to read or write that well."

Before he landed this permanent job, Bo managed to get to know all the different automotive shops in the area. He arranged to have work at each of these sites. "Once I got to go to one shop, I knew the guy in the next shop. The guy was upset that I didn't come back the next year, but I wanted to see what a different shop was, and it was totally different."

Individual Resources

One of Bo's assets was his directness and willingness to help a person in need. He has managed to be quite visible in the community as a responsible adult. His honesty, strong work ethic, willingness to try things, and his desire to help people in need have been well received by family and community members. He is protective of people who are vulnerable, as evidenced in his doing errands and work for his fragile grandmother.

Bo developed his ability to do household repairs, and his mother now counts on him for this help. He has substantial carpentry skills that he somehow acquired. He is a visual learner, probably in response to his learning disability, and has good math skills enabling him to manage money well. Two years into the study, Bo was able to fulfill his grandmother's and his own dream of building a log cabin. Building the log house involved some reading, but mostly he relied on pictures about how to put the pieces together.

Today, Bo is well liked in his community despite a reputation for speaking his mind. Although he did not appear to be the easiest student to accommodate during his school years, as a young adult in the world of work and his social network, he is rather sociable and likeable.

Lessons Learned From Bo

Bo's many assets have been the critical factors that enabled him to be successfully employed, to be an owner of a beautiful log house that he built, and to have positive relationships with his partner and family. Although he had a period in his high school days when he associated with a group of friends who got themselves into trouble, he is currently a successful citizen in his little community.

There are several lessons to be learned from Bo's story. Bo became a successful citizen in his community just as Ky did, despite their differences in race, living location, family factors, and so on. Bo had the support and advocacy of a caring and assertive parent, some support from his school and community and he had managed to develop skills and opportunities in his small community on which he could capitalize. The interplay of support, opportunity, and his own skills of building and working with his hands provided a positive youth developmental outcome.

In a little rural town where everyone seems to know one another, the building of Bo's log cabin was quite an interesting event. His mother somewhat bitterly says that teachers who once gave Bo a hard time now say to her, "I knew he would turn out well." People who have seen or heard of the log cabin speak of Bo with great admiration. The building of the home is symbolic of his development as a young adult. It is a physical product showing his talents, his ability to problem solve, his adeptness in finding the necessary resources, his appreciation for a beautifully designed home, and his value of perfection.

Throughout his transition to adulthood, his mother was an advocate for him. She promoted and empowered him and sought others to assist her. She continues to tell him that he's loved and that he can do it, no matter what the current challenge. She tells him what a worthy person he is and reinforces the belief that hard work does pay off.

❖ PROMOTING POSITIVE YOUTH DEVELOPMENT FOR YOUTH WITH DISABILITIES

These case studies demonstrate the importance of individual resources, neighborhood and community support, adult advocacy, and access to being productive and satisfied through work. The literature on assets building for youth highlights the importance of the roles that supportive and significant adults and communities play in promoting positive youth development. For youth with disabilities to a greater extent than with other youth, adult professionals often may play a significant role in their lives.

Although youth with disabilities represent a relatively small proportion of the overall youth population, they are an important segment for professionals interested in promoting positive youth development. First, as the case studies above underscore, the successful engagement of professionals in the lives of adolescents with disabilities requires the participation of multiple adults over time. These adults may cross institutional boundaries and represent different sectors of society, but they nonetheless embrace the notion of creating a community of support around these adolescents and their families.

Second, adults who work with adolescents with disabilities must exhibit extreme patience. Although developmental milestones may be achieved by youth with disabilities, the critical periods of transition are unpredictable with respect to when they are achieved. For adults, this means a longer period of engagement with youth, which is extremely important and can be beneficial to the individual and the family. These adults become important anchors (Garbarino, 1999) in the life of youth over the life span, not just for a brief period of time.

In addition to serving as anchors in the lives of adolescents with disabilities, these adults must assume the role of advocate. In other words, these adults become a type of "community wizard" (McLauglin, Irby, & Langman, 1994) for the individual, creating linkages and bridges across institutions while identifying learning environments that can promote positive development.

Finally, adults who work with youth who have disabilities must create a vision that is based on the assets of youth and help create a path to success. With the ultimate objective of this relationship being independent living and optimal development in the areas of work and social relationships, these adults serve as the stewards of growth.

Ironically, the outcome of this close relationship is that adults benefit perhaps more than the youth themselves. These relationships provide unique insights into the development of individuals that most of society would prefer to forget or render invisible or useless. People who choose to devote their time to working with youth with disabilities have the potential to become ambassadors for structuring environments that promote positive youth development. By committing to these long-term relationships, these adults are able to see beyond limitations and discover the arenas for optimal individual development. As adult providers, they become knowledgeable of policies and opportunities that can promote developmental outcomes. In the course of working with youth and families, these adults develop an ability to advocate not only for the individuals with whom they are working closely, but also for the larger community of youth with disabilities. These adults become community resources who strive to facilitate an institutional capacity to promote positive youth development.

From the stories of Ky and Bo and countless other youth with disabilities, we can only conclude that the model for positive youth development is being haphazardly implemented in the institutional world. The success of both these young people depended in great part on the advocacy and the support of family and community members.

Adults in multiple settings made substantive contributions to their positive development, but it did not appear to be either systematic or consistent across institutional systems. Thus, professionals who care deeply for the youth that they serve must continue to find the means and opportunity to implement a strengths-based approach. And, more important, there is still opportunity for the systems in which these professionals are employed to embrace a model of positive youth development that allows both time and opportunity to apply the strategies for promoting positive youth development in young people with disabilities.

The two case studies that are provided in this text underscore the importance of first- and second-order effects in the lives of youth with disabilities (Small & Supple, 2001). As this chapter demonstrates, the families of youth with disabilities must create a seamless web of support between themselves and their young adults to enhance the likelihood of successful and positive outcomes.

❖ REFERENCES

Benson, P. L. (1997). *All kids are our kids*. San Francisco: Jossey-Bass.

Blackorby, J. (1993). Participation in vocational education by students with disabilities. In M. Wagner (Ed.), *The secondary school programs of students with disabilities: A report from the National Longitudinal Transition Study of Special Education Students*. Menlo Park, CA: SRI International. (ERIC Document Reproduction Service No. ED 365 084)

Blackorby, J., & Wagner, M. (1996). Longitudinal postschool outcomes of youth with disabilities: Findings from the national longitudinal transition study. *Exceptional Children, 62*, 399-413.

Garbarino, J. (1995). *Raising children in a socially toxic environment*. San Francisco: Jossey-Bass.

Garbarino, J. (1999). *Lost boys: Why our sons turn violent and how we can save them*. New York: Free Press.

Halpern, A. S. (1992). Transition: Old wine in new bottles. *Exceptional Children, 58*, 202-211.

Hayden, M. F., & Heller, T. (1997). Support, problem-solving/coping ability, and personal burden of younger and older caregivers of adults with mental retardation. *Mental Retardation, 35*, 364-372.

Kretzmann, J. P., & McKnight, J. L. (1993). *Building communities from the inside out: A path toward finding and mobilizing a community's assets*. Evanston, IL: Northwestern University, Center for Urban Affairs & Policy Research, Neighborhood Innovations Network.

McLaughlin, M. W., Irby, M. A., & Langman, J. (1994). Urban sanctuaries: neighborhood organizations in the lives and futures of inner city youth. San Francisco: Jossey-Bass.

Schorr, L. B. (1997). *Common purpose: Strengthening families and neighborhoods to rebuild America*. New York: Anchor Books.

Small, S., & Supple, A. (2001). Communities as systems: Is a community more than the sum of its parts? In A. Booth & A. C. Crouter (Eds.), *Does it take a village? Community effects on children, adolescents, and families*. New Jersey: Lawrence Erlbaum.

Part II

The Intersection Of Youth And Community Programs

9

A Serious Look at Leisure

*The Role of Leisure Time and Recreation
Activities in Positive Youth Development*

Linda L. Caldwell and Cheryl K. Baldwin

Approximately 40% to 50% of a young person's time can be categorized as free and unobligated, making the leisure context a critical one just in terms of the bulk of time it consumes for a young person. The leisure context, however, is much more important to youth than just filling time. What youth do in their free time and their concomitant experiences derived from time use are important to their healthy development. The purposes of this chapter are to discuss why the leisure context is important to positive youth development, identify the need for leisure education, and describe issues related to community-based recreation and leisure programs.

A brief historical account of recreation and youth services will be presented first. This history will be followed by a discussion of how researchers have addressed the developmental relevance of leisure time and recreational activities, considering both developmental benefit and risk. A useful strategy for examining developmental consequence is to relate youth's self-reported perception of the overall quality of leisure with indicators of health and development status. Ironically, there is less research on the developmental benefits of activities that are experienced positively than on activities perceived negatively. This may be due to the typical but biased belief that all adolescents experience their leisure positively. It may also have to do with the fact that, recently, studies have been conducted to shed light on preventing developmentally unproductive and unhealthy behaviors from co-occurring with leisure activity. The next section of this chapter, therefore, provides a discussion of why many youth need help in learning how to use their free time constructively. Finally, we consider recreation-based community programs and provide some practical considerations in providing leisure services.

❖ A HISTORICAL PERSPECTIVE

The historical events leading to the professionalization and academic study of recreation and leisure are likely familiar to those committed to the field of youth development. From a leisure perspective, the pioneering work of reform era leaders such as Jane Addams, Luther Gulick, and Joseph Lee are hailed as advancing play and recreation as essential elements in the quality of life in a community. Of course, these pioneers are also viewed as instrumental to a number of other fields such as social work, early childhood development, youth development, and outdoor recreation and education. In the case of recreation and leisure it is also necessary to recognize John Muir, Gifford Pinchot, and Frederick Law Olmstead, among others, who were instrumental in ensuring that wilderness, outdoor areas, and community parks were preserved for public use.

These early leaders all had one thing in common. They believed that the conditions associated with an increasingly urbanized United States were detrimental to the quality of life of U.S. citizens, and in particular, children. Through these leaders' efforts, the first parks, playgrounds, open spaces, after-school programs, and recreation centers were established through government sanction and provision. Tax-based governmental action supporting community parks and recreation coincided with the development of a number of nonprofit agencies serving youth and families (e.g., Boy Scouts, established in 1910; Girl Scouts, 1912; YMCA/YWCA, 1851). Service strategies varied, including community-based centers, residential outdoor experiences, and weekly meetings of troops or groups in schools, churches, or other gathering places. Program formats were activity based, and the need for trained professional leadership to administer and provide recreation programs was a primary concern of the early leadership. Responding to this need, the American Playground Association, the predecessor to today's National Recreation and Parks Association, was established in 1906.

In contemporary American society, many of these issues and concerns about youth and quality of life remain. At an academic level, the study of adolescent development in leisure contexts has continued to grow over the past 15 years. The interest in this area is so keen that recently, the *Journal of Park and Recreation Administration* published a special issue on Youth and Leisure (see Volume 18, Issues 1 and 3, 2000). Articles in this special issue all contained research focused on youth development, and many of these articles emanated from a protective factors or developmental assets framework. As well, the *Therapeutic Recreation Journal* has issued a call for papers on the topic of youth and therapeutic recreation.

Historically and in the present day, the context of leisure and recreation affords youth with opportunities for engagement in meaningful activity pursuits. Youth development organizations play a critical role in introducing and facilitating experiences that can promote healthy development and lead to lifelong leisure pursuits. Research continues to confirm that personally meaningful free time activity is essential to overall health and well-being throughout the life course (Kleiber, 1999). In the next section of this chapter, we highlight aspects of the theoretical and empirical base that supports viewing leisure as a unique developmental context.

❖ LEISURE AS A POSITIVE DEVELOPMENTAL CONTEXT

Examining the anatomy of a leisure experience suggests that the conditions are right to facilitate positive growth and development. Research confirms that the adolescent views leisure as a chance to relax, do what one wants, be free from external pressures, be with friends, express oneself, experience competence, and of course have fun (e.g., Kleiber, Caldwell, & Shaw, 1993; Mobily, 1989). In short, self-determination, intrinsic motivation, perceived self-competence, and pleasurable experiences are defining elements of leisure pursuits (e.g., Iso-Ahola, 1980; Mannell & Kleiber, 1997; Neulinger, 1981) for adults and adolescents alike. Leisure has been called the fourth developmental context (Silbereisen, Todt, & Rudinger, 1994), highlighting the fact that issues such as the development of autonomy, experimentation with social roles, valuing achievement, and identity development are often associated with leisure behavior and the leisure experience (e.g., Harter, 1990; Kleiber, 1999; Kleiber & Kirshnit, 1991; Larson, 1994; Shaw, Kleiber, & Caldwell, 1995).

In a recent book on leisure and human development, Kleiber (1999) describes the value of leisure for youth development extensively. He suggests that leisure is important because it is a context for freely chosen engagement and the serious investment of attention. Two theoretical models in particular encompass this sense of engagement: self-determination and intrinsic motivation theory (Ryan & Deci, 2000) and the theory of optimal experience (Csikszentmihalyi, 1990) both address this engaging and absorbing character of leisure activity.

Intrinsic Motivation and Self-Determination

Ryan and Deci (2000) suggest that intrinsic motivation is fundamental in meeting three basic human needs: competence, autonomy, and relatedness. Of all the contexts in a youth's life, the leisure context allows for maximal probability of intrinsically motivated behavior. That is, youth are likely to choose to do things in their free time because they find the activities pleasurable, interesting, and inherently enjoyable. Even if their participation includes some feelings of obligation to friends or family, youth are still likely to be self-determined in their activity (that is, participating by choice).

The opportunity for intrinsic motivation is important developmentally for a number of reasons. Larson (2000), for example, links being self-determined with initiative, which he calls a "core quality of positive youth development" (p. 170). Furthermore, Larson links initiative to the development of creativity, leadership, altruism, and civic engagement and suggests that structured settings such as arts, sports, hobbies, and participation in voluntary organizations are uniquely situated to achieve these outcomes. Intrinsic motivation is linked with the behavioral action of persistence, suggesting that, in the pursuit of personally meaningful activities, youth will learn to overcome constraints and challenges to their continued participation, learn to solve problems, and develop lifelong skills that will assist them in the transition to adulthood.

Optimal Experience: Flow

The leisure context is one that is most conducive to feelings of "flow" (e.g., Csikszentmihalyi, 1990) and less likely to produce feelings of boredom (although these do occur and will be discussed in the next section). Flow, like leisure, is associated with positive affect and intrinsically motivated and self-determined behaviors. Being optimally challenged is associated with the positive emotional state of flow. Essential to this state is a match between challenge and skill, clear goals, and immediate feedback. The flow experience acts as a motivator for an individual to embark upon greater challenges and improve skills. As Csikszentmihalyi and Rathunde (1993) suggest, these conditions are "readily available in most games, sports, and in many artistic and religious performances" (p. 59).

❖ THE DARK SIDE OF LEISURE AND NEED FOR INTERVENTION

Despite the developmental potential associated with the leisure context, it is also necessary to recognize the darker side of leisure time use. The Carnegie Council on Adolescent Development's (1992) report on time use of youth and adolescents calls time "a matter of risk and opportunity," pointing to the paradoxical nature of leisure. The report states that, despite compelling evidence suggesting that participation in leisure activities contributes to healthy development for youth, leisure is also a context for adolescent rebellion, boredom, vandalism, and participation in unhealthy activities such as using drugs and alcohol, violent activities, and sexual behavior (e.g., Caldwell & Smith, 1995; Levin, Smith, Caldwell, & Kimbrough, 1995).

The freedom that adolescents experience in leisure settings provides a catalyst for experimentation with social roles, behaviors, and ideas, all of which contribute to a successful transition to adulthood. The experimentation that takes place in this context is essential for healthy development but also includes behaviors that may be developmentally maladaptive. For example, drinking, illegal drug use, delinquency, and sexual experimentation most often occur in the context of social leisure settings (Caldwell & Smith, 1995, 1996). The tensions between developing autonomy, responding to peer pressure, and living up to parental expectations and rules are often played out in social leisure contexts. For example, actively using one's leisure to rebel has been associated with increased substance use (Caldwell & Darling, 2000).

One of the reasons leisure is risky is that some adolescents experience leisure negatively. Boredom, for instance, is a negative leisure experience. Perceptions of nothing to do, no place to go, and boredom have been linked with a number of problem behaviors such as alcohol and drug abuse (Brake, 1997; Iso-Ahola & Crowley, 1991; Orcutt, 1985), higher rates of dropping out of school (Farrell, Peguero, Lindsey, & White, 1988) and vandalism (Caldwell & Smith, 1995). Although it may be tempting to view risky behavior as aligned with self-directed (albeit misguided) fun and excitement, what is compelling about this line of research is that individuals engaging in these behaviors report higher levels of boredom in leisure.

Unfortunately, many youth do not know how to participate in or create opportunities for constructive leisure. In an era in which TV watching, video game playing, and considerable (if not maximal) structure of leisure time imposed by parents (e.g., soccer games, music lessons, and church groups) dominate the leisure of youth, it is not surprising that the ability to self-initiate meaningful activities alone or with peers is a skill that seems to be decreasing. Youth's leisure today is so often tightly structured and controlled that by the time young people reach the age at which they are developing autonomy from parents and are concomitantly faced with blocks of "freedom" (i.e., leisure time), they are often unprepared and ill equipped to construct meaningful activities. Often, youth who tend to just "hang out" (not have anything meaningful to do) and whose peers use substances are highly likely to use substances themselves (Caldwell & Darling, 1999). Thus, there is a need to balance structured leisure time and self-initiated activities in leisure time.

To reiterate, many recreation and leisure activities foster intrinsic enjoyment, engagement, challenge, identity development, autonomy, and relatedness, whether these activities are self-directed (during free time at home or with peers) or a component of structured youth programs. These feelings are conditions of experience that are implicated in healthy development. Unfortunately, many of the typical ways that youth fill their time, including TV watching, hanging out, and other forms of passive engagement, do not demonstrate these developmentally relevant characteristics. Research comparing overall leisure activity profiles and the quality of the leisure experience indicates that some of the most negative free-time endeavors, such as engaging in risky behavior, are associated with the sense of nothing to do and passive leisure time. This is compelling evidence for greater guidance in helping youth structure their leisure time.

❖ THE NEED FOR LEISURE EDUCATION

In light of the leisure time paradox, the Carnegie Council report suggests that making creative and constructive use of the free time available to youth by participating in "high-yield" leisure and recreational activities is an important task because such high-yield leisure leads to an increase in future educational and life achievement. John Dewey (1916) argued that schools should be educating youth for the wise use of leisure time. One of the seven cardinal principles of education, he said, is "to educate for worthy use of leisure time." Unfortunately, Dewey's plea has been largely ignored, and today's schools do not teach youth how to be prepared for using their free time in a positive manner. Therefore, parents, families, and community agencies must address this issue.

Community agencies provide open spaces, playgrounds, recreation centers, and sports fields as opportunities for recreational activity, and some youth make adequate use of these facilities. However, the constructive use of blocks of free time requires adequate leisure skills, and not all youth possess these skills. Self-determined action and leisure skills must be fostered and facilitated so that youth have a well-rounded repertoire of intrinsically satisfying and meaningful things to do.

The constructive use of time is a developmental asset based on youth participation in creative activities, youth programs, and religious activities (Benson, Leffert, Scales, & Blyth, 1998). The developmental assets approach pioneered by Benson and his colleagues implicates the need for leisure education. We view leisure education for youth as the development of interest and skills in leisure activities that are personally meaningful, appropriately challenging and engaging, and can grow in complexity. Leisure education helps youth understand the implications of being self-determined and intrinsically motivated in leisure. Thus, leisure education is developing skills for managing time wisely, both in terms of learning to initiate action in a purposeful way and in terms of managing spontaneous or unstructured free time. Finally, leisure education for youth helps youth identify resources (e.g., personal, family, at home, and in the community) to engage in leisure activity, learn leisure skills, and surmount roadblocks that get in the way of participation. The development of leisure and time use skills requires guidance and more than casual attention.

Structure and Guidance

From a leisure education perspective, adults (parents, coaches, friends, and agency personnel) will be most effective if they facilitate the development of leisure skills. Before we go on, it needs to be recognized in this discussion that often parents do not or are unable to provide the guidance and structure necessary for healthy development to occur. Although ideally parents play this vital role, often it is up to other adults in a youth's life to provide guidance or to complement parental guidance. The leisure context, and community recreation opportunities in particular, are vital in fostering the perception in youth that there are caring adults in their lives. The way adults relate to youth is important and will be discussed next.

Adults can influence the type of activities engaged in, choices of those with whom to share activities, and ways a youth may manage free time. Of importance here is that adults are essential in guiding youth in how to use their free time wisely, as long as the guidance is not overbearing. This guidance includes helping youth learn to be good consumers of what is available in the community, to choose what is personally meaningful, to negotiate with friends, and to structure free time in the home environment. Adults can also teach activity skills to help facilitate ongoing interests.

Thus, adult guidance is an essential element to positive youth development in a leisure context. Too much guidance, however, can have a negative effect. Many parents dedicate a fair amount of their time to coordinating and supporting daily activities or even to deciding in which activities a child should participate. As more opportunities arise and daily schedules grow in complexity, parents may tend to overstructure the lives of their children, usurping their self-determined action. Habitual guidance by parents may lead to youth being unable to make their own decisions and solve their own problems.

In formal programs, leaders may similarly overstructure experiences, and there may be relatively little opportunity for youth to contribute in meaningful ways to what transpires in the program. For most youth, continued participation in structured programs with little or no opportunity to be part of the decision-making process has negative outcomes. The skills and perspective needed to self-direct activities, make good decisions, overcome obstacles, and coordinate one's actions with those of others do not develop if parents (or other adults) take too active a role in structuring or limiting free time activities.

Finally, overstructuring may be an unavoidable consequence when youth are restricted to the home during after-school hours because it is the safest place to be while parents are working. In this way, the structure presents a limit to the child's opportunities. Recognizing that this is a necessity in many households, we advocate that parents or adults help youth prepare for home-based free time by helping them discover personal interests that can be pursued at home.

Thus far, we have addressed how leisure can be developmentally productive. We recognized that problem behaviors do occur in leisure, and we suggested that many youth need leisure education to help them navigate their free time in positive ways as they move from early to later adolescence. In the next section, we will describe the role of, and issues related to, community-based recreation programs and developmentally productive leisure.

❖ COMMUNITY-BASED RECREATION
   AND LEISURE PROGRAMS

Our use of the term "leisure" is purposely broad and implies that recreation and leisure (sports, arts, music, hobbies, volunteer service) may be incorporated in different types of agencies and program formats. A particular recreation activity may be the main focus of a program or a subcomponent of broad-based programs. The latter configuration is characteristic of Boys and Girls Clubs, Big Brothers Big Sisters, outdoor education programs, and organized camping. In addition, some agencies use site-based programming, whereas others use outreach strategies that coordinate volunteers or staff in a manner such that all youth have at least some access to programming. In any given community, for example, the school district, the parks and recreation agency, or any of the many nonprofit youth-serving organizations could run an after-school program. We advocate that any agency offering recreation programming, or any program that includes recreational activities as part of the whole program, be deliberate in facilitating or programming for developmental outcomes.

Whether recreation is the central focus or an element of programming, community-based youth programs are uniquely situated to support a number of developmental outcomes. Programming for developmental benefit is a deliberate and challenging endeavor, and we highlight five issues in the provision of services: (1) program focus, (2) program format, (3) program leadership, (4) inter-agency collaborations, and (5) outcome evaluation. Examples of current programs and research will be incorporated in this discussion, and we cite examples primarily from the field of parks and recreation with which we are most familiar. Although there are many examples of excellent programs that we could have discussed, we chose those that seemed to best represent our discussion in this chapter (see Witt & Crompton, 1996, for a discussion of other types of programs that work).

Program Focus

Returning to their historical roots, many public parks and recreation departments are actively pursuing a community youth development approach to recreation programming. In doing so, they are adopting a "beyond fun and games" philosophy. Concomitant with the increased interest in the recent positive youth development approach to recreation programming is the related interest in seeing recreation as an intervention to decrease risk behaviors and promote resiliency, the hallmarks of prevention science. From both a research and a practical perspective, using a developmental or resiliency framework has shaped the way recreation programs are offered and evaluated.

A benefit of outcome based program design is that scholars have begun to identify what works and what doesn't in terms of youth development in a leisure context. For example, using the Protective Factors Scale (e.g., Witt et al., 1996) and the Benefits-Based Programming (BBP) framework, the multi-site study conducted by Hurtes, Allen, Stevens, & Lee (2000) found that "Although the results vary widely by site, the overall pattern of results suggests that the BBP philosophy, incorporating a resiliency framework, is appropriate and effective in programs where the level of contact between participants and recreation professionals is high." (p. 34).

Despite the focus on resiliency and developmental assets, agencies that offer recreation programs must not neglect the critical aspect of fun. Recent studies by Carruthers and Busser (2000) and King (2000), for example, stress the importance of making sure the overall experience is fun, even if other more developmental ultimate goals are the focus of the program. The fun aspect is what keeps overall interest high and keeps youth voluntarily coming back for more.

Program Format

Structured programs vary in format, creating notable variation in the time, frequency, and intensity of opportunity for participation. Bronfenbrenner and Morris (1998) argue that if recreation, leisure, and athletic activities are to be effective, they must take place on a regular basis, over an extended time period, and become increasingly more complex. Programmatically, this suggests that long-term involvement with an activity is important. This long-term engagement can occur via contact with a single agency or by use of multiple agencies, or long-term engagement can occur in self-directed activities such as hobbies. The main point is that the opportunity for continued engagement must be present.

Programs that are limited in scope, however, also can be developmentally relevant. As they try to find out what interests them, youth need opportunities to experience different types of activities before they can meaningfully pursue greater involvement in any particular pursuit. Structured programs that provide a sampling of different types of experiences may help to spark interest even if they do not provide in-depth skill development.

Conversely, agencies involved in providing skill development may become overly focused on skill enhancement and achievement, raising a concern for the quality of adult-to-youth and peer-to-peer interaction. Overemphasis on competition may also occur. These skill-based programs may fail to capitalize on the critical social development aspects of peer relations that are an important developmental component of these contexts. A proper balance of long-term challenge, skills, complexity, and competition is important to positive youth development.

Program Leadership

Perhaps one of the greatest concerns with community-based recreation and leisure activities is supervision by skilled and well-trained professionals, part-time staff, and volunteers. Research on the development of interest in achievement domains is beginning to examine the ways in which feedback on performance may enhance or suppress interest and intrinsic motivation (Eccles, 1993). The form and content of program leader communication is linked to the youth's subsequent continued participation or decision to drop out (e.g., Hurtes et al., 2000).

Although the character of the activity may be engaging for a youth, far greater developmental outcomes will be achieved when skilled leaders foster experiences that encourage growth and reflection. For example, Green, Kleiber, & Tarrant (2000) found that youth who had adults help them process their recreation experience (an adventure-based recreation program) increased their resiliency scores (as measured by the Protective Factors Scale; Witt et al., 1996) significantly more than two comparison groups (one that had no recreation programming, and one that had a recreation program but did not involve processing).

The evaluators conducting a study of the Big Brothers Big Sisters (Tierney, Grossman, & Resch, 1995) program made the following observations concerning the adult-youth relationship. Although these were not hypotheses explicitly tested in their evaluation, they concluded that, compared with less successful relationships, the stronger adult mentor and youth relationships were characterized by a high level of contact. In addition, the more positive relationships were characterized by adults who attempted to support the youth rather than explicitly act as "teacher or preacher" and change the youth's behavior.

Similarly, as mentioned previously, research has provided evidence that youth leadership and ownership of a program or space is very important (King, 2000; Patterson, Pegg, & Dobson-Patterson, 2000). Lerner, in particular, advocates that even though doing something positive for youth may hold value, positive youth development occurs when youth are enabled to achieve on their own (Lerner, 2002).

Interagency Collaboration

Effective partnerships are often necessary for providing services in a holistic and coordinated manner to youth and their families. In many communities, what works is to have one of the agencies designated as the coordinator of recreation-based youth development efforts. This broader perspective of community cooperation assures greater access and types of opportunities to everyone in the community.

These interagency partnerships take time to evolve and have challenges associated with them (Langman & McLaughlin, 1993). One of the challenges to partnering with a number of agencies is that all stakeholders, including the youth and parents, as well as administrators and staff, must share in the recognition of common goals and desired outcomes of program participation. Recently, research has shown that often parents, staff, youth, and administrators have different perspectives on what is important in recreational programming (Baker & Witt, 2000; Carruthers & Busser, 2000). Therefore, a clear identification of the concerns of each stakeholder group and agreement on program goals are necessary to the formation of effective partnerships.

The Philadelphia Recreation Department (PRD) is one example of a department that collaborates with other organizations and agencies and adopts a recreation-as-prevention perspective. This new prevention perspective arose several years ago when the PRD conducted a needs assessment of its clientele and discovered that there were several large community-based social problems that they could be addressing in partnership with other local agencies. Coordinated by the PRD, the partners began by targeting crime prevention in general. As a result, the partnership has developed an impressive after-school program that now serves about 3,000 children in approximately 150 different programs. Furthermore, they have 20 community partners such as churches, police, merchants, and residents who work toward common goals of youth development and prevention.

Outcome Evaluation

Demonstrating program outcomes is an ever-present necessity in recreation and youth programming. Conducting outcome evaluations provides support for the benefit of participation in community-based programs. However, a number of challenges inhibit the generalization of outcome studies to participation in general.

There are notable differences across studies in program goals and format, scope of participation, and the characteristics of participants. In fact, given the way "leisure and recreation" is used in everyday language, it is often difficult to determine what programs should be considered in this category. For example, many would consider research in the area of youth and single activity domains (e.g., media, sport) or community-based programs on a specific developmental issue (e.g., drug prevention) to be related to how youth spend their leisure time.

Similarly, many might include research on adult supervision versus self-care in the nonschool hours. How the problem of leisure time is framed obviously influences the community-based programs that are included. We have limited our discussion to recreation-based community programs and more general youth development programs that have a recreation aspect.

Because it is difficult to synthesize and summarize findings across studies, we have opted to highlight factors to be considered in outcome evaluation. In addition to distinguishing program format, goals, and participants, studies providing evidence of the benefit of participation in community leisure programs can also be distinguished by the method used to conduct the evaluation. Using existing studies, we highlight issues surrounding qualitative, cross-sectional, and longitudinal research.

One of the more extensive research programs addressing the value of community youth programs for urban youth is the work of Heath and McLaughlin (1993; McLaughlin, 2000). Their research on the role of urban community-based programs supports many of the common beliefs youth workers hold about the role of these programs. These urban-based programs offer a space separate from school in which to involve and engage youth. The centers offer a context for the development of life skills, positive self-worth, and positive sense of future opportunity (McLaughlin, 2000). The research is richly descriptive and compelling, particularly in its ability to present the contextual complexity of urban youth programming. As persuasive as this work is, the sociocultural and qualitative method used may leave some feeling that these studies offer little more than anecdotal evidence.

In contrast, program evaluation designs that compare participants and nonparticipants in a pretest and posttest manner offer a different form of evidence for program benefits. For example, the study conducted by a private research firm for Big Brothers Big Sisters (Furano, Roaf, Styles, & Branch, 1993; Tierney, Grossman, & Resch, 1995) clearly demonstrates program impact in terms of differences between participants and nonparticipants. A few of the results from this study included findings that participants were less likely to start using drugs and alcohol, were less likely to hit someone, had improved school attendance and performance, and had improved peer and family relationships. In addition to gleaning information on positive impacts, this type of cross-sectional study can also demonstrate that some outcomes believed to be occurring are in fact not happening.

Other well-designed cross-sectional studies focusing on different program formats also demonstrate similar positive results (Baker & Witt, 1996; Hurtes et al., 2000). However, two concerns surround this line of research. First, the studies often include an unbounded and long list of program outcomes. The long list of outcomes often reflects lack of theoretical foundation for programming and is methodologically problematic. Second, there is a lack of consistency in outcomes studied. Although some variation is expected, it is difficult to integrate findings across studies if sense of self-worth or academic achievement is measured in a different manner in each study.

Many national youth-serving agencies have commissioned cross-sectional outcome studies. These studies, often conducted by private research firms, are also generally well designed and offer support for the developmental benefit of participation. However, complete study results are usually not widely distributed, and unfortunately, in all but a few cases, these studies do not represent sustained programs of research.

An improvement over the one-time cross-sectional evaluation designs are longitudinal studies that track participants and nonparticipants for an extended period of time, often 2 to 5 years. These recent studies offer some evidence for the benefit of participation in community programs (e.g., Eccles & Barber, 1999). For example, using the activity categories of "athletics," "arts and hobbies," and "youth organizations," Larson's (1994) longitudinal analysis suggests that participation in youth organizations reduced participation in antisocial behavior. Participation in arts and hobbies (for boys only) also led to reduced antisocial behavior. This positive benefit, however, was not associated with participation in athletics.

Longitudinal studies provide stronger evidence than one-time cross-sectional designs that participation does indeed lead to positive development. However, many of the challenges previously discussed still exist in the longitudinal design. Whereas many cross-sectional studies examine participation in a single program format, longitudinal studies assess participation in a wide range of organized activities. Therefore, classifying participation is much more challenging, and researchers use different classification schemes to represent participation in organized programs, which further complicates generalization.

Finally, an overriding challenge to research is the segmented nature of youth development services. As interests of youth develop and diverge, a single agency may not be able to sustain depth, breadth, and frequency of participation. Since a child may enter and leave a number of programs sponsored by different types of agencies, continuity may be difficult to capture. Counting the number of participants served by an agency or by agencies in a community may not capture the continuity of experience at the individual level. Also, because many agencies offer drop-in programs, the dose effect of service delivery is almost impossible to calculate.

Furthermore, research related to activities generally considered to be recreation may occur in separate academic departments and separate professional fields. This segmentation also seems to work against the synthesis of research on youth programming. Similarly, youth workers associated with a particular youth-serving agency may not have easy access to the work and publications of other youth-serving agencies. This segmentation, in combination with the challenges to conducting good-quality research, makes it difficult to develop or find a careful, comprehensive, and detailed synthesis of developmental benefits associated with participation in community-based programs.

❖ CONCLUSION

This chapter has focused on the role recreation and leisure time activities play in positive youth development. A leisure education focus has been advocated, and a community development perspective has been used to highlight the various roles and opportunities that community-based agencies have to contribute to youth development through recreation. Combining youth development, leisure, human development, and prevention perspectives seems important in developing effective programs to meet the needs of youth. These perspectives suggest practical ways to help youth use their free time constructively and to help agency personnel offer opportunities and guidance to facilitate positive growth and development.

The context of leisure and all that can happen to youth in the leisure context are powerful. As a young person develops, the leisure context allows a self-determined approach to learning about the self. Lifelong interests and skills can be developed and can help offset some of the challenges to positive development that youth face. Adults and agencies are critical in helping youth through this process, but in the end, the leisure context affords the ideal context for self-determined development.

Youth need to learn how to use their free time wisely. This does not come naturally to most people.

- A balance between structure and guidance is needed. Structure is needed to provide opportunities for the development of interests. Guidance is needed to help youth learn how to take responsibility for their activities.
- Although a sampling of activities is necessary to develop interests, consistent and regular long-term engagement is necessary for development to occur.
- Fun is an essential component of community youth development recreation-based programs.
- Leadership must go beyond activity skill development to include processing of experiences.
- More rigorous studies are needed to understand the developmental benefits of participation in recreation-based community youth services.
- Continued efforts at partnerships and interdisciplinary research are needed to strengthen community-based recreation service provision and evaluation.

❖ REFERENCES

Baker, D. A., & Witt, P. A. (1996). Evaluation of the impact of two after-school recreation programs. *Journal of Park and Recreation Administration, 14*, 23-44.

Baker, D. A., & Witt, P. A. (2000). Multiple stakeholders' views of the goals and content of two after-school enrichment programs. *Journal of Park and Recreation Administration, 18*, 68-86.

Benson, P. L., Leffert, N., Scales, P. C., & Blyth, D. A. (1998). Beyond the "village" rhetoric: Creating healthy communities for children and adolescents. *Applied Developmental Science, 2*, 138-159.

Brake, S. B. (1997). *Perspectives on boredom for at risk adolescent girls.* Unpublished master's thesis, Pennsylvania State University, University Park.

Bronfenbrenner, U., & Morris, C. (1998). The ecology of developmental processes. In W. Damon (Series Ed.) & R. M. Lerner (Vol. Ed.), *Handbook of Child Psychology: Vol. 1: Theoretical models of human development* (5th ed., pp. 993-1028). New York: Wiley.

Caldwell, L. L., & Darling, N. (1999). Leisure context, parental control, and resistance to peer pressure as predictors of adolescent partying and substance use: An ecological perspective. *Journal of Leisure Research, 31*, 57-77.

Caldwell, L. L., & Darling, N. (2000, March 30-April 2). Adolescent problem behavior as a function of leisure experience and motivation. Paper presented at the meeting of the Society for Research on Adolescents, Chicago.

Caldwell, L. L., & Smith, E. A. (1995). Health behaviors of leisure alienated youth. *Society and Leisure, 18,* 143-156.

Caldwell, L. L., & Smith, E. (1996, May). Adolescent problem behavior and leisure participation. Paper presented at the 8th Canadian Congress on Leisure Research, Ottawa, Ontario.

Carnegie Council on Adolescent Development. (1992). *A matter of time: Risk and opportunity in the nonschool hours.* New York: Carnegie Corporation of New York.

Carruthers, C. P., & Busser, J. A. (2000). A qualitative outcome study of Boys and Girls Club program leaders, club members, and parents. *Journal of Park and Recreation Administration, 18,* 60-67.

Csikszentmihalyi, M. (1990). *Flow: The psychology of optimal experience.* New York: Harper/Collins.

Csikszentmihalyi, M., & Rathunde, K. (1993). The measurement of flow in everyday life: Toward a theory of emergent motivation. In R. Dienstbier & J. E. Jacobs (Eds.), *Nebraska Symposium on Motivation: Vol. 40. Developmental perspectives on motivation* (pp. 145-208). Lincoln: University of Nebraska Press.

Dewey, J. (1916). *Democracy and education: An introduction to the philosophy of education.* New York: MacMillan.

Eccles, J. S. (1993). School and family effects on the ontogeny of children's interests, self-perceptions, and activity choices. In R. Dienstbier & J. E. Jacobs (Eds.), *Nebraska Symposium on Motivation: Vol. 40. Developmental perspectives on motivation* (pp. 145-208). Lincoln: University of Nebraska Press.

Eccles, J. S., & Barber, B. L. (1999). Student council, volunteering, basketball, or marching band: What kind of extracurricular involvement matters? *Journal of Adolescent Research, 14,* 10-43.

Farrell, E., Peguero, G., Lindsey, R., & White, R. (1988). Giving voice to high school students: Pressure and boredom, ya know what I mean? *American Education Research Journal, 4,* 489-502.

Furano, K., Roaf, P. A., Styles, M. B., & Branch, A. Y. (1993). *Big Brothers/Big Sisters: A study of program practices.* Philadelphia: Public/Private Ventures.

Green, G. T., Kleiber, D. A., & Tarrant, M. A. (2000). The effect of an adventure-based recreation program on development of resiliency in low income minority youth. *Journal of Park and Recreation Administration, 18(3),* 76-97.

Harter, S. (1990). Self and identity development. In S. S. Feldman, G. R. Elliott (Eds.), *At the threshold: The developing adolescent* (pp. 352-387). Cambridge, MA: Harvard University Press.

Heath, S. B., & McLaughlin, M. W. (Eds.). (1993). *Identity and inner-city youth: Beyond ethnicity and gender.* New York: Teachers College Press.

Hurtes, K. P., Allen, L. R., Stevens, B. W., & Lee, C. (2000). Benefits-based programming: Making an impact on youth. *Journal of Park and Recreation Administration, 18(1),* 34-49.

Iso-Ahola, S. (1980). *The social psychology of leisure and recreation.* Dubuque, IA: Wm. C. Brown.

Iso-Ahola, S. E., & Crowley, E. (1991). Adolescent substance abuse and leisure boredom. *Journal of Leisure Research, 23,* 260-271.

King, K. (2000). From the precipice: Recreation experiences of high risk adolescent girls. *Journal of Park and Recreation Administration, 18(3),* 19-34.

Kleiber, D. (1999). *Leisure experience and human development: A dialectical interpretation.* New York: Basic Books.

Kleiber, D. A., Caldwell, L. L., & Shaw. S. M., (1993). Leisure meanings in adolescence. *Society & Leisure, 16,* 99-114.

Kleiber, D. A., & Kirshnit, C. E. (1991). Sport involvement and identity formation. In L. Diamant (Ed.), *Mind-body maturity: Psychological approaches to sport, exercise and fitness* (pp. 193-211). New York: Hemisphere.

Langman, J., & McLaughlin, M. W. (1993). Collaborate or go it alone? Tough decisions for youth policy. In S. B. Heath & M. W. McLauglin (Eds.), *Identity and inner-city youth: Beyond ethnicity and gender* (pp. 147-175). New York: Teachers College Press.

Larson, R. W. (1994). Youth organizations, hobbies, and sports as developmental contexts. In R. K. Silbereisen, E. Todt, & G. Rudinger (Eds.), *Adolescence in context* (pp. 46-65). New York: Springer-Verlag.

Larson, R. W. (2000). Toward a psychology of positive youth development. *American Psychologist, 55,* 170-183.

Lerner, R. M. (2002). The potentials of adolescence: The role of community programs and public policy. In R. M. Lerner (Ed.). *Adolescence: Development, diversity, context, and application.* Upper Saddle River, NJ: Prentice Hall.

Levin, D., Smith, E. A., Caldwell, L. L., & Kimbrough, J. (1995). High school sports participation and violence. *Pediatric Exercise Science, 7,* 379-388.

Mannell, R. C., & Kleiber, D, A. (1997). *A social psychology of leisure.* State College, PA: Venture.

McLaughlin, M. (2000). *Community counts: How youth organizations matter for youth development.* Washington, DC: Public Education Network. Retrieved September 25, 2002, from www.publiceducation.org/cgi-bin/download-manager/publications/p72.asp

Mobily, K. E. (1989). Meanings of recreation and leisure among adolescents. *Leisure Studies, 8,* 11-23.

Neulinger, J. (1981). *The psychology of leisure* (2nd ed.). Springfield, IL: C. C. Thomas.

Orcutt, J. D. (1985). Contrasting effects of two kinds of boredom on alcohol use. *Journal of Drug Issues, 14,* 161-173.

Patterson, I., Pegg, S., & Dobson-Patterson, R. (2000). Exploring the links between leisure boredom and alcohol use among youth in rural and urban areas of Australia. *Journal of Park and Recreation Administration, 18*(3), 53-75.

Ryan, R. M., & Deci, E. L. (2000). Self-determination theory and the facilitation of intrinsic motivation, social development, and well-being. *American Psychologist, 55,* 68-78.

Shaw, S. M., Kleiber, D. A., & Caldwell, L. L. (1995). Leisure and identity formation in male and female adolescents: A preliminary examination. *Journal of Leisure Research, 27,* 245-263.

Silbereisen, R. K., Todt, E., & Rudinger, G. (Eds.). (1994). *Adolescence in context.* New York: Springer-Verlag.

Tierney, J. P., Grossman, J. B., & Resch, N. L. (1995). *Making a difference: The impact study of Big Brothers/Big Sisters.* Philadelphia: Public/Private Ventures.

Witt, P. A., Baker, D., & Scott, D. (1996). *The Protective Factors Scale.* Texas A&M University: Unpublished instrument. College Station: Texas A&M University, Department of Recreation, Park and Tourism Sciences.

Witt, P. A., & Crompton, J. L. (Eds.). (1996). *Recreation programs that work for at-risk youth: The challenge and shaping the future.* State College, PA: Venture.

10

Working Hand in Hand

Community Youth Development
and Career Development

Theresa M. Ferrari

W orkforce preparation has become a major concern in our society. The rapid pace of social and technological change and globalization of the economy have contributed to the changing nature of work. Moving from school to work is one of the most important transitions that young people face. Some have argued that current educational systems do not adequately support this transition for young people (American Federation of Teachers, 1997; Murnane & Levy, 1996; U.S. Department of Education, 1996; U.S. General Accounting Office, 1993). Many organizations (e.g., school-to-work initiatives, state education departments, youth organizations such as 4-H) have responded to this concern by using the report of the Secretary's Commission on Achieving Necessary Skills (SCANS) to develop recommendations to guide program development and evaluation. The SCANS (1991) report outlined the skills and competencies that are viewed as necessary prerequisites for success in today's workplace, such as working well with others, acquiring and using information, and critical thinking. Although many reform efforts focus on changes that school systems should undertake, schools alone cannot and should not bear the total responsibility for preparing youth for work. The job of workforce preparation needs to be addressed by all sectors of youth's social world, including family, school, and community; and these individuals and organizations must work together. Therefore, the involvement of community-based youth organizations in the process of workforce preparation represents an opportunity to enhance an important aspect of development.

A growing trend that is affecting youth programs is a focus on community youth development (Hughes & Curnan, 2000; Perkins, Borden, Keith, Hoppe-Rooney, & Villarruel, 2003, this volume). From this perspective, development of positive skills, promotion of positive relationships, and engagement in one's emerging development, rather than simply the prevention of negative outcomes, is stressed. The emphasis is not only on whether youth are problem free but also on whether they are fully prepared for life and therefore able to reach their optimal development (Pittman & Wright, 1991). One aspect of life for which they must be fully prepared is the world of work.

The community youth development framework can be applied to the area of workforce preparation and career development.[1] In fact, workforce preparation is considered a component of the broader spectrum of youth development (Pittman, Cahill, & Zeldin, 1994; Vondracek, Lerner, & Schulenberg, 1986; Zuckerman, 2000). Also, effective workforce programs make an effort to incorporate youth development principles (National Youth Employment Coalition, 2002). Programs that incorporate career-focused activities can serve as the means to reach developmental competencies, skills, and goals such as developing specific life skills, establishing positive relationships with adults and peers, and contributing through partnerships in the community. By consciously applying a community youth development framework to program development, the likelihood increases that the programs created will not only accomplish workforce-related goals but will also make the connection to broader community youth development outcomes. To ensure that these goals are achieved, the connection between career development and positive youth development should be intentional, not just a side effect of participation in an event or activity. Workforce preparation programs for youth need to make sure that key elements are reflected in program design and content to realize positive youth development goals.

Table 10.1   Common Threads Connecting Career Development
and Positive Youth Development

Key Elements of Career Development Experiences	Key Elements of Positive Youth Development Programs
Are intentional	Contain clearly stated goals
Are developmentally appropriate	Are based on developmental theory and focus on specific needs of young people
Use the experiential learning model and involve active exploration of the world of work	Engage youth in active, participatory, and reflective learning experiences
Provide exposure to a wide variety of career options	Include a diversity of activities and experiences that address multiple learning styles
Provide exposure to career role models	Establish positive, ongoing relationships with adults
Focus on skills that would be required for any job	Emphasize development of practical life skills, with focus on skills and competencies
Are of sufficient frequency, duration, and intensity (i.e., once is not enough)	Occur on a frequent and ongoing basis
Provide appropriate training for adults who work with youth	Managed by well-trained staff
Source: Ferrari (2000)	Source: Perkins and Borden (2003, this volume)

Conversely, programs with primarily a youth development focus can incorporate key elements of workforce preparation practices. Both sets of practices are complementary (see Table 10.1).

The chapter by Perkins and Borden in this volume describes the key elements of positive youth development programs. These elements serve as an important set of promising practices that, when combined with specific recommendations related to the program content (i.e., career development), will help to ensure high quality programs that enhance youth development. In this chapter, I will discuss how workforce preparation practices can reflect an understanding of what it means to be based on a community youth development model. By using the example of workforce preparation in 4-H,[2] it is my aim to demonstrate how the key elements can be applied when creating and conducting educational programs for youth. However, a similar process could be followed by other community-based youth organizations and could apply to other content areas besides career development.

Building on Perkins and Borden's more extensive review of the key elements, I will discuss both the process of designing learning opportunities and the process of determining the content of these experiences. Hughes (1994) points out that, whereas the content of an educational program is important, equally important are the strategies for how it should be designed and presented. In other words, it is not just *what* you do but *how* you do it that counts. The first part of the chapter examines the target audience of youth and the role of adults. This is followed by a discussion of program design and delivery issues including experiential learning, life skills, and specific activities for career development. The chapter concludes by identifying several principles of practice.

❖ TARGETING THE AUDIENCE: A RATIONALE FOR WORKING WITH ELEMENTARY-AGE YOUTH

A review of literature and practical experience (e.g., conducting local focus groups with educators and business people) provides evidence that comprehensive workforce preparation strategies must build on an early foundation of knowledge, skills, attitudes, and experiences to achieve the desired long-term results. Such a developmental approach favors intervention at earlier rather than later points in the life span. The influence begins at the particular point of intervention, but it affects the future course of development as well, what is often referred to as a developmental trajectory. Therefore, program developers should focus attention on events, processes, and life periods that are antecedents to actual decisions. Such a focus is consistent with a community youth development approach. This approach targets youth before they become at risk; by anticipating the developmental milestones and challenges they will face, it allows one to deal with situations in a proactive manner. This approach also acknowledges that the development of skills such as leadership and decision making is not a one-time event but is part of an ongoing process, with each experience building on previous ones.

In the case of career development, much attention has been focused on adolescents and college students. Perhaps these age groups are highlighted because their transition from school to work is imminent. However, as a report by the American Federation of Teachers (1997) has noted, high schools cannot be expected to magically provide a solution to the effective transition from school to work. Those who are "serious about preparing youngsters for work and citizenship when they graduate from high school must make sure changes extend all the way down to the elementary grades" (p. 6). Although the importance of a comprehensive approach to workforce preparation is acknowledged, few educational efforts have directly addressed this younger age group (U.S. Department of Education, 1996).

There is ample support for the notion that the school-age years represent a unique opportunity for the development of workforce preparation skills and competencies. Experiences in the early years can help to prepare youth for later career exploration and decision making. Early experiences may limit or create options in the world of work. During this time, children will develop preferences and specialized abilities that influence the choices they make; in turn, these choices will significantly shape the course of their development. Young children are motivated to learn about the world around them, and this includes the world of work. Furthermore, when they participate in organized career-related learning experiences, they often rate them positively (Ferrari, 1998; Ferrari & Farrell, 1998). Career-related learning experiences are important contributors to the process of workforce preparation for young people. Actual participation in career preparation activities, more so than indirect influences, has been positively related to youths' career efficacy beliefs (Ferrari, 1998).

Emphasizing the elementary-age youth as a target audience in no way diminishes the need to direct programs to older youth. Ideally, career education programs begin early and continue across the age spectrum. Clearly the target age group will determine what is developmentally appropriate. This connection to developmental theory is what is needed for high-quality youth programs (Perkins & Borden, 2003, this volume; Yohalem, 2003, this volume). For example, the National 4-H Council (1993) developed a model for youth experiences that includes all phases of the life cycle along with recommended learning experiences for each. Specific developmentally appropriate activities for elementary-age youth are considered in more detail later in this chapter.

❖ WORKING HAND IN HAND:
ADULT ROLES AND RELATIONSHIPS

The review by Perkins and Borden (2003, this volume) established that programs should provide opportunities to build positive and ongoing relationships with adults. There are key components to such relationships. Adults who work with youth should be grounded in the knowledge base of positive youth development principles and practices, be able to establish trust with youth, and understand their needs and respect them (Astroth, 2000; Yohalem, 2003, this volume). Because adults' roles and relationships are so important, those who develop curricula and programs for youth should pay close attention to how adults will interact with youth during the course of these experiences. It is important that these interactions promote, not hinder, the development of positive relationships. Youth are looking for adults who are willing to work with them, that is, adults who see themselves as partners with youth.

Adults play an important role in creating an environment that fosters engagement in learning. A positive climate is one of the key factors in youth groups that are successful (Astroth, 1997). This climate may be accomplished in groups that have leaders who are autonomy oriented, as they are more likely to foster opportunities for youth to take charge of their own learning (Astroth, 1997). Autonomy-oriented adults operate as guides more than leaders, providing opportunities for youth to make their own decisions rather than taking control of the group. This is a shift from seeing adults as the experts. In their role as career coaches, adults are not telling children what to think, but helping them learn how to learn (Ferrari, 1997). Curriculum materials should describe the rationale for this approach as well as provide directions for conducting activities based on this philosophy. The directions should be outlined in such a way that adults can guide youth through a process, such as creating a list of questions to ask a guest speaker, rather than doing it themselves (i.e., making the list ahead of time and telling the youth what questions to ask). However, adults without previous experience may need to be coached to adopt a facilitative style; this idea is discussed when the experiential model is presented later in the chapter.

Adults play a crucial role when working with youth to help them achieve positive workforce preparation and youth development outcomes. The encouragement provided by adults may be a significant factor in the beliefs that youth develop about their abilities to tackle career-related tasks. Through their words and actions while engaged in activities with youth, adults can facilitate the development of positive attitudes toward learning and can demonstrate the importance of teamwork. They can set up situations that foster cooperation and team-work rather than competition, such as working together in small groups to solve a problem. Activities can be structured to emphasize the concept that people in a group need to work together to accomplish their goal. Creating this climate is particularly important when the focus is on workforce preparation, because attitudes toward learning, teamwork, and cooperation are important workplace competencies (SCANS, 1991), yet these attitudes and behaviors are hard to teach directly. Dealing with these workforce competencies explicitly through curriculum development, activities, and training ensures that they will happen by design and not by default.

From a program design and delivery standpoint, another aspect of adult relationships bears mentioning here: preparing adults to assume their role. Dewey (1938) pointed out that it is the responsibility of the educator to create the conditions for experiences that result in growth for young people. This responsibility requires a knowledge of youth development, an understanding of the types of experiences that could help them learn, and the ability to anticipate and respond to situations that develop as an experience unfolds. A key element appears to be training for those adults (and teen leaders) who will facilitate activities, not just in the content area of career development, but in the process of working with groups of children. For example, observations of college student facilitators who were working with youth in after-school career clubs showed that they were not aware of how to get the group started and how to create a feeling of group cohesion (Ferrari & Farrell, 1998). Some of the students had difficulty leading group discussions, even though the activity directions listed several discussion questions. While they could ask the first question listed, they were often unsure of what to do next, and the discussion would be limited. The observations also indicated that the student facilitators needed preparation for dealing with group management issues, such as establishing ground rules for behavior and techniques for conflict resolution.

Evidence indicates that a positive learning climate is partly deter-mined by adults' beliefs in their ability to create mastery experiences for young people (Fritz, Miller-Heyl, Kreutzer, & MacPhee, 1995). These beliefs, or sense of efficacy, can be influenced by providing opportunities to practice new skills and to receive feedback and encouragement. Therefore, training sessions should discuss and demonstrate the importance of processing the educational experience (i.e., the "reflect" portion of the experiential model described in this chapter) and should provide an opportunity for facilitators to role play group situations. Observations of and coaching by skilled facilitators also may be helpful. Additionally, training sessions can help make adults aware of the rationale behind particular education techniques (e.g., nonformal and experiential) that may be used in the curriculum. In-service training programs need to go beyond simply providing new knowledge and skills and address confidence in performing the teaching role and providing support to take risks in new program areas.

❖ HANDS-ON AND MINDS-ON LEARNING: UNDERSTANDING THE EXPERIENTIAL LEARNING MODEL

Learning experiences that are active, participatory, and reflective are recommended elements of the positive youth development model (Perkins & Borden, 2003, this volume). Experiences of this nature are suggested because they are the source of learning and development. Education theorists conceive of learning as a continuous process grounded in interaction with the social and physical environment (Berk, 2000; Dewey, 1938; Kolb, 1984). The complete cycle of learning takes place when a person is involved in an activity, looks back at it critically, determines what was useful or important to remember, and uses this information to perform another activity. Kolb (1984) emphasized that "learning, and therefore knowing, requires *both* a grasp or figurative representation of experience and some transformation of that experience. Either the figurative grasp or operative transformation alone is not sufficient" (p. 42).

Learning of this nature is particularly important in today's workforce. The new skills needed for the workplace do not emphasize knowing specific information, because the facts of today may not be the facts of tomorrow. Instead, it is important to know how to acquire and use information, to work with others to use that information creatively to solve problems and make decisions, and to have the motivation to continue to learn and adapt as conditions change. Youth who merely acquire current knowledge will be inadequately prepared for the future. Today's workers need to apply what they have learned to real-life situations, and the ability to do this is fostered by the experiential learning process outlined here. Workforce preparation activities should be designed to be hands-on and minds-on, thereby accomplishing both workforce preparation and youth development goals. Certain strategies (such as advance organizers, cooperative learning, and using real experiences) have been shown to be particularly effective across a variety of content areas and age levels (Marzano, Pickering, & Pollock, 2001).

Experiential education consists of any structured learning activities that engage students directly in the subject being studied. Its principles serve as a guide for planning the active, participatory learning experiences that are an important component of the community youth development approach. A model for developing experientially based curricula has been described by Horton, Hutchinson, Barkman, Machtmes, and Myers (1999), and it is one way to ensure that skills, objectives, and activities are congruent with youth development principles. The experiential learning model consists of five phases:

1. Experience the activity.

2. Share the experience by describing what happened.

3. Process the experience to identify common themes.

4. Generalize from the experience to form principles or guidelines that can be used in real-life situations.

5. Apply what was learned to another situation.

To simplify even further, this model is often presented using the three concepts of "do–reflect–apply" (see Figure 10.1). A central idea in this model is that simply having an experience—doing something—is *not* enough to guarantee that learning occurs. The following statement aptly summarizes this concept:

> To say that experience is a good teacher, however, does not imply that it's easily or automatically so. . . . It's true that we can learn from experience. We may also learn nothing. Or we may, like Mark Twain's cat who learned from sitting on a hot stove lid never to sit again, learn the wrong lesson. The key, as Aldous Huxley explained, is that "experience is not what happens to a man; it is what a man does with what has happened to him" (Conrad & Hedin, 1987, p. 39).

Figure 10.1   Steps in the Experiential Learning Model

1. DO   The youth do or experience an activity. This could involve
making something, playing a game, or solving a problem.

2. REFLECT   Next, youth share what they think happened in the
experience. They think about what they did, how it felt,
whether it was easy or difficult. They also analyze the
experience by reflecting on problems or issues that came up
for them.

3. APPLY   In this step, youth generalize the experience by connecting it
to real-world examples. This is the "so what" portion of
experiential learning. Finally, they apply what they have
learned by thinking about it in terms of new situations that
might happen now or in the future.

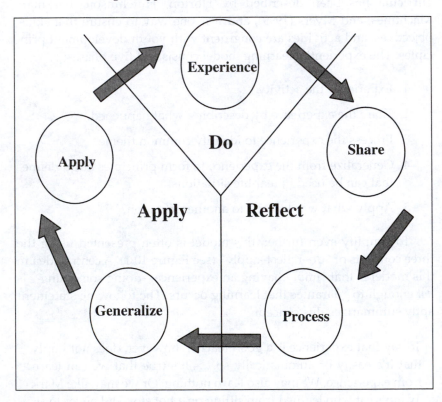

To have a meaningful experience, the "do" phase may need to be
conceptualized as a series of activities (Horton et al., 1999). Relating
activities through a common theme facilitates children's generalization
of knowledge and skills from one experience to another (Kostelnik,

Soderman, & Whiren, 1993). For example, several shorter introductory activities may prepare youth for a field trip to interact with workers in their community (see Box 10.1 for an example; other examples are provided in Beale, 2000, and Beale & Nugent, 1996). Reflection afterwards is needed to give meaning to the experience (Steps 2 and 3), but sufficient amount and depth of experience must have transpired for meaningful reflection to occur. Finally, it is the application to other experiences (Steps 4 and 5), or what Dewey (1938) called the continuity of a learning experience, that is important; in this way, what a person "has learned in the way of knowledge and skill in one situation becomes an instrument of understanding and dealing effectively with situations which follow" (p. 44). It may help to think of an activity, such as a field trip, as the "filling" for a sandwich. The filling provides the flavor, but it is held together by two slices of "bread"—in this case, what you do before and after the trip. The complete "sandwich" is a more meaningful learning experience. Reflective discussions are possible when the learning climate is based on positive adult relationships— a necessary ingredient in this process. Young people are quite eager to share their thoughts, provided there is such an opportunity.

Box 10.1   Job Shadowing and the "Sandwich" Approach of Experiential Learning

---

The curriculum *WOW! Wild Over Work* (Ferrari, 1997) includes an activity titled "Only the Shadow Knows" that will be helpful to those organizing a workplace visit. The goal of job shadowing is to learn about careers through active engagement in a work setting.

❖ BEFORE YOU GO

Plan ahead. A little advance planning goes a long way. Bring up the idea early enough so any necessary permission from employers can be secured. Help them think about the types of experiences that will help the children learn about what occurs in the workplace. Children will get bored if they simply sit and watch other people do things all day. The younger the child, the more concrete and structured the experience needs to be. The handout "Making the Most of Job Shadowing" that is included in the *WOW!* job shadowing activity can be copied and shared.

Review workplace etiquette. Interpersonal skills are necessary in the workplace. Schedule time in advance to talk about the appropriate way to behave on the job. Review simple manners such as how to respond when introduced, shaking hands when you meet someone, and thanking people for their help.

❖ IT'S OFF TO WORK WE GO

To focus their attention during the experience, children can do a job skills scavenger hunt (a sample is included in the curriculum).

❖ REFLECT ON THE LEARNING EXPERIENCE

Don't forget this part of the "sandwich." Children can learn by thinking about their experience and comparing it with others. Here are some questions to help start the discussion:

- What surprised you about the visit?

- How is your day like a worker's day? How are they different?

- What was the most important thing you learned?

- What other work-related experiences would you like to have?

Training sessions with adults are an opportunity to model an experiential approach and encourage its use. For example, learning stations can be set up where adults have the opportunity to experience at least part of several activities in a curriculum. When the group comes back together, it is much easier to talk about the activities because the participants have actually experienced them, rather than having to discuss them in the abstract. Then a discussion could take place about how they see themselves using the activities in their own settings. Experience with this technique using the *Wild Over Work* curriculum (Ferrari, 1997) has shown that participants respond positively to the format and that it is flexible enough to work well with groups of different size and composition and with a variety of time frames.

❖ LIFE SKILLS FOR THE 21ST CENTURY

Another key element is for youth programs to have a focus on the development of practical life skills (Perkins & Borden, 2003, this volume). Life skills are those skills that develop over time and in multiple contexts. Although there is no one set of life skills that is universally accepted, there are a number of skills that are mentioned repeatedly for which there is widespread support, both practical and empirical, such as communication, decision making, and interpersonal skills. Youth development professionals have made efforts to consider appropriate sets of life skills for different age groups (Scheer, 1997) and to incorporate SCANS (1991) workforce preparation competencies and skills with other sets of important skills (Barkman, Machtmes, Myers, Horton, & Hutchinson, 1999; Horton et al., 1999).

A focus on workforce preparation has heightened the attention given to life skills development. The challenges of a rapidly changing society demand that today's children become lifelong learners. Dewey (1938) has stated that "the most important attitude that can be formed is that of desire to go on learning" (p. 48). The need for learning how to learn and for lifelong learning (the ability to adapt to continuous change) take on particular significance in career development programs, as they are considered a cornerstone for success in the workforce (Murnane & Levy, 1996). Much of what employers say they are looking for is not found in a book but is gained by experience. Problems encountered in the workplace are not those posed in textbooks with answers at the end of the chapter; they involve integrated responses.

Although a focus on life skills will inevitably prepare youth for the world of work, the development of life skills is not an automatic outcome of program participation. Specific attention to youth development and world-of-work concepts is necessary to make this assumption a reality. Life skills are not new skills, but the current workplace climate gives them a new emphasis. For example, interpersonal skills, once called "soft," are now considered among the "new basic skills"

(Murnane & Levy, 1996). Levin (1994) suggested that a broad-based set of skills—which includes interpersonal skills, thinking and learning skills, and communication skills—would not only meet workplace needs but are the same skills that are needed for active citizen participation and positive human development. Furthermore, a conscious reliance on youth development principles is one of the hallmarks of effective workforce development programs (National Youth Employment Coalition, 2002). Again, career development and community youth development are complementary.

❖ DESIGNING ACTIVITIES FOR WORKFORCE PREPARATION

Although children in the school-age years have given thought to their future, this is not the time to push them into decisions that restrict future occupational exploration and attainment. Development is enhanced when individuals have the opportunity to be exposed to the widest possible array of learning experiences. Youth need to participate in learning opportunities that are goal directed, ongoing (i.e., more than occasional), important and meaningful, challenging, and fun. Furthermore, human development theory suggests that processes that encourage development should occur over time, involve contact with an ever-widening sphere of peers and adults, and become progressively more complex (Bronfenbrenner & Morris, 1998). It follows, then, that program planners should design a comprehensive approach to career development, building in longer-term experiences that provide time for relationships to form.

Drummond and Ryan (1995), provided suggestions for career preparation objectives for elementary level students (see Box 10.2). These objectives can form the basis for specific workforce preparation activities and strategies. Activities in a workforce preparation curriculum should help children think about themselves, their skills, and relevant careers; provide a means to develop self-awareness; provide exposure to role models; provide positive support for pursuing educational and career goals; and provide a means to acquire career information. Activities can focus on current interests and how those interests might develop into jobs in the future. They can help children see work as an outlet for their talents, abilities and interests. It is not unusual to hear about adults whose career interests were sparked during their elementary school years.

Box 10.2   Career Preparation Objectives for Elementary-Age Youth

1. Develop an appreciation for and positive attitude toward work.

2. Demonstrate understanding of the importance of jobs in the community and the importance of preparing for a job.

3. Discuss work-related activities necessary in the home and school, importance of community workers, and how these workers help everyone.

4. Develop skills to locate, evaluate, and interpret information about vocational and career opportunities.

5. Describe work of family members.

6. Describe jobs that are unique to their community.

7. Identify work activities that are appealing.

8. Recognize the interdependence of jobs.

9. Study local employers, their working conditions, and the skills necessary for workers in these businesses.

10. Examine the relationship of personal values and abilities to occupational interests.

11. Recognize the role educational planning has on one's life.

12. Identify goals and outline steps for achieving a plan of action.

SOURCE: Drummond and Ryan, 1995.

Often a disparity exists between intent and reality. Although workforce skills and competencies appear as intended program outcomes, they are not necessarily provided for in the program's structure or activities (El Sawi & Smith, 1997). Many times activities such as career days and field trips can become isolated learning experiences if they are done without preparation and follow-up and if they are not connected to some larger goals or framework of career development or youth development. It is assumed that key concepts about the world of work have been gained, but there has been no mechanism built in to ensure that this has occurred. Using a curriculum based on the experiential learning model already discussed can strengthen these tried-and-true formats. Also, because issues such as program frequency, intensity, and duration matter, there is a need to focus on delivery methods that extend adult and youth interaction; one-shot deals just don't cut it.

An after-school-club format is one way to incorporate several elements of positive youth development. Daily or weekly meetings provide a program delivery structure that builds in frequent contact. One such pilot program, Career Coaches, enlisted college student volunteers in service-learning classes to conduct weekly activities after school (Ferrari & Farrell, 1998). From the elementary students' perspective, a key aspect was that the activities were viewed as fun. They really enjoyed interacting with the college students, and they learned something about future careers. Overall, the findings from the evaluation indicated that college students working with elementary students can be a successful delivery model for career development programs, with benefits for both groups of students. Furthermore, the after-school club was an experience that complemented others (such as job shadowing) that were conducted throughout the school year through a collaboration between a university and a school district (Keith, Perkins, Greer, McKnight Casey, & Ferrari, 1998). Taken together, these activities were engaging to youth and provided multiple points of contact with caring adults and positive role models.

The way that children approach learning tasks can determine if they will continue to approach challenges in a healthy and adaptive way or give up before they have even tried (Berk, 2000). Experiences that foster the development of positive self-concept and assist children with the challenges of learning important life skills can contribute to future success in the world of work. In summary, instructional strategies in a workforce preparation curriculum should incorporate team activities and encourage children to interact with each other, should help them view learning as an active process, should emphasize that learning is a skill they will continue to use throughout life (not just while they are in school), should build generic workplace skills such as teamwork and decision making, and should enable them to envision themselves in the future. Not only are these strategies important for success in the workforce, they are also an essential part of overall positive youth development.

❖ WHAT YOU SEE IS WHAT YOU GET: EXPOSURE TO CAREER OPTIONS AND ROLE MODELS

In many cases, children can state what they want to be when they grow up and why, but few can state specifically what they would have to do to attain their career goals (Phipps, 1995). The content of career choice is often the focus (i.e., "What do you want to be when you grow up?"), and little attention has been given to the way one goes about making those choices. Children's preferences for particular areas of work may change, but the process of gathering information and making decisions can be repeated. Whether or not their specific *choices* persist into adulthood, the childhood years are important ones in the *process* of workforce preparation. Experiential activities will help to create an understanding of the process rather than simply focusing on gaining specific information.

When it comes to career choice, what you see is what you get. Exposure to career options would benefit children in several ways. Children's knowledge of jobs is based on what is available for them to observe directly (in their environment) or indirectly (e.g., books and TV). It's quite simple: If you don't know that a particular career exists, you are not going to envision yourself doing it. It also follows that their interests may be limited by the amount and type of models with whom they come in contact. Exposure to role models is an important factor in career decision making, particularly for women who have made nontraditional career choices such as skilled trades (Greene & Stitt-Gohdes, 1997). Because occupational stereotypes still exist, both boys and girls will benefit from exposure to a wide variety of career options (Ferrari, 1998). The name of the game is exposure.

Experience with elementary-age youth suggests that their career interests are often tied to knowing someone with that career. Here is where the connection to caring adults again becomes particularly important. Furthermore, learning from people on the job is a method that youth prefer (Ferrari, 1998; McKenna & Ferrero, 1991). Whereas these are activities that youth enjoy, one study found that these active exploration activities (i.e., talking to workers, visiting a worksite) were those that youth felt least sure of their ability to do (Ferrari, 1998). Activities such as guest speakers, career fairs, and worksite visits can introduce students to the range of options available in the world of work. To be most effective, however, they must be done with positive youth development principles in mind.

Worksite visits, often called job shadowing, provide a way for children to observe and interact with role models in their work environment. Exposure to nontraditional role models has been found to prompt children's interest and questions about their work (Bailey & Nihlen, 1989). Although they are beneficial for all students, shadowing experiences may be particularly useful for children who lack adequate role models in their families (Phipps, 1995). Therefore, activities should be designed to make children aware of the broad range of opportunities in the world of work, including options that may not be traditional for their gender, race, or ethnicity. Furthermore, as discussed previously, exposure to role models should be followed up with opportunities for reflection and discussion. My observations of classroom visits and job-shadowing activities indicated that students who participated in organized job-shadowing experiences were able to recognize skills people used on the job and how those skills are related to what students learn in school (Ferrari & Farrell, 1998). This strategy was effective with teachers as well (Ferrari, 1996). The focus of the educational experiences should be on developing attitudes and skills that will be important for their success in whatever path they choose.

The anticipation of adult careers at some distant point in the future does not have enough pull to serve as a motivating force for youth to sustain interest in many career-focused activities (Larson, 2000). When youth are involved in activities that have intrinsic motivation, that are challenging enough to engage their attention, and that occur over time, they develop initiative (Larson, 2000). Larson contends that these conditions occur during what he calls "structured voluntary activities," which include activities organized by adults and those that youth participate in on their own (p. 174). Obviously, community-based youth organizations, working with youth as partners to learn what motivates, challenges, and engages them, can play a major role in structuring activities of this nature.

❖ PRINCIPLES OF PRACTICE

This chapter has highlighted several concepts about career development that are relevant to the community youth development perspective.

First, there is ample support that the school-age years represent a unique opportunity for the development of workforce preparation skills and competencies. Creating a developmentally appropriate curriculum requires knowing the target audience and taking into account how children develop and learn. Second, the activities should also help children develop attitudes and skills that will help them be successful now and in their future. In addition to the general practices described above, specific recommendations have been made about activities to guide children's career development. However, goals and objectives must be specified, and specific developmentally appropriate activities must be designed to make the curriculum usable for the intended audience. Finally, implicit in this discussion is the idea that educational opportunities provided by community-based youth organizations can play a role in supporting career development outcomes for youth.

From the preceding discussion of program design considerations, several principles of practice emerge. These principles may be applied to a variety of youth development programs.

- Provide training for adults in both the program content and the process of working with groups of children to facilitate experiential learning experiences.
- Use a combination of current research literature tempered with real voices and experience as a foundation for program development.
- Strengthen programs and the activities that comprise them through the use of a conceptual framework.
- Plan the timing of programs to take into account the developmental milestones and challenges faced by youth.
- Aim to enhance life skill development not only by starting programs early but also by having them available over the life span, with developmentally appropriate activities designed to accommodate the needs and interests of each age group.
- Recognize that adults play multiple roles as facilitators and role models.
- Be explicit about strategies for positive interaction between youth and adults. Don't assume that relationships will happen on their own.
- Use experiential learning activities to foster career development, life skill development, and youth development outcomes.

Activities must meet the standards of both youth (e.g., fun) and
adults (e.g., education).
- Activities must be of sufficient frequency, duration, and intensity to achieve long-term outcomes and to allow for relationships to develop.

Work remains central to our society, but what it takes to be
successful in the workforce is changing (Murnane & Levy, 1996;
U.S. Department of Education, 1996). Attention to the key elements of
positive youth development programs will enhance efforts aimed at
promoting preparation for the world of work. This chapter has outlined some of the ways that the concepts of a community youth development model can be applied to this important topic. There must be a
conscious effort on the part of youth development educators to apply
key elements of positive youth development and to examine existing
and new programs based on the extent to which they meet these
elements.

Career development and community youth development are connected. They truly do work hand in hand.

❖ NOTES

1. The terms "workforce preparation" and "career development" are
used interchangeably in this chapter.
2. 4-H is the youth development program of the Cooperative Extension
System based at land grant universities in the United States. The 4-H program
includes curriculum and experiences to help youth explore career options.

❖ REFERENCES

American Federation of Teachers. (1997). *Reaching the next step: How school-to-
career can help students reach high academic standards and prepare for good jobs.*
Washington, DC: Author.

Astroth, K. A. (1997). Beyond resiliency: Fostering vibrancy in youth groups.
New Designs for Youth Development, 13(4), 4-11.

Astroth, K. A. (2000). Measuring your vibrancy index: A simple self-assessment
tool. *Community Youth Development Journal, 1*(2), 30-35.

Bailey, B. A., & Nihlen, A. S. (1989). Elementary school children's perceptions
of the world of work. *Elementary School Guidance and Counseling, 24,*
135-145.

Barkman, S. J., Machtmes, K., Myers, H., Horton, R. L., & Hutchinson, S. (1999). *Evaluating 4-H curriculum through the design process: Pilot testing and collecting data for the 4-H national jury review process* (4H-898). West Lafayette, IN: Purdue University.

Beale, A. W. (2000). Elementary school career awareness: A visit to a hospital. *Journal of Career Development, 27*(1), 65-72.

Beale, A. W., & Nugent, D. G. (1996). The pizza connection: Enhancing career awareness. *Elementary School Guidance and Counseling, 30,* 294-303.

Berk, L. E. (2000). *Child development* (5th ed.). Boston: Allyn & Bacon.

Bronfenbrenner, U., & Morris, P. A. (1998). The ecology of human developmental processes. In W. Damon (Series Ed.) & R. M. Lerner (Vol. Ed.), *Handbook of child psychology: Vol. 1. Theoretical models of human development* (5th ed., pp. 993-1028). New York: Wiley.

Conrad, D., & Hedin, D. (1987). Learning from service: Experience is the best teacher—or is it? In *Youth service: A guidebook for developing and operating effective programs* (pp. 39-45). Washington, DC: Independent Sector.

Dewey, J. (1938). *Experience and education.* New York: Macmillan.

Drummond, R. J., & Ryan, C. W. (1995). *Career counseling: A developmental approach.* Englewood Cliffs, NJ: Prentice Hall.

El Sawi, G., & Smith, M. F. (1997). Skills and competencies in 4-H curriculum materials. *Journal of Extension, 35*(2). Retrieved September 24, 2002, from www.joe.org/joe/1997april/a1.html

Ferrari, T. M. (1996). *JOBS—Joining Our Businesses and Schools.* Unpublished report, Michigan State University, Department of Family & Child Ecology.

Ferrari, T. M. (1997). *WOW! Wild Over Work: A helper's guide for workforce preparation activities.* Minneapolis: University of Minnesota, 4-H Cooperative Curriculum System. (Ordering information retrieved September 24, 2002, from www.n4hccs.org/shop/products.asp?action=list&cat=4&subcat=13)

Ferrari, T. M. (1998). *Career preparation self-efficacy of elementary-age children: An examination of person, social context, and career preparation learning experience variables.* Unpublished doctoral dissertation, Michigan State University, East Lansing.

Ferrari, T. M. (2000, November). Close encounters with the world of work: Best practices for designing workforce preparation experiences for elementary-age youth. Poster session presented at the annual conference of the National Association of Extension 4-H Agents, Denver, Colorado.

Ferrari, T. M., & Farrell, P. (1998). *Career Coaches (Final Program Narrative).* Unpublished report. East Lansing: Michigan State University, Department of Family & Child Ecology.

Fritz, J. J., Miller-Heyl, J., Kreutzer, J. C., & MacPhee, D. (1995). Fostering personal teaching efficacy through staff development and classroom activities. *Journal of Educational Research, 88*(4), 200-208.

Greene, C. K., & Stitt-Gohdes, W. L. (1997). Factors that influence women's choices to work in the trades. *Journal of Career Development, 23,* 265-278.

Horton, R. L., Hutchinson, S., Barkman, S. J., Machtmes, K., & Myers, H. (1999). *Developing experientially based 4-H curriculum materials* (4-H 897). Columbus: Ohio State University.

Hughes, D. M., & Curnan, S. P. (2000). Community youth development: A framework for action. *Community Youth Development Journal, 1*(1), 7-13.

Hughes, R., Jr. (1994). A framework for developing family life education programs. *Family Relations, 43,* 74-80.

Keith, J. G., Perkins, D. F., Greer, J. C., McKnight Casey, K., & Ferrari, T. M. (1998). The Young Spartan Program: Building a bridge between the ivory tower and the community. In R. M. Lerner & L. A. K. Simon (Eds.), *Creating the new outreach university for America's youth and families: Building university-community collaborations for the twenty-first century* (pp. 289-314). New York: Garland.

Kolb, D. A. (1984). *Experiential learning: Experience as the source of learning and development.* Englewood Cliffs, NJ: Prentice Hall.

Kostelnik, M. J., Soderman, A. K., & Whiren, A. P. (1993). *Developmentally appropriate programs in early childhood education.* New York: Merrill.

Larson, R. W. (2000). Toward a psychology of positive youth development. *American Psychologist, 55,* 170-183.

Levin, H. M. (1994). Educational workplace needs. *Theory into practice, 33*(2), 132-138.

Marzano, R. J., Pickering, D. J., & Pollock, J. E. (2001). *Classroom instruction that works: Research-based strategies for increasing student achievement.* Alexandria, VA: Association for Supervision and Curriculum Development.

McKenna, A. E., & Ferrero, G. W. (1991). Ninth-grade students' attitudes toward nontraditional occupations. *Career Development Quarterly, 40,* 168-181.

Murnane, R. J., & Levy, F. (1996). *Teaching the new basic skills: Principles for educating children to thrive in a changing economy.* New York: Free Press.

National 4-H Council & USDA Extension Service (1993). *Preparing youth for employable futures.* Washington, DC: Author.

National Youth Employment Coalition. (2002). *Promising and effective practices network (PEPNet): Index to effective practices.* Retrieved October 4, 2002, from www.nyec.org/pepnet/practices.htm

Perkins, D. F., & Borden, L. M. (2003). Key elements of community youth development programs. In F. A. Villarruel, D. F. Perkins, L. M. Borden, & J. G. Keith (Eds.), *Community youth development: Programs, policies, and practices.* Thousand Oaks, CA: Sage.

Perkins, D. F., Borden, L. M., Keith, J. G., Hoppe-Rooney, T. L., & Villarruel, F. A. (2003). Community youth development: Partnership creating a positive world. In F. A. Villarruel, D. F. Perkins, L. M. Borden, & J. G. Keith

(Eds.), *Community youth development: Programs, policies, and practices.* Thousand Oaks, CA: Sage.

Phipps, B. J. (1995). Career dreams of preadolescent students. *Journal of Career Development, 22*(1), 19-32.

Pittman, K. J., Cahill, M., & Zeldin, S. (1994). *Youth employment preparation through a youth development lens: Broad recommendations for sustaining change.* Washington, DC: Center for Youth Development and Policy Research.

Pittman, K. J., & Wright, M. (1991). *Bridging the gap: A rationale for enhancing the role of community organizations promoting youth development.* Washington, DC: Center for Youth Development and Policy Research.

Scheer, S. D. (1997). Programming parameters for 5-to-8-year-old children in 4-H. *Journal of Extension, 35*(4). Retrieved September 24, 2002, from www.joe.org/joe/1997august/a2.html

Secretary's Commission on Achieving Necessary Skills. (1991). *What work requires of students.* Washington, DC: U.S. Department of Labor.

U.S. Department of Education. (1996). *Study of school-to-work initiatives: Studies of educational reform.* Retrieved October 4, 2002, from www.ed.gov/pubs/SER/SchoolWork/index.html

U.S. General Accounting Office. (1993, September). *Transition from school to work: States are developing new strategies to prepare students for jobs* (GAO Publication No. HRD-93-139). Washington, DC: Author.

Vondracek, F. W., Lerner, R. M., & Schulenberg, J. E. (1986). *Career development: A life-span developmental approach.* Hillsdale, NJ: Lawrence Erlbaum.

Yohalem, N. (2003). Adults who make a difference: Identifying the skills and characteristics of successful youth workers. In F. A. Villarruel, D. F. Perkins, L. M. Borden, & J. G. Keith (Eds.), *Community youth development: Programs, policies, and practices.* Thousand Oaks, CA: Sage.

Zuckerman, A. (2000). The more things change, the more they stay the same: The evolution and devolution of youth employment programs. In *Youth development: Issues, challenges, directions* (pp. 301-324). Philadelphia: Public/Private Ventures.

11

Workforce and Youth Development for Court-Involved Youth

Barriers and Promising Approaches

David Brown, Edward DeJesus,
Sarah Maxwell, and Vincent Schiraldi

With youth crime and juvenile justice receiving increased attention and study, employment and training programs for delinquent youth have received scrutiny as possible answers to some of the challenges facing the juvenile justice system. In 1997, the U.S. Department of Labor's Employment and Training Administration and

AUTHORS' NOTE: This chapter is a revised version of a portion of the Toolkit (copyright 2002) developed by the Annie E. Casey Foundation, www.aecf.org, called "Barriers and Promising Approaches to Workforce and Youth Development for Young Offenders." Used by permission.

the Department of Justice's Office of Juvenile Justice and Delinquency Prevention (OJJDP) sponsored a Task Force on Employment and Training for Court-Involved Youth. The Task Force was convened by the Home Builders Institute "to explore and examine practices and problems crossing a range of disciplines that could result in developing an effective strategy for improving vocational preparation, reducing youth crime and recidivism and improving the attachment between court-involved youth and the labor market" (Task Force on Employment Training, 2000, p. 1).

In 1999, the Annie E. Casey Foundation asked the National Youth Employment Coalition (NYEC),[1] in cooperation with the Youth Development and Research Fund (YDRF)[2] and the Justice Policy Institute (JPI),[3] to build on the work of the Task Force by developing a report grounded in exemplary programmatic and policy initiatives designed to enable young people involved in the juvenile justice system to become economically self-sufficient. To that end, we undertook a national study to identify workforce development/youth development programmatic and policy initiatives targeting court-involved youth. The study consisted of three parts, which are reflected in this chapter:

1. An identification of barriers to reform and review of the literature pertaining to the nexus of youth employment/development and juvenile justice

2. An examination of 15 exemplary youth employment/development programs explicitly serving juvenile offenders

3. A survey and synthesis of innovative state and local policy initiatives that promote effective programming

This chapter provides a summary of that effort.

❖ HISTORICAL AND STATISTICAL CONTEXT OF THE JUVENILE JUSTICE SYSTEM

From its very inception, the juvenile justice system has struggled to find a happy medium between protection and rehabilitation of young people, on one hand, and the punishment and incapacitation aspects inherent in the sentencing function, on the other. Early reformers built upon the core tenets of separating juveniles from adults, as well as treating juveniles as qualitatively different from adults and therefore more malleable and deserving of rehabilitative efforts. Yet from the first juvenile court, established in Chicago in 1899, there is evidence that such courts were also viewed by some as a means for removing youth from the adult courts, where some felt that youth were the recipients of excessively lenient treatment.

Nonetheless, the juvenile court concept spread like wildfire, and in 25 years, all but two states had created juvenile court systems where none had previously existed. But during the 1950s and 1960s, the tension between the rehabilitative and procedural aspects of the court came into sharp focus. Public confidence in the rehabilitative aspects of the court declined, while concerns over procedural safeguards were heightened. In 1964, when Jerry Gault, a 15-year-old Arizona boy, was given an indeterminate 6-year sentence for making a prank telephone call for which the maximum adult sentence was 60 days, the Supreme Court extended to juveniles basic protections such as the right to notice and counsel, cross-examination of witnesses, and protection against self-incrimination. *In re Gault* (1967) was the most important in a series of decisions that gave juveniles greater constitutional protections and rendered juvenile court more like adult court.

As powerful as these changes were, they have been dwarfed by changes that began in the late 1970s and early 1980s and have come into full power in the 1990s. States around the country began to statutorily exclude certain categories of youth from juvenile court, beginning with New York in the 1970s (Butterfield, 1995), or to give prosecutors primary discretion over whether a youth should be tried in adult or juvenile court, beginning with Florida in the early 1980s (Schiraldi & Ziedenberg, 1999).

This coincided with exponential growth in adult prison populations, and some of the more punitive aspects of the adult system spilled over to the juvenile system. For example, California, often considered a bellwether state for public policy, removed rehabilitation as a goal of its adult correctional system and added punishment as a goal for its juvenile justice system in the late 1970s. Whereas most juvenile codes originally emphasized rehabilitation and prevention, by 1997, the philosophical goals of 32 states included a mixture of punishment and treatment, compared to 9 states that emphasized punishment and 8 states and the District of Columbia that emphasized treatment (Snyder & Sickmund, 1999).

By the 1990s, a full-blown crackdown on juvenile crime, fueled in part by the crack cocaine epidemic and a spike in juvenile homicides, was under way. Between 1992 and 1997, legislatures in 47 states and the District of Columbia enacted laws that made their juvenile justice systems more punitive, facilitating the transfer of youth to adult court (45 states) or removing traditional confidentiality protections (47 states) (Snyder & Sickmund, 1999). A recent Justice Department report revealed that in 1997, 7,100 youth were housed in adult prisons, nearly double the 1984 number. A one-day count revealed that 9,100 juveniles were held in America's adult jails in 1997, up from 1,630 in 1985. An additional 106,000 youth were held in residential placement facilities in 1997, 71 percent of whom were held in locked facilities. Data such as these led Amnesty International, the international human rights organization, to decry what it considered human rights violations in the U.S. juvenile justice system. Fortunately, the response is positive: More recent data indicate that waivers to adult court are on the decline. Although increases in waivers increased dramatically from 1988 to 1993, the current trend is a reversal of this policy. Between 1993 and 1997, for example, a 23 percent and 29 percent decline in waivers to adult court were recorded for person and property crimes committed by youth (Puzzanchera et al., 2000).

Although the transfer of large numbers of youth into the adult system is apparently improving, the deteriorating state of the juvenile justice system itself is of equal, if less well publicized, concern. For example, in his book *No Matter How Loud I Shout*, journalist Ed Humes (1996) wrote,

> In Los Angeles, the judges, prosecutors and defense attorneys can't remember individual kids anymore, or faces or histories. They look at you as if you're insane if you name a juvenile and ask what happened to his or her case. . . . The kids have been reduced to categories. (pp. 325-326)

In a report by R. A. Mendel (2000) entitled "Less Hype, More Help: Reducing Juvenile Crime, What Works—And What Doesn't," the American Youth Policy Form categorized a litany of woes facing the U.S. system of justice for juveniles, that thwart the goals of rehabilitation and are anathema to youth development. These include overwhelmed courts, a glaring imbalance between institutional and community-based resources, underinvestment in community-based services, and counterproductive "net widening"(Mendel, 2000).

As the United States moves into the 21st century, we continue to grapple with our ambivalence about our own invention, the juvenile court—a struggle that clearly impacts policymaking and program design. Despite a 68% decline in juvenile homicides since 1993, nearly two thirds of Americans believe that youth crime is on the increase; and despite the fact that youth are involved in less than 1 in 10 homicides, polls show that the public believes that they are responsible for nearly half of all homicides (Belden, Russonello, & Stewart, 1999).

Conversely, focus group sessions conducted by the Building Blocks for Youth Coalition and polling by the California Wellness Foundation consistently show that the public is not willing to give up on young people. Both groups found that the rehabilitative ethic is still very much alive in the hearts of U.S. citizens when it comes to the treatment of young people who have run afoul of the law.

Absent trust in the juvenile justice system, the public has shown a reluctant willingness to support adult court waivers so that at least "something is done" with youthful offenders. Thus, the juvenile justice system is caught in a quandary—the more poorly it functions, the more the adult system will siphon off youth and resources, and the more starved it is in terms of resources and public confidence, the more poorly it will function.

In sum, as it enters its second hundred years, the juvenile court and juvenile justice system, founded on paternalistic notions of "doing to" rather than "collaborating with" young people, are at best at cross-purposes to (and at worst, directly in conflict with) a youth development approach, a philosophy that fosters caring and youth empowerment. Far from engaging young people in creating thriving communities, the juvenile justice system often hobbles their ability to do so. In a sense, the juvenile justice system, as it currently exists, is the very definition of a deficit-focused approach.

The challenge for youth development and juvenile justice efforts is to meaningfully engage young people in creating programs that have a measurable impact on *both* asset building and risk reduction, to collect and quantify the impact of those programs, and to educate the public on the effectiveness of those efforts. The "Promising Practices" section of this chapter discusses a diverse set of programs that have made great strides toward that end.

❖ RESEARCH ON YOUTH
JUSTICE AND WORKFORCE DEVELOPMENT

The notion of work as a means of preventing delinquency and reforming delinquent youth has been promoted since at least the 1960s (Krisberg & Pearce, 1997). In its more simplistic iteration, it was felt that if young people have a little money in their pockets and are productively occupied in employment activities, they are less likely to commit delinquent acts and more likely to become productive members of society.

The research and experimentation with employment and training programs over the ensuing years suggest a much more complex picture of the relationship between youth employment and delinquency. There is strong evidence in a macro sense from the work of researchers such as Robert Freeman (1995) that there is a connection between poverty, unemployment, and delinquency. Yet it cannot be said that all employment or all jobs programs have a salutary effect on delinquency.

Research by Wofford (1988) and Elliott (1992) found that the duration and intensity of work had negative outcomes on delinquency. Steinberg and Dornbusch (1991) also found evidence that employment in excess of 15 to 20 hours per week during the school year led to diminished school performance and increased alcohol and drug use. Wofford (1988) suggests that youth employment is problematic in that it tends to be repetitive and provides little in the way of skill building. To rephrase Pittman's (2000) assertion that "Problem free is not fully prepared" (para. 6), the research has shown that gainfully employed is not problem free.

Still, there is ample research that connects meaningful employment with better outcomes for delinquent youth. Laub and Sampson (1993) and Elliott (1992) have found that meaningful, gainful employment correlates significantly with youthful offenders maturing out of delinquent behavior as they age into young adulthood, effectively wiping out differences in the rates at which whites and blacks commit violent behavior as young adults. Perhaps this is why, as black youth disproportionately benefited from economic upturns in the 1990s, the decline in arrest rates for African American youth outstripped the decline in arrest rates for white youth (Elliott, 1992).

Troy Duster also considers the disproportionate number of black youth who are both unemployed and involved in the criminal justice system to be no accident. The shift in the workforce from manufacturing jobs traditionally located in inner cities populated by blacks, to service sector jobs increasingly located in suburbs populated by whites, has led to a potentially permanent "underclass" (Duster, 1987).

It is clear that well thought out and implemented programs that help youth attain economic self-sufficiency can have a positive effect on delinquency and a number of other measures, such as earnings. One of the nation's largest federally funded employment programs, Job Corps, has been found not only to work, but work well (Mallar, Kerachsky, Thornton, & Long, 1982). Within six months of program completion, Job Corps graduates were five times as likely to have earned a high school diploma or GED than a comparison group (Mallar et al., 1982). They also experienced reduced criminality, improved health, and better employment and earning outcomes. Both the 70001, Inc. (now WAVE Inc.) program and the Youth Incentive Entitlement Pilot Projects showed increased earnings and employment for participants versus their comparison groups, although those impacts diminished over time (Corporation for Public/Private Ventures, 1983).

In addition to findings that well-designed, comprehensive, and well-implemented workforce development programs can help find youth meaningful employment and reduce delinquency, research has also shown that incarceration can worsen job prospects (Laub & Sampson, 1993). According to Freeman, it is incarcerations, not just arrests, that are associated with poorer employment prospects in adults (Freeman, 1995).

The research shows the following:

- Economic self-sufficiency is key to a youth's ability to mature out of delinquency.
- Not just any job or any job program will help delinquent youth attain economic self-sufficiency and eschew a delinquent lifestyle.
- A comprehensive approach to employment, youth development, and rehabilitation shows the most promise.
- The increased use of incarceration correlates with reduced career prospects, which in turn correlates with increased criminality.

The Practitioner's View

The practitioners we interviewed echoed much of what was found in the research. Youth justice experts were interviewed individually and in a focus group about the challenges faced by the system in helping youth attain economic self-sufficiency. We organized their responses into five categories: the need to make workforce development a higher priority; the stigma attached to delinquent youth; geographical obstacles; shifting, sometimes inconsistent juvenile justice philosophies; and the need for creativity.

The Need to Make Workforce Development Issues a Higher Priority. As our nation's juvenile justice system has focused more on institutionalization through locked care and has shifted from a rehabilitative to a more punitive focus, programs of all kinds have suffered.

The Stigma Attached to Delinquent Youth. Many practitioners indicated that the stigma of juvenile justice system involvement posed significant challenges for workforce development. As societal attitudes have shifted from rehabilitation to punishment and as community attitudes have hardened against youthful offenders, youth corrections practitioners have found that acceptance of youth employment and training programs has suffered.

Geographical Obstacles. Many administrators reported that the training schools and residential programs they operated were located a prohibitive distance from many of the juveniles' home neighborhoods. Furthermore, the increased attention paid to security in the modern era of juvenile corrections is such that youth are less able to transition to their home communities through furloughs, halfway houses, or independent living settings.

Shifting, Sometimes Inconsistent, Juvenile Justice Philosophies. In this era of shifting youth corrections mandates, current policies that guide youth justice are clearly not helping to create viable, long-term access to meaningful employment. Punitive mandates can require that youthful offenders simply "do time" or participate in community service efforts designed more to enact retribution than to enhance career development.

The Need for Creativity. Despite the challenges presented by these obstacles, the youth corrections administrators evidenced a commitment to the rehabilitative ethic and viewed employment and training efforts as a key element toward that end. Some emphasized the importance of entrepreneurial efforts to teach young people job skills and job creation creativity, giving examples of enterprises operating out of their training schools in cooperation with local business people.

Summary

In summary, then, preparing youth for economic self-sufficiency, like youth development overall, cannot be viewed in isolation from other strengths and needs youth possess. Temporary employment programs, devoid of other services, do little to reduce delinquency. To maximize the potential for employment and training programs to realize their delinquency-reduction potential, numerous barriers inherent to the juvenile justice system need to be creatively overcome. For such programs and policies to maximize their potential, balance must be restored to the decades-old debate between punishment and rehabilitation, which has swung dangerously in the direction of punishment.

❖ PROMISING AND EXEMPLARY PRACTICES

As the previous section suggests, few systematic efforts have been undertaken to identify the key elements of programs that effectively prepare court-involved youth for economic self-sufficiency. Public and private institutions have usually focused on preventive and crisis intervention measures designed to mitigate the societal costs of juvenile crime and delinquency, rather than exploring how to more effectively habilitate, rehabilitate, and reintegrate these young offenders so they can become productive members of society. Most juvenile justice entities are primarily concerned with public safety and security. Although most juvenile justice administrators understand the importance of promoting economic self-sufficiency, this goal is often overshadowed by the bottom-line need to provide mandated services, maintain institutional order, and address overcrowding.

In contrast to many programs in the juvenile justice system, youth development programs are guided by comprehensive sets of operating principles that view young adults and their needs in holistic terms. Many workforce development programs are restructuring to more effectively equip youth with the necessary academic, vocational, and work readiness skills, as well as the life skills and developmental opportunities that will enable their successful transition to adulthood and careers. These programs are increasingly reflecting the consensus emerging from both research and practice, that preparing youth for careers and adult roles requires more than the narrow range of training-related services commonly provided by youth employment and training programs. This new wave of youth employment development programs is grounded in an assets-based approach that stresses young people's strengths and works to empower youth, instead of focusing on their perceived deficits. Some of the key program elements that reflect the core principles of youth development include mentoring, community service, leadership development, positive peer-centered activities, and long-term follow-up and supports.

Through the course of this project, we examined 15 exemplary youth programs that serve juvenile offenders, to establish a set of common practices that effective youth programs employ. And although the following section outlines the results of our endeavors, perhaps the more encompassing finding is that, at least in these case examples, the fields of youth development and juvenile justice have each accommodated the other's goals, creating opportunities for youth to thrive in the process. As a result, these programs not only accomplish the goals of juvenile justice—a minimal re-arrest and reincarceration rate—but they prepare youth offenders for economic self-sufficiency and provide youth with the skills and resources necessary to achieve long-term success. These programs demonstrate that youth development principles can be applied to the field of juvenile justice, because such principles further the bottom-line outcomes that practitioners, administrators, and policymakers in both fields are responsible for producing.

❖ EFFECTIVE YOUTH PROGRAMS: COMMONALITIES

There have been few systematic efforts to identify the key elements of programs that prepare court-involved youth for economic self-sufficiency. In contrast to many programs offered within the juvenile justice system, the programs highlighted below are guided by a comprehensive set of principles that view young adults and their needs holistically.

Commitment to Rehabilitation

It may seem obvious that successful youth offender programs are committed to the development and achievement of young adults. The reality is that many youth-serving organizations neither exhibit a clear sense of purpose nor possess a firm dedication to a stated mission. In contrast, the youth-serving organizations examined see themselves as rehabilitation projects rather than disciplinary programs (despite the difficult population they serve), resources rather than crutches, and organizations intent on empowering youth offenders rather than taking control and running their lives.

For example, the Texas Youth Commission's Project RIO-Y has a stated mission to "provide incarcerated youth with post-release career and training opportunities and with youth development skills necessary for them to find and maintain employment as productive members of society" (Re-Integration of Offenders Youth Project, n.d., para. 1). Its staff follow through on this mission through a resocialization program that goes beyond discipline to encompass education, work training, and therapeutic measures. The mission of the Career Exploration Project (New York) is to "help young offenders gain the self-confidence they need to exit the justice system as responsible, productive members of their communities" (Career Exploration Project, n.d., para. 1). The Omega Boys Club structures all its programming around one powerfully simple idea: that young adults should be free. Such mission statements help organizations to stay focused on their outcomes and drive a set of appropriate actions that will help them fulfill their goals.

Continuum of Care

Service providers that demonstrate successful outcomes for youth offenders provide a continuum of services. This continuum should include preventive care, assessment, and interventions that meet the various needs of different youth populations, but the most fundamental aspect of this continuum is the emphasis on postprogram support and services that help youth achieve their long-term goals.

All of the reviewed programs have a host of postprogram supports and services that extend for an average of 1 year after graduation and are designed to help youth offenders reintegrate themselves into society. For instance, the Dayton, Ohio, YouthBuild program helps its graduates transfer their credits to a 2-year college, apply to a 4-year college, or find viable employment opportunities that provide skills and career development. Additionally, alumni continue to receive counseling and can draw upon YouthBuild's various educational and vocational resources. The Gulf Coast Trade Center in New Waverly, Texas, provides emergency shelters to facilitate independent living. Fresh Start (Baltimore) has established a workforce development center manned by transition specialists who provide support and follow-up for 3 years, and the Omega Boys' Club in San Francisco provides more than $250,000 per year in scholarships to support the college education of its most motivated participants.

Integrated Education

Education is the gateway to economic self-sufficiency. Although traditional job programs have predominantly trained and prepared youth for the workforce in isolation, a wraparound service model necessitates a holistic educational curriculum that acts as a bridge between the anti-achievement culture and learning deficits of youth offenders and the skills, behaviors, and attitudes necessary to succeed in the workplace.

At the same time, the school-to-work movement in both public and alternative educational systems has demonstrated that preparing any young person for economic self-sufficiency requires that they be equipped not only with academic credentials but also with the hard skills (field-specific expertise), soft skills (pre-employment skills and appropriate workplace beliefs and behaviors), and the work-based experience necessary to succeed on the job.

Fresh Start educates youth through a chair production business that simulates a real-world working environment; YouthBuild participants learn appropriate workplace behaviors, construct houses for low-income residents, and get certified in construction trades. And the Gulf Coast Trade Center instructs young people in soft skills and provides a multitude of vocational training and work experience options, including auto maintenance and culinary arts.

Another important element of the workplace preparation components of the reviewed programs are their deliberate efforts to connect vocational training with the demands of an ever-changing economy and to collaborate with employers in designing and shaping the curriculum to ensure this type of responsiveness. As a result, Corrections Clearinghouse (Olympia, Washington) connects youth offenders with computer training and repair workshops, the Avon Park (Florida) Youth Academy and the Tampa Marine Institute educate youth in the use and application of various computer software, and Dayton

YouthBuild contracts with local technology firms to provide youth with training and employment opportunities.

Finally, the reviewed programs recognize that workforce development is an important medium for connecting youth with positive adult role models. Many of these programs (such as the Career Exploration Project, which trains youth in workforce readiness and then provides internships with small minority business owners who act as mentors) connect youth with caring adults who can supervise, support, and guide a young person's career and life path. In this way, youth are imbued with the skills they need to climb the workforce ladder and have the confidence and the references to take those first key steps.

Collaboration

Youth offender programs that achieve on a high level not only offer a wide range of services but also recognize that they cannot offer, and are not experts in, all aspects of youth development. As a result, effective youth programs collaborate and form connections with other agencies to strengthen their outcomes and enable them to refer youth offenders to agencies and programs better suited to attend to their other needs. The key here is that youth programs do not allow participants to fail simply because the organization's resources or expertise may not be adequate to meet their needs.

One-stop service is demonstrated most clearly through the Community Assessment and Referral Center in San Francisco (implemented by the Delancey Street Foundation). This program is a point of collaboration for all city agencies working with juvenile offenders. It enables service providers, in conjunction with a participant's family, to develop an individualized and comprehensive care plan that addresses the offender's current problems and educational and vocational goals.

Another vital, more specific form of collaboration is the development of formal connections with employers. Programs such as Corrections Clearinghouse, Project RIO-Y and YouthBuild contract with job placement agencies to help youth put their education to practice and find viable employment opportunities.

Support Structures

Effective youth service providers, regardless of their mission, connect youth offenders with a support network that is consistent, compassionate, and challenging in its efforts to motivate and counsel young adults toward success. The absence of connection with caring adults apparent in the life of many youthful offenders can lead to emotional problems such as depression and poor anger management skills, which can emerge as roadblocks to their positive development. Mentoring and counseling programs can offer youth the one-on-one attention they crave and can be the most powerful mechanisms for reinforcing a program's educational philosophy.

The Ferris School for Boys (Wilmington, Delaware) helps adjudicated juvenile delinquents overcome their problems primarily through the HOSTS (Help One Student To Succeed) mentoring program. HOSTS mentors are trained in nationally standardized curricula that encompass academic, social, and life skills training. They meet with students at least 1 hour per week for a commitment of no less than 6 weeks.

A similar program that heavily uses support structures is T-CAP North (Fort Worth, Texas). T-CAP (Tarrant County Advocate Program) North pairs each participant with a paid advocate from the community who coordinates the implementation of an individualized treatment plan, establishes links between family and community resources, and acts as a mentor for a participant and his or her family.

Accountability

Youth offender programs that strive to serve their participants in the most effective way possible constantly challenge their own success and search for new ways to improve. Quality youth service organizations recognize the extraordinary needs of youth in this country and are committed to holding themselves accountable.

One key aspect of this accountability is setting high standards for youth offenders. Effective youth programs make a specific effort to disengage youth from a self-defeating philosophy by setting high expectations for them and high standards for their achievement. For instance, Fresh Start requires students to attend the program on time, without fail, every day for the first 2 weeks, or they are discharged from the program. Additionally, as already mentioned, students are given full responsibility for the daily affairs of the Fresh Start construction businesses (including a different student foreman each day) and are challenged with daily assignments regardless of skill level. In this way, students put pressure on themselves and each other to achieve on a high level and, through the profits they receive from the business, can directly see the returns on their efforts. By setting these high standards, Fresh Start allows youth to fail; but rather than expecting failure, Fresh Start expects its students to achieve. Most often, these expectations transform into reality.

Outcome Measurement

Programs that successfully serve juvenile offenders recognize the value of measuring clear and consistent outcomes of performance. Indeed, all of the reviewed programs are exemplary not simply because their practices are ideologically sound, but also because they have developed case management systems to track their program participants and to produce tangible, measurable outcomes of success.

As mentioned earlier, the average juvenile justice institution has a recidivism rate between 50% and 70%. The Tampa Marine Institute, Gulf Coast Trade Center, Fresh Start, and Friends of Island Academy (New York) all have recidivism rates below 20%. In addition, for youth that participate in Crispus Attucks YouthBuild (York, Pennsylvania), only a 5% recidivism rate was reported for 74 participants previously involved with the juvenile justice system, and three fourths of all participants are employed after graduation. Almost 90% of participants in Dayton YouthBuild are employed or in school after graduation. Avon Park Youth Academy has a 78% successful program completion rate; 40% of its participants earned GEDs or high school diplomas. Seventy-eight percent of Avon Park's participants receive vocational certification, and 81% are still employed after 6 months. Eighty percent of Project RIO-Y graduates are engaged in a "constructive activity," defined as part-time employment or attending school or vocational training. All Career Exploration Project (CExP) graduates continue to pursue educational goals, and two thirds of them eventually proceed to other internships or jobs; half of these young adults continue to work 6 months after completion of the program.

It seems clear, then, that the reviewed youth programs, by focusing on youth development principles, are extremely successful in providing for both juvenile justice as well as youth development goals and outcomes. In this way, anyone who wants to be tough on crime should consider these programs not only as mechanisms for reintegrating juvenile offenders into society but also as diversionary programs that can act as a substitute for institutionalizing, and forever stigmatizing, young adults.

❖ POLICY INITIATIVES

The programs in the previous section represent efforts of entrepreneurial, committed, creative, and determined individuals to craft and implement innovative and effective programs, sometimes despite public policy. All too often, these innovators assert, public policy is a major barrier to effective programs rather than an enabler of good programming. If we are to move beyond "islands of excellence in seas of mediocrity" (Zuckerman, 1998), public policy must acknowledge, advance, sustain, and build environments that promote effective practice.

Promising approaches sometimes evolve in part from policy strategies that, even in the broadest sense, provide the flexibility of workforce and juvenile justice systems. This section is a look at those policies, providing descriptive accounts of the processes that allowed the systems to contribute to enabling the development of economically self-sufficient youth.

The examples follow in four sections that detail the key areas in which policymakers felt they made the most progress. They are (1) funding, support, and replication, with a special section devoted to the Workforce Investment Act; (2) system collaboration, either between systems or between systems and the private sector; (3) system flexibility that promotes youth development; and (4) other innovative approaches.

Promising Funding Allocations and Resource Development

Anyone interested in starting a new initiative or affecting public policies must contend with the perennial problem of funding. A number of systems and agencies are developing creative partnerships and avenues to tap into funding streams that have not traditionally supported juvenile justice programming.

In 1997, the California Legislature enacted legislation that authorized county juvenile probation departments to receive Temporary Assistance for Needy Families (TANF, or welfare funds) to be utilized in a flexible manner to serve the needs of youth on probation. Recognizing that delinquent youth were at risk of becoming welfare recipients, Assembly Bill 1542 block-granted funds to counties promoting the innovative creation of youth development programs, as well as intervention programs for delinquent youth.

On the federal level, Congress enacted the Workforce Investment Act (WIA) in 1998, which promotes a new approach to youth employment and training informed by the latest research. The act also combines the 35-year old Summer Youth Employment and Training Program and the Job Training Partnership Act's year-round youth employment and training program and replaces Private Industry Councils with Workforce Investment Boards. The youth provisions of WIA reflect much of what has been learned in recent years about how to prepare young people for adulthood. Implementation of the WIA, therefore, provides an opportunity for states and communities to begin to combine traditional youth employment and training services with activities grounded in the principles of youth development, such as mentoring, community service, leadership development, positive peer-centered activities, and long-term follow-up and supports. Furthermore, to promote a new vision of youth programming, the law requires each local workforce investment board to establish a youth council to provide expert advice on the selection and oversight of youth programs.

System Collaboration

Once the policy or initiative is launched, the next step is efficacious implementation. The simple problem of systems not connecting or not understanding each other is a major reason for the lack of collaboration between the juvenile justice and workforce development systems. Therefore, an effort was made to locate systems that were successfully pursuing a shared vision, to find out how the systems converged to provide services to court-involved youth.

Many state governments provide a range of resources and services that can be accessed by juvenile offenders if the opportunities are identified and mutually beneficial interagency agreements can be hammered out. Just Work is a cooperative agreement between the Nebraska Vocational Rehabilitation Department and Health and Human Services, Office of Juvenile Services. Initiated in 1998, the collaboration serves Omaha area youth, ages 14 to 19, who are involved in the juvenile justice system through experiential employment training. The youth are low-to-moderate risk and represent those who tend to fall through the cracks, that is, youth who find themselves in a commitment facility when community placements may be more appropriate.

Prior to this initiative, the Vocational Rehabilitation Department had not worked with court-involved youth; its focus had traditionally been on serving adults with disabilities. To promote communication and cooperation, staff members of the two agencies were assigned to the same location. This initiative benefits hard-to-serve youth who might otherwise have been passed over for employment due to their disabilities. In the process, the two agencies had to learn the terminologies of each other's systems so that each would understand the eligibility requirements of the program.

In many states, workforce development and juvenile corrections agencies are barely aware of each other's existence and rarely work together. However, in 1995, Texas launched a unique program involving a collaboration between the state's juvenile correctional agency, the Texas Youth Commission (TYC), and its consolidated workforce development agency, the Texas Workforce Commission (TWC). The goal of Project RIO-Y is to prepare adjudicated youth committed to the state's custody to enter the workforce and/or to access educational/training opportunities that will ultimately lead to meaningful employment. Project RIO-Y reintegrates TYC youth into the community by linking TYC's resocialization, educational, training, and specialized treatment services while they are incarcerated to TWC's job placement and training programs in the community upon their release on parole or to a transitional placement facility.

For years, juvenile justice professionals have been critical of the Job Corps policy that discouraged court-involved youth from entering Job Corps programs. Most youth workers recognize that Job Corps youth and juvenile justice youth face similar challenges and backgrounds. In 1997, the New York Office of Children and Family Services (formerly the Division for Youth) and the U.S. Department of Labor, New York Office of Job Corps, signed a formal agreement detailing the conditions under which a youth being released from the juvenile justice system could enter Job Corps. By agreeing to certain conditions under which these youth might be successful in Job Corps, the two agencies were able to formalize a policy that in many eyes was long overdue.

Effectively addressing juvenile crime at the community level requires a comprehensive strategy that engages the full range of key stakeholders. Such strategies focus not only on primary prevention but also target youth who have already penetrated the juvenile justice system and are living in the community. The Comprehensive Strategy for Youth, Family and Community, in San Diego, is predicated upon a philosophy of shared responsibility and coordinated action to prevent juvenile delinquency and promote positive development of youth. Through intense assessments and data collection, these stakeholders were able to build an impressive partnership to address a variety of community needs, including data-driven efforts to address the workforce development needs of court-involved youth.

In today's tight labor market, many employers are seeking nontraditional sources to find workers. If they are assured that the potential employees are prepared and screened, they are increasingly open to hire individuals, such as welfare recipients and offenders, whom they would not have considered in the past.

However, linking business and government has always proven an arduous challenge. Business leaders do not conform well to task forces and meetings with social service workers. They are task oriented and require projects that can be accomplished effectively and efficiently. However, in one case, it was the business leaders, in the form of the Florida Business Partners for Prevention, who initiated the project. The business leaders formed a "policy community" and approached the Florida Department of Juvenile Justice (DJJ) with an idea to ameliorate crime in the state. DJJ immediately rejected the status quo, enabling the agency to adapt to a business, rather than bureaucratic, culture. Florida Business Partners works to create, sponsor, promote, and support programs and services targeted at youth identified as being at risk of entering the juvenile justice system.

System Flexibility and Reform

Systemic change is also the result of deliberate courses of action. In juvenile justice, these policies usually fall under the guise of regulatory policies, or those that attempt to alter or control the behavior of individuals or groups. Recently, a number of policies have been initiated that step outside the usual criminal justice codes (such as incarceration) and focus instead on programmatic or systemwide changes that support positive workforce approaches for youth. Ultimately, these reform efforts have the same goal as any other juvenile justice policy: to reduce recidivism. Yet these initiatives surface as new and effective ways to accomplish that goal.

Youth development initiatives build upon a range of competencies that complement the youth's connection to his or her community. Many policy initiatives are geared toward vocational training or employment, but the ones that build human and social capital are highlighted as youth development initiatives. Unlike systemic reform initiatives, youth development projects can be implemented without any type of formal policy. In fact, youth development projects serve numerous youth, not just those involved in the juvenile court system. Youth development encompasses a philosophy that spills over into numerous systems that serve youth, no matter what the ultimate goal is of each.

The Iowa Division of Criminal and Juvenile Justice Planning (CJJP) is spearheading a statewide initiative to focus on the broad goal of developing assets for youth. When a group of service providers heard that federal funding was available from the Family and Youth Services Bureau (FYSB) at the U.S. Department of Health and Human Services, they decided to eliminate the fragmentation status quo that had ruled the individual systems. More than 30 partners convened, all with different individual goals, to form one goal: youth development.

When broadscale collaborations are the goal, the challenge is ultimately to contend with multiple partners and agencies and the corresponding competing interests. Iowa's Youth Development initiative is still in the planning stages, but partners are making rapid progress in shaping a shared vision. Those from the workforce development system are learning juvenile justice terminology in Iowa, and the juvenile service providers are acquiring knowledge of the workforce development system. A common language that specifies the vision and goals is proving advantageous to the group's progress.

Other New and Innovative Approaches

The development and adoption of new approaches to combating crime and promoting self-sufficiency can originate at any point and from anyone. In fact, innovative approaches to enhancing economic opportunities for youth in the juvenile justice system are more likely to be the result of individuals with a vision, such as policy entrepreneurs, or the result of a perceived need.

For example, the Florida Juvenile Justice Accountability Board (JJAB) was created to measure, evaluate, and report on outcomes of youth referred to the Department of Juvenile Justice, and to assess the degree to which juvenile justice practices support the policies laid out by the Legislature. JJAB recently released a study of vocational programs for delinquent youth, which includes an analysis of effective programs nationwide and research on what makes programs effective.

Although there are some national workforce trends, most labor markets are regional and local, making it necessary for the juvenile justice and workforce development systems to work together to provide the information each requires. The State of North Carolina has launched a system to ensure that skills training is responsive to the local labor market. The Office of Juvenile Justice and its training schools across the state partnered with ExploreNet, a Raleigh-based nonprofit organization, to provide students the opportunity to learn computer skills and turn their lives around. Students learn marketable skills by building computers that are installed and wired in the training schools.

Similar to that of North Carolina, but operating on a larger and more involved scale, is a broad-based initiative in Oregon that allows the juvenile justice system to receive updated labor market information for vocational planning purposes. The University of Oregon and Oregon's workforce development system use labor market predictions to guide program development for youth in the juvenile justice system. This process assists transition specialists who work with the Department of Vocational Rehabilitation to develop appropriate job-training programs and to locate employment for youth leaving the justice system.

❖ CONCLUSION

Despite (or perhaps because of) massive changes in the juvenile justice system over the past decade, the system too often failed to alter the trajectories of troubled youth or to prepare them to assume productive adult roles. The combination of confinement, supervision, surveillance, and treatment commonly provided to youth in the system has not achieved the desired results. Nevertheless, many states continue to increase spending on juvenile corrections, with little result.

This chapter suggests that state and local policymakers and the juvenile justice system promote initiatives that combine the principles of youth development and workforce development. The traditional approaches to academic and vocational education, anchored in the industrial age, need to be abandoned. The juvenile justice system needs to more broadly adapt practices and policies that reflect what has been learned from the youth development and workforce development fields. The young people who find themselves tangled in the juvenile justice system must be given the same opportunities to establish nurturing relationships with adults; be buoyed by positive peer support; assume leadership roles; contribute to the well-being of their communities; and develop the same academic, vocational, and work readiness skills and competencies as youth who have not been similarly disadvantaged. In addition, the many public systems charged with serving their needs must partner with business and community-based organizations to more effectively collaborate and share their resources and expertise to realize their shared and unique goals. As a nation, we cannot continue to cast off such large segments of our youth population and thereby commit them to the margins of our society.

❖ NOTES

1.   NYEC is a 21-year-old member organization representing over 170 youth employment/development organizations. It is dedicated to promoting policies and programs that help youth succeed in becoming lifelong learners, productive workers, and self-sufficient citizens. David Brown is Executive Director of NYEC, and Sarah Maxwell serves as a consultant for NYEC. (For more information on NYEC, visit its website at www.nyec.org.)

2.   YDRF was formed by a multicultural group of young professionals (TEAMYOUTH) with expertise in youth programming, research, and policy in response to the need to reclaim the lost economic fortunes of at-risk young adults. The YDRF mission is to improve programs, policies, and opportunities for youth through research, training, and culture. YDRF takes its programs and strategies to juvenile justice systems, schools, community-based organizations, foundations, corporations, and government agencies to help maximize successful outcomes for youth and youth service providers. Edward DeJesus is President and Founder of YDRF. (For more information on YDRF, visit www.teamyouth.com.)

3.   JPI is a policy development and research body that promotes effective and sensible approaches to the U.S. justice system. It conducts research, proffers model legislation, and takes an active role in promoting a rational criminal justice discourse in the electronic and print media. Vincent Schiraldi is Founder and President of JPI and former President of the Center on Juvenile and Criminal Justice (CJCJ). (See www.justicepolicy.org for more information about JPI.)

❖ REFERENCES

Belden, N., Russonello, J., & Stewart, K. (1999). *Americans consider juvenile crime, justice, and race: Executive summary.* Unpublished report commissioned by Building Blocks for Youth, Washington, DC.

Butterfield, F. (1995). *All God's children: The Bosket family and the American tradition of violence.* New York: Alfred Knopf.

Career Exploration Project. (n.d.). Mission. Retrieved September 28, 2002, from www.nyec.org/pepnet/awardees/cexp.htm

Corporation for Public/Private Ventures. (1983). *Longer-term impacts of pre-employment services on the employment and earnings of disadvantaged youth.* Philadelphia: Author.

Duster, T. (1987). Crime, youth unemployment, and the black urban underclass. *Crime and Delinquency, 33*(2), 300-316.

Elliott, D. S. (1992). Longitudinal research in criminology: Promise and practice. In E. G. Weitekamp and K. Hans-Jurgen (Eds.), *Cross-national longitudinal research on human development and criminal behavior.* London: Kluwer.

Freeman, R. B. (1995). The labor market. In J. Q. Wilson & J. Petersilia (Eds.), *Crime* (pp. 171-191), San Francisco: ICS Press.

Humes, E. (1996). *No matter how loud I shout: A year in the life of juvenile court.* New York: Touchstone.

In re Gault, 387 U.S. 1 (1967).

Krisberg, B., & Pearce, G. (1997). *Employment-based youth violence prevention: A review of the literature.* San Francisco: National Council on Crime and Delinquency.

Laub, J. H., & Sampson, R. J. (1993). *The long-term effect of punitive discipline.* Revised version of paper presented at the Life History Research Society Meeting, May 6, 1992.

Mallar, C. S., Kerachsky, C., Thornton, C., & Long, D. (1982). *Evaluation of the economic impact of the Job Corps Program* (3rd follow-up report). Princeton, NJ: Mathematica Policy Research.

Mendel, R. A. (2000). *Less hype, more help: Reducing juvenile crime, what works—and what doesn't.* Washington, DC: American Youth Policy Forum.

Pittman, K. (2000, Winter). Balancing the equation: Communities supporting youth, youth supporting communities. *Community Youth Development, 1*(1). Retrieved September 28, 2002, from www.cydjournal.org/2000Winter/pittman.html

Puzzanchera, C., Stahl, A. L., Finnegan, T., Snyder, H., Poole, R., & Tierney, N. (2000, May). *Juvenile court statistics 1999.* Washington, DC: Office of Juvenile Justice and Delinquency Prevention.

Re-Integration of Offenders Youth Project. (n.d.). Retrieved September 28, 2002, from www.nyec.org/pepnet/awardees/rioy.htm

Schiraldi, V., and Ziedenberg, J. (1999). *The Florida experiment*. Washington, DC: Justice Policy Institute.

Snyder, H. N., & Sickmund, M. (1999). *Juvenile offenders and victims: 1999 national report*. Washington, DC: Office of Juvenile Justice and Delinquency Prevention.

Steinberg, L., & Dornbusch, S. (1991). Negative correlates of part-time work during adolescence: Replication and elaboration. *Developmental Psychology, 27*(2), 304-313.

Task Force on Employment Training for Court-Involved Youth. (2000). *Employment training for court-involved youth*. Washington, DC: Office of Juvenile Justice and Delinquency Prevention. Retrieved September 28, 2002, from www.ncjrs.org/pdffiles1/ojjdp/182787.pdf.

Wofford, S. (1988). *A preliminary analysis of the relationship between employment and delinquency/crime for adolescents and young adults*. (National Youth Survey Report No. 50.) Boulder, CO: Institute of Behavioral Science.

Zuckerman, A. (1998). *The more things change, the more they stay the same: The evolution and devolution of youth employment programs*. Washington, DC: National Youth Employment Coalition.

12

The Character of Moral Communities

A Community Youth Development Approach to Enhancing Character Development

Karen L. Pace

Moral development is quite possibly the area of youth development that has been explored for the longest period of time. Philosophers, ethicists, and religious leaders have grappled with various aspects of values and ethics for thousands of years, and people have been concerned about the perceived decline in the moral development of children for a very long time. Contemporary literature on moral development and character education spans several decades and includes rich discussion, debate, and controversy among psychologists, educators, politicians, and child development experts (Damon, 1995; Damon & Colby, 1996; Gilligan, 1993; Goble & Brooks, 1983; Hartshorne & May, 1928, 1929, 1930; Kilpatrick, 1992; Kohn, 1997; Lickona 1993; Nucci, 1989; Vessels, 1998; Walberg & Wynne, 1989). Central to this debate are issues related to whose responsibility it is to teach children about values, which values ought to be taught, and what methods and approaches ought to be employed in helping young people learn about and internalize ethical values. This debate remained largely unresolved through most of the 20th century, and consequently, character and values-based education fell in and out of favor with many educators and youth development professionals.

The 1990s brought about a resurgence of interest in character education across the country. This renewed focus was fueled largely by concerns of parents, educators, youth development professionals, politicians, community members, and scholars about negative and risky behaviors of children and adolescents. Surveys indicated that adults believe children and youth were not learning and internalizing essential moral values that would assist in their development toward becoming respectful, compassionate, and honorable adults (Public Agenda Report, 1999). Many believe that today's young people are more likely than youth of past generations to act cruelly toward others, disregard authority and rules, use crude language, and bully peers who are different from themselves (Garbarino, 1995; Hersch, 1998). Scholars and observers of youth culture are concerned about high levels of aggression and violent behaviors, nastiness, an ethic of cheating to get ahead, and a frightening lack of conscience when it comes to incidences of lying, cheating, and stealing (Bronfenbrenner, McClelland, Wethington, Moen, & Ceci, 1996; Damon, 1995; Garbarino, 1995; Hersch, 1998, Josephson Institute of Ethics, 2000).

Although it is understandable that adults are concerned about these and other behaviors, for too many the tendency has been to blame young people for the lack of ethical values and moral direction in their lives. This focus on bad behaviors and lack of morals has contributed to the creation of character education programs that focus heavily on fix-the-kids approaches, including methods of inculcation, unquestioning deference to authority, and obedience (Kohn, 1997). It is important to note that the so-called teenage problems that many people are concerned about actually mirror adult behaviors around them and in society as a whole (Males, 1999). Adult attitudes and behaviors create a tone and set standards for communities. More important, the quality and nature of the environments in which children are developing and learning contribute significantly to their ability to understand, internalize, and apply ethical values to the context of their lives. Efforts that knowingly or unwittingly blame, demonize, and punish youth for being part of communities that are morally ambivalent at best and morally toxic at worst add to the moral chaos and confusion in the lives of too many children.

In addition to the emphasis on competencies and skill development, youth professionals and educators are charged with sorting through the debate surrounding character education efforts to implement and strengthen programs that can have a positive influence on the social, emotional, and moral development of children. A good place to begin is with research on asset-based positive youth development, which emphasizes the importance of nurturing internal qualities such as positive values and social competencies and strengthening external support systems such as caring neighborhoods and school environments (Benson, 1997). In addition, a community youth development framework provides a powerful lens through which to view the relationships, opportunities, skills, and sense of purpose that all young people need to increase their chances of growing into physically, emotionally, and morally healthy individuals (Hughes & Curnan, 2000).

This chapter will discuss salient aspects of moral development theory, explain effective character education, and suggest promising practices that can assist in creating strategies and programs that support a community youth development approach to enhancing character development. Last, a discussion of the role of researchers, program evaluators, and policymakers will be presented.

❖ DEFINITION OF TERMS

Much of the confusion and controversy surrounding the areas of moral development and character education have to do with how the constructs are defined and understood. To set the stage for further discussion, several important terms are presented as they are described in the literature on moral development and character education.

Morals. Unlike manners or mores, morals are a system of beliefs and conduct based on accepted principles of what is considered right, virtuous, or just (Rich & DeVitis, 1994).

Values. Values are deep personal beliefs and commitments that ultimately guide how a person tends to behave. Ethical, prosocial, and positive values refer to principles that reflect widely shared beliefs that, when put into action, benefit individuals and the larger society (Scales & Leffert, 1999).

Ethics. Rooted in a philosophical approach, *ethics* refers to the nature of morality and how one ought to be and act to live a moral life (Rich & DeVitis, 1994).

Character. Character is defined in three parts—moral knowing, moral feeling, and moral behavior. Good character consists of knowing the good, loving the good, and doing the good (Lickona, 1991). Character is that within a person which governs moral choices (Pipher, 1996).

Moral development. Moral development is a lifelong process that begins at birth. This complex process of establishing a system of ethical values and actions involves cognitive and affective development and is highly influenced by everyday social interactions with peers and adults (Damon, 1988).

Character education. Character education is a term that is used to describe a wide variety of purposeful, direct, planned approaches to helping children learn about positive, ethical, and prosocial values. For some, it is a narrow construct that refers to the indoctrination and transmission of traditional values that often are rooted in a traditional-ist conservative agenda (Kohn, 1997). Character and moral education, to most contemporary scholars, refers to the mobilization of many community institutions to endorse and promote shared ethical values that are essential building blocks of a true and just democracy. These shared values consist of concepts such as trustworthiness, respect, responsibility, fairness, caring, and citizenship, and are presented and modeled in ways that come alive in the hearts, minds, and relation-ships between children, youth, and adults (Garbarino, 1999).

❖ A HISTORICAL PERSPECTIVE ON CHARACTER EDUCATION

As mentioned earlier, character education is not a new idea or the latest educational fad. Philosophers, religious leaders, and community members have rigorously debated—and rarely agreed—for thousands of years about various issues related to ethics, values, and morality. However, centuries of diverse philosophers, thinkers, and scholars have believed in the critical importance of teaching about issues of character to children (Heslep, 1995). Many indigenous people of this country have valued the powerful teaching of consensus community values through rich stories and traditions for millennia. Throughout time, most cultures have had, as a part of their very fabric, ethical values and truths that bind members together, and imparting these values and truths to young people has long been an essential role of adults, elders, and other community members.

❖ CHARACTER EDUCATION IN SCHOOLS

When the system of compulsory public school education was first created in the United States, the teaching of character was at its very foundation. Helping children become smart and good people are goals as old as education itself (Lickona, 1991). Character education in its earliest form relied on methods of inculcation and coercion that were grounded in Christian philosophy and teachings. In the small homogeneous communities of the 18th and 19th centuries, it was not unusual for children to receive similar messages about right and wrong—based in Christian teachings—in their families, schools, churches, and other community organizations.

As the population of the United States became increasingly diverse and began to embrace and value the notion of pluralism, people began to question the practice of teaching Christian-based principles in public-funded institutions. Teaching only one religious perspective in public schools infringes on the First Amendment guarantee of religious liberty and the separation of church and state. Teaching and promulgating one particular set of religious ideals is unconstitutional and is disrespectful to those who find their religious and spiritual paths through other ideologies and organizations.

Without a religious-based framework for teaching about and enforcing values, educators were unsure about how to approach issues of morals, ethics, and values in schools. One comprehensive study of character education conducted in the 1920s showed that didactic, indoctrination styles of transmitting specific values were not effective strategies (Hartshorne & May, 1928, 1929, 1930). Progressive education theories and methods were also entering the educational arena during this time, as was growth in scientific methodologies for studying human development and psychology. The social justice movement of the 1950s and 1960s profoundly influenced such notable moral development theorists as Lawrence Kohlberg, whose seminal and enduring theory of moral development is rooted in justice reasoning in a true and just democracy. These and other historical and social factors in the United States had a significant impact on the character education movement. For decades, character education was like a tide, its popularity ebbing and flowing throughout much of the 20th century.

❖ VALUES CLARIFICATION MAKES ITS DEBUT

By the 1970s, the term *character education* was rarely used, and many educators had adopted a very relativistic, nonjudgmental approach to teaching about values. Values clarification was introduced in the late 1960s by Rath, Harmin, and Simon with the publication of the book *Values and Teaching* (1966). As a values-neutral approach, values clarification quickly became popular based on the growing belief at that time that schools and other public-funded institutions had no right to teach specific ethical values to children. Teachers or leaders of values clarification programs are instructed in ways to help young people recognize what their personal values are and to explore how people make decisions based on their values. One major aspect of values clarification is to remain completely neutral and never judge anyone else's values.

Values clarification programs helped organizations avoid controversies about which values ought to be taught. Lack of consensus about which values ought to be taught had fueled the character education debate in previous years. At its best, values clarification helped students think about what values they possessed and align their values with their actions (Lickona, 1991). According to Damon (1988), values clarification is itself an irresponsible moral choice because it does nothing to help children understand the difference between ethical and unethical values. Values clarification programs seemed only to add to the mounting moral confusion in schools and communities.

The 1980s brought a return to a more myopic focus on academics and achievement in schools, and many communities relegated the intentional teaching of values to the back burner. This was largely a result of a lack of consensus in the literature and in communities about how to effectively teach values. By the late 1980s, the debate about whose responsibility it is to teach young people values began to rage again in response to mounting youth violence, substance abuse, and serious discipline problems in many communities. The 1990s brought a willingness among many scholars, educators, ethicists, politicians, business people, faith-based leaders, parents, and other community members to come together to explore common foundations on which to build effective character development efforts.

❖ THE LITERATURE ON MORAL DEVELOPMENT AND CHARACTER EDUCATION

A review of the scientific literature reveals what appears to be a chasm between two primary approaches—moral development and character education. At the heart of the discussion of these approaches are differing theories of human development; for example, psychoanalytic and cognitive developmentalism versus social learning theory and behaviorism. A great deal of energy has been expended over the past several decades by researchers and theorists who claim their particular perspectives are more helpful than others in explaining and predicting human thinking and behavior. What is more helpful, and infinitely more useful, for youth development practitioners is a careful eye toward many theories of human development. Program developers and educators need to pay attention to cognitive, social, emotional, behavioral, physical, and contextual influences on youth development. Promising practices for effective character education are grounded in multiple theories of moral development and character education and use principles of community youth development as guides for developing comprehensive, community-wide approaches to character development.

❖ COMMUNITY YOUTH DEVELOPMENT AND CHARACTER EDUCATION

The six Cs of community youth development presented earlier in this volume—competence, confidence, connection, character, caring, and contribution—all relate in critically important ways to the process of healthy emotional, social, and moral development of young people. Using this framework as a guide, the following is a discussion of how moral development theory relates to community youth development and how people can integrate effective character education strategies into their work with and on behalf of young people.

The First *C*: Competence

When one thinks of competence, the first tendency may be to focus on observable skills and accomplishments. Also important to healthy human development, however, are competencies in the moral realm—including the domains of cognitive, affective, and behavioral development. For example, in Native American Indian cultures, one goal of education includes competencies in the areas of physical, social, and spiritual development (Brendtro, Brokenleg, & Van Bockern, 1998). Moreover, youth development experts are coming to understand important relationships between healthy moral, social, and emotional development, and motivation and achievement. Though the research in this area is limited, the internalization of positive values such as caring, responsibility, social justice, and honesty seems to improve children's mental health, social skills, and performance in school (Scales & Leffert, 1999).

Moral competencies include the ability to think and reason about ethical matters and the capacity to feel empathy and understand others' perspectives, make ethical decisions based on positive values, and take moral action in one's daily life. The process of development of these competencies is complex, beginning at birth and developing through age-related stages throughout the life span (Damon, 1988; Havighurst, 1953; Kohlberg, 1984; Piaget, 1965). At younger ages, children's ability to think and act morally tends to be grounded in their fear of punishment, then moves toward their desire to please others. In adolescence, young people begin to understand the importance of rights and responsibilities, abstract principles of justice and care, and the importance of these values in healthy relationships of all kinds.

Studies show that didactic, inculcative character education methods alone, such as lectures, pledges, and codes, are unlikely to work (Hartshorne & May, 1928, 1929, 1930; Kohn, 1997; Vessels, 1998). Moreover, simply helping young people develop reasoning skills through the discussion of ethical dilemmas does not necessarily transfer to their behaviors and attitudes outside the learning environment. Clear rules of conduct that are fairly enforced; student ownership of rules and satisfaction in complying with them; supportive, caring environments; cooperative learning; and just community strategies that enhance a sense of belonging and create group cohesiveness show promise for character education (Damon, 1988; Leming, 1993; Vessels, 1998).

Adults who work with young people can create environments that help build and strengthen moral competencies. Strategies for enhancing moral thinking and reasoning include creating opportunities for reflection, discussion, and problem solving with peers and adults on ethical matters that surface naturally in the day-to-day life of groups, classrooms, and communities. Giving young people a voice in the creation of guidelines and rules increases their understanding of the importance of group norms and standards and increases their commitment to them. Creating opportunities that expose young people to moral thinking that is slightly higher than where they currently are enhances their ability to develop higher moral reasoning skills. Respectful engagement on complex issues that create cognitive dissonance increases the ability to think and reason about moral matters. Young people benefit from active decision making about difficult issues (Carnegie Council on Adolescent Development, 1992). Interestingly, character education efforts also seem to help adults who are involved enhance their understanding of and commitment to moral principles and increase their competencies in ethical decision making.

The Second C: Confidence

Helping youth develop confidence in who they are becoming is an important part of positive youth development. A community youth development framework encourages the involvement of young people in their own development—making use of their talents and actively involving them in the process of their own identity, independence, and self-worth (Hughes & Curnan, 2000). An important part of developing a positive identity is developing a moral identity—a sense of being or becoming a moral person (Damon & Gregory, 1997; Vessels, 1998). Developing a strong, positive moral identity can be challenging in a media-drenched society that promotes rampant materialism and "lookism"—resulting in more emphasis on what you own and how you look than on who you are and what you do. Indeed, rampant materialism nurtured through television may be the most serious new threat to children at a time when too many young people lack strong adult attachments and positive role models (Larson & Brendtro, 2000). Another factor that presents challenges to strong moral identity development is that many youth development practitioners, educators, and parents have misunderstood and misused the concept of self-esteem by overemphasizing *feeling* good and underemphasizing *doing* good. Through emphasizing self-esteem instead of character and good works, society is promoting narcissism. "Self-esteem, if real, is self regard and comes from ethical behavior" (Pipher, 1996, p. 158).

Also strongly related to positive identity development and healthy moral development is the development of trust. Trust is critically important to moral development because one must have trust in order to act in ways that show concern for the welfare and interest of self and others (Erikson, 1968). Young people who feel that the world cannot be trusted may be more likely to meet violence with violence than to rely on teachers, parents, police, or others to help resolve their disputes (Bronfenbrenner et al., 1996).

Another serious threat to positive moral identity is the misunderstood aspect of racial and ethnic identity. A moral goal not often articulated by moral educators is the dual appreciation of the importance of people's racial or ethnic identity to them—a combined appreciation of their individuality and their connection and attachment to racial groups and communities (Blum, 1999). To overcome the poison of a socially toxic environment, it is critical for youth to have pride in who they are as individuals and as part of a group (Garbarino, 1995). Moreover, Holloway (1995) discusses the tragic implications of a society that reinforces and enables racism. She writes, "Whether psyches and spirits are disabled, or prejudice and hatred are enabled, color and character have become linked in an abusive construction" (p. 142). Overt and covert racism take a tragic toll on the identity development process of adolescents of color, often contributing to feelings of anger, resentment, alienation, and inadequacy (Tatum, 1997). In addition, young people who are perceived as "different" because of race, ethnicity, gender, sexual orientation, or physical abilities are often assaulted with degrading names, slurs, and put-downs in schools and communities. These are the real threats to safe schools and communities because of the common escalation from words to violence and the destructive impact of hateful language on those who are targeted. People who are part of traditionally targeted groups understand that sticks and stones may break one's bones, but words of hate break souls (Wessler, 2000/2001). Adults have a responsibility to interrupt and stop harassment and destructive language and behaviors that degrade and debase others. Communities committed to helping young people develop confidence in who they are becoming are engaged in active processes that affirm the individual and group identities of young people, nurture a sense of social justice, and create multicultural communities of care, responsibility, and shared loyalties (Blum, 1999).

Identity development is a complex process that includes discovering and deepening one's commitment to personal beliefs and values. Many adolescents develop confidence in who they are becoming through active experimentation and risk-taking behaviors. No teenager reaches higher levels of moral reasoning without some experimentation with right and wrong (Prothrow-Stith, 1991). Rebelliousness is often a reaction in adolescence to a demanding conscience at work—not necessarily a sign of lawlessness and low moral standards (Freud, cited in Coles, 1997). Adults need to remember that a certain amount of risky and negative behaviors and attitudes are developmentally appropriate. However, the world young people are growing up in makes it dangerous for many adolescents to carry out their risk-taking behavior (Prothrow-Stith, 1991). Rather than punish and label youth as "bad," youth development professionals can encourage growth and healthy development by creating opportunities for young people to reflect on their beliefs and values and by helping them to learn from their decisions and mistakes.

The Third C: Connection

It is important to remember that the need for connection and belonging is such a strong part of the human experience that young people may seek negative peer groups and gangs to meet this need if positive moral alternatives are not available to them. A positive community youth development framework stresses the connections between young people, adults, family, community, the earth, and the sacred (Hughes & Curnan, 2000).

Moral development, like all human development, proceeds through social experience, and character development is strongly tied to connections that young people have with significant people in their lives. It is not enough, however, to simply create opportunities to connect young people with peers and adults. Children's natural moral inclinations are strengthened and enhanced through *positive* relationships and interactions (Damon, 1988). Connections with adults that foster moral development include equitable, democratic processes and respectful engagement that allow young people full and active participation in open, egalitarian procedures. Moreover, moral development is enhanced when children have opportunities to apply ethical principles, moral learnings, and decision making in a variety of social contexts including family, school, faith-based organizations, youth programs, and the wider community.

Moral and character education efforts that only focus on children's behaviors and the development of young people are doomed to fail. The role of adults and adult development are critically important as well. As stated earlier, adult attitudes and behaviors set a tone and create standards in communities. A "do as I say, not as I do" approach to moral and character education is not effective, nor are power-based, authoritarian methods. Adults need character education as much or more than the young people whose lives they touch so that adults may deepen their understanding of the importance of modeling and the role they play in creating social climates that promote character development. Young people yearn for the time and attention of adults who are willing to involve them fully in respectful, caring relationships and who are willing to ensure that the groups of which they are a part are safe, morally rich environments that promote genuine caring and affirmation for all members.

Connections to the sacred and the cultivation of spirituality are also important aspects of moral and character education. Young people's need for spirituality is grounded in transcendence, an orientation of service to others, and an intimation of life's deeper meaning (Damon, 1995). Even the most lost and troubled youngsters can be powerfully affected by attachments to self and others that are grounded in the spiritual character of the human child (Garbarino, 1999). Religious institutions are not the only venue for potential positive development. Spiritual development in public institutions can be enhanced by focusing away from punitive, insidious, and materialistic aspects of the culture toward empathy and socially engaged moral thinking. Opportunities to identify and reflect on noble values that strengthen relationships and serve the common good in communities are important parts of this process. Reflection, meditation, discussion, and creative expression through poetry, music, inspirational readings, drama, writing, and art can provide powerful pathways to spiritual understanding, which enhances moral and character development.

A deep respect and spiritual connection to the larger community and to the earth are important aspects of community youth development. Ensuring balance in one's life involves the appreciation, understanding, and importance of the concept of belonging—in terms of human relationships and connections and of belonging to the natural environment, as well (Brendtro et al., 1998). Effective moral and character education efforts help young people understand the importance of their attitudes and actions in the context of interdependent human relationships—and as they relate to their interdependence and connections with the earth's ecology.

The Fourth C: Character

Character is that within a person which guides and governs decision making and moral choices. As important as character is to one's healthy emotional, social, and moral development, people have largely disagreed for decades about *how* to impart ethics and values to young people. In the past, many claimed that the responsibility to teach children values lies only in the domain of the family. Some believed that ethical values should only be taught in the context of religious institutions. Those attitudes have changed as concerns about negative behaviors in communities have risen. Values move to center stage—and everyone wants to talk about character—with every school shooting, political scandal, and controversy surrounding entertainment and media messages. A statewide survey of Michigan citizens conducted by Michigan State University Extension's 4-H Youth Development program showed that 95% of the respondents believe that teaching character education in the community is very important (1997). People have begun to see that teaching about character is *everyone's* responsibility, including families, schools, youth organizations, faith-based groups, and other community organizations (Benson, 1997). Many youth organizations across the country are finding that character education can be a powerful catalyst for bringing a wide variety of community organizations—along with the powerful voices and involvement of young people—together to create partnerships for positive community change.

Which values to emphasize in character education programs is another common area of disagreement. Controversy tends to rise when values that are not widely shared, or universal, are discussed (such as unquestioning obedience to authority, cleanliness, and orderliness). Building community consensus on core ethical principles is important for effective character development programs. Moreover, healthy human development is enhanced when children experience shared common values in the multiple contexts of their lives (Bronfenbrenner, 1979). Creating community-wide approaches to character development can provide the consistency, redundancy, and common language that help people learn and internalize ethical values. When young people experience community organizations delivering the same kind of messages about expected behavior and providing support to act on those expectations, their behaviors become healthier and their risks decrease (Benson, 1997; Scales, 1996).

How do practitioners decide which values to incorporate into character education programs? Although it may be impossible to ever claim total universality for any ethical value, there is widespread agreement about some ethical principles among psychologists, educators, and ethicists. Some values have "universal currency," such as caring, honesty, and responsibility, which are affirmed by nearly all people regardless of age, income, race, or ethnicity (Benson, 1997). The literature on moral development and character education clearly emphasizes the ethical values of fairness, justice, care, respect, and responsibility. In his book *Shared Values for a Troubled World*, Kidder (1994) presents eight values that are the moral glue holding humanity together: love, truthfulness, fairness, freedom, unity, tolerance, responsibility, and respect. The philosophy of community youth development is rooted in justice and compassion (Hughes & Curnan, 2000)—critically important foundations for moral development. Thousands of educators, youth development professionals, and volunteers across the country are using the framework of CHARACTER COUNTS!—a popular character education program of the Josephson Institute of Ethics. The framework focuses on six pillars of character—trustworthiness, respect, responsibility, fairness, caring, and citizenship.

It is important to note that even though character education approaches and programs exist that include ethical values that are largely agreed on, it is still important to build community consensus on the values to be emphasized. In addition, special attention must be paid to cultural differences and the ways in which core values may be expressed in different racial, ethnic, and cultural groups. Respect in one culture, for example, may include looking adults in the eyes while speaking. Respect in other cultures may include looking down when a young person is speaking to an adult. Respect may well be one of the most universal of ethical values, but it also means respecting the *differences* in how varying cultures and communities embody and live ethical values.

Character is not about blind adherence to rigid principles and values. Moreover, character development doesn't happen through a simple didactic process of telling young people how to be and how to behave. Moral behavior tends to be situational and developmental (Elkind, 2000/2001), and character development is a complex process that begins at birth and progresses throughout the life span. Most experts believe that moral growth is a result of maturation, socialization, and education. Humans generally possess an ethical sense of things—a kind of moral intuition—and children are naturally drawn to moral clues from their families, teachers, and others (Coles, 1997). Youth development practitioners need to be well aware that adults and children are on this journey of moral development together—learning, growing, making mistakes, and learning some more. Moreover, children can be the moral guides of adults as powerfully and effectively as adults can guide youngsters in a mutually respectful atmosphere of trust, care, and support. Adults honor children by taking the moral and spiritual sides of their lives seriously and by thinking how best to respond to those aspects of young people with tact and intelligence (Coles, 1997). A community youth development approach to character development recognizes that young people are full and active participants in their own moral growth as well as that of those around them.

The Fifth C: Caring and Compassion

Caring and compassion are critically important aspects of community youth development, moral development, and character education. Much of moral learning happens throughout social experience, and several studies have shown that the development of empathy in children increases prosocial behaviors toward others (Goleman, 1995; Roberts & Strayer, 1996). Beginning in infancy, humans have an inclination toward empathy that develops through a natural progression as children grow (Hoffman, 1984). Children who are abused, neglected, and do not experience strong, caring, loving relationships may fail to acquire the sense of trust and belonging that are prerequisites for the healthy development of empathy. Empathy and caring are highly linked. People are more likely to act on moral principles if they are able to put themselves in another's place. When one has the capacity to feel empathy—to actually feel or experience the perspective or pain of others—the likelihood of acting in caring and altruistic ways is increased. To feel with another is to care—and the roots of morality are found in empathy (Goleman, 1995; Hoffman, 1984). Moreover, the morality of care assumes that the welfare of others is connected to one's own welfare, thereby strongly connecting the notions of care, attachment, and responsibility (Damon, 1988; Gilligan, 1993).

Encouraging the development of caring and compassion in a community youth development framework includes helping young people to bridge feelings of empathy to include people different from themselves. Morality can be hampered by "bounding" or limiting children's contact with the world only to people who are like them, as opposed to bridging or exposing them to people of different backgrounds. Limiting young people's exposure to people who are just like them can cause them to exclusively empathize with people similar to themselves and exclude everyone else (Springen, 2000). Character education efforts grounded in an ethic of care and compassion create moral climates that encourage perspective-taking and empathy-building opportunities that allow young people to work side by side with diverse groups of adults and peers in service to their communities.

The Sixth C: Contribution

A community youth development approach creates opportunities for young people to put important aspects of positive youth development (competence, confidence, connection, character, caring) to work in communities through meaningful and purposeful contribution (Perkins, Borden, Keith, Hoppe-Rooney, & Villarruel, 2003, this volume; Pittman, 2000). Taking responsibility and meeting obligations is the pathway to finding purpose and meaning in life, which is the essence of human existence (Frankl, 1986). Learning and living ethical values through moral action, service to others, and meaningful contribution are critically important to healthy character development. One cannot reason one's way to virtuous conduct, and values cannot be learned without actually living them through daily tasks, responsibilities, and actions (Frankl, 1986; Leming, 1993).

Simply providing opportunities for young people to work is not enough. In fact, young people who work excessively for money in low-skilled jobs dominated by uncommitted employees are at risk for educational failure and the hedonism of a materialistic society (Brendtro et al., 1998). Economic exploitation and crafty advertising campaigns lure many teens into a culture dominated by lookism and materialism—two enemies of healthy character development.

Young people need and yearn for opportunities for meaningful involvement, contribution, and learning (Pittman & Irby, 1996).

Deprived of these opportunities, youth may come to believe that they are unimportant and that they cannot make a difference in their world. Feelings of isolation, powerlessness, and apathy can be addressed through opportunities to work in service to others and to contribute to causes that benefit the common good in communities. Authentic, respectful partnerships with youth and adults based on shared power and shared leadership give young people the chance to practice ethical decision making and strengthen moral skills. Adults often underestimate the passion and commitment of young people to be actively engaged in solutions to problems and issues that affect them, the groups to which they belong, and their communities as a whole. Young people are not the problem in communities—they are part of the solution. Adults "must give young people as much support as they need, balanced with as much freedom as they can manage. To do anything less is to court disaster, for individuals and for society" (Comer, 1992, p. 19).

Community youth development in a truly just and democratic society includes the voices of diverse groups of young people—not only those who are natural leaders and high achievers. Young people need to be recognized and valued both as individuals and as members of the cultural groups to which they belong, along with an emphasis on the power of community—an intense sense of shared responsibility and obligation to the group and to the greater society. In addition, youth development practitioners can help to create environments in which all young people are actively involved in creating guidelines, rules, and policies that affect them, and where they feel a sense of shared belonging and care for one another. Caring, respectful, moral communities fully engage youth and adults in experiences and processes that unite their efforts for positive social change and contribution to the common good.

❖   RESEARCH AND POLICY

The research on the impacts of character education programs is limited, and most of the studies that have been done in the area have focused on school settings. There is also wide variation on how programs are implemented, the style and personality of the teachers, and the overall tone or climate of the classrooms. All of these factors make it difficult to make comparisons and generalizations about what is most effective. Furthermore, there is a lack of solid research that examines the effectiveness of a community youth development approach to character education—one that involves many community organizations working along with youth to create caring, moral environments in all contexts in which young people live, learn, work, and grow. Anecdotal and informal data seem to indicate that efforts incorporating many of the aspects discussed in this chapter can be effective in creating effective community-wide and community-driven approaches to character education. Rigorous research and program evaluation are needed to further develop, strengthen, and inform practice and to encourage replication of approaches to character development that are effective.

Although not specific to character education, the Search Institute data involving more than a half million young people illustrate the importance of internal assets such as ethical values and social competencies and external assets that include community building and relationship building (Benson, 1997; Vessels, 1998). Further research is needed to contribute to an understanding of the elements of character education initiatives and of programs that enhance moral development in a variety of community contexts in a framework of community youth development.

Character education is increasingly important to many politicians and educators. Those involved with public policy can advocate for federal and state character education legislation to support community youth development approaches to character development that include program development, implementation, and research. All too often, public grants, initiatives, and programs have been heavily tied to in-school settings—leaving out programs that reach young people during critical out-of-school time. Policy advocates can also help to ensure funding for research-based, nonpartisan approaches to character development that are appropriate for public-funded institutions. These initiatives ought to blend a variety of traditional and progressive approaches to character education. Last, public policy advocates can enrich the character education agenda by making strong connections with efforts to combat bullying, hateful language, prejudice, bias, and discrimination to promote positive community change and social justice—the essence of caring, moral communities.

❖ PROMISING PRACTICES FOR MOVING FORWARD WITH CHARACTER EDUCATION

There is no more critical indicator of the future of a society than the character, competence, and integrity of its youth (Bronfebrenner et al, 1996). Over the past several years, volumes have been written about the socially toxic and ethically polluted nature of the U.S. culture and the challenges communities face in helping young people navigate toward healthy and productive futures (Benson, 1997; Brendtro et al., 1998; Garbarino, 1995; Hersch, 1998; Larson & Brendtro, 2000; Pipher, 1996). It is critically important that those who work with and care about the positive development of young people pay special attention to ethical and moral development. Currently, many educational and youth development organizations are urgently seeking promising approaches for integrating concepts and methods of moral and character education into their work with children and adolescents. The character of communities that support healthy moral development include the following promising practices.

- *Youth and Adult Partnerships:* A community youth development approach involves youth and adults in learning together, applying ethical principles to their daily lives, and taking action to teach others and work in authentic partnerships in communities.

- *Community-Wide Approach:* Efforts in communities need to be comprehensive and inclusive. As many people as possible in the lives of children need to be brought into the process, including parents and other family members, school staff and administrators, youth organization professionals, volunteers and teens, faith-based leaders and youth groups, youth and family agencies, businesses, community leaders and politicians, representatives of local media, recreation leaders, sports groups, coaches, and other community members. People representing these groups need to be involved right from the start in helping to create a vision and plan to encourage community-wide buy-in and commitment. Young people need to be involved—up front and all along the way—as resources and partners in any community-wide approaches to character education. Youth development practitioners would do well to explore possible linkages and connections with other community youth development and asset-building efforts in local communities.

- *Widely Shared Ethical Values:* A person's character is largely a reflection of the ethical values he or she uses as guides for decision making and actions. A process needs to be implemented for coming to consensus about what values will be included in a community-wide character education effort. The values chosen to be the framework for the effort can make or break it. Ethical values must have widely shared meanings and universal appeal, and coming to agreement on these values can be a challenging process. Youth development practitioners are encouraged to explore what other credible organizations devoted to community-wide character education efforts have developed. Building consensus with a variety of people and organizations about the ethical values to use is a critically important part of successful character education efforts.

- *Thinking, Feeling, Doing:* Opportunities for young people to be engaged in learning about ethical values must focus on multiple domains—cognitive, affective, and behavioral. Children need opportunities to become more *conscious* of the right thing to do, more *committed* to doing it, and more *competent* in integrating ethical values into their actions. They need opportunities to think, feel, and do—and additional opportunities to apply ethical decision-making processes and actions to their daily lives.

- *Adult Development and Learning:* Adults who live with, work with, and care about young people need opportunities to reflect on their own ethical values and behaviors. They need opportunities to learn how they and others in the community can positively affect the ethical climate of groups—and the community as a whole—through what they say and do every day. Adults need community learning opportunities that increase awareness, strengthen relationships, nurture a sense of belonging and commitment, and help them learn how to teach and model ethical values to others.

- *Family Involvement:* Families are important influences on children's moral development. Most parents want their children to avoid negative behaviors such as lying, cheating, stealing, and fighting. Youth development practitioners need to explore respectful, authentic, and effective ways to involve families as full partners and resources in community character education efforts.

- *Youth Development and Learning:* Young people need opportunities for meaningful, purposeful learning with peers and adults about ethical values and how these values influence their thinking, feelings, and behaviors. Adults should not take for granted that children already know what values are important to the community and how those values play out in everyday decisions and actions. Many resources are available that include engaging, awareness-boosting, skill-building activities and materials that focus on ethical values and decision making. Practitioners need to remember the developmental nature of moral and character development and choose materials and processes for learning that are age appropriate.

• *Morally Rich Learning Environments:* In addition to specific activities and opportunities to learn about ethical values, adults need to explore ways to integrate ethical values into almost everything children learn in formal and nonformal educational settings. Many content areas easily lend themselves to the exploration of ethical values in the subject matter, including environmental education, natural and biological sciences, life skills, history, animal science, pet care, social science, creative arts, literature, cultural heritage, career exploration and workforce preparation, communication, leadership, health, and sports and recreation. Adults can embed character education into ongoing lessons, activities, and projects through reflection, discussion, and action on important ethical values as they relate to the subject at hand.

• *Caring, Moral Climates:* Enduring ethical principles need to encompass and influence the very culture and climate of groups. How the group makes decisions; how rules and discipline issues are created and handled; how members treat one another; how honest and trustworthy people are in the group; and the amount of caring, kindness, and compassion members experience all contribute to (or detract from) the moral climate and ethical tone of groups. One of the most important things a youth leader can do is to help nurture and foster connections and caring relationships among all group members—including adults and youth. All humans have an innate need to belong to groups that make them feel cared for and respected. Isolation and disconnectedness breed loneliness, despair, depression, and anger. Caring, moral "communities" are families, clubs, classrooms, Sunday-school classes, youth groups, sport teams, neighborhoods—and the community as a whole.

• *Multiple Learning Approaches:* When planning character education opportunities for young people, group leaders and teachers need to consider multiple learning styles. Long lectures about values and simply *telling* young people what to do are not effective. What does work are learning opportunities that actively engage young people such as group activities, lively discussions, role-plays, dramatic presentations, creative multimedia campaigns, art projects, music and songwriting, movies, reflective writing, literature, engagement with social justice issues, meaningful opportunities to work in service to others, and opportunities to learn from moral mentors in communities. Practitioners, teachers, and group leaders are encouraged to use an experiential learning model that involves young people in doing, sharing, processing, generalizing, and applying what they've learned in meaningful ways.

• *Youth as Leaders:* Peer pressure is not always bad (contrary to popular thinking), and young people are powerful role models for peers and younger children. Youth development practitioners can harness the spirit, energy, and enthusiasm of young people and involve them in a variety of ways in character education efforts as teachers, mentors, coalition members, speaker's bureau representatives, and participants in community service projects that focus on putting ethical values into action. Invite young people into the process of helping to create policy and rules that ultimately affect them most. Insist that young people's voices are heard loud and clear and that their opinions are taken into account in all aspects of character education planning and implementation.

• *Outcomes and Evaluation:* Character education efforts need to be outcome driven and evaluated to ascertain if program goals are met, to inform program improvements and to help replicate models that work. One strategy is to gather baseline data about incidences of conflict in a group, attendance, achievement, or other existing information to use for comparative purposes. Other strategies include pretest and posttest surveys, focus groups, and case studies involving leaders, parents, community members, and young people. Process evaluation strategies including program logs and lesson plans will help others implement programs that work. Evaluators may be interested in the impact on attitudes and behaviors of children, the impact on adults who are working with the program, and the changes in the overall culture and climate of the group or community. Evaluation of community youth development programs with a community-wide emphasis is a complex process, and practitioners are encouraged to involve evaluation specialists in their efforts.

❖ REFERENCES

Benson, P. L. (1997). *All kids are our kids: What communities must do to raise caring and responsible children and adolescents.* San Francisco: Jossey-Bass.

Blum, L. (1999). Race, community and moral education: *Journal of Moral Education, 28,* 125-143.

Brendtro, L. K., Brokenleg, M., & Van Bockern, S. (1998). *Reclaiming youth at risk: Our hope for the future.* Bloomington, IN: National Educational Service.

Bronfenbrenner, U. (1979). *The ecology of human development: Experiments by nature and design.* Cambridge, MA: Harvard University Press.

Bronfenbrenner, U., McClelland, P., Wethington, E., Moen, P., Ceci, S. (1996). *The state of Americans: This generation and the next.* New York: Free Press.

Carnegie Council on Adolescent Development. (1992). *A matter of time: Risk and opportunity in the nonschool hours.* New York: Carnegie Corporation.

Coles, R. (1997). *The moral intelligence of children.* New York: Random House.

Comer, J. (1992). A growing crisis in youth development. In *A matter of time: Risk and opportunity in the nonschool hours.* New York: Carnegie Corporation.

Damon, W. (1988). *The moral child: Nurturing children's natural moral growth.* New York: Free Press.

Damon, W. (1995). *Greater expectations: Overcoming the culture of indulgence in America's homes and schools.* New York: Free Press.

Damon, W., & Colby, A. (1996). Education and moral commitment. *Journal of Moral Education, 25,* 31-37.

Damon, W., & Gregory, A. (1997). The youth charter: Towards the formation of adolescent moral identity. *Journal of Moral Education, 26,* 117-130.

Elkind, D. (2000/2001). The cosmopolitan school. *Educational Leadership, 58,* 12-17.

Erikson, E. (1968). *Identity: Youth and crisis.* New York: W.W. Norton.

Frankl, V. E. (1986). *The doctor and the soul.* New York: Vintage Books.

Garbarino, J. (1995). *Raising children in a socially toxic environment.* San Francisco: Jossey-Bass.

Garbarino, J. (1999). *Lost boys: Why our sons turn violent and how we can save them.* New York: Free Press.

Gilligan, C. (1993). *In a different voice: Psychological theory and women's development.* Cambridge, MA: Harvard University Press.

Goble, F., & Brooks, B. (1983). *The case for character education.* Ottawa, IL: Green Hill.

Goleman, D. (1995). *Emotional intelligence.* New York: Bantam Books.

Hartshorne, H., & May, M. A. (1928, 1929, 1930). *Studies in the nature of character.* New York: Macmillan.

Havighurst, R. J. (1953). *Human development and education.* New York: Longmans, Green.

Hersch, P. (1998). *A tribe apart.* New York: Ballantine.

Heslep, R. D. (1995). *Moral education for Americans.* Westport, CT: Praeger.

Hoffman, M. L. (1984). Empathy, social cognition, and moral action. In W. Kurtines and J. Gerwitz (Eds.), *Moral behavior and development: Advances in theory, research, and applications.* New York: Wiley.

Holloway, K. F. (1995). *Codes of conduct: Race, ethics, and the color of our character.* New Brunswick, NJ: Rutgers University Press.

Hughes, D. M., & Curnan, S. P. (2000). Community youth development: A framework for action. *Community Youth Development Journal, 1,* 7-11.

Josephson Institute of Ethics (2000). *2000 Report Card on the Ethics of American Youth.* Marina del Ray, CA: Author.

Kidder, R. M. (1994). *Shared values for a troubled world: Conversations with men and women of conscience.* San Francisco: Jossey-Bass.

Kilpatrick, W. (1992). *Why Johnny can't tell right from wrong.* New York: Simon & Schuster.

Kohlberg, L. (1984). *The psychology of moral development.* New York: Harper & Row.

Kohn, A. (1997). How not to teach values: A critical look at character education. *Phi Delta Kappan, 78,* 429-439.

Larson, S., & Brendtro, L. (2000). *Reclaiming our prodigal sons and daughters: A practical guide for connecting with youth in conflict.* Bloomington, IN: National Educational Service.

Leming, J. S. (1993). In search of effective character education. *Educational Leadership 51,* 63-71.

Lickona, T. (1991). *Educating for character: How schools can teach respect and responsibility.* New York: Bantam Books.

Lickona, T. (1993). The return of character education. *Educational Leadership, 51,* 6-11.

Males, M. (1999). *Framing youth: 10 myths about the next generation.* Monroe, ME: Common Courage Press.

Michigan State University Extension. (1997). *Community needs assessment of character education.* Unpublished report on a statewide survey. East Lansing: Michigan State University.

Nucci, L. (1989). *Moral development and character education.* Berkeley, CA: McCutchan.

Perkins, D. F., Borden, L. M., Keith, J. G., Hoppe-Rooney, T. L., & Villarruel, F. A. (2003). Community youth development: Partnership creating a positive world. In F. A. Villarruel, D. F. Perkins, L. M. Borden, & J. G. Keith

(Eds.), *Community youth development: Programs, policies, and practices.* Thousand Oaks, CA: Sage.

Piaget, J. (1965). *The moral judgment of the child.* New York: Free Press.

Pipher, M. (1996). *The shelter of each other: Rebuilding our families.* New York: Ballantine Books.

Pittman, K. J. (2000). Balancing the equation: Communities supporting youth, youth supporting communities. *Community Youth Development Journal, 1,* 32-36.

Pittman, K. J., & Irby, M. (1996). *Preventing problems or promoting development: Competing priorities or inseparable goals?* Takoma Park, MD: International Youth Foundation.

Prothrow-Stith, D. (1991). *Deadly consequences.* New York: HarperCollins.

Public Agenda Report. (1999). *What Americans really think about the next generation.* New York: Public Agenda.

Rath, L., Harmin, M., & Simon, S. (1966). *Values and teaching: Working with values in the classroom.* Columbus, OH: Charles E. Merrill.

Rich, J. M., & DeVitis, J. L. (1994). *Theories of moral development.* Springfield, IL: Charles C. Thomas.

Roberts, W., & Strayer, J. (1996). Empathy, emotional expressiveness, and prosocial behavior. *Child Development, 67,* 449-470.

Scales, P. C. (1996). A responsive ecology for positive young adolescent development. *Clearing House: A Journal of Educational Research, Controversy and Practices, 69,* 226-230.

Scales, P. C., & Leffert, N. (1999). *Developmental assets: A synthesis of the scientific research on adolescent development.* Minneapolis, MN: Search Institute.

Springen, K. (2000, Fall/Winter). Raising a moral child. *Newsweek,* 71-73.

Tatum, B. D. (1997). *Why are all the black kids sitting together in the cafeteria? And other conversations about race.* New York: Basic Books.

Vessels, G. (1998). *Character and community development.* Westport, CT: Praeger.

Walberg, H., & Wynne, E. A. (1989). Character education: Toward a preliminary consensus. In L. P. Nucci (Ed.), *Moral development and character education* (pp. 37-50). Berkeley, CA: McCutchan.

Wessler, S. L. (2000/2001). Sticks and stones. *Educational Leadership, 58,* 28-33.

13

Youth Civic Development

A Logical Next Step in
Community Youth Development

Constance Flanagan and Beth Van Horn

I n this chapter we focus on the theme of youth civic development as a logical next step in community youth development. Civic development builds on the positive development framework of community youth development, in which young people are conceived as assets to their communities. In concert with a community youth development approach, we assert the importance of moving beyond prevention toward practice that prepares youth to be informed and committed participants in the affairs of their communities (Perkins, Borden, Keith, Hoppe-Rooney, & Villarruel, 2003, this volume; Zeldin, 2000). To accomplish this goal, communities need to create "free spaces" (Evans & Boyte, 1992) in which young people from different backgrounds can mingle and find common ground that stretches beyond the borders of their family backgrounds. We further enforce the civic dimension of community youth development by arguing that developing the assets of individuals is not enough. Community youth development must also foster youths' identification with the common good and with values such as tolerance, compassion, and skills such as perspective taking that undergird a democratic and civil society.

We have two overarching goals in this chapter. One is to unpack the unique role that nonformal youth groups (including extracurricular activities at school and voluntary youth organizations in the community) play in modern democratic societies. Membership in such organizations lays the foundation for a political community because, as we shall argue, such groups provide opportunities to work toward common goals in a context where the status of all members is equal.

Our other goal is to raise the question of equal access to extracurricular activities and community youth development programs. If such programs are the informal "schools for democracy" (Tocqueville, 1848/1966) in which the next generation gains civic practice, then it is incumbent on those committed to community youth development to advocate policies which ensure that meaningful opportunities to engage in such groups are broadly available and culturally relevant.

❖ POLITICAL ROLE OF
   YOUTH ORGANIZATIONS

Historically, youth groups have shared a common mission in fostering the character of the next generation of citizens by integrating young people into the norms and mores of the social order. Besides encouraging constructive prosocial norms, youth organizations also stabilize political and social systems either overtly, by emphasizing specific ideological commitments, or more subtly, by communicating an affinity with national values (Kahane, 1997; Yogev & Shapira, 1990). The practices of these organizations emphasize those principles which the organization considers central to the development of citizenship and character. For example, at every meeting, members of the 4-H organization pledge "my head to clearer thinking, my heart to greater loyalty, my hands to greater service, and my health to better living for my club, my community, my country, and my world."

The affinity with a community that typifies the everyday practices of community youth groups provides a solid foundation for the political system, one that assumes a more palpable patriotic quality when the times call for it. For example, in the 1950s, during the height of the Cold War, the Young Pioneers and Comsomol organizations in Central and Eastern Europe played an overt political role, encouraging the patriotic proclivities of young Soviet citizens. In contrast, during the 1960s and 1970s, the political role of the Young Pioneers was less overt. The organization was known primarily for the camping they sponsored. In this latter context, youth assumed responsibility for public work such as environmental reclamation projects (Flanagan, Jonsson, et al., 1998). The good citizen was less likely to be called on to defend the nation and more likely to be someone who cared about the quality of public spaces that citizens share.

In a similar way, the patriotic role of the 4-H organization has been apparent in particular epochs (Van Horn, Flanagan, & Thomson, 1998). For example, during the two world wars, the agrarian skills of 4-H members were called into service for the nation. With the military and defense industries draining older youth and young adults from the farm, younger 4-H members assumed additional responsibilities in their communities. In fact, during World War I, 4-H Club work was partially abandoned so that the energy of the members could be devoted to raising food for the war effort. Victory gardens became a way that 4-H members could do their part in War World II as well. They grew essential war crops, raised animals, and canned millions of jars of fruits, vegetables, and meats. Their war slogan was "Food for Freedom," and it was estimated that from 1943 until the end of the war, 4-H club members produced enough food to feed a million soldiers serving in the U.S. forces (Rasmussen, 1989), giving special meaning to the concept of youth as assets to their communities. In short, the mores and practices of community youth organizations coupled with the infrastructure of such groups makes them ideal for rallying large numbers of young people toward patriotic and political ends.

In less politically charged times, these groups assume a more subtle political role but one that nonetheless benefits the social order. Youth groups serve a socially integrative function by providing structure for free time, a prosocial peer reference group, and adult mentors who typically are volunteering their own time to a community organization. In fact, as Storrmann (1991, 1993) has pointed out, a political agenda of social integration and conforming citizenship was at the heart of the reform efforts in the early days of the outdoor recreation and playground movements in this country. And the politics of gender in general and masculinity specifically have figured in debates and decisions of the Boy Scouts of America from the date of its founding in 1910 through contemporary times (Mechling, 2001).

Interpretations of the civic values that youth organizations presume to foster can also be contested, as was evident in the recent controversy caused by the Boys Scouts of America's decision to exclude gay leaders from the organization. One side in this debate saw tolerance, inclusion, and respect for diversity as civic values that youth organizations should promote. The other, represented by the Boy Scouts organization's leadership, held that including gay leaders was tantamount to endorsing a gay lifestyle and would run counter to the Boy Scouts' core values. These core values recall the role the organization played in the early 20th century, when the Boy Scouts organization was promoted as a counterbalance to what many worried was a dissolution of masculinity and an erosion of traditional male roles brought on by urbanization and white-collar work (Hantover, 1978).

The traditions, mores, or habits that bind members of an organization in a common identity and purpose can, consciously or not, exclude newcomers. The very processes that bring benefits to members (strong ties, solidarity, and trust) may restrict access to the organization for those on the outside. In some instances, those exclusionary practices are intentional (McLaughlin, 1993). More typically, exclusion is unintended but results from the unwillingness of an organization's leaders to accommodate well-worn practices so that they are more meaningful to an increasingly diverse population of young people. The core tenets and traditions of a youth organization can be translated into practices that are responsive to the changing demography of the youth population as organizations such as the Girl Scouts have shown. In either case, exclusionary practices send messages about who is welcome, who belongs, and who counts in the community. And such messages have broader political implications. When one is treated with mistrust or rejected as an outsider, that individual will have more negative feelings for the political system, as some have argued is the case for youth from ethnic minority groups (Abramson, 1983; McLaughlin, Irby, & Langman 1994; Sanchez-Jankowski, 1992). An excerpt from an interview with a Chicano adolescent says it all: "Before I knew anything about how the American government worked, I could tell Chicanos didn't have much say in how things got done, 'cause of the way Anglo people would treat us" (Sanchez-Jankowski, 1992, p. 84).

Given the demographic changes predicted for the next 50 years, exclusion of ethnic minority youth from having a voice in the affairs of the mainstream undermines the stability of democracy. National studies of high-school students indicate that racial differences in political efficacy and trust persist even when socioeconomic factors are controlled. Both Latino and African American high school students are more skeptical than their white peers about the amount of attention the government pays to the average person (Niemi & Junn, 1998). However, when political issues hit close to home as they did in California's antidocumented immigrant Proposition 187, ethnic minority youth have strong and yet diverse opinions on the issue (Bedolla, 2000). Insofar as politics is grounded in interest group activity, ethnic solidarity experienced in local community action is an important means by which youth would develop political awareness. As Sanchez-Jankowski (1992) points out, the politicization of ethnic minority youth is very much played out in the context of local politics and their group's position in the local social order.

In summary, community youth organizations stabilize the polity by providing a prosocial reference group and a core set of values with which the younger generation can identify. Their contribution to society is widely recognized. However, there are times when an organization, pressed to take a stand, uncovers contention in the interpretation of principles that bind its members together. But such discord is inevitable insofar as community youth organizations, like any institutions of Civil Society, serve a dual function of maintaining traditions and contributing to social change (Flanagan & Campbell, in press).

❖ THE ROLE OF YOUTH ORGANIZATIONS AND EXTRACURRICULAR ACTIVITIES IN ADULT CIVIC ENGAGEMENT

The connection between extracurricular involvement in one's youth and adult civic involvement has been well documented. Participation in an array of extracurricular activities at school and community-based organizations in youth predicts later adult involvement in community affairs (Hanks & Eckland, 1978; Otto, 1976; Van Horn, Flanagan. & Willits, 2002; Verba, Schlozman, & Brady, 1995; Youniss, McLellan, & Yates, 1997). Although young people are less likely to be involved in political organizations, longitudinal studies also have shown that participation in such activities in high school predicts political activity in the college years (Flanagan, 1998) and later in adulthood (DeMartini, 1983). Why this connection exists is a matter for speculation. We discuss several plausible explanations, noting at the outset that the empirical evidence for any of these theses is sparse.

❖ SOCIOECONOMIC ADVANTAGE
AND POLITICAL PARTICIPATION

One possibility is that, because involvement in extracurricular activities and community clubs is voluntary, those who join are different in some systematic way from the nonjoiners. For example, there may be dispositional biases, with those who join being more outgoing or exhibiting more initiative (Larson, 2000), or there may be social inequities in the availability of groups. Groups may be more available in privileged communities, or the activities they offer may seem meaningless for young people from different cultural backgrounds. In any case, if the opportunities and invitations to join are not broadly available, then such groups may contribute to adult civic participation but would not equalize that participation.

Socioeconomic inequalities in political participation are higher in the United States than in other democracies (Verba, Nie, & Kim, 1978), and education plays a multifaceted role in those participatory inequities (Verba et al., 1995). Among adults, higher levels of education are related to higher levels of political interest and activity (Delli Carpini & Keeter, 1996). Formal education also is associated with the likelihood of working in professional jobs, from which recruitment into community associations tends to occur. As Verba and colleagues (1995) show, recruitment into community associations is mainly a matter of being asked to join, and the likelihood of being asked is higher for the better educated and for those with jobs, especially professional jobs.

Might participation in extracurricular activities or community youth organizations increase the political advantages of groups with higher socioeconomic status? National studies indicate that 29% of early adolescents are not reached by community youth programs at all (U.S. Department of Education, 1990) and that youth from more advantaged families are more likely to be involved in such programs (Hart, Atkins, & Ford, 1998). Nonformal groups such as Little League, the YMCA, 4-H, and Boys and Girls Clubs are typically less represented, with fewer resources, in poorer neighborhoods (Connell & Halpern-Felsher, 1997). Even when programs do exist in disadvantaged communities, they tend to reach youth for far less time (1 or 2 hours per week) than that needed to provide a sustained connection for them (Carnegie Council on Adolescent Development, 1992). Similarly, several studies indicate that youth from higher socioeconomic backgrounds and from higher academic ability groups are more likely to participate in extracurricular activities at school (Carnegie Council, 1992; McNeal, 1995) and that such programs are cut back or eliminated when communities experience economic declines or increases in unemployment (Flanagan, 1990).

On the other hand, there is some evidence that extracurricular activities keep students connected to school, undoubtedly preventing some from dropping out and ultimately predicting higher levels of educational attainment in their early adulthood (Barber, Eccles, & Stone, 2000). Two longitudinal studies of adults in the 1970s found that, when socioeconomic status and academic achievement were controlled, involvement in extracurricular activities (drama, debate, student government, academic, service, artistic, or religious clubs) was related to adult involvement in community associations such as trade union, farm, and professional or educational organizations, youth groups, and communities of faith (Hanks & Eckland, 1978; Otto, 1976). Furthermore, membership in these adult civic, community, and religious associations decreased political alienation and increased the likelihood of voting (Hanks & Eckland, 1978).

❖ ORGANIZATIONAL MEMBERSHIP AND THE SOCIAL INTEGRATION OF YOUNG PEOPLE

Returning to the question of why youth participation in voluntary groups may be related to adult civic participation, we move next to a discussion of the integrative function of such groups. The civic commitment and engagement of the next generation depends on some level of social integration into the broader society. Community youth organizations serve this function in part by keeping young people supervised and connected to prosocial reference groups. The after-school hours from 3:00 to 6:00 p.m. are the times when most juvenile misdemeanors occur—a time of greatest need for community supervision and a niche filled by many after-school clubs and organizations (Carnegie Council, 1992).

Social control is one of the primary functions that community associations fulfill. In fact, nearly 70 years ago, Waller (1932) reflected that extracurricular activities were a means by which school systems could co-opt adolescent social structure and keep young people on a straight and narrow path. With the possible exception of athletics, youth who are involved in organized youth activities are less likely to be involved in antisocial acts or substance abuse (Allen, Kuperminc, Philliber, & Herre, 1994; Eccles & Barber, 1999; Larson, 1992).

However, distracting youth from more deviant pursuits seems to oversimplify the connection between youth-serving institutions and adult civic life. In our view, the civic function of community organizations runs much deeper. Even risk prevention studies suggest that the protective role of these institutions is not merely to distract but to enable youth to bond with others in their communities. The evidence is clear: When institutions provide caring and cohesive settings with ample opportunities for young people to bond with others, those young people are less likely to cause harm to themselves or to others in their communities (Blyth & Leffert, 1995; McBride et al., 1995; Roth & Brooks-Gunn, 2000). Population-based studies confirm that feelings of connectedness remain a significant protector across all major risk domains, even after demographic factors are controlled (Eccles & Gootman, 2002; Neumark-Sztainer, Story, French, & Resnick, 1997; Resnick et al., 1997) and that a bonding environment protects youth from substance use and other risk factors when school policies and rules do not (Resnick et al., 1997).

When young people lack an emotional bond to their community, we refer to them as disaffected or alienated, as if estranged from their society. Our very choice of words reveals the fundamental importance we accord to feelings of affection for one's community, culture, or nation. The absence of such emotional bonds is considered a problem not only for the individual but for the community as well. Why are emotional or affective bonds important to a civil society? And what role might community youth development play in fostering the civic affection that carries over into adulthood? We answer these questions by linking political scientists' discussions of diffuse support for democratic societies with a psychological explanation of the civic processes that we believe take place in nonformal youth organizations.

❖ DIFFUSE SUPPORT FOR THE POLITY AND FEELINGS OF MEMBERSHIP AND MATTERING IN YOUNG PEOPLE

According to political socialization theory, the stability of democratic polities depends on widespread support in the population for the principles that bind the polity together (Easton & Dennis, 1969). Scholars in this tradition argued that such support was rooted in the early affinity children felt for their nation and the benevolence of its leaders. According to Easton (1953), diffuse system support bred in this way remains stable and independent of any specific rewards that may or may not accrue to individual citizens. However, after Watergate there were precipitous declines in children's and adolescents' faith in political leaders (Dennis & Webster, 1975; Sigel & Hoskin, 1981). Indeed, polls since September 11, 2001, suggest that trust in elected leaders waxes and wanes with the times.

What, then, might be the mechanism ensuring stability of the political system? We contend that the diffuse support that stabilizes political systems is rooted in children's experiences of membership in the institutions of their communities and of mattering to fellow citizens in those communities. Rather than relying on the benevolence of national leaders, we believe that children learn by firsthand and repeated encounters to trust in the goodwill of other members of their communities. Furthermore, the ties that bind younger generations to the broader community are reciprocal, that is, when young people feel that the community cares about them and that they have a say in community affairs, they are more likely to identify with the community's goals and to want to commit to its service.

❖ ADULTS MODELING THE PRINCIPLES OF CIVIL SOCIETY

Theorists in the political socialization tradition referred to the president and the police as the "head and tail" symbols for children's image of the state and its authority (Easton & Dennis, 1969). But young people's beliefs in such symbols have eroded over the years, calling into question their viability as mechanisms whereby diffuse support for the polity develops. Instead, we have argued that it is in everyday relationships with more proximal adult authorities (teachers, principals, youth workers, counselors, coaches, and parents) that children come to adopt a basic belief that they live in a just society. Our studies have focused on the teacher's role in this regard, but the results apply broadly to adults who work with and are in some position of authority in their interactions with youth.

In particular, we have argued that when teachers hold the same high standards for and respect the ideas of all students, insist that students listen to and respect one another, and actively intervene to stop any incivility, they play a critical role in promoting the younger generation's support for the polity (Flanagan, Gill, & Gallay, 2001). Across different racial/ethnic groups, when students felt their teachers practiced this ethic, they were more committed to the kinds of public interest goals that would sustain a democratic polity, that is, contributing to their communities and serving their country, working to improve race relations, and helping the disenfranchised. Other work indicates that, across social class groups, students' social integration, role commitment, and academic achievement are fostered by a sense of trust, by confidence, and by expectations of extracurricular involvement from their teachers and administrators (Hilles & Kahle, 1985). New models of youth-adult partnerships in community-based organizations also indicate that the healthy integration of younger generations into the polity is supported by relationships with adults who genuinely respect young people and their voice in governance of the organization (Camino & Zeldin, 2002).

In summary, the social integration of younger generations and their support for the principles that bind the polity together develop via respectful and fair relationships with adult authorities (parents, teachers, youth workers) and via the opportunities that youth organizations provide for negotiating with peers on an equal footing.

❖ EQUALITY AND THE TRANSFORMATION OF INDIVIDUAL INTERESTS INTO GROUP GOALS

Political socialization has typically been conceived as a vertical process across generations, but democracies imply an egalitarian quality in social interaction. Thus, voluntary youth organizations play a unique role in modern societies (Kahane, 1997). Aristotle himself described the polity as a network of friends bound together by the mutual pursuit of a common good. Whereas vertical relationships between patrons and clients are the structure underlying an authoritarian social order, horizontal networks that build trust between equals are the basis for a democratic social order (Putnam, 2000).

By virtue of their nonhierarchical structure, community youth groups afford unique opportunities to practice the skills that citizens in democracies need. In contrast to the other major institutions of socialization (families and schools), in which relationships of power and authority are essentially asymmetrical, in youth groups the status of the members is the same. Such egalitarian relationships are basic to the democratic enterprise. On this even playing field, youth can learn how members of a group can disagree, debate, negotiate differences, and ultimately reach a group decision. They can gain experience in admitting and resolving differences of opinion in an atmosphere in which the consequences of disagreeing are the same for everyone in the group.

However, although an attainable ideal, equal status is not the norm in all peer groups and, as the research on intergroup relations has shown, status differences based on age, physical size, language, race/ethnicity, or sexual preference do not level themselves by default. A laissez-faire attitude can reinforce inequities of power in youth groups. To overcome those inequities, active intervention by adults may be needed (Schofield, 1995). In fact, young people want adult involvement in their organizations in the form of coaching, mentoring, and dialogue, and they want those relationships to reflect equality and mutual respect (Camino & Zeldin, 2002).

❖ SOCIAL TRUST/GROUP
    SOLIDARITY/COLLECTIVE EFFICACY

The importance of generalized social trust (defined as a standing decision to give others the benefit of the doubt) is considered essential to a strong civil society. Among adults, higher levels of trust are related to civic engagement, and the disposition to trust others is increased by such engagement (Putnam, 2000; Verba et al., 1995). Yet, to our knowledge, there has been no research on the developmental foundations of social trust. Nor has attention to the developmental roots of trust figured in the civil society discourse.

We believe that nonformal youth organizations provide a unique opportunity for developing social trust. In a study of a large and diverse sample of adolescents, we have found that involvement in at least one extracurricular activity or community organization is related to higher levels of trust in fellow community members (Flanagan, Gill, & Gallay, in press). Our explanation for this relationship is twofold. First, when youth are not spending their time in some organized groups, they are likely to be spending more time watching television, which reinforces stereotypes about others as untrustworthy. Second, in the activities of nonformal youth organizations, young people come to understand the reciprocal relationship between trust and trustworthiness. Trust among peers is earned by working together toward goals defined in common, by working through differences that could otherwise divide them. As a member of the group, an individual helps to define its identity and has a say in defining its goals. Thus, in a very real way, participation in nonformal organizations is an opportunity for youth to define what it means to be a member of the public. Such groups are an opportunity for each new generation to work through the reciprocity between rights and obligations that constitute the essence of citizenship. They exercise their rights by having a voice in the organization. However, to achieve group goals, individuals typically have to forego some personal preferences. Democratic societies rely on persons with "democratic dispositions," that is,

a preparedness to work with others different from oneself toward shared ends; a combination of strong convictions with a readiness to compromise in the recognition that one can't always get everything one wants; and a sense of individuality and a commitment to civic goods that are not the possession of one person or one small group alone. (Elshtain, 1995, p. 2)

In the give-and-take of peer group negotiations, young people learn that people (fellow citizens and members of the public) have different perspectives. They learn that (as in community affairs and in politics) resolving differences of opinion may require bargaining and compromise. For example, group projects provide an opportunity for negotiating. In such collective endeavors, ownership of the project is enhanced when each member has a say. By working together, young people can see how their individual efforts contribute to the group as well as how the collective efforts of several people can produce a better product (Youniss et al., 1997).

Members can hold one another accountable for the project as well. Thus, the obligations citizens owe by virtue of their membership in the group are learned via such practices among peers. Political goals are rarely accomplished by the efforts of one individual, and the group projects of community youth organizations are a means by which young people gain civic practice. Reiterating the point we made at the beginning of this chapter: Community youth development not only provides an opportunity for individuals to practice life skills and develop their own assets; it also provides a unique opportunity for civic practice, including the chance for individuals to identify as members of groups with mutually defined goals for which all members are held accountable.

❖ GROUP SOLIDARITY

In his treatise on identity, Erikson (1968) held that individuals sought an internal coherence in their self-concepts but also needed to find solidarity with a group and its ideals. As young people become members of groups, we believe two interrelated phenomena occur. First, they take on the norms of the group and integrate into their own self-concept aspects of the group's identity. Second, the sense that they belong to the group and feel a solidarity with fellow members is essential if they are going to make the values of the group their own. As Lewin (1951) observed, group norms affect individual values, but their efficacy depends on a sense of group cohesion and solidarity.

In other work, we have conceived of young people's experiences of membership in institutions and organizations as the developmental foundation for a political community and for the ties that bind members of that community together. The importance of student solidarity as a factor in developing identification with the common good emerged in our comparative study in which adolescents from four fledgling democracies and three stable democracies participated. Across countries, youth were more likely to commit to public interest goals such as serving their communities and country *if* they felt a solidarity with peers at school and *if* they felt that most students in the school were proud to be part of an institution where caring transcended the borders of social cliques (Flanagan, Bowes, Jonsson, Csapo, & Sheblanova, 1998).

We should note that student solidarity is not a property of individuals. Similar to the collective efficacy of communities where residents feel that their neighbors generally act in the public interest (Sampson, Raudenbush, & Earls, 1997), ours is a measure of the collective properties of the student body. As such, it taps young people's perceptions of an inclusive climate in which youth feel that they and their fellow students matter to one another and to the institution. Other research has pointed to similar opportunities for group solidarity and social bonding for adults in community volunteer organizations. Clary and Miller (1986) found that, in adults who did not have particularly close relationships with their own parents, social bonding and cohesion with fellow volunteers were important aspects that sustained their commitment to the organizational work.

According to political scientists, a sense of shared values is more important than self-interest as the driving force behind political ideas, commitments, involvement, and even voting (Verba & Orren, 1985). Group solidarity and collective action also may sustain individuals engaged in political activism insofar as the likelihood of achieving political objectives is uncertain. In particular, when people are engaged in social change and the odds are against them, identification with a group and its cause may help them to overcome the anxiety inherent in the uncertainty of their situation (Keniston, 1968).

But there is a downside to group solidarity that warrants attention as well. Bonding strengthens the internal ties of group members and reinforces their organizational identity. But if bonding precludes the abilities of members to bridge to other individuals or groups, then it can undermine democracy. As Erikson (1968) warned, social cliques pose dangers to democracy if youth have no opportunities to connect to others beyond their narrow borders. Dewey (1916) listed two aspects of groups that make them democratic. First, to the extent that the interests of the members are numerous and varied, it should be more likely that everyone would play an integral role in the group and less likely that only a few people would take charge. Second, to the extent that interactions with others outside the group were "full and free," the group should be less likely to be isolationist and exclusive. Isolationist groups, Dewey warned, were not only undemocratic but also antisocial. Dewey's thesis as it applies to adults' civic engagement was supported in some of our recent work (Van Horn, 2001). One of the strongest predictors of the community and political involvement of young adults in this study was the number of *different* extracurricular clubs and activities in which individuals had participated in their high school years. If community youth development programs are going to fulfill their civic potential, Dewey's two conditions could provide a useful benchmark for program assessment.

The everyday contexts in which U.S. teens spend their time are rather homogeneous settings, and this fact can have consequences for democracy. According to social development research, whereas teenagers learn about such qualities as reciprocity in peer relationships, that learning is typically with friends who share their values (Berndt, 1982). Only in late adolescence do they learn to integrate and resolve *different* points of view (Selman, Watts, & Schultz, 1997). This may be due to the age, class, and culturally segregated worlds they inhabit. As a result of decreasing family size, age grading practices, social homogenization of neighborhoods, and school tracking, adolescents have fewer opportunities to interact with people who are different from them on a wide range of dimensions. Thus, there may be few natural opportunities for young people to develop skills that are fundamental to the functioning of democratic societies, including perspective taking, negotiation, and compromise. If community youth organizations reach out to include youth from different backgrounds and encourage activities that would link across generations or otherwise motivate adolescents to engage with others in their communities, they would not only enable youth to develop personal competencies but would be strengthening democracy as well.

❖ COMMUNITY SERVICE

Community service presents another opportunity to expand the awareness of others in a youth's community—their needs, conditions, customs, histories, contributions, and perspectives. In fact, when asked what they learned from service, young people note that their stereotypes broke down and their trust of 'others' increased because they had the opportunity to get to know individuals who were 'elderly' or 'homeless'. An ethic of service is common to most community youth organizations and is the kind of practice that makes real the principles embodied in a pledge such as that of the 4-H organization—service to my club, my community, and my world. When programs are well conceived, service can move young people beyond the confines of their world, expose them to the needs of the larger community, and at the same time, enable communities to see youth as a resource rather than a liability. But these outcomes are not inevitable. Organizations can maximize the civic learning potential of service projects by making sure that the experience is not isolated but instead is integral to both the lives of the youth and their communities. In other words, service should not be random acts of kindness. Rather, it should be a means whereby young people can form a sustained connection to their communities.

A set of best practices has now been identified in the literature on service learning (Billig, 2000; Youniss & Yates, 1999). These include meaningful activities (rather than busywork) that youth have a voice in choosing. These activities should be connected to the curriculum, and reflection on the service should be integral to the curriculum. If the reflection is done collectively rather than privately, the content of the work and the community issue it addresses becomes a public discussion. Discussion by the group raises service that could be a private act of charity to a level of public discourse. Thus, to the extent that community service is addressing a community problem (e.g., homelessness), group reflection can raise it to the level of public debate. When homelessness is viewed as a public issue rather than as a problem of individuals, the solution can move beyond the soup kitchen to discussions of affordable housing and a living wage. Youniss and Yates (1999) also emphasize the importance of connecting the service with the history of the organization providing it. The decision to engage in service reflects the organization's ideology. By making that connection salient for young people, they can see that they are members of a group with a history and, as members participating in the organization's actions, they are also contributing to history.

❖ SCHOOLS OF DEMOCRACY

An early observer of American mores, Alexis de Tocqueville noted that community associations in which citizens of all stripes worked through the issues and made decisions for their communities were the "schools of democracy" in the United States. In a similar vein, contemporary scholars have argued that engagement in youth clubs and extracurricular activities provides hands-on training for citizenship (Verba et al., 1995). We list some specific skills that young people are likely to develop as members of youth groups that would qualify community youth development programs as nonformal "schools of democracy."

Many practices common in nonformal youth groups are opportunities for developing organizational skills. These include electing club leaders, deciding together and following through on group projects, often making decisions using parliamentary procedure and learning to resolve disagreements in a civil fashion. In short, young people can learn how organizations operate, such as how meetings are conducted and committee work is accomplished. In addition, the project-based structure of voluntary youth activities includes facets such as goal setting; connecting concrete action steps to goal attainment; and reflecting on, evaluating, and refining activities so that goals are more likely to be attained (Rogoff, Baker-Sennett, Lacasa, & Goldsmith, 1995). And, by studying the community, its history, and knowing its services and resources, young citizens can get a picture of some of the players with whom one would have to work to effect local change. Meeting and visiting with elected officials might help to humanize the bureaucracy or demystify politics. It should make public servants seem less like politicians and more like fellow citizens. There have been many attempts to connect young people with elected officials and the work of government but few evaluations of such efforts. Hamilton and Zeldin (1987) evaluated a youth internship in local government and found that, compared to their peers in conventional civics classes, the interns' knowledge of local government increased, although their image of government did not become more positive. The Annenberg Student Voices project connected high school students from urban schools to candidates running in local mayoral elections. Evaluations of this program across multiple sites found that it increased students' interest in local politics and lowered their cynicism about politicians (Romer, 2002).

Opportunity to interact with public officials is a means by which stereotypes about politicians can break down. Youth may learn that those officials are ordinary citizens like themselves whose job is to serve the public. They may also get more interested in the political process if they come to believe that a citizen has a right to hold those officials accountable.

❖ CIVIC DEVELOPMENT: A LOGICAL NEXT STEP IN COMMUNITY YOUTH DEVELOPMENT

Throughout this chapter, our discussion of the civic potential of community youth development has assumed a participatory rather than a representative framework for democracy. In this spirit, we have argued that such groups afford unique opportunities for the practice of citizenship. We end the chapter by summarizing why we refer to this potential as a logical next step rather than a given or inevitable outcome of the community youth development movement.

Interest and belief in the political process is at an all-time low, especially among younger cohorts of Americans. The generation gap in social trust has grown as well (Smith, in press). These trends in younger generations bode poorly for democracy. At the same time, volunteerism in the community has become more normative among young people over the past decade (Sagawa, 1998). The results of an annual nationwide study of college freshman found that 81% of the class of 2000 had done volunteer work and 45% had participated in an organized demonstration, but only 28% said that they were interested in keeping up with politics (Kellogg, 2001).

Local communities are the space in which citizens are most likely to effect change and community youth development programs can be a major force for connecting the service in which youth engage to the local issues and political processes with which they need to grapple as citizens. But this bridge between service and political affairs is one that community youth development organizations (possibly in collaboration with schools, which also are engaged in service-learning opportunities for their students) have to think through and build into their programs.

We believe that an overriding reason why young people who participate in community programs become adults who are civically engaged is that they identify with the common good and value what they do for the community. Being a citizen with rights and obligations is who they are. The ethos of commitment is carried with them no matter how modern conditions of mobility may change the community in which they live. Evidence that this ethos is transmitted across generations is provided in two recent studies. Chan and Elder (2001) found that parents' participation in community affairs was a significant predictor of their adolescent's participation in community youth groups, and Van Horn et al. (2002) showed that this ethic carries over into adult life. The strongest predictor of the engagement of adults in their late 20s and early 30s in the affairs of their communities was their parents' involvement in community affairs when they were young.

The disconnection of younger generations from the political process is of concern in a democracy such as the United States. An even bigger issue in the diverse democracy that the 2000 Census paints is the possibility of unequal participation in the political process by different groups of citizens. There was a time when access to entry-level jobs with the potential for mobility provided a bridge for those in disadvantaged communities to connect to mainstream America. That era is over (Wilson, 1996). If an uneven distribution of community youth development programs reinforces the belief that the United States has turned its back on some groups of youth, the costs to those young people, as well as to U.S. democracy, are considerable.

The times call for innovation in community youth development. In his book, *Bowling Alone: The collapse and revival of American community* Robert Putnam (2000) urges a new civic inventiveness. He points to the parallels between the conditions of life in the United States today and those at the turn of the last century including disparities in wealth, growing corporate power, waves of immigration and massive change in the demographics of the population, new forms of technology, commerce, and communication, and a restructured workplace. At the close of the 19th century, optimism about the potential for social change was balanced by pessimism about seemingly intractable social ills.

But there was a boom in the building of community associations that revitalized the civic culture. In the late 19th and early 20th centuries, U.S. citizens created and joined an unprecedented number of voluntary associations, not the least of which were new youth organizations. In less than a decade (1901-1910), most of the nationwide youth organizations that were to dominate the 20th century were founded—the Boy and Girl Scouts, Campfire Girls, the 4-H, Boys Clubs and Girls Clubs, Big Brothers and Big Sisters, and the American Camping Association (Putnam, 2000).

If the community youth development approach is to realize its full potential for nurturing the next generation of local and national leaders—of engaged, committed citizens—we need to take seriously the need for greater innovation in the development of new youth institutions that respond to and build on the wealth of assets of our increasingly diverse population of young people.

❖ REFERENCES

Abramson, P. R. (1983). *Political attitudes in America.* San Francisco: W. H. Freeman.

Allen, J. P., Kuperminc, G., Philliber, S., & Herre, K. (1994). Programmatic prevention of adolescent problem behaviors: The role of autonomy, relatedness, and volunteer service in the teen outreach program. *American Journal of Community Psychology, 22,* 617-638.

Barber, B. L., Eccles, J. S., & Stone, M. R. (2000). *Whatever happened to the jock, the brain, and the princess? Young adult pathways linked to adolescent activity involvement and social identity.* Manuscript submitted for publication.

Bedolla, L. G. (2000). They and we: Identity, gender, and politics among Latino youth in Los Angeles. *Social Science Quarterly, 81,* 106-122.

Berndt, T. J. (1982). The features and effects of friendship in early adolescence. *Child Development, 53,* 1447-1460.

Billig, S. H. (2000, May). Research on K-12 school-based service learning: The evidence builds. *Phi Delta Kappan,* 658-664.

Blyth, D. A., & Leffert, N. (1995). Communities as contexts for adolescent development: An empirical analysis. *Journal of Adolescent Research, 10(1),* 64-87.

Camino, L. A., & Zeldin, S. (2002). Everyday lives in communities: Discovering citizenship through youth-adult partnerships. *Applied Developmental Science, 6(4).*

Carnegie Council on Adolescent Development. (1992). *A matter of time: Risk and opportunity in the nonschool hours.* New York: Carnegie Corporation of New York.

Chan, C. G., & Elder, G. H. (2001). Family influences on the social participation of youth: The effects of parental social involvement and farming. *Rural Sociology, 66,* 22-42.

Clary, E. G., & Miller, J. (1986). Socialization and situational influences on sustained altruism. *Child Development, 57,* 1358-1369.

Connell, J., & Halpern-Felsher, B. (1997). How neighborhoods affect educational outcomes in middle childhood and adolescence: Conceptual issues and an empirical example. In J. Brooks-Gunn, G. Duncan, & J. Aber (Eds.), *Neighborhood poverty: Context and consequences for children* (pp. 174-199).

Delli Carpini, M. X., & Keeter, S. (1996). *What Americans know about politics and why it matters.* New Haven: Yale University Press.

DeMartini, J. R. (1983). Social movement participation: Political socialization, generational consciousness, and lasting effects. *Social Forces, 64,* 1-16.

Dennis, J., & Webster, C. (1975). Children's images of the president and of government in 1962 and 1974. *American Politics Quarterly, 3(4),* 386-405.

Dewey, J. (1916). *Democracy and education: An introduction to the philosophy of education.* New York: Free Press.

Easton, D. (1953). *The political system: An inquiry into the state of political science.* New York: Alfred A. Knopf.

Easton, D., & Dennis, J. (1969). *Children in the political system.* New York: McGraw-Hill.

Eccles, J. S., & Barber, B. L. (1999). Student council, volunteering, basketball, or marching band: What kind of extracurricular involvement matters? *Journal of Adolescent Research, 14,* 10-43.

Eccles, J. S., & Gootman, J. A. (Eds.). (2002). *Community programs to promote youth development*. Report for the National Research Council and Institute of Medicine, Committee on Community-Level Youth Programs for Youth, Board on Children, Youth and Families. Washington, DC: National Academies Press.

Elshtain, J. B. (1995). *Democracy on trial*. New York: Basic Books.

Erikson, E. H. (1968). *Identity: Youth and crisis*. New York: W. W. Norton.

Evans, S. M., & Boyte, H. C. (1992). *Free spaces: The sources of democratic change in America*. Chicago: University of Chicago Press.

Flanagan, C. A. (1990). Families and schools in hard times. In V. C. McLoyd & C. A. Flanagan (Eds.), *New directions for child development: Vol. 46. Economic stress: Effects on family life and child development* (pp. 7-26). San Francisco: Jossey-Bass.

Flanagan, C. A. (1998). Exploring American character in the sixties generation. In A. Colby, J. James, & D. Hart (Eds.), *Competence and character through life* (pp. 169-185). Chicago: University of Chicago Press.

Flanagan, C.A., Bowes, J., Jonsson, B., Csapo, B., & Sheblanova, E. (1998). Ties that bind: Correlates of male and female adolescents' civic commitments in seven countries. *Journal of Social Issues, 54,* (pp. 457-476).

Flanagan, C. A., & Campbell, B. (in press). Social class and adolescents' beliefs about justice in different social orders. In J. Ostrove & E. Cole (Eds.), The psychological meaning of social class. *Journal of Social Issues*.

Flanagan, C. A., & Gallay, L. S. (1995). Reframing the meaning of "political" in research with adolescents. *Perspectives on Political Science, 24,* 34-41.

Flanagan, C.A., Gill, S., & Gallay, L. (2001). *Adolescents' social integration and affection for the polity: Processes for different racial/ethnic groups*. Unpublished manuscript.

Flanagan, C. A., Gill, S., & Gallay, L. S. (in press). Social participation and social trust in adolescence: The importance of heterogeneous encounters. In A. Omoto (Ed.), *Claremont Symposium on Applied Social Psychology: Vol. 19. Social participation in processes of community change and social action*. Thousand Oaks, CA: Sage.

Flanagan, C. A., Jonsson, B., Botcheva, L., Csapo, B., Bowes, J., Macek, P., Averina, I., & Sheblanova, E. (1998). Adolescents and the "social contract": Developmental roots of citizenship in seven countries. In M. Yates & J. Youniss (Eds.), *Community service and civic engagement in youth: International perspectives* (pp. 135-155). Cambridge University Press.

Hamilton, S. F., & Zeldin, R. S. (1987). Learning civics in the community. *Curriculum Inquiry, 17*(4), 407-420.

Hanks, M., & Eckland, B. K. (1978). Adult voluntary associations and adolescent socialization. *The Sociological Quarterly, 19,* 481-490.

Hantover, J. P. (1978). The Boy Scouts and the validation of masculinity. *Journal of Social Issues, 34,* 184-195.

Hart, D., Atkins, R., & Ford, D. (1998). Urban America as a context for the development of moral identity in adolescence. *Journal of Social Issues, 54,* 513-530.

Hilles, W. S., & Kahle, L. R. (1985). Social contract and social integration in adolescent development. *Journal of Personality and Social Psychology, 49,* 1114-1121.

Kahane, R. (1997). *The origins of postmodern youth: Informal youth movements in a comparative perspective.* New York: De Gruyter.

Kellogg, A. (2001, January 26). Looking inward, freshmen care less about politics and more about money. *The Chronicle of Higher Education,* A47-A49.

Keniston, K. (1968). *Young radicals: Notes on committed youth.* New York: Harcourt, Brace, & World.

Larson, R. W. (1992). Youth organizations, hobbies, and sports as developmental contexts. In R. K. Silbereisen & E. Todt (Eds.), *Adolescence in context: The interplay of family, school, peers, and work in adjustment* (pp. 46-65). New York: Springer-Verlag.

Larson, R. W. (2000). Toward a psychology of positive youth development. *American Psychologist, 55,* 170-183.

Lewin, K. (1951). *Field theory in social science: Selected theoretical papers.* New York: Harper.

McBride, C. M., Curry, S. J., Cheadle, A., Anderman, C., Wagner, E. H., Diehr, P., & Psaty, B. (1995). School-level application of a social bonding model to adolescent risk-taking behavior. *Journal of School Health, 65,* 63-68.

McLaughlin, M. W. (1993). Embedded identities: Enabling balance in urban contexts. In S. B. Heath & M. W. McLaughlin, *Identity and inner city youth.* New York: Teacher's College Press.

McLaughlin, M. W., Irby, M. A., & Langman, J. (1994). *Urban sanctuaries: Neighborhood organizations in the lives and futures of inner-city youth.* San Francisco: Jossey-Bass.

McNeal, R. B. (1995). Extracurricular activities and high school dropouts. *Sociology of Education, 68,* 62-81.

Mechling, J. (2001). *On my honor: Boy Scouts and the making of American youth.* Chicago: University of Chicago Press.

Neumark-Sztainer, D., Story, M., French, S. A., & Resnick, M. D. (1997). Psychosocial correlates of health compromising behaviors among adolescents. *Health Education Research, 12*(1), 37-52.

Niemi, R. G., & Junn, J. (1998). *Civic education: What makes students learn.* New Haven, CT: Yale University Press.

Otto, L. B. (1976). Social integration and the status attainment process. *American Journal of Sociology, 81,* 1360-1383.

Perkins, D. F., Borden, L. M., Keith, J. G., Hoppe-Rooney, T. L., & Villarruel, F. A. (2003). Community youth development: Partnership creating a positive world. In F. A. Villarruel, D. F. Perkins, L. M. Borden, & J. G. Keith

(Eds.), *Community youth development: Programs, policies, and practices.* Thousand Oaks, CA: Sage.

Putnam, R. D. (2000). *Bowling alone: The collapse and revival of American community.* New York: Simon & Schuster.

Rasmussen, W. (1989). *Taking the university to the people: Seventy-five years, of cooperative extension.* Ames: Iowa State University Press.

Resnick, M. D., Bearman, P. S., Blum, R. W., Bauman, K. E., Harris, K. M., Jones, J., Tabor, J., Beuhring, T., Sieving, R. E., & Shew, M. (1997). Protecting adolescents from harm: Findings from the National Longitudinal Study on Adolescent Health. *JAMA, 278*(10), 823-832.

Rogoff, B., Baker-Sennett, J., Lacasa, P., & Goldsmith, D. (1995, Spring). Development through participation in sociocultural activity. *Cultural practices as contexts for development: New directions for Child Development, 67,* 45-65.

Romer, D. (2002, March). *Evaluation of student voices: What have we learned and what are we going to do?* Presentation for the Student Voices Advisory Board meeting, Grand Cayman, BWI.

Roth, J., & Brooks-Gunn, J. (2000). What do adolescents need for healthy development? Implications for youth policy. Society for Research in Child Development. *Social Policy Report, 14*(1).

Sagawa, S. (1998). Ten years of youth in service to America. In S. Halperin (Ed.), *The forgotten half revisited: American youth and young families, 1988-2008* (pp. 137-158). Washington, DC: American Youth Policy Forum.

Sampson, R. J., Raudenbush, S. W., & Earls, F. (1997). Crime: A multilevel study of collective efficacy. *Science, 277,* 918-924.

Sanchez-Jankowski, M. (1992). Ethnic identity and political consciousness in different social orders. In H. Haste & J. Torney-Purta, (Eds.), *New directions in child development: Vol. 56. The development of political understanding.* San Francisco: Jossey-Bass.

Schofield, J. (Ed.). (1995). *Promoting positive intergroup relations in school settings.* San Francisco: Jossey-Bass.

Selman, R. L., Watts, C. L., & Schultz, L. H. (1997). *Fostering friendship: Pair therapy and prevention.* New York: Aldine de Gruyter.

Sigel, R. S., & Hoskin, M. (1981). *The political involvement of adolescents.* New Brunswick, NJ: Rutgers University Press.

Smith, T. (in press). The transition to adulthood and the generation gap from the 1970s to the 1990s. In F. F. Furstenburg, R. G. Rumbaut, & R. A. Settersten, Jr. (Eds.), *On the frontier of adulthood: Theory, research, and public policy.* Chicago: University of Chicago Press.

Storrmann, W. (1991). The ideology of the American parks and recreation movement: Past and future. *Leisure Sciences, 13,* 137-151.

Storrmann, W. (1993). The recreation profession, capital, and democracy. *Leisure Sciences, 15,* 49-66.

Tocqueville, A. C. de. (1848/1966). *Democracy in America*. New York: Harper & Row.

U.S. Department of Education, Office of Educational Research and Improvement, National Center for Education Statistics. (1990). *National education longitudinal study of 1988: A profile of the American eighth grader* (pp. 50–54). Washington, D.C.: U.S. Government Printing Office.

Van Horn, B. (2001). Youth, family and club experiences and adult civic engagement. Unpublished doctoral dissertation, Pennsylvania State University, University Park.

Van Horn, B., Flanagan, C., & Thomson, J. (1998, December). Changes and challenges in 4-H: Part 1. *Journal of Extension*.

Van Horn, B., & Flanagan, C. A., & Willits, F. K. (2002). *Youth, family and club experiences and adult civic engagement*. Manuscript submitted for publication.

Verba, S., Nie, N. H., & Kim, J. (1978). *Participation and political equality: A seven nation comparison*. Cambridge, MA: Harvard University Press.

Verba, S., & Orren, G. R. (1985). *Equality in America: The view from the top*. Cambridge, MA: Harvard University Press.

Verba, S., Schlozman, K. L., & Brady, H. E. (1995). *Voice and equality: Civic voluntarism in American politics*. Cambridge, MA: Harvard University Press.

Waller, W. (1932). *The sociology of teaching*. New York: Wiley.

Wilson, W. J. (1996). *When work disappears: The world of the new urban poor*. New York: Vintage Books.

Yogev, A., & Shapira, R. (1990). Citizenship socialization in national voluntary youth organizations. In O. Ichilov (Ed.), *Political socialization, citizenship education, and democracy* (pp. 205-220). New York: Columbia University Teacher's College Press.

Youniss, J., McLellan, J. A., & Yates, M. (1997). What we know about engendering civic identity. *American Behavioral Scientist, 40*, 620-631.

Youniss, J., & Yates, M. (1999). Youth service and moral-civic identity: A case for everyday morality. *Educational Psychology Review, 11(4)*, 363-378.

14

Giving Youth a Voice in Their Own Community and Personal Development

*Strategies and Impacts
of Bringing Youth to the Table*

*Melissa S. Quon Huber, Jeff Frommeyer,
Amy Weisenbach, and Jennifer Sazama*

This chapter describes the benefits for communities and organizations when youth are included in key decision-making roles or youth governance roles. Then we examine common reasons youth have been excluded from these roles and how to successfully overcome

AUTHOR'S NOTE: The authors wish to thank the editors of this chapter for their instructive and thoughtful reviews and revisions. In addition, we gratefully acknowledge Sarra Baraily and Shelley Moore for their editorial assistance.

these barriers. Finally, examples are provided of youth as advocates, grantmakers, and policymakers in their own communities.

The field of positive youth development has drawn attention to the importance of recognizing and building on youth assets so that youth can be "fully prepared" rather than just "problem free" (Pittman & Irby, 1998). This suggests that youth have many talents, skills, behaviors, and attitudes that will contribute to their own success. The field also recognizes the important role that community contexts play in helping youth to develop (Bronfenbrenner, 1977). As Zeldin (2000) has noted, communities are important settings that can help to determine how well youth succeed and fully develop their assets. This next section provides an overview of the important social, human, and economic capital assets that youth and communities can derive from each other. Human capital investments in positive youth development have benefits for youth as well as the community.

❖   HOW DO COMMUNITY YOUTH
        INVESTMENTS BENEFIT YOUTH?

Communities have many ways of investing in youth collectively as individuals or as a municipal entity. For instance, the amount of time that individual adults (e.g., family members, friends, teachers, neighbors, and other community members) spend with youth contributes to the development of positive academic and social behaviors for those same youth (Scales, Benson, Leffert, & Blyth, 2000). Also, the types and quality of out-of-school settings that a community provides for youth to constructively use their time (Scales & Leffert, 1999) have positive benefits beyond what may be found at school (Larson, 2000), reconnecting youth to adults (Camino, 2000) and to their communities (Zeldin, 2000). Such mentoring and development of social ties are critical investments in youth. In addition, the access to quality health care that a community provides is also an important determinant of youth physical health and well-being (Malone, 1994).

Economic opportunities and investments in youth are also important to their success and thriving. The quality of local education and job conditions can shape young people's aspirations and economic well-being in their future careers (Huber, 2000). These community economic conditions can even influence the quality of peer relationships that children develop during childhood (Brody et al., 2001). These economic conditions will also determine whether or not youth will be able to remain in their home communities near their support (such as family, friends, and religious institutions) when they seek employment as young adults, or whether they will migrate to another community for gainful employment and experience the loss of tangible assistance and social support, which can lead to sadness and depression (Elder, King, & Conger, 1996; Lichter, McLaughlin, & Comwell, 1993). Clearly, community and economic development investments in programs, resources, and relationships can have a positive impact on the quality of life and future for youth in the community. It is also clear that the quality of community facilities, education, health, and economic and neighborhood conditions may affect the overall positive development of youth in a community. Therefore, strategies to improve youth development must also include community and economic development strategies.

❖ HOW DO YOUTH DEVELOPMENT INVESTMENTS BENEFIT COMMUNITIES?

Although the benefits of positive youth development investments for youth may be clear, it is also important to realize that these positive youth developments are also in the best interest of the community, providing both economic and social returns. Communities benefit economically and socially by supporting positive youth development strategies and investing in the economic future of their youth. When youth migrate to other communities, it results in a great loss of youth skills and economic contributions to the community (Mullet & Neto, 1991). Communities depend on their youth to contribute to the current and future economy through their purchases and payment of taxes as productive workers (Maier, 1988). However, communities must help to provide youth with the education, skills, and assets that will enable them to contribute to the local economy rather than draining it as unemployed or incarcerated citizens (Beker, Eisikovits, & Guttmann, 1987). In this way, fully thriving youth can contribute not only their economic resources but also their human capital resources to the leadership, permanence, and social fabric of the community through their social and civic engagement as youth as well as when they become adults.

In addition to the benefits of positive youth development investments in creating productive citizens, these same youth investments are also quality of life investments that attract businesses and help stimulate economic growth. All other factors being equal, companies seek to locate their businesses in communities that have quality education, programs, and cultural enrichment opportunities for their employees' families (Ward, 2000). The presence of positive youth development programs and strategies can help communities become more economically competitive.

Furthermore, these quality of life investments in youth activities (e.g., summer camps, leisure activities, and recreation programs) can generate income for the community. For example, a high school of nearly 1,000 youth was found to spend at least $600,000 annually on recreation and leisure activities alone, with half of this money being spent outside the community because few youth activities or venues were available locally (Huber, 2001). By providing affordable activities in the local community, communities can derive economic benefit from the revenue to local youth-serving organizations, which in turn is spent in the local community economy and recirculated to provide additional revenue throughout the community (Carter, Huber, LaMore, Lemer, Lichty, & Rosenbaum, 1997). Community revenue can also be generated through employment of youth and other adults in these youth-serving organizations. The connectedness of community and thriving youth outcomes points to the importance of community-wide approaches to investing in and planning for positive youth development.

❖ WHY IS YOUTH PARTICIPATION IMPORTANT?

As important as these investments are in positive youth development, it is even more important to actively engage youth in the development of strategies and priorities for these investments. Unfortunately, adults often complete the development of programs and activities designed for youth without engaging youth in the development and identification of priorities and implementation strategies (Hart, 1992). Similarly, across the nation, youth report that they have little value to the community and have few opportunities for meaningful roles (Scales et al., 2000). As one middle school female remarked after participating in a community-planning process involving youth, "This is really cool! No one has asked us our opinions before" (Huber, 2001, p. 8). There is a great opportunity to support positive youth development in both the process and outcomes of engaging youth in planning ways for communities and organizations to address their needs and desires. The process of involvement will give youth opportunities for growth, learning, leadership, and mentoring through their meaningful involvement in these planning and implementation processes. The hope is that the end results will also be beneficial in providing programs, activities, and organizational and community changes that reflect the needs and priorities of the local youth and that this will generate greater participation and a better fit for their needs. To achieve these levels of youth participation, both the community development and the youth infusion models provide useful frameworks for understanding the importance of youth participation in these processes.

❖ WHAT IS A COMMUNITY DEVELOPMENT APPROACH TO YOUTH PARTICIPATION?

The community development approach provides a useful framework for thinking about youth development (see Table 14.1). First, it recognizes the need to address economic, social, environmental, political, and psychological issues in promoting healthy communities. As noted earlier, community development strategies and decisions can have an impact on the present and future quality of life for youth. Therefore, this comprehensive community-level perspective is needed to create the community contexts that can nurture youth and help them thrive academically, socially, physically, and vocationally, as set forth in the first chapter of this book (Perkins, Borden, Keith, Hoppe-Rooney, & Villarruel, 2003, this volume). Second, it seeks to build the capacity of a diverse group of local community members and "promote active and representative participation toward enabling all community members to meaningfully influence the decisions that affect their lives" (Community Development Society, 2000). In principle, youth are members of this diverse group of participants, although they have often been underrepresented in community development initiatives (Israel, Coleman, & Ilvento, 1993). When youth are involved in these community initiatives, not only does this type of involvement increase youths' empowerment and decrease their alienation from their community (Calabrese & Schumer, 1986; Zimmerman, 1990; Zimmerman & Rappaport, 1988), but it can also provide important benefits to the community (Beker et al., 1987; Zeldin, McDaniel, Topitzes, & Calvert, 2000). Overall, this community development perspective of youth participation recognizes

Table 14.1   Community Development Society Principles of Good Practice

- Promote active and representative participation toward enabling all community members to meaningfully influence the decisions that affect their lives.
- Engage community members in learning about and understanding community issues and the economic, social, environmental, political, psychological, and other impacts associated with alternative courses of action.
- Incorporate the diverse interests and cultures of the community in the community development process; and disengage from support of any effort that is likely to adversely affect disadvantaged members of a community.
- Work actively to enhance the leadership capacity of community members, leaders, and groups within the community.
- Be open to using the full range of action strategies to work toward the long-term sustainability and well-being of the community.

SOURCE: Community Development Society (2000).

the need for youth to be involved in shaping their own community contexts.

❖ WHAT IS THE YOUTH INFUSION APPROACH TO DECISION MAKING?

Similar to the community development approach, the youth infusion model has a strong philosophical emphasis on participation; however, this model focuses specifically on involvement of youth members of the community. The goals of youth infusion are "to integrate youth and young adults into all spheres of community life and to ensure that their voice and actions are valued and utilized in efforts aimed at social or community change" (Zeldin et al., 2000, p. 3). Youth governance, or youth decision making, is a strategy used to help achieve this goal of infusion. This notion of youth governance refers to youth-adult partnerships in organizations, institutions, or coalitions where youth have an active role in setting the overall policy directions. This type of policy-making involvement is exemplified by boards of directors, advisory groups, committees, and other planning bodies that include youth members (Zeldin et al., 2000).

❖ WHAT ARE THE BENEFITS OF THIS YOUTH INFUSION APPROACH?

Practitioners of youth involvement have long touted the benefits of such involvement for young people. Many also point to the fact that adults and the organizations in which youth are involved benefit as well. A recent study commissioned by the Innovation Center for Community and Youth Development and conducted by Shepherd Zeldin and colleagues (2000) at the University of Wisconsin—Madison backs up these assertions (see Box 14.1).

Box 14.1   The Synergy of Youth and Adult Contributions to Decision Making

---

Zeldin, McDaniel, Topitzes, and Calvert (2000) explored the experiences of 19 youth and 29 adults from 15 U.S. organizations, each with varying degrees of youth involvement. Their findings also build on other literature from past research.

In addition to impacts and conditions that facilitate them, the research (Zeldin, et al., 2000) also identified the unique contributions that youth and adults bring to decision-making roles. The following ideas are summarized from their report.

Effective decision-making in organizations requires the complementary skills, experience, and contributions of both youth and adults.

- *Youth bring energy, fresh perspectives, knowledge of young people, and a sense of community to decision-making processes.* The adolescent stage of development suits the needs of organizations. During adolescence, young people are driven to explore issues of social justice. They are creating and experimenting with their own principles and political ideas, leading many to become involved in cause-based action. Young people have a way, rarely subtle and often inventive, of bringing attention to their needs and concerns, and they often say things that challenge people and institutions.

Adolescence is also a time for deepening relationships and intimacy with peers. Young people bring a firsthand knowledge of youth that simply is not accessible to adults. They bring connections to other young people and can leverage the participation and skill of their peers. Almost every adult interviewed stressed that young people often bring a sense of community and energy to decision-making processes.

- *Adults bring organizational and administrative experience, allowing youth to concentrate on more mission-driven and action-oriented aspects of decision making.* The young people and adults in this study most often used words such as *guidance* and *support* when describing the contributions of adults. By virtue of years of work experience, adults bring a range of administrative and programming skills to the table. Adults also bring lessons learned from other organizations.

Young people especially value this knowledge and often seek the advice, instruction, and direction that adults can offer. What's more, adults' organizational expertise often allows youth to concentrate their expertise, interest, and time on the more mission-driven and action-oriented aspects of the organization. Many adults have institutional power not accessible to young people. With this power come access and connections to a fuller range of human, community, and financial resources. According to those interviewed, whereas youth had important connections with other youth in the community, adults were more connected—because of age and institutional power—to other community resources, such as money, status, and legitimacy.

- *Working together creates synergy between youth and adults.* The mutual contributions of youth and adults can result in a synergy, a new power and energy that propels decision-making groups to greater innovation and productivity. The researchers reported that in this atmosphere, youth and adults become more committed to attending meetings and create a climate that is grounded in honest appraisal, reflection, and ongoing learning.

Source: Zeldin, McDaniel, Topitzes, & Calvert (2000).

Zeldin and colleagues contend that young people do benefit, but that the impacts on adults, organizations and communities are significant as well. For adults, the benefits include changed attitudes about young people, including a greater confidence in young people's abilities. In addition, adults develop a deeper commitment to the organization and a stronger sense of community. In general, the adults interviewed expressed an enthusiasm for their role that they attributed to their partnership with young people.

Organizations in the study also pointed to positive outcomes they have experienced from involving young people. Nearly all those interviewed mentioned young people's ability to focus on the fundamentals, such as the fit of the organization's mission with programs and activities. In the case of the National 4-H Council's Board of Trustees, they went so far as to create a formal role for youth (the position of vice president for mission and performance).

Oftentimes, involving youth is the first step toward a more inclusive decision-making body overall. For example, many organizations cited that once they considered youth involvement, they began to question the absence of other stakeholders as well. As a result, they invited other previously underrepresented groups to participate. Also, as organizations realized the benefits of youth involvement, they further increased opportunities for youth involvement. Many organizational representatives interviewed for the study shared that they had a newfound ability to attract financial resources as a result of involving youth. For some, this came as a result of young people serving as convincing spokespersons to representatives of potential funding sources. For others, it allowed them to apply for grants from funding sources that require youth involvement.

The study was unable to consistently identity community level outcomes due to a variety of conceptual and methodological issues. However, there were some promising examples that point to positive community impacts. One organization the report featured was the Hampton (Virginia) Coalition for Youth. Hampton began youth involvement efforts nearly a decade ago by involving young people as city planners. Now young people are engaged in decisions across the community that affect youth, serving on everything from nonprofit boards to a citywide advisory board. Hampton has created a community culture of youth involvement that reaches well beyond the original role of youth as city planners (Zeldin et al., 2000).

❖ WHAT ARE THE BARRIERS TO INVOLVING YOUTH IN DECISION MAKING?

Despite the many benefits to involving youth in community decision making, youth have often been left out of these decision-making processes in the community (Israel et al., 1993). There are many reasons why youth have been excluded from decision making in many areas, not just community development strategies. Youth have been excluded from decision-making roles in schools and other organizations where they are involved as participants or service recipients. Adult attitudes as well as structural issues are common barriers to youth involvement in decision making, and these barriers are explored.

Adult Perceptions of Youth Capacities

One of the reasons that youth are not often involved in community decision making is because adults often question whether or not youth will possess the capacities needed to be involved in important decision making (Young & Sazama, 1999). Adults have often underestimated the capacities of youth (Boggiano & Katz, 1991; Midgley, Feldlaufer, & Eccles, 1988) and their desire to participate in decision making (Eccles et al., 1993). Adults may also have concerns about youths' ability to make decisions, to follow through on assignments, or to deal with sensitive or confidential matters. However, these fears and perceptions are not consistent with the actual capacities of most youth. Research has found that youth have sound decision-making and comprehension skills by the age of 9, and these skills are equivalent to adult skills by age 14 to 16 (Belter & Grisso, 1984; Grisso, 1980; Lewis, 1981; Weithorn & Campbell, 1982). What youth may lack is the accompanying experiences of making these decisions in adult settings (Young & Sazama, 1999). Therefore, it is beneficial to give youth more opportunities to make decisions with adults so that they can gain these experiences that will continue to develop their decision-making abilities (Hart & Pavlovic, 1991).

Use of Tokenism

The lack of confidence in youth capacities may lead youth to be excluded entirely from decision making, but it may also lead to token participation of youth. Token participation occurs when adults include youth in committees or groups that make decisions but do not act on their suggestions or give them real opportunities to participate in the decision-making process (Hart, 1992). It may also occur when adults have inappropriately stepped in and taken over tasks previously assigned to youth members. Labeling theory suggests that such tokenism can diminish the role of the youth and ultimately decrease their motivation (Scheff, 1975). Therefore, youth advocates recommend that a minimum of two youth members be included on boards or other decision-making bodies to prevent such tokenism (Young & Sazama, 1999).

Structural Issues

Structural issues may be considerable barriers for youth involvement in community decision-making opportunities. Adults have not often shared power and resources with youth (Melton, 1987a), and children have historically had an inferior social, political, and legal status in modern society. They have not been able to advocate for their own resources (Bikson, 1978; Melton, 1987b; Takanishi, DeLeon, & Pallak, 1983; Tremper & Kelly, 1987). Therefore, organizational bylaws and budgets have not have been designed to regularly include youth and institutionalize their participation (Young & Sazama, 1999).

Practical barriers prevent their participation as well. Many community meetings take place during the school day and preclude youth involvement. It can be difficult for students to leave school grounds to attend meetings, and it may be even more difficult for them to obtain transportation to such meetings. Furthermore, communication with students outside community meetings is often restricted. School districts have varying policies on student communications, with some barring the use of even pay phones during the day and many barring personal communication devices, such as cellular phones and pagers, that are common office tools for adults. Schools also have varying policies on whether or not messages can be left for students. Unlike adults, youth do not have office locations where they can make calls and receive phone and electronic messages throughout the day, making it difficult to involve youth members on committees that have planning activities or tasks to conduct outside the actual meeting times.

Legal Barriers

Another concern that may arise is the legal ability of youth to participate in decision-making opportunities, such as being voting members of boards or organizations that require the ability to sign contracts. Although youth can be members of committees and boards without voting privileges, the age at which they can be legal voting members varies from state to state (Young & Sazama, 1999) and should be verified with current state legislation as changes continue to occur. It may also be necessary for an organization to revise its bylaws to formally institutionalize the role of youth as legitimate voting members.

❖ HOW CAN THESE BARRIERS BE OVERCOME?

As beneficial as it is for adults and organizations to involve youth as decision makers, these positive outcomes do not occur spontaneously; rather, they require much hard work. Young and Sazama (1999) identified the key factors in organizations that promote young people's full involvement in decision making and provide tools and strategies for addressing those issues. Based on this research, 14 points identified as ways to overcome barriers and successfully involve youth in decision making are highlighted in Table 14.2. These key points address the need to examine organizational goals, practices, and structures that will facilitate creation of a climate conducive to bringing youth on board, as well as eliminating barriers that could turn youth away. They also highlight the importance of training and orientation for both youth and adults to better equip them with the knowledge, skills, and attitudes needed to work together effectively. Additional mentoring between individual adults and youth and the inclusion of parents are also cited as factors helping to foster youth involvement in such organizations.

Even more than just removing and addressing barriers to youth participation, Zeldin and colleagues (2000) found that the organization must have several "necessary conditions" in place to effectively involve youth (see Table 14.3). These conditions include strong support from the leaders in the organization as well as the presence of adult advocates for youth and youth who are willing to advocate for themselves. There need to be mechanisms for advancing youth through a series of increasingly more advanced responsibilities. These conditions

Table 14.2   Ways to Overcome Barriers to Youth Involvement in Decision Making

Steps to Overcoming Barriers for Organizations	Step Descriptions
1. **Know why you want to involve young people.**	Be aware of the civil rights issues that have lead to discrimination based on age. Develop clear goals and objectives that are tangible, attainable, and specific.
2. **Assess your readiness.**	Identify aspects of the governance structure that need to be modified to include youth. Engage the board and staff in preparations for their involvement to gain their support for youth involvement.
3. **Determine your model for youth involvement.**	Determine whether youth will be incorporated into the existing decision-making structure or whether a separate group comprised of and run by youth should be formed.
4. **Identify organizational barriers.**	Create a permanent structure, such as bylaws, that will ensure consistent involvement of youth through administrative changes. Identify changes in budgets that may be needed to incorporate costs of transportation, refreshments, etc., that will facilitate youth involvement in the meetings.
5. **Overcome attitudinal barriers.**	Help adults overcome their negative stereotypes of youth and help youth recognize their own value. Avoid the use of terms and abbreviations that youth will not understand. Present information in ways that youth will understand.
6. **Address legal issues.**	Know the legal obligations of board members and identify the age in your state at which youth are allowed to be voting members and sign contracts.
7. **Recruit young people.**	Identify characteristics needed for members of the governing body and characteristics needed to diversify the team. Choose youth who are committed and motivated. Have at least two young people in the governing body to provide peer support and prevent feelings of isolation.

(Continued)

Table 14.2   Continued

Steps to Overcoming Barriers for Organizations	*Step Descriptions*
8. **Create a strong orientation process for youth and their parents.**	Develop a new member orientation to help youth understand the purpose of the group along with their roles and responsibilities. Provide orientation for parents to help them be comfortable with their youth's involvement.
9. **Provide training for youth and adults.**	Provide training for youth so they can develop skills such as reading budgets and working on committees. Provide training for adults to explore their assumptions and stereotypes about youth. Use innovative training methods that are suitable for your group.
10. **Conduct intergenerational training.**	Pair youth with adults to help them learn to work together and build relationships during training. Keep the training fun and help create spaces for youth and adults to listen to one another.
11. **Make meetings work.**	Conduct meetings at times that enable youth to attend, recognizing that they often have less control over their time than adults do. Provide opportunities for everyone to speak and provide feedback. Review budgets in teams and provide time for questions.
12. **Develop a mentoring plan.**	Provide buddies for all new members to help them learn about the organization and its culture. Help mentors know their responsibilities to their new youth member. Remind youth to ask questions and rely on their mentor for assistance.
13. **Build youth-adult relationships.**	Build strong relationships between youth and adults to create a caring environment. Remind adults to go easy on themselves as they learn how to interact and involve youth. Build relationships with parents and include them in events and keep them informed.
14. **Create support networks.**	Help youth to network with other youth leaders who will help them find support from their peers. Remind adults to be supportive of one another to support their own growth as well.

SOURCE: Young & Sazama (1999).

suggest that organizations must have clear plans and strong support to lay the foundation for youth involvement.

An overall community youth development perspective is needed to examine how a broad range of youth are engaged across many domains of the community to invest in their own development and the development of their community context. As noted in this chapter, communities, organizations, and youth benefit when communities invest in youth and when youth are engaged in the development of their communities. To examine how these benefits can be achieved, two examples of youth decision-making organizations will be examined.

❖ YOUTH ADVOCATES—TEEN COURT

A teenager stands before a County Probate Judge and a jury of his peers, awaiting the jury's verdict on the crime with which he has been charged (malicious destruction of property). The teen jury then hands down the sentence: 4 months' probation; 38 hours of community service; counseling; and more than $300 in restitution and court costs. He also must attend school regularly and improve his grades (Butts & Buck, 2000). This example refers to a teen court case in one U.S. city, just one of approximately 675 youth courts in communities across the nation (a number that has grown considerably, beginning with only a handful of such programs in the 1960s). Teen courts are examples of settings in which youth have actual decision-making powers and the ability to influence their own community social climate by reinforcing norms and seeking alternative ways of solving problems in their communities.

What Are Positive Impacts for Youth Involved in Teen Court?

Teen courts can have positive youth development benefits for the court members as well as the offending youth. Because adolescence is a time when young people are developing skills, habits, and attitudes that will remain with them throughout their lives, the experiences that offending youth encounter are critical to this development. Teen courts can be a positive experience where first-time juvenile offenders (with no criminal record) are provided an opportunity for a second chance, provided they fulfill the requirements of their sentence. By providing an opportunity for

Table 14.3   Necessary Conditions for Change to Involve Youth in
Decision-Making

Conditions Necessary for Change	*Description of Conditions*
1. **Organizations are committed to youth governance.**	The top decision-making body in the organization needs to be committed to youth governance and youth-adult partnership and must change their ways of operating accordingly. The data are clear: If a governance body is focused on vision and learning, there is room for young people to make substantial contributions. If it is more traditionally focused on rule making and management, then it is less likely that young people will have a significant influence on the board.
2. **A visionary adult leader is present.**	Organizational change is facilitated by an adult visionary leader, one with institutional power and authority, to strongly advocate for youth decision making. Without this leadership, traditional management structures and stereotypic views about young people are too powerful to overcome.
3. **Youth organize and demand participation.**	Although an adult typically leads the initial change process, the movement takes on greater power and influence as young people begin to organize and demand increasing participation in governance.
4. **Adults change their views by watching youth do adult work and community service and by working with youth toward meaningful outcomes**	Adult views about young people are difficult to change, and this is true even for adults in governance positions. Change occurs when the organization offers three types of experiences to adults: a) *Adults perceive a good reason to work with youth.* The governance work must be purposefully oriented toward meaningful outcomes. Adult attitudes do not change when the decision making is perceived as symbolic or as tokenism. b) *Adult attitude change occurs most readily when young people perform well in the boardroom* or in other places that adults regard as their turf. It is important for

Conditions Necessary for Change	Description of Conditions
	adults to witness youth succeeding in the nuts and bolts of organizational improvement.
	c) *Adults change their views of young people when they have the opportunity to observe youth engaged in community action that has real payoffs for community residents.*
5. Youth leaders are carefully selected.	Organizational change occurs most rapidly when adults perceive the young people as effective decision makers. For this reason, the young people who were nominated to take on key governance roles were selected carefully, just as the adults were. Most of the organizations in the study created a kind of scaffolding for youth to work their way up through the organization, engaging in a variety of leadership-building and decision-making opportunities.
6. Organizations foster change by including older youth in the organization first	According to developmental research, organizations begin the change process by first involving older youth in governance roles. Age matters. A 14-year-old differs significantly from an 18- or 19-year-old across multiple domains (cognitive, physical, societal, psychological, economic, and legal). The organizations in this study recognized this difference. Although decision makers ranged in age from 12 to 23, the majority fell between the ages of 17 and 21. The mean age of those whom the organizations chose to be their spokespersons for this study was 18 years. It seems that the organizations in the study, in their desire to ensure the early success of youth governance, decided to begin with older youth and to eventually integrate younger adolescents into governance.

SOURCE: Zeldin, McDaniel, Topitzes, & Calvert (2000).

juvenile offenders to be judged by their peers, teen courts can aid in interrupting patterns of negative behavior by promoting self-esteem, self-improvement, and a healthy attitude toward authority. Juvenile offenders must assume responsibility for their behavior and accept the consequences imposed by the teen jury. The teen court will aid in the learning process by providing an educational experience for both juvenile offenders and the teen jury.

Teen court members also derive benefits. Through this process, juveniles can also gain an understanding of our legal system, as can the teen jurors and others in attendance. In addition, teen court programs capitalize on peer influence. Formerly called "peer pressure," it is now recognized as a normal, healthy, and necessary part of teen behavior, as well as a powerful tool in helping redirect and solve problem behavior (Godwin, 2001).

Teen courts provide a hands-on approach to learning the basic juvenile justice procedures. Teen courts educate both juvenile offenders, who would otherwise go through the traditional court process, and teen jurors, who experience the deliberation process knowing that their decisions will have an impact on the juvenile offender they face. Juvenile offenders not only learn some of the consequences of delinquent behavior without acquiring a formal record, but they may also be ordered to jury duty, which gives them the opportunity to experience the responsibility of the deliberation process as well.

How Can Youth Positively Affect
Their Communities Through Teen Courts?

Through teen courts, youth participate in the creation of a better community context. Teen courts often seek to address key problems in communities, including but not limited to the following:

- Increased numbers of juveniles entering the formal court process and the inability of counties to provide appropriate sanctions
- Lack of diversion programs for first-time juvenile offenders
- The need for intervention during early adolescence
- The desire for more hands-on education
- The need for community collaboration to tackle fundamental issues

What Actual Decision-Making Roles Do Teen Court Members Have?

The general mission of teen courts is to rehabilitate juvenile offenders through peer justice, parental, and community collaboration while teaching ownership and accountability for inappropriate actions. Teen courts around the country provide nonviolent juvenile misdemeanor offenders (with no prior felony adjudications or pending felony charges) an opportunity to appear in court without establishing a formal court record. Actual county judges preside over every case. A jury of area high school teens questions the defendant, victim, and his or her parent/guardian/custodian to determine the ultimate disposition of the case. The teen jury does not determine guilt or innocence but deliberates only on an appropriate disposition for the juvenile offender. The teen jurors must come to a two-thirds majority decision with regard to the disposition of a case and have several options to aid them in reaching a decision.

Each community with a teen court must have a system of referrals and screening of teen court candidates. When developing a teen court program, determinations that must be made include the following: types of offenses that can be referred, age limitations, involvement of juvenile offenders' parents or guardians, prior records to be considered, and requirements for offenders to fulfill before their court dates. Age constraints should also be considered when determining jurors so that offenders and jurors are of similar age. If a juvenile is ordered to jury duty, the juvenile must complete the remainder of the disposition before serving on a jury. Jurors are judicial representatives through their participation in teen courts and must act in a manner that reflects this status. In case there are any legal questions regarding the trial, the judge should be consulted. The judge is always ready and available to determine all questions of law pertaining to the case.

In sum, the teen court system provides youth with meaningful opportunities to influence the lives of their peers and their community in ways that can be long-lasting. These decision-making opportunities are real and legitimized by the court system, indicating the high level of trust and investment placed in community youth. Such decision-making opportunities reflect solid commitments to youth infusion goals in the public sector.

❖ YOUTH POLICYMAKERS—YOUTH ADVISORY COUNCIL TO THE MAYOR

Leaders in many communities have begun to focus on youth in an effort to ensure that the next generation of young people will reach adulthood prepared to be productive workers, effective parents, and responsible citizens. Focusing on the theme of positive youth development, city leaders are seeking to establish youth advisory committees, which consist of a group of young people who have a strong interest in their schools and communities and would like to express their views and concerns at the top level of city government. Through discussion and action, these groups of youth may begin to develop positive ties between themselves and city leaders while learning about city government and gaining self-esteem and confidence from the realization that they are valued as productive and successful citizens. These youth play an important leadership role of identifying youth issues, developing youth programming, and representing the young student population in their community. In this sample community, we describe one youth advisory council that advises the local mayor on a variety of issues.

How Are Students Recruited and Who Are Members?

The composition of a mayor's youth advisory council (MYAC) is intended to be representative of students in the community. Depending on the size of a community, it is important that there are committee representatives from all schools in the target group. Diversity on the committee is also necessary, including diversity in gender, race, ethnicity, personality, and academic achievement. Program coordinators should develop their own strategies to ensure proper representation, such as meeting with administrators and teachers at each school and asking them to recommend a student for the committee. It may be beneficial to indicate that you are looking for students to whom other students listen, rather than students who are the obvious leaders, to recruit students from a variety of peer groups in the school.

To help with the recruiting of a diverse group of students and establishment of a successful youth advisory committee, community support is needed from entities such as the city council, city departments, school district, media, parents, and other active community members. One way to gain support is by organizing an event/luncheon/press conference in which all of the aforementioned people can come together to learn about the intentions of this newly established group. This is also a good way for all of those invited to get to know each other.

How Are Youth Roles as Decision Makers Legitimized?

Another important concept to consider in establishing a youth advisory committee is to make sure that youth are involved in decision making from the beginning. Decisions that need to be made include creating a charter and developing vision and mission statements, goals and objectives, and applications for new members. To ensure positive relationships among committee members from all schools in the area, it may be beneficial to hire a facilitator to organize team-building activities, which will take place at the beginning of monthly committee meetings.

How Is a Mayor's Youth Advisory Council Structured?

Youth advisory committees should meet at least monthly with the mayor or city manager to advise on issues that are affecting young people in their schools, neighborhoods, and communities. Students meet as a large group and also in committees that are focused on specific issues. The committees meet within the larger group and, on occasion, outside the regular monthly meeting.

What Is the Role of Adults?

In one successful example of an MYAC, an adult intern serves as the program coordinator of the MYAC and provides administrative assistance in running and preparing the meetings. To prepare an agenda for these meetings, program coordinators meet with the mayor or city manager to discuss specific items on which he or she would like input from the committee. At least one week before each meeting, members of the committee meet with each other and the program coordinators to discuss issues they would like to present to the mayor or city manager. Based on the ideas that emerge from these meetings, the program coordinators prepare a complete agenda for the meeting. In addition to serving as the administrator and liaison, the program coordinator often coordinates and personally implements transportation for students attending the meetings in keeping with the need to address structural barriers to youth participation in meetings (Young & Sazama, 1999).

What Kind of Training Do Youth Receive for Their Roles?

Training and orientation to organizations have been documented as important precursors to successful youth involvement in organizational decision making (Young & Sazama, 1999). To accomplish the goal of teaching youth about city government, program coordinators may organize training sessions in which students meet with city council members and representatives from various city departments. Coordinators should ask for input from committee members on how to structure these meetings and what information they would like to learn. Each committee, of course, establishes meeting times and dates in which all come together. However, it is important to create subcommittees of youth to work on various tasks so that significant work is done outside full committee meetings. Full committee meetings should primarily include subcommittee reports and critical planning decisions.

**How Is the Mayor's Youth Advisory Council
Sustained Over Time, Given Changing Membership?**

Because there is significant turnover in these types of committees, youth are given the freedom to establish new goals and objectives for themselves each year, primarily related to specific projects in which they would like to become involved. However, it is important to keep as much continuity as possible so that the efforts of youth in years past are not wasted. For this reason, it is generally beneficial to groups to avoid turnover in the coordinator position and to have several returning members each year who can help initiate new members and keep group continuity. Common general goals for youth advisory committees include the following:

- Empowering youth to have a proactive voice in youth programming
- Providing youth with an opportunity to develop a meaningful understanding of city government
- Developing a strong, positive relationship between youth and city leaders

- Establishing more communication and exchange among students and administrators in their schools.

How Can a Mayor's Youth Advisory Council Positively Affect the Community?

An example of the impact that youth involvement through a youth advisory committee can be found in one example of a successful MYAC. This MYAC has had an interest in starting a teen center in the community. One of the major concerns of many of the 20 MYAC members was that there was not enough for teens to do for entertainment on weekdays after school and on weekends. Out of this concern came an idea to create a teen center, which the students proposed to the mayor and the superintendent of the local school district. The students' collective voice was heard, because the teen center was included in the bond issue on which city residents voted, though its primary objective was to improve the quality of local schools. Although the bond issue was not passed, students continued to work with their peers and other adults to move this agenda forward. Additionally, students became empowered through their involvement with the MYAC and used their newly found power to demand that a junior city council be created for youth voices to be heard on broader city issues. With the support of some adult council members, the youth were successful in creating this venue for their participation. Furthermore, following high school graduation, one alumnus of the MYAC ran a successful primary campaign to enter the local city council race, with the teen center as one of the issues on his platform.

This example of youth involved in city government shows the potential for youth to influence policies that affect their lives and their communities. Through the MYAC just discussed, students have gained access to adult power centers in many departments of the local government. Youth have become more visible in city issues and have learned about the ups and downs of the political process through their partnership with adults in this organization.

This example of youth decision making in the community demonstrate how youth can have meaningful roles in creating and proactively developing programs to meet the needs of local youth. It also shows how students develop their own assets, because students in that community have begun to ask for more opportunities to serve in youth governance roles. One student was able to advocate for a seat on his own school board, another ran for a regular (adult) seat on the city council, and still other youth created new positions of power through a local junior city council. Clearly, these examples of youth involvement as decision makers in a variety of organizations highlight the increasing responsibilities and opportunities that youth are afforded as they participate in these key decision-making and leadership roles in the community.

❖ REFERENCES

Beker, J., Eisikovits, Z., & Guttmann, E. (1987). Economic considerations in supporting preventive services for troubled youth: The case of adolescents on the farm. *Children & Youth Services Review, 9*(3), 187-206.

Belter, R., & Grisso, T. (1984). Children's recognition of rights violations in counseling. *Professional Psychology, 15*, 899-910.

Bikson, T. K. (1978). The status of children's intellectual rights. *Journal of Social Issues, 34*, 69-86.

Boggiano, A. K., & Katz, P. (1991). Maladaptive achievement patterns in students: The role of teachers' controlling strategies. *Journal of Social Issues, 47*, 35-51.

Brody, G. H., Ge, X., Conger, R., Gibbons, F. X., Murray, V. M., Gerrard, M., Simmons, R. L. (2001). The influence of neighborhood disadvantage, collective socialization, and parenting on African American children's affiliation with deviant peers. *Child Development, 72*, 1231-1246.

Bronfenbrenner, U. (1977). Toward an experimental ecology of human development. *American Psychologist, 32*, 513-531.

Butts, J. A., & Buck, J. (2000, October). *Teen courts: A focus on research.* Office of Juvenile Justice and Delinquency Prevention Juvenile Justice Bulletin NCJ 183472. Retrieved September 29, 2002, from www.ncjrs.org/html/ojjdp/jjbul2000_10_2/contents.html

Calabrese, R. L., & Schumer, H. (1986). The effects of service activities on adolescent alienation. *Adolescence, 21*(83), 675-687.

Camino, L. A. (2000). Youth-adult partnerships: Entering new territory in community work and research. *Applied Developmental Science, 4*(Suppl. 1), 11-20.

Carter, F. S., Huber, M., LaMore, R., Lemer, S., Lichty, J., & Rosenbaum, R. P. (1997). *Community income and expenditures model: Linkages and leakages among businesses, households, and nonprofit organizations in Southwest Detroit ZIP code area 48209.* (Available from Michigan State University, Center for Urban Affairs, Community and Economic Development Program, 1801 West Main Street, Lansing, MI 48915)

Community Development Society. (2000, July). *Principles of good practice.* Revised and adopted by the Community Development Society during its 32nd annual conference, Saint John, New Brunswick.

Eccles, J. S., Midgley, C., Wigfield, A., Buchanan, C. M., Reuman, D., Flanagan, C., & MacIver, D. (1993). Development during adolescence: The impact of stage-environment fit on young adolescents' experiences in schools and families. *American Psychologist, 48,* 90-101.

Elder, G. H., Jr., King, V., & Conger, R. D. (1996). Attachment to place and migration prospects: A developmental perspective. *Journal of Research on Adolescence, 6,* 397-425.

Godwin, T. M. (2001). *The role of restorative justice in teen courts: A preliminary look.* Unpublished report. (Available from National Youth Court Center c/o American Probation and Parole Association, P. O. Box 11910, Lexington, KY 40578-1910, www.youthcourt.net)

Grisso, T. (1980). Juveniles' capacities to waive Miranda rights: An empirical analysis. *California Law Review, 68,* 1134-1166.

Hart, R. A. (1992). Children's participation: From tokenism to citizenship. UNICEF Innocenti Essays No. 4. (Available from UNICEF, International Child Development Centre, Piazza S.S. Annunziata 12, 50122 Florence, Italy).

Hart, S. N. (1991). From property to person status: Historical perspectives on children's rights. *American Psychologist, 46,* 53-59.

Hart, S. N., & Pavlovic, Z. (1991). Children's rights in education: An historical perspective. *School Psychology Review, 20,* 345-358.

Huber, M. S. (2000). *Testing an ecological model of career aspirations: The role of community, family, and individual human capital variables among pre- and mid-adolescent children of public assistance recipients.* Unpublished doctoral dissertation, Michigan State University, East Lansing.

Huber, M. S. Q. (2001, June). *Enhancing out-of-school activities in Barry County: Improvements desired by middle, high school, and alternative school students.* Unpublished manuscript. (Available from the Department of Family and Child Ecology, Michigan State University, 203A Human Ecology Building, East Lansing, MI 48824-1030).

Israel, G. D., Coleman, D. L., & Ilvento, T. W. (1993). Student involvement in community needs assessment. *Journal of Community Development Society, 24*(2), 249-271.

Larson, R. W. (2000). Toward a psychology of positive youth development. *American Psychologist, 55,* 170-183.

Lewis, C. (1981). How adolescents approach decisions: Changes over grades seven to twelve and policy implications. *Child Development, 52,* 538-544.

Lichter, D. T., McLaughlin, D. K., & Comwell, G. T. (1993). Migration and the loss of human resources in rural America. In L. J. Beaulieu & D. Mulkey (Eds.), *Investing in people: The human capital needs of rural America.* Boulder, CO: Westview Press.

Maier, F. (1988). Battling rural "brain drain": a small Illinois town fights to keep talented youth. *Newsweek, 112*(26), 46.

Malone, F. S. (1994). Building mental health services into the public school. *Journal of Emotional and Behavioral Problems, 3*(3), 45-48.

Melton, G. B. (1987a). Children, politics, and morality: The ethics of child advocacy. *Journal of Clinical and Consulting Psychology, 16*, 357-367.

Melton, G. B. (1987b). The clashing of symbols: Prelude to child and family policy. *American Psychologist, 42*, 345-354.

Midgley, C., Feldlaufer, H., & Eccles, J. S. (1988). The transition to junior high school: Beliefs of pre- and post-transition teachers. *Journal of Youth and Adolescence, 17*, 543-562.

Mullet, E., & Neto, F. (1991). Intention to migrate, job opportunities, and aspirations for better pay: An information integration approach. *International Journal of Psychology, 26*, 95-113.

Perkins, D. F., Borden, L. M., Keith, J. G., Hoppe-Rooney, T. L., & Villarruel, F. A. (2003). Community youth development: Partnership creating a positive world. In F. A. Villarruel, D. F. Perkins, L. M. Borden, & J. G. Keith (Eds.), *Community youth development: Programs, policies, and practices.* Thousand Oaks, CA: Sage.

Pittman, K., & Irby, M. (1998). Reflections on a decade of promoting positive youth development. In S. Halperin (Ed.), *The forgotten half revisited: American youth and young families, 1988-2008* (pp. 159-169). Washington, DC: American Youth Policy Forum.

Scales, P. C., Benson, P. L., Leffert, N., & Blyth, D. A. (2000). Contribution of developmental assets to the prediction of thriving among adolescents. *Applied Developmental Science, 4*, 27-46.

Scales, P. C., & Leffert, N. (1999). *Developmental assets: A synthesis of the scientific research on adolescent development.* Minneapolis: Search Institute.

Scheff, T. J. (1975). *Labeling madness.* Englewood Cliffs, NJ: Prentice-Hall.

Takanishi, R., DeLeon, P. H., & Pallak, M. S. (1983). Psychology and public policy affecting children, youth, and families. *American Psychologist, 38*, 67-69.

Tremper, C. R., & Kelly, M. P. (1987). The mental health rationale for policies fostering minors' autonomy. *International Journal of Law and Psychiatry, 10*, 111-127.

Ward, J. (2000, May). Come one! Come all! *The American City & County: Pittsfield, 115*(6), 35-42.

Weithorn, L., & Campbell, S. (1982). The competency of children and adolescents to make informed treatment decisions. *Child Development, 53*, 1589-1599.

Young, K. S., & Sazama, J. (1999). Fourteen points: Successfully involving youth in decision-making. Unpublished report. (Available from Youth on Board, 58 Day Street, Third Floor, P. 0. Box 440322, Somerville, MA 02144)

Zeldin, S. (2000). Integrating research and practice to understand and strengthen communities for adolescent development: An introduction to the special issue and current issues. *Applied Developmental Science, 4*(Suppl. 1), 2-10.

Zeldin, S., McDaniel, A. K., Topitzes, D., & Calvert, M. (2000). *Youth in decision-making; A study on the impact of youth and adults on organizations*. Chevy Chase, MD: Center and Innovation Center for Youth and Community Development and University of Wisconsin Extension.

Zimmerman, M. A. (1990). Toward a theory of learned hopefulness: A structural model analysis of participation and empowerment. *Journal of Research in Personality, 24*, 71-86.

Zimmerman, M. A., & Rappaport, J. (1988). Citizen participation, perceived control, and psychological empowerment. *American Journal of Community Psychology, 16*, 725-750.

Part III

Youth Professionals, Communities, And Youth

15

Key Elements of Community Youth Development Programs

Daniel F. Perkins and Lynne M. Borden

Throughout the country, the school bell signals the end to another day of formal education in the lives of youth. Young people and their parents make critical choices about the use of their time during the after-school hours. They may chose to go straight home, go to a part-time job, hang out with friends, or participate in a wide range of community programs sponsored by community organizations and schools.

During adolescence, young people have a significant amount of free time available to them. For instance, one research study found that approximately 40% of the waking hours of a sample of high school youth was spent in leisure time (Csikszentmihalyi & Larson, 1984). With the exception of school and sleep, youth in the United States spend more time watching television then doing anything else (Carnegie Council on Adolescent Development, 1992; Hofferth, 1998 Robinson & Godbey, 1997). Other uses of this discretionary time include sports, hobbies, reading, talking on the phone with friends, playing computer games, and participating in youth-serving organizations and in faith-based activities (Robinson & Godbey, 1997). It is also important to note that much of that time may be spent without companionship or supervision from adults (Carnegie Council on Adolescent Development, 1995).

Out-of-school time can be either an opportunity for youth to engage in positive activities that enhance their development and foster their competency, or a time to participate in negative activities that increase their chances of yielding to social pressures to engage in drug use, sex, and antisocial activities (Villarruel & Lerner, 1994). For example, FBI statistics indicate that 47% of violent juvenile crime occurs on weekdays, between the hours of 2:00 and 8:00 p.m. (Snyder & Sickmund, 1997). In contrast, Larson (2000) suggests that important life skills may be gained more readily in out-of-school contexts than in school. The focus of this chapter will be on one of the out-of-school contexts—youth programming—and the elements of youth programming that seem to enhance positive youth development.

Whereas schools provide a formal structured learning environment, nonformal, community-based youth organizations offer important opportunities for socialization and learning. That is, quality youth programs offer young people a context in which to develop critical life skills and competencies. Youth programs employ structured activities as a vehicle or strategy for promoting the positive development of youth. These programs occur during out-of-school hours at times that include before and after school, evenings, weekends, and during the summer. If designed appropriately, youth programs offer a safe environment that provides opportunities for young people to explore their world, develop skills, and gain a sense of belonging with peers and adults as well as within themselves.

This chapter will present the importance of youth development programs as contexts for positive development and will then give an overview of the key components of high-quality programs. Youth development programs are defined here as any structured learning activity offered during the out-of-school hours. They include, but are not limited to, sports programs, before- and after-school clubs, service clubs, faith-based organizations, 4-H Youth Development programs, Boys and Girls Clubs, Boy Scouts and Girl Scouts, YMCA, and those sponsored by other community and/or youth-serving organizations.

❖ IMPORTANCE OF YOUTH PROGRAMS

Youth development programs offer young people one arena for positive development, that is, an opportunity to meet their developmental needs while decreasing the likelihood that they will engage in risky behavior that threatens their life chances (Benson, Leffert, Scales, & Blyth, 1998). These programs also provide youth with the chance to develop positive relationships that connect them to peers and adults in their communities. In a recent review of the literature, Scales and Leffert (1999) suggest that a positive relationship with an adult can be indirectly or directly related to higher levels of self-esteem and self-efficacy, reduced drug and alcohol use, as well as positive and improved school outcomes. Moreover, these contexts enhance the likelihood of youth developing sustained and positive peer relationships, which, in turn, contribute to increased academic achievement (McLaughlin, 2000), increased development of social maturity, and buffered depressive symptoms (Scales & Leffert, 1999). Indeed, as McLaughlin (2000) points out, youth development programs "provide community sanctuaries and supports that enable youth to imagine positive paths and embark upon them" (p. 7). Adult and peer relationships developed in conjunction with the structured activities provided by youth development programs increase the likelihood that youth will successfully navigate challenges as they move toward adulthood.

In addition, high-quality youth development programs engage young people in reflective learning experiences, experiences that enhance youths' understanding of self and others. Moreover, these experiences encourage youth to see themselves as a part of their community, become invested, and engage in activities that better the community (McLaughlin, 2000). For example, McLaughlin notes, "Youth that have high levels of participation in community service activities— as parts of arts programs, sports, leadership initiatives, dedicated community service projects such as 'Weed and Seed,' work with elderly residents or rehabilitation efforts—were eight times more likely to respond that it is very important to get involved with community than were representative American youth" (p. 6).

McLaughlin's (2000) longitudinal study of youth and youth development programs provides strong evidence of the positive influence that participation in youth development programs can have on young people. Moreover, Scales and Leffert (1999), in their review of more than 30 research studies about the impact of involvement in youth programs on young people, found that involvement in youth programs was linked to the following:

1. Increased self-esteem, sense of personal control, and enhanced identity development

2. Better-developed life skills, leadership skills, public-speaking skills, decision-making skills, and increased job dependability and responsibility

3. Increased academic achievement

4. Improved protection of students at risk of dropping out of school

5. Improved likelihood of college attendance

6. Increased involvement in constructive activities in young adulthood

7. Increased safety

8. Increased family communication

9. Decreased psychological problems, such as loneliness, shyness, and hopelessness

10. Decreased involvement in risky behaviors

Programs do more than occupy the idle time of youth; they provide a playing field on which youth can learn essential life lessons, develop practical life skills, and build strong, positive relationships with adults and peers (Perkins & Borden, 2001). Thus, youth programs provide opportunities for youth to develop the "five Cs" identified by Lerner and his colleagues (Lerner, 2002; Lerner, Fisher, & Weinberg, 2000; Lerner, Sparks, & McCubbin, 1999). These include (1) competence in academic, social, emotional, and vocational areas; (2) confidence in who one is becoming (identity); (3) connection to self and others; (4) character that comes from positive values, integrity, and strong sense of morals; and (5) caring and compassion. Along those lines, Pittman (2000) highlights a sixth C, contribution. By contributing to their families, neighborhoods, and communities, youth are afforded practical opportunities through participation in youth programs to make use of the other five Cs. Yet, not all youth programs are the same in their effectiveness. The impact that participating in a youth program has on a young person is determined in part by the quality of that program.

❖ KEY COMPONENTS OF QUALITY YOUTH PROGRAMS

In a recent study, engagement in youth development programs was found to be the most pervasive positive influence and common predictor of positive youth outcomes (Scales, Benson, Leffert, & Blyth, 2000). The positive influences that youth programs have on youth are dependent on several factors, such as focus of the program, degree of participation by youth, adults involved with the program, and context in which the program takes place.

Pittman (1991), for example, notes that programs focusing on promotion of skills and competencies in addition to prevention of negative behaviors are more likely to have a positive influence on youth. In other words, programs must seek to address risk behaviors but must also seek to build new skills that are related to positive developmental outcomes. High-quality youth programs are those efforts that conduct activities, establish environments, and develop sustained peer-peer and youth-adult relationships that are intentional and deliberately focused on youth's capacity building. As Pittman & Irby (1996) state, "Problem-free youth are not fully prepared youth" (p. 2).

Through the establishment of these quality programs, as well as through greater participation, youth increase the number of opportunities to build their skills and competencies. For example, in her 10-year study of youth and youth programs, McLaughlin (2000) found that youth with higher levels of participation in community youth organizations were approximately 15% more likely to view themselves as worthy persons.

Clearly, the quality of community youth development programs is highly related to the skills and competencies of the adults who devote their expertise, time, and energy to them (Halpern, Barker, & Mollard, 2000; see Yohalem, 2003, this volume, for an extended discussion). Adults who are successful at fostering positive youth development possess a strong sense of commitment to youth and their engagement in program planning, implementation, and evaluation, facilitating youth empowerment as well as skill development. A community youth worker who emphasizes the growth and development of each participant through multisensory experiential programs creates a positive learning experience. For example, a community youth worker who designs activities to meet the developmental, physical, emotional, and intellectual needs of the participants offers them an opportunity for positive learning experiences. Such programs provide experiences that enable youth to learn life skills (e.g., decision making, teamwork, problem solving) and establish positive relationships with adults and peers. On the other hand, a community youth worker who ignores the developmental needs of young people may create an environment that leads to negative learning experiences. A negative learning experience increases the likelihood of youth learning inappropriate behaviors that could negatively influence their life trajectory.

As McLaughlin (2000) notes, successful community youth programs are not entirely dependent on the adults and youth themselves. Rather, the context that surrounds the youth program can either foster the success of the program or create barriers to the program's success. For example, communities that provide ongoing resources to community youth-serving organizations—those that engage youth during their free time, prevent risk behavior, and promote opportunities for positive development—are creating an environment for successful positive youth programs. Communities that support a variety of youth programs addressing diversity and acknowledging cultural and gender differences shape youth preferences and developmental needs (McLaughlin, 2000). The key components of youth development programs will be presented in the next section as it addresses program development, program implementation, program evaluation, and program staffing.

Program Development

Youth development programs and the staff who conduct them must establish a clear focus that intentionally includes time for positive relationship building among adults and youth. Besides offering access to caring adults and responsible peers, high-quality youth programs provide skill-building activities that reinforce positive values and skills. Indeed, creating effective youth development programs involves several steps.

First, youth must be partners, fully engaged in the development of programs. Youth should be engaged in the process of seeking input about what is needed and wanted in terms of programs, and they should also have a strong voice in the structure and operation of the programs. Fully engaging young people in the development, planning, and evaluation of youth programs is critical to the success of the program. In addition, youth can be workers in the program.

Second, the program must begin with a clear focus that emphasizes specific skills, competencies, and assets. The clear focus is derived from identified needs and strengths of potential participants. It is critical that young people be a part of the identification process. Whereas some skills are universal (regardless of the targeted youth), others are specific to a group in a particular context. For example, communication skills are needed by all young people. However, theatrical skills may represent a specific need of a subgroup of youth in the community.

The third step in creating a high-quality youth development program involves the variety of activities and experiences that address the multiple learning styles of young people. For example, when teaching about leadership, one may present the content through a minilecture followed by a paper-and-pencil test, and another may offer an experiential problem-solving exercise that enables a leader to emerge from the group.

Fourth, programs should offer youth the opportunity to build positive and sustainable relationships with adults and peers. Creating meaningful projects that fully engage both adults and peers can foster these relationships. Moreover, thinking strategically about developing activities that pair individuals who live close to one another may foster a relationship that goes beyond the program hours.

In summary, the following characteristics are important components to consider when creating a youth development program. These characteristics have been either identified through research and/or highlighted by scholars (Benson, 1997; Carnegie Council on Adolescent Development, 1992; Catalano, Berglund, Ryan, Lonczak, & Hawkins, 1999; Dryfoos, 1990, 1998; Durlack, 1998; Galavotti, Saltzman, Sauter, & Sumartojo, 1997; Halpern et al., 2000; International Youth Foundation, 1993; Lerner, 1995; McLaughlin, 2000; Pittman, 1996; Quinn, 1995; Roth, Brooks-Gunn, Murray, & Foster, 1998). These characteristics are also factors to which time and attention should be devoted by adults who are seeking to establish high-quality community youth development programs. High-quality youth programs provide youth with an opportunity to have ongoing, one-on-one, positive relationships with caring adults. These interactions are organized around concrete productive purposes. In addition, the program offers frequent opportunities for youth to interact with other adults through intergenerational events and activities.

• High-quality youth programs provide youth with social support by connecting youth to positive peer groups.

• High-quality youth programs create a strong sense of belonging, with clear rules and expectations, responsibilities, and flexibilities. Flexibility is the ability to adapt a program to meet the unique needs of young people in the program. Rules are embraced by youth who have direct input in their development.

• High-quality youth programs focus on the specific needs and interests of young people. Therefore, a quality program engages youth as partners in the identification of needs, the planning, the implementation, and the evaluation of the program. Youth can be engaged in these processes through various methods (e.g., focus groups, concept mapping, and coleadership).

• High-quality youth programs offer young people the opportunity to hold meaningful leadership roles within the program and organization.

• High-quality programs also engage youth in organized service activities within the community. This affords youth the opportunity to contribute and further build their competence, confidence, connection, character, and compassion.

• High-quality youth programs provide an accessible safe haven for youth, both physically and emotionally. They provide youth with a sense of a positive group experience.

• High-quality youth programs provide learning opportunities that are active and participatory. Therefore, programs use experiential learning opportunities and encourage young people to take positive risks. All attempts, successful or unsuccessful, are viewed as part of the learning process. Thus, learning how to take risks also involves learning how to *fail courageously*. This approach empowers youth to consistently take new risks without fear of being rejected.

• High-quality youth programs focus on recruiting and retaining young people from diverse backgrounds (e.g., race, ethnicity, family income, family structure, and gender) by intentionally designing activities that address their needs. In addition, such programs do not wait for participants to appear; rather, they reach out to youth.

• High-quality youth programs provide multiple opportunities for youth to engage in activities with their families and communities.

• High-quality youth programs encourage parental involvement by offering a variety of possibilities for participation (e.g., social events, parental workshops, volunteer opportunities).

• High-quality youth programs are designed and conducted based on theories of adolescent development. Theory acts as a guide in determining activities and expected outcomes for targeted audiences.

• High-quality youth programs strive to assist youth in avoiding identified problem behaviors by providing them with alternative opportunities. These opportunities are designed to enhance skills (e.g., goal setting, decision making, problem solving, and delayed gratification), civic responsibility, and prosocial behavior.

• High-quality youth programs offer relevant skill-building activities that reinforce the values and skills linked with doing well in school and maintaining good physical health.

• High-quality youth programs are ongoing and occur on a frequent basis (e.g., twice a week, twice a month, etc.). They are at least a year in length and have built in follow-up sessions.

• High-quality youth programs offer a variety of resources through collaboration with other youth-serving community organizations and schools.

• High-quality youth programs have clearly stated goals that are assessed on a regular basis. These goals are linked to outcomes for youth (e.g., decision-making skills, problem-solving skills, and conflict resolution skills) that emphasize the benefits of program participation. The evaluation strategy being used allows for midcourse corrections in the program.

- High-quality youth programs have well-trained staff, as evidenced by appropriate educational backgrounds, diversity of staff, frequent staff in-services, and low staff turnover. Staff are visible advocates for youth.

- High-quality youth programs have a visible organizational structure and are well organized and managed.

- High-quality youth programs have established strategies to recognize the accomplishments of their participants.

It should be recognized that no one program can address all the needs of young people, nor does one program necessarily possess all of the dimensions of quality programs that are presented above. Nonetheless, quality programs can easily point to the previously mentioned programmatic elements in their curriculums.

The research is clear—youth who are engaged in high-quality programs are making a difference in their world now, and they are increasing their chances of being successful as adults (McLaughlin, 2000; Scales & Leffert, 1999). Similarly, too much of a good thing can be unhealthy. Larner, Zippiroli, and Behrman (1999) have found that youth who are engaged in more than 20 hours of extracurricular activities a week are more likely to engage in risky behaviors than are youth who engage in 5 to 19 hours of extracurricular activities. Therefore, young people's participation in youth programs must be balanced with other demands on their time (e.g., school and family).

❖ CONCLUSION

This review of research underscores an array of possible outcomes, as well as the importance of community-based youth programs; the outcomes should be interpreted with caution. Unfortunately, not all programs can claim these or any outcomes as benefits of programs, given the realities and challenges of any program. First, not all programs attempt to address, let alone promote competencies in, these skills and areas. Second, the duration of some youth-based programs is not sufficient by itself to promote skill development in these areas. Moreover, whereas some programs claim to address these areas, conclusions about what is actually accomplished are somewhat controversial.

Specifically, the evaluation employed in positive youth development programs is an area to which additional emphasis must be devoted (Roth, 2000; Roth et al., 1998). Nevertheless, the accumulation of multiple research studies seems to overcome methodological issues, and, taken together, the results of these studies provide strong evidence of the positive influence that programs can have on young people's development (Benson et al., 1998; Lerner, 1995; McLaughlin, 2000; Roth, 2000; Scales & Leffert, 1999).

Like schools, community youth programs offer young people a context for development that deserves society's attention (Larson, 2000). Young people develop as the result of their core experiences with diverse people, systems, communities, and the institutions in those communities. Communities and institutions can be supportive influences in the lives of youth through policies and programs that promote positive development. Communities that offer a variety of programs and encourage youth participation are more likely to harness youthful energy for the common good. Programs, through positive connections and activities, empower youth to develop their skills, build their capacity to be resourceful, and increase their self-confidence. Moreover, these communities experience the positive power of youth as they contribute to their families, neighborhoods, and communities.

In order for programs to provide *all* youth with the developmental opportunities that they need, communities and citizens must commit themselves to expanding those programs. For example, some 29%, approximately 5.5 million young adolescents, are not being served by any existing youth program (Carnegie Council on Adolescent Development, 1995). Most of these young people are in impoverished neighborhoods and are in dire need of safe places in which to be challenged (Carnegie Council on Adolescent Development, 1995). Thus, barriers to participating in youth programs should be addressed, and equal access is required to ensure that all youth have the developmental opportunities they need.

If we as citizens want our children and youth to do more than avoid risky behaviors and to become contributing, engaged members of society, then we must be intentional about creating places and opportunities that nurture their development. The core experiences that young people gain from participating in high-quality youth development programs during the out-of-school hours can provide them with a clear sense of direction, both now and in the future.

❖ REFERENCES

Benson, P. L. (1997). *All kids are our kids.* San Francisco, CA: Jossey-Bass.

Benson, P. L., Leffert, N., Scales, P. C., & Blyth, D. A. (1998). Beyond the "village" rhetoric: Creating healthy communities for children and adolescents. *Applied Developmental Science, 2*(3), 138-159

Carnegie Council on Adolescent Development. (1992). *A matter of time: Risk and opportunity in the nonschool hours.* New York: Carnegie Corporation.

Carnegie Council on Adolescent Development. (1995). *Great transitions: Preparing adolescents for a new century.* New York: Carnegie Corporation.

Catalano, R. F., Berglund, M. L., Ryan, J. A., Lonczak, H. S., & Hawkins, J. D. (1999). *Positive youth development in the United States: Research findings on evaluations of positive youth development programs.* Seattle: University of Washington, School of Social Work, Social Development Research Group. Retrieved September 25, 2002, from aspe.hhs.gov/hsp/Positive YouthDev99

Csikszentmihalyi, M., & Larson, R. (1984). *Being adolescent: Conflict and growth in the teenage years.* New York: Basic Books.

Dryfoos, J. G. (1990). *Adolescents at risk: Prevalence and prevention.* New York: Oxford University Press.

Dryfoos, J. (1998). *Safe passage: Making it through adolescence in a risky society.* New York: Oxford University Press.

Durlack, J. A. (1998). Common risk and protective factors in successful prevention programs. *American Journal of Orthopsychiatry, 68,* 512-520.

Galavotti, C., Saltzman, L., Sauter, S., & Sumartojo, E. (1997). Behavioral science activities at the Centers for Disease Control and Prevention. *American Psychologist, 52*(2), 154-166.

Halpern, R., Barker, G., & Mollard, W. (2000). Youth programs as alternative spaces to be: A study of neighborhood youth programs in Chicago's West Town. *Youth & Society, 31,* 469-506.

Hofferth, S. (1998). The American family: Changes and challenges for the 21st century. In H. Wallace, G. Green, K. Jaros, M. Story, & L. Paine (Eds.), *Health and welfare for families in the 21st century* (pp. 3-12). Sudbury, MA: Jones and Bartlett.

International Youth Foundation (1993). *Guidelines regarding the 17 criteria for successful programs.* Baltimore: Author.

Larner, M. B., Zippiroli, L., & Behrman, R. E. (1999). When school is out: Analysis and recommendations. *The Future of Children, 9,* 4-20.

Larson, R. W. (2000). Toward a psychology of positive youth development. *American Psychologist, 55,* 170-183.

Lerner, R. M. (1995). *America's youth in crisis: Challenges and options for programs and policies.* Thousand Oaks, CA: Sage.

Lerner, R. M. (2002). *Adolescence: Development, diversity, context, and application.* Upper Saddle River, NJ: Prentice Hall.

Lerner, R. M., Fisher, C., & Weinberg, R. (2000). Toward a science for and of the people. Promoting civil society through the application of developmental science. *Child Development, 71,* 11-20.

Lerner, R. M., Sparks, E., & McCubbin, H. (1999). *Family diversity and family policy: Strengthening families for America's children.* Norwell, MA: Kluwer Academic.

McLaughlin, M. (2000). *Community counts: How youth organizations matter for youth development.* Washington, DC: Public Education Network. Retrieved September 25, 2002, from www.publiceducation.org/cgi-bin/download-manager/publications/p72.asp

Perkins, D. F., & Borden, L. M. (2001). Programs for adolescents. In J. V. Lerner & R. M. Lerner (Eds.), *Adolescence in America* (pp. 535-540). Santa Barbara, CA: ABC-CLIO.

Pittman, K. J. (1991). *Promoting youth development: Strengthening the role of youth-serving and community organizations.* Washington, DC: Center for Youth Development and Policy Research.

Pittman, K. J. (1996). *Programs that work: What is youth development?* Baltimore: International Youth Foundation.

Pittman, K. J. (2000, March). *Grantmaker strategies for assessing the quality of unevaluated programs and the impact of unevaluated grantmaking.* Paper presented at Evaluation of Youth Programs symposium at the Biennial Meeting of the Society for Research on Adolescence, Chicago.

Pittman, K. J., & Irby, M. (1996). *Preventing problems or promoting development: Competing priorities or inseparable goals?* Takoma Park, MD: International Youth Foundation.

Quinn, J. (1995). Positive effects of participation in youth organizations. In M. Rutter (Ed.), *Psychosocial disturbances in young people: Challenges for prevention* (pp. 274-303). New York: Cambridge University Press.

Robinson, J., and Godbey, G. (1997). *Time for life: The surprising ways Americans use their time.* University Park: Pennsylvania State University.

Roth, J. (2000, April). *What we know and what we need to know about youth development programs.* Paper presented at Evaluation of Youth Programs symposium at the Biennial Meeting of the Society for Research on Adolescence, Chicago.

Roth, J., Brooks-Gunn, J., Murray, L., & Foster, W. (1998). Promoting healthy adolescents: Synthesis of youth development program evaluations. *Journal of Research on Adolescence, 8,* 423-459.

Scales, P. C., Benson, P. L., Leffert, N., & Blyth, D. A. (2000). Contribution of developmental assets to the prediction of thriving among adolescents. *Applied Developmental Science, 4,* 27-46.

Scales, P. C., & Leffert, N. (1999). *Developmental assets: A synthesis of the scientific research on adolescent development.* Minneapolis, MN: Search Institute.

Snyder, H., & Sickmund, M. (1997). *Juvenile offenders and victims: 1997 update on violence.* Washington, DC: U.S. Department of Justice, Office of Juvenile Justice and Delinquency Prevention.

Villarruel, F. A., & Lerner, R. M. (Eds.). (1994). *Promoting community-based programs for socialization and learning* (New Directions for Child Development, No. 63). San Francisco: Jossey-Bass.

Yohalem, N. (2003). Adults who make a difference: Identifying the skills and characteristics of successful youth workers. In F. A. Villarruel, D. F. Perkins, L. M. Borden, & J. G. Keith (Eds.), *Community youth development: Programs, policies, and practices.* Thousand Oaks, CA: Sage.

16

Positive Youth Development: The Role of Competence

Angela J. Huebner

The introduction to this volume provides a wonderful overview of the importance of community youth development, which refers to the supports, opportunities, and structures communities provide to promote positive youth development. Youth development, at its core, is the work of young people. It refers to the idea that young people find ways to meet their needs and to develop the competencies they perceive as necessary for survival and transition to successful adulthood. Positive youth development refers to the notion that youth will develop in ways that are healthy and positive for both themselves and their communities.

The introductory chapter describes two critical components of positive youth development: (1) positive and sustained relationships with peers and adults and (2) opportunities to develop competence. The goal of this chapter is to examine the central role of competence in the framework of community youth development. Specifically, this chapter will review the definition of competence, review relevant research findings on specific competence domains, and make recommendations on how communities can create environments that support the development of competence in young people.

❖ WHAT IS COMPETENCE?

Several researchers have provided useful definitions of competence. For example, Garbarino (1985) defines competence as

a set of skills, attitudes, motives, and abilities needed to master the principal setting that individuals can reasonably expect to encounter in the social environment of which they are a part, while at the same time maximizing their sense of well-being and enhancing future development. (p. 80)

He further suggests that competence is "the ability to succeed in the world" and that competence is the "goal of socialization and development" (p. 81).

According to Schaie & Willis (1999), competence can be thought of as

a construct that implies action that may change the environment as well as adapt to the environment. . . . Attributes of competence include (a) the ability to select those features from the environment that are needed to process information, (b) initiating a sequence of movements to achieve the planned objectives, and (c) learning from successes and failures to form new plans. (p. 175)

In his work on adolescent competence and adult success, Clausen (1991) suggests the following:

Competence entails knowledge, abilities, and controls. It entails knowing something about one's intellectual abilities, social skills, and emotional responses to others. It entails knowing about available options and thinking about how to maximize or expand those options. Competence obviously also entails the ability to make accurate assessments of the aims and actions of others in order to interact responsibly with them in pursuit of one's objectives. Further, the person must have sufficient self-confidence to pursue his or her goals and desires. (p. 808)

As these definitions clearly suggest, competence can be thought of as the outcome of community youth development, because all three definitions suggest the skills needed to become a successful contributing member of the community. It is important, however, to recognize that competence does not develop in a vacuum—different environments necessitate the mastery of different skills for successful development. In other words, competent behavior occurs when the resources of the individual are a fit with environmental influences or demands.

The development of competence is also dependent on the individual's level of cognitive development (Danish, Petitpas, & Hale, 1990; Schaie & Willis, 1999). Given that competence is an interplay between the individual and the environment, it makes sense that an individual's stage of cognitive development would influence how he or she interprets and interacts with the environment. According to Danish and colleagues (1990),

As one progresses through the stages, certain demands or social expectations are placed upon the individual by society. The effort to adjust to these demands produces a state of tension that provokes action. This action is the use of a set of developmental skills just recently acquired. Successful achievement or learning of a task promotes happiness and suggests that the individual is likely to be successful at mastering other developmental tasks. Failure to acquire the skills necessary to task mastery can lead to personal unhappiness, societal disapproval, and difficulty in achieving later developmental tasks. Thus with age individuals begin to adopt external assessments of their performance that then influence their perceptions of their competence. (p. 171)

Finally, it is important to recognize that the development of competence is an ongoing process (Masten et al., 1995). Mastery of any skill takes time, repetition, and encouragement. For this reason, adults must provide young people with multiple opportunities to learn, practice, and relearn skills as they grow and develop. Moreover, community youth development demands that competencies are used by youth to contribute to the betterment of their community.

Given this definition and the contextually specific nature of competence, the question becomes "What specific competencies are relevant for adult success?" Furthermore, what can communities do to enhance successful acquisition of these competencies?

❖ WHAT DO WE KNOW ABOUT COMPETENCE?

There is general agreement that competence is context specific, such that certain skills are relevant for certain environments or settings (e.g., Garbarino, 1985; Masten et al., 1995). For example, the ability to read bus schedules could be an important skill for a person living in the city but not as important for an individual living in a rural area where public transportation is not available. If, however, the country dweller moves to the city, the ability to understand bus schedules may become important. The ability to identify different types of snow might be important for an Alaskan but less so for a Hawaiian. The ability to swim might be an important competence for those living near the ocean, but less so for those living in the desert.

Most research has examined the phenomenon of competence in specific domains, and there is general agreement about the existence of multiple competence areas (Dishion, Patterson, Stoolmiller, & Skinner, 1991; Harter, 1982, 1985; Masten et al., 1995; Morrison & Masten, 1991; Patterson & Capaldi, 1990; Sameroff, Bartko, Baldwin, Baldwin & Seifer, 1998). Additionally, most of the competence domains are related to developmental tasks (Masten et al., 1995). Generally, these domains can be connected to those referenced in the positive youth development framework described by Pittman and Irby (1996): (a) civic and social, (b) cultural, (c) physical health, (d) emotional health, (e) intellectual, and (f) employability. As the descriptions below will illustrate, each of these competence areas is important for community youth development, and each has application to a wide variety of contexts. As mentioned earlier, it is important to keep in mind that each competence listed below has the potential to look different depending on the setting. As Blum (1998) points out, "Prosocial behavior is one of the hallmarks of the resilient individual, but what is prosocial varies dramatically depending on the community norm" (p. 369).

Civic Competence

Civic competence has been defined as working collaboratively with others for the larger good, and sustaining caring friendships and relationships with others. The emphasis on civic competence for youth has been gaining momentum over the past several years. Civic competence can be fostered through participation in a variety of opportunities such as neighborhood beautification projects, volunteering at local nursing homes, organizing a playground equipment building day, mobilizing the youth vote, and understanding local political issues. Increasing numbers of schools are requiring demonstration of civic competence via completion of community service hours. America's Promise, an initiative of the Alliance for Youth, is an example of one national initiative that focuses on giving young people the opportunity to serve others.

Research related to civic competence suggests that service-learning experiences contribute to a young person's sense of personal competence and efficacy as they see how their efforts can make a tangible difference in the community and in the lives of others (Scales & Leffert, 1999). Community service can also promote a sense of personal and collective identity (Youniss & Yates, 1997). Specific studies have demonstrated that youth who have meaningful roles exhibit a higher self-concept (Bernard, 1990; Price, Cioci, Penner & Trautlein, 1993), a greater sense of optimism about the future (Kurth-Schai, 1988; Nettles, 1991), decreased delinquency (Bilchik, 1995) and increased problem-solving skills (Conrad, 1980). Service-learning experiences also have the potential to strengthen the connections between youth and their community, fostering a sense of ownership and meaningful membership. Research suggests that those youth who do not feel a connection to their communities are at greater risk of not achieving outcomes related to positive youth development (Gottfredson & Hirschi, 1990; Hirschi, 1969). Finally, those youth who do participate in community service projects are more likely to vote and join community organizations as adults (Youniss, McLellan & Yates, 1997).

Social Competence

Social competence has been defined as the ability to sustain caring friendships and relationships with others. It refers to skills adolescents use to interact effectively and appropriately with others in multiple settings (Scales & Leffert, 1999). Examples of social competence include planning and decision-making skills, empathy, conversation skills (the ability to listen and respond appropriately to others), good status in one's peer group, a willingness to accept responsibility, following through on commitments, and the ability to handle conflict with others peacefully (Downs, 1990; Scales & Leffert, 1999).

It could be argued that social skills are critical for development, because learning and further development are enhanced through our relationships with others. Our degree of social competence influences how others perceive us—if we will be taken seriously, if we will be liked, or if we will be avoided in future interactions. For example, a young person who has poor social skills will most likely have difficulty making friends. Research suggests that lack of positive peer group interactions is predictive of later association with antisocial peers and that association with antisocial peers is linked with participation in delinquent activity and academic failure (Dishion et al., 1991). Although the logical link between peer acceptance and romantic relationship competence is just beginning to be examined (Neeman, Hubbard, & Kojetin, 1991), other researchers have found that peer acceptance is a predictor of job competence (Morrison & Masten, 1991).

Cultural Competence

Cultural competence has been defined as respecting and affirmatively responding to differences between groups and individuals of diverse backgrounds, interests, and traditions. Because of the growing number of immigrants in the United States, our increasingly global economy, worldwide news coverage, and increased use of the Internet, cultural competence is critical. Cultural competence can be thought of globally as interactions with those from other countries or locally as interacting with those from other neighborhoods. Essentially, people can interact with others who are different from themselves in nonjudgmental and respectful ways. Empathy skills are a critical component of cultural competence (Scales & Leffert, 1999).

Cultural competence can be fostered by providing opportunities for interracial and intercultural friendships (DuBois & Hirsch, 1990). Examples of such opportunities may come in the form of exchange programs with youth or families from other countries or the encouragement of pen pals or e-mail pals with youth from other countries or other states. Volunteering in programs located in other parts of the community can also be helpful. In short, any opportunity that allows culturally different types of youth to interact in positive ways can foster the development of cultural competence.

Physical Health

Physical health has been defined as acting in ways that ensure current and future physical health for self and others. It includes making informed decisions about nutrition, diet, exercise, birth control, and engagement in risky behaviors such as drinking, smoking, and other drug use. As several researchers have pointed out, adolescence is a critical time for establishing health-related habits that will persist into adulthood (Maggs, Schulenberg, & Hurrelmann, 1997).

Factors that influence health-enhancing behaviors have been identified. These factors include having a positive value of health, having accurate information about the effects of healthy behavior, having parents who model healthy behaviors (Jessor, Turbin, & Costa, 1998), and having high levels of parent-family connectedness and school connectedness (Resnick et al., 1998).

The availability of and access to organized sports, community club teams, and recreational equipment are important for helping youth to establish patterns of physical fitness. Access to supervised high-risk activities (e.g., rock climbing, skateboard or roller-blading parks) can help youth to fulfill their need for excitement with limited probability of physical harm. Access to accurate information about diet, nutrition, and methods of birth control are also important for the promotion of healthy habits.

Emotional Health

Emotional health is defined as the ability to respond affirmatively and cope with positive and adverse situations, to reflect on one's emotions and surroundings, and to engage in leisure and fun. As teens get older, they experience increased emotional stress (Blum & Rinehart, 1998). Coping refers to an individual's ability to manage stressors encountered in the environment. Adolescents' coping strategies depend on several factors, including their level of cognitive development, temperament, available resources, frequently used strategies, aspects of particular situations, and the time frame in which the stress occurs (Cohen & Lazarus, 1983; Hauser & Bowlds, 1990).

Leisure activities can provide an important venue for practicing emotional health. Youth need to be encouraged to find leisure activities that are fun! Specific studies have shown that individuals with more positive attitudes about engagement in leisure activities experienced less general psychological distress, anxiety, depression, and hostility. They also experienced higher levels of positive affect and reported feeling physically healthier (Cassidy, 1996). Adolescents' choices of and participation in leisure activities can also influence their leisure pursuits as adults (Scott & Willits, 1989). Thus, exposure to a variety of leisure activities is important during youth.

Intellectual Competence

Intellectual competence has been defined as the ability to learn in school and in other settings; to gain the basic knowledge needed to graduate from high school; to use critical thinking, creative, problem-solving, and expressive skills; and to conduct independent study. Research has demonstrated that academic achievement is a strong predictor of adult occupational success (Masten et al., 1995). Youth who are at academic risk report lower occupational aspirations and expectations than their academically successful counterparts (Rojewski & Hill, 1999). Critical thinking skills are also important for youth. Improved media coverage and Internet connectivity allow youth and adults instant access to millions of pieces of information at any time. Unfortunately, not all of this information is accurate. Youth need to be able to evaluate what they read and hear. Because information and technology are changing so rapidly, young people also need to become lifelong learners. They need to know how to reinvent and upgrade their skills and how to solve problems creatively.

It is important to recognize that learning does not just take place in the classroom. There is a growing literature on the importance of nonformal educational settings (McLaughlin, 2000; Villarruel & Lerner, 1994). Nonformal educational settings are different from formal educational settings in several significant ways. First, participation in nonformal educational programs is voluntary. This means that youth will only participate if they find the program appealing. Second, nonformal educational settings involve adults as facilitators or partners rather than as didactic teachers (Dubas & Snider, 1993). Nonformal educators provide the experiences and guided questions needed for the young person to learn on his or her own. Third, nonformal education usually incorporates experiential learning techniques (Resnick, 1987). Experiential learning involves direct interaction between the learner and the content. The experiential process involves three phases: (1) having a concrete experience and describing it, (2) reflecting on the experience, and (3) making generalizations about how what was learned can be applied to other settings (Moote & Wodarski, 1997). It is only through such reflection that true learning occurs.

Employability

Employability can be thought of as vocational competence. It has been defined as the ability to gain the functional and organizational skills necessary for employment, including an understanding of careers and options with the steps necessary to reach goals. Employability skills are critical for all youth in the 21st century. In the early 1990s, the Secretary of Labor convened the Secretary's Commission on Achieving Necessary Skills (SCANS) to examine the gap between what employers were looking for in new workers and the types of preparation young people were receiving. The SCANS (1991) study revealed five consistent workplace competence areas: (1) managing resources, (2) working with others, (3) using information, (4) understanding systems, and (5) using technology. It also identified three "foundation skills" necessary for good job performance: (1) basic skills (reading, writing, math, etc.), (2) thinking skills (creativity, making decisions, solving problems, knowing how to learn), and (3) personal qualities (individual responsibility, sociability, self-management, integrity). According to the 1991 SCANS report, "Good jobs depend on people who can put knowledge to work. New workers must be creative and responsible problem solvers and have the skills and attitudes on which to build" (p. v).

Unfortunately, too few youth have the opportunity to interact with adults in the workplace. There seems to be an increasing gap between young people and adults such that both remain with their age-mates in work, school, and social settings. This makes it difficult for youth and adults to foster appropriate role modeling relationships. The Ms. Foundation's Take Your Daughter to Work Day and the America's Promise Groundhog Job Shadowing Day are two examples of efforts to expose youth to adult workplace settings. Unfortunately, one or two days of exposure are not enough. The National 4-H Council's Workforce Preparation Program and the Career Exploration and Job Ready programs of the Boys and Girls Clubs of America are promising programs that take a developmental approach to career exploration and development.

Motivation for Success

How important is each of these competence areas? It depends on how each is perceived by the individual. Harter and Connell (1984) suggest that one's overall sense of self is determined by the interplay of one's ability or competence in specific domains with the perceived importance of that domain. Following this rationale, if the adolescent deems athletic ability as unimportant, it will not really matter if that youth is a poor basketball player. On the other hand, if athletics is deemed important by that young person, then an inability on the basketball court may be devastating. Other researchers suggest that the choice to participate in competence-building activities depends in part on one's appraisal of the situation or opportunity. If the opportunity is viewed as a challenge, the individual may engage in competence-building activities; if the situation is viewed as a threat, it is likely the individual will not engage in the activity (Lazarus & Folkman, 1984). Finally, research also suggests that an individual's concept of what is important is also shaped by gender, social class, and culture (Eccles, Wigfield, & Schiefele, 1998).

Given such individual differences in importance, the question becomes one of how to motivate youth to achieve competence across multiple domains. Larson (2000) suggests that "a central question of youth development is how to get adolescents' fire lit, how to have them develop the complex of dispositions needed to take charge of their lives" (p. 170). He suggests that the notion of "initiative," described as self-motivation for mastery of a goal, is key in youth development. He further suggests that initiative consists of three parts: (1) intrinsic motivation—such that youth want to be involved in activities that ultimately increase their competencies; (2) concrete engagement with the environment—such that the task is sufficiently challenging enough to warrant concentration, but not so difficult as to create frustration; and (3) participation over time. Unfortunately, most daily experiences of youth do not provide sufficient opportunities to develop initiative.

❖ ENVIRONMENTS THAT SUPPORT THE ACQUISITION OF COMPETENCE

How then can youth be encouraged to develop competence? How can we "light their fires" enough to motivate them to achieve? Part of the answer lies in examining our communities.

A trend over the past decade has been a shift in focus from youth problem behaviors or deficits to a focus on competence or assets. As mentioned earlier, we know that an individual's environment plays a critical role in determining the acquisition of competence. "Even a capable individual can appear incompetent when functioning in a resource-limited, demanding environment" (Schaie & Willis, 1999, p. 181). In fact, characteristics of the individual's environment or community can sometimes be more powerful than any individual's level of competence. In their study of 500 families, Sameroff et al. (1998) found that, regardless of race or gender, "resourceful" adolescents (defined as those having good problem-solving skills, an ability to overcome difficulties and recover from setbacks) who found themselves in high-risk environments fared *worse* on measures of mental health, self-competence, problem behaviors, activity involvement and academic performance than less resourceful youth in low-risk environments. Similar findings were reported for academically high-achieving youth. These findings further emphasize the important role of environment in the promotion of community youth development.

Another trend over the past decade has been the recognition of community development and youth development as intertwined endeavors. People are becoming more aware that youth develop in communities and that community sustainability and growth depends on youth growing to successful adulthood. "There is no doubt that community and youth development belong together and that as partners they can achieve a far greater and more enduring change than either one alone" (Armistead & Wexler, 1997, p. 3). Given these trends, what can parents, teachers, faith communities, youth development professionals, community members, policy makers, and business leaders do?

❖ IMPLICATIONS FOR WORK WITH YOUTH, FAMILIES, AND COMMUNITIES

So what does this mean for our work with communities and families? The five *P*s of youth development proposed by the Center for Youth

Development (Pittman & Zeldin, 1995) provide a good starting point for assessing our tasks. The associated questions are examples of those that should be asked in helping communities to establish themselves as promoters of positive youth development.

The Five *P*s of Positive Youth Development

1. *Possibilities and Preparation.* What opportunities are available for youth in this community? Are a diverse range of opportunities available? Have youth opinions been surveyed? Given what we know about the multiple domains of competence necessary for positive youth development, it is critical that youth have multiple opportunities to develop a wide array of skills. Programs and opportunities should be available to youth with varying skill levels and innate abilities. Program staff must actively encourage youth to try new experiences and to persist (not give up) even when they become frustrated.

2. *Participation.* Do we know how youth are spending their out-of-school time? Do we know what programs are already available for youth? Who are our current programs designed for? Are all young people actively recruited for group membership? Are relationships within programs encouraged? Are adults viewed as mentors and role models? Do we think about transportation issues in getting young people to and from activities? Are activities located in inviting places?

3. *People.* Who are the people interacting with our youth daily? Who is in charge of our community's youth programs? Does that person have training in youth development practices? How do adults in the community view young people? Are they seen as a threat or a resource? What special talents or skills are adults in the community willing to share? Have they been asked to share their talents? What does successful development look like in our community? Do youth get a clear picture of acceptable and unacceptable behavior from community members? Do adults model healthy behaviors? Are the unspoken messages louder than the spoken messages to youth?

4. *Places and Pluralism.* What resources are available in the community for young people? What can they access on their own? Is transportation an issue? In a study of leisure activities among youth, it was discovered that the number one issue for adolescent participants,

regardless of locality (i.e., urban, rural, suburban), was transportation to leisure activities and having access to appropriate spaces to pursue leisure activities (McMeeking & Purkayastha, 1995). Can multiple organizations work together for the greater good of youth? Can agencies that do not traditionally see themselves in the business of youth work be convinced that young people are important? Can groups be convinced to let go of their turf issues?

5. *Partnerships.* Are youth included as partners in the planning and implementation process of programs? Do adults believe that youth can make valuable contributions to their own development and to the community? Too often adults plan *for* youth, assuming that they always know what is best for young people, rather than planning *with* them. Youth and adults bring different but complimentary skills to the planning table—youth have enthusiasm and creativity, and adults have the resources and knowledge of how the system works. Working in a partnership in which both are respected and valued, youth-adult teams can generate creative solutions to issues and create exciting and innovative programs that will attract other youth.

❖ CONCLUSIONS

As we work to implement this framework in our communities, it is imperative that we focus on providing youth with the supports, opportunities, and services needed to promote the development of competence in multiple domains. We can begin to accomplish the task of promoting competence in youth by taking inventory of our communities, using the framework of questions provided above as a starting point. In addition, we can begin to incorporate young people's definitions of what successful community youth development should encompass. Few researchers have attempted to take the youth perspective into consideration (for exceptions see Huebner, 1995; Hauser, 1999) when defining community youth development and, specifically, necessary youth competencies. Definitions of competence tend to be generated by adults for youth, rather than by youth for youth. Future efforts in this arena should strive to include youth as partners in shaping their future.

❖ REFERENCES

Armistead, P., & Wexler, M. (1997). Community development and youth development: The potential for convergence. *Community & youth development: Complimentary or competing priorities for community development organizations* (Paper No. 1). Ford Foundation and International Youth Foundation. Retrieved September 26, 2002, from www.forumforyouthinvestment. org/cydseriescommyouthdev.pdf

Bernard, B. (1990). *Turning the corner: From risk to resiliency.* Portland, OR: Northwest Regional Educational Laboratory, Western Regional Center for Drug-Free Schools and Communities. Retrieved September 26, 2002, from www.nwrac.org/pub/library/t/t_turning.pdf

Bilchik, S. (1995). *Delinquency prevention works.* Washington, DC: Department of Justice, Office of Juvenile Justice and Delinquency Prevention.

Blum, R. (1998). Healthy youth development as a model of health promotion. *Journal of Adolescent Health, 22,* 368-275.

Blum, R., & Rinehart, P. (1998). *Reducing the risk: Connections that make a difference in the lives of youth* (Monograph). (Available from Division of General Pediatrics and Adolescent Health, University of Minnesota, Box 721, 420 Delaware St. S.E., Minneapolis, MN 55455)

Cassidy, T. (1996). All work and no play: A focus on leisure time as a means for promoting health. *Counseling Psychology Quarterly, 9*(1), 77-90.

Clausen, J. (1991). Adolescent competence and the shaping of the life course. *American Journal of Sociology, 96*(4), 805-842.

Cohen, F., & Lazarus, R. (1983). Coping and adaptation in health and illness. In D. Mechanic (Ed.), *Handbook of health, health care, and the health professions* (pp. 608-635). New York: Free Press.

Conrad, D. (1980). The differential impact of experiential learning programs on secondary school students. (Doctoral dissertation, University of Minnesota, 1980). *Dissertation Abstracts International, 41,* 919.

Danish, S., Petitpas, A., & Hale, B. (1990). Sport as a context for developing competence. In T. Gullotta, G. Adams, & R. Montemayor (Eds.), *Developing social competence in adolescence: Advances in adolescent research* (Vol. 3, pp. 169-194). Newbury Park, CA: Sage.

Dishion, T., Patterson, G., Stoolmiller, M., & Skinner, M. (1991). Family, school, and behavioral antecedents to early adolescent involvement with antisocial peers. *Developmental Psychology, 27,* 172-180.

Downs, C. (1990). The social biological constructs of social competence. In T. Gullotta, G. Adams, and R. Montemayor (Eds.), *Developing social competence in adolescence* (pp. 43-94). Newbury Park, CA: Sage.

Dubas, J., & Snider, B. (1993). The role of community-based youth groups in enhancing learning and achievement. In R. M. Lerner (Ed.), *Early* adolescence: Perspectives on research, policy, and intervention (pp. 150-174). Hillsdale, NJ: Lawrence Erlbaum.

DuBois, D., & Hirsch, B. (1990). School and neighborhood friendship patterns of Blacks and Whites in early adolescence. *Child Development, 61*, 524-536.

Eccles, J., Wigfield, A., & Schiefele, U. (1998). Motivation to succeed. In W. Damon & N. Eisenberg (Eds.), *Handbook of child psychology: Vol. 3. Social, emotional, and personality development* (pp. 1017-1095). New York: Wiley.

Garbarino, J. (1985). Human ecology and competence in adolescence. In J. Garbarino (Ed.), *Adolescent development: An ecological perspective* (pp. 40-86). Columbus, OH: C. E. Merrill.

Gottfredson, M., & Hirschi, T. (1990). *A general theory of crime.* Stanford, CA: Stanford University Press.

Harter, S. (1982). The perceived competence scale for children. *Child Development, 53*, 87-97.

Harter, S. (1985). Competence as a dimension of self-evaluation: Toward a comprehensive model of self-worth. In R. L. Leahy (Ed.), *The development of the self* (pp. 55-121). Orlando, FL: Academic Press.

Harter, S., & Connell, J. (1984). A model of children's achievement and related self-perceptions of competence, control and motivational orientation. In J. Nicholls (Ed.), *Advances in motivation and achievement* (Vol. 3, pp. 219-250). Greenwich, CN: JAI Press.

Hauser, S. (1999). Understanding resilient outcomes: Adolescent lives across time and generation. *Journal of Research on Adolescence, 9*(1), 1-24.

Hauser, S., & Bowlds, M. (1990). Stress, coping, and adaptation. In S. Feldman & G. Elliott (Eds.), *At the threshold: The developing adolescent* (pp. 388-413). Cambridge, MA: Harvard University Press.

Hirschi, T. (1969). *Causes of delinquency.* Berkeley: University of California Press.

Huebner, A. (1995). *A contructivist approach to evaluation methodology: Implications for positive youth development.* Unpublished doctoral dissertation, University of Arizona, Tucson.

Jessor, R., Turbin, M., & Costa, F. (1998). Protective factors in adolescent health behavior. *Journal of Personality and Social Psychology, 75*(3), 788-800.

Kurth-Schai, R. (1988). Collecting the thoughts of children: A Delphic approach. *Journal of Research and Development in Education, 21*, 53-59.

Larson, R. (2000). Toward a psychology of positive youth development. *American Psychologist, 55*(1), 170-183.

Lazarus, R., & Folkman, S. (1984). *Stress, appraisal and coping.* New York: Springer.

Maggs, J., Schulenberg, J., & Hurrelmann, K. (1997). Developmental transitions during adolescence: Health promotion implications. In J. Schulenberg, J. Maggs, & K. Hurrelmann (Eds.), *Health risks and developmental transitions during adolescence* (pp. 522-546). New York: Cambridge University Press.

Masten, A., Coatsworth, J., Neemann, J., Gest, S., Tellegen, A., & Garmezy, N. (1995). The structure and coherence of competence from childhood through adolescence. *Child Development, 66*, 1635-1659.

McLaughlin, M. (2000). *Community counts: How youth organizations matter for youth development.* Washington, DC: Public Education Network. Retrieved September 25, 2002, from www.publiceducation.org/cgi-bin/download-manager/publications/p72.asp

McMeeking, D., & Purkayastha, B. (1995). "I can't have my Mom running me everywhere": Adolescents, leisure, and accessibility. *Journal of Leisure Research, 27*(4), 360-378.

Morrison, P., & Masten, A. (1991). Peer reputation in middle childhood as a predictor of adaptation in adolescence: A seven-year follow-up. *Child Development, 62*, 991-1007.

Moote, G., & Wodarski, J. (1997). The acquisition of life skills through adventure-based activities and programs: A review of the literature. *Adolescence, 32*(125), 143-167.

Neemann, J., Hubbard, J., & Kojetin, B. (1991, April). *Continuity in quality of friendships and romantic relationships from childhood to adolescence.* Paper presented at the biennial meeting of the Society for Research in Child Development, Seattle.

Nettles, S. (1991). Community contributions to school outcomes of African-American students. *Education and Urban Society, 25*, 132-147.

Patterson, G., & Capaldi, D. (1990). A mediational model for boys' depressed mood. In J. Rolf, A. Masten, D. Cicchetti, K. Nuechterlein, & Y. Weintraub (Eds.), *Risk and protective factors in the development of psychopathology* (pp. 141-163). New York: Cambridge University Press.

Pittman, K., & Irby, M. (1996). *Preventing problems or promoting development: Competing priorities or inseparable goals?* Takoma Park, MD: International Youth Foundation.

Pittman, K., & Zeldin, S. (1995). *Premises, principles, practices: Defining the why, what, and how of promoting youth development through organizational practice.* Washington, DC: Academy for Educational Development.

Price, R., Cioci, M., Penner, W., & Trautlein, B. (1993). Webs of influence: School and community programs that enhance adolescent health and education. *Teachers College Record, 94*, 487-521.

Resnick, L. B. (1987). The 1987 presidential address: Learning in school and out. *Educational Researcher, 16*(9), 13-20.

Resnick, M., Bearman, P., Blum, R., Bauman, K., Harris, K., Jones, J., Tabor, J., Beuhring, T., Sieving, R., Shew, M., Ireland, M., Bearinger, L., & Udry, J. (1998). Protecting adolescents from harm: Findings from the National Longitudinal Study of Adolescent Health. In R. Muuss & H. Porton (Eds.), *Adolescent behavior and society: A book of readings* (5th ed., pp. 376-395). New York: McGraw-Hill.

Rojewski, J., & Hill, R. (1999). Influence of gender and academic risk behavior on career decision making and occupational choice in early adolescence. *Journal of Education for Students Placed At Risk (JESPAR), 3*(3), 265-287.

Sameroff, A., Bartko, W., Baldwin, A., Baldwin, C., & Seifer, R. (1998). Family and social influences on the development of child competence. In M. Lewis and C. Feiring (Eds.), *Families, risk and competence* (p. 161-185). Mahwah, NJ: Lawrence Erlbaum.

Scales, P., & Leffert, N. (1999). *Developmental assets: A synthesis of the scientific research on adolescent development.* Minneapolis: Search Institute.

Schaie, K., & Willis, S. (1999). Theories of everyday competence and aging. In V. Bengtson & K. Schaie (Eds.), *Handbook of theories on aging* (pp. 174-195). New York: Springer.

Scott, D., & Willits, F. (1989). Adolescent and adult leisure patterns: A 37-year follow-up study. *Leisure Sciences, 11*(4), 323-335.

Secretary's Commission on Achieving Necessary Skills. (1991). *What work requires of schools.* Washington, DC: U.S. Department of Labor. (NTIS No. PB 92-146711/INZ).

Villarruel, F. A., & Lerner, R. M. (Eds.). (1994). *Promoting community-based programs for socialization and learning.* San Francisco: Jossey-Bass.

Youniss, J., McLellan, J., & Yates, M. (1997). What we know about engendering civic identity. *American Behavioral Scientist, 40*(5), 620-631.

Youniss, J., & Yates, M. (1997). *Community service and social responsibility in youth.* Chicago: University of Chicago Press.

17

Adults Who
Make a Difference

*Identifying the Skills and
Characteristics of Successful Youth Workers*

Nicole Yohalem

Few would argue with the assertion that youth-serving organizations have historically been influential in the lives of young people.
Since the 1950s, however, a profound set of economic, demographic,
and social changes have contributed to a dramatic reduction in the
amount and quality of time that many young people spend with caring
adults. "The most stunning change for adolescents today is their alone-
ness. The adolescents of the nineties are more isolated and more unsupervised than other generations" (Hersch, 1998, p. 19). At the same
time, young people today are faced with career options that require
unprecedented levels of educational and technological expertise if
they hope to achieve economic self-sufficiency. As social and economic
pressures on traditional institutions such as extended family and
cohesive neighborhoods increase, a variety of formal and informal

community-based youth programs are assuming an increasingly critical role in the healthy development of today's youth (Wallace–Reader's Digest Fund, 1996).

The developmental process is "influenced by environments and mediated through relationships" (Pittman & Irby, 1996). The previous chapter addressed critical aspects of youth program environments, one of the many contexts in which young people develop; this one will focus on the relationships that occur within such environments, or specifically, the role that youth development professionals play in promoting positive development. Until recently, and in many places to this day, the preparation of youth development professionals has been relatively haphazard. Although teachers participate in a formal, systematic certification process, there is neither a structured process nor a clearly defined disciplinary framework when it comes to training people for careers in youth work or nonformal education. Therefore, individuals who play a critical role in nurturing the healthy development of young people often find themselves lacking the necessary knowledge, support, and resources to meet the staggering needs they face daily.

As awareness grows (both in the field and in the general public) concerning the central themes of youth development and the need for a shift from a deficit or problem-focused framework to one based on assets, discussions are also taking place concerning the role of youth development professionals. The paradigm shift to positive youth development—recognizing that "Problem free is not fully prepared" (Pittman & Fleming, 1991)—has explicit implications for staffing and training. As strategies, preventing problems and promoting development reflect different philosophies that require different skills on the part of practitioners.

This leads to an important question requiring further exploration by practitioners, researchers, those who oversee funding, and young people. What are the skills, knowledge, and characteristics that youth development professionals need in order to support the development process and achieve desirable youth outcomes? For the purposes of this chapter, the terms "youth development professional" and "youth worker" will be defined broadly and used interchangeably to include those individuals who have selected careers in direct service, program development, or management.

By synthesizing the results of several worthy efforts to respond to this question with some of my own experiences working at different levels within the field, I aim to articulate a straightforward model for successful youth development professionals. Such a model can serve several purposes: assisting practitioners in developing staff training plans, informing funding sources and policymakers as to the professional development needs within the field, and helping youth workers themselves reflect on the strengths and challenges that they bring to their work with young people.

The combination of knowledge, skills, and characteristics that I discuss in the next sections reflect recent efforts of several national youth-serving organizations to identify core competencies, such as the National 4-H Council (1997) and the Center for Youth Development and Policy Research (1996). It also includes factors that have allowed me to experience some degree of success in my work with youth over the past decade. These fall into two broad categories:

1. Knowledge and skills

2. Characteristics and beliefs

Successful youth development professionals possess the following knowledge and skills:

- The ability to build and sustain meaningful relationships with and on behalf of youth and families
- An understanding of relevant theory (i.e., educational, ecological, social) and current cultural trends affecting youth
- The ability to create and maintain positive, safe learning experiences and environments in which youth have meaningful roles and responsibilities

In addition to knowledge and skills, successful youth workers tend to bring a similar set of characteristics and beliefs to their work. More difficult to describe in words but obvious to the observer, these qualities push the boundaries of what are traditionally considered "job skills." They are critical, however, to the success of effective youth programs, and they are also those qualities that inevitably emerge when young people are asked to describe caring adults. Although they cannot be packaged neatly into a curriculum as could a module on adolescent development, these are qualities that can be developed over time and nurtured by employers.

Successful youth development professionals are

- optimistic, seeing youth as positive, productive contributors (or potential ones) rather than problems or liabilities;
- consistent, yet flexible; and
- passionate about their work and committed to young people.

I hesitate to label any one skill or characteristic more important than another. There is a certain primacy to the ability of youth development professionals to build and sustain positive relationships, for it is only with such relationships in place that meaningful interactions follow. However, such relationships are more likely to be effective when adults possess an understanding of relevant theory and trends, the second skill area to be explored. Although I describe the three skill areas and three characteristics discretely for the purpose of clarity, the categories are much more fluid and interdependent in practice than they appear on paper. Just as development is itself a nonlinear process, the skills and characteristics that youth development professionals need to be successful are complex and interrelated.

❖ SKILLS AND KNOWLEDGE

Successful youth development professionals draw on a multidisciplinary set of theoretical and applied ideas in their work with young people, as noted in the following sections.

The Ability to Build and Sustain Meaningful Relationships With and on Behalf of Youth and Families

The need for young people to have supportive, accessible adults (in addition to their parents) in their lives has been well documented (Benson, Scales, Leffert, & Roehlkepartain, 1999). Such relationships give young people a sense of security and safety, access to resources, and models of future options and life choices. The need for such relationships is clear, but the process through which they evolve is less so.

When young people sense that adults do not respect them, they are unlikely to turn to those adults for support or guidance. Respect and trust are the critical ingredients of meaningful relationships between youth and adults, and as even the most well-meaning youth workers know, they are not always easy to come by. Research conducted by the Search Institute has demonstrated that most teenagers think adults have a negative view of them (Roehlkepartain, 1992). Teenagers are regularly the subject of negative media attention, cartoons, comedy routines, and adult complaints. Adolescence itself is a developmental stage typically portrayed as something parents and teens must survive. Two of the broad societal messages teens receive today are "We're scared of you" and "You're not a valuable member of society until you grow up." Against this backdrop, the challenge for youth workers as they attempt to develop trusting, respectful relationships often includes overcoming healthy skepticism, low expectations, and even resistance on the part of young people.

Another important ingredient of successful youth-adult relationships is time, an increasingly scarce commodity in today's fast-paced society. It takes time for relationships to develop, and in programs with high youth-adult ratios and/or high staff turnover, this can present a significant challenge. Time spent informally "hanging out" with youth and time spent participating in shared experiences is what creates the groundwork for two critical aspects of effective programs—positive youth-adult interactions and a sense of community. In addition to trust, respect, and time, adults working with youth need strong communication skills. They need to know when and how to approach youth in nonthreatening ways, how to listen, how to ask open-ended questions, when and how to share from their own experiences, and how to support youth through tough decisions without telling them what to do.

Through relationships, youth gain experiences, develop a sense of identity, access resources, and develop interpersonal skills. Many youth arrive at programs with a history of unhealthy, broken, or nonexistent relationships with key adults in their lives, both increasing the need for positive relationships and making their formation more difficult. In order to put any of the above-mentioned communication skills to work, adults must first genuinely connect with youth. This often means stepping out of our comfort zone—often literally, by going where youth are instead of expecting them to come to us, and figuratively, by exposing ourselves to popular culture and teens' ideas and realities so that we have enough familiarity with their perspectives to make meaningful connections.

In addition to relationships between youth workers and young people, the critical ability to cultivate other kinds of relationships is also implied by the first skill area. In fact, a recent survey of youth workers in Indiana indicated that many frontline workers spend a majority of their day working on *behalf* of youth rather than directly *with* youth (Indiana Youth Institute, 2001). Descriptions of effective programs almost universally point to the importance of engaging family members. Successful youth workers must be able to forge connections with family members and other key adults in the lives of the youth with whom they work. In addition, the success of many youth development professionals will depend on their ability to develop relationships with organizations and individuals who can be resources for their programs or for youth and families in the communities they serve (National 4-H Council, 1997). Seeking such connections and fostering them over time can exponentially increase the impact we have as youth professionals, by adding and strengthening critical layers and links within the complex contexts of young people's lives.

An Understanding of Relevant Theory and Current Cultural Trends Affecting Youth

Jane Addams has been credited with noting that the best social workers "keep one foot in the library and one foot in the street." To develop positive relationships with youth and, more broadly, to plan and implement successful youth programs, adults need a solid understanding of theory and research concerning the physical, emotional, social, moral, and cognitive processes of development. In addition, they should have a working knowledge of basic theories related to education, such as peer group relations and active and cooperative learning. A clear understanding of such theory and research is not only necessary in guiding program development on an organizational level; it should influence the day-to-day and moment-to-moment decisions that youth workers make as they lead activities, respond to behaviors, and facilitate discussions with groups of youth. Programs, activities, and specific interactions are most effective when they are developmentally appropriate. Operating from a developmental framework, youth professionals plan activities and opportunities in which youth are likely to engage and to experience success, based on realistic expectations of the interests and abilities of young people of different ages.

In addition to a basic grounding in theories of development, youth professionals should be familiar with a growing body of knowledge that increasingly points to the power of the youth development approach, including research related to risk and protective factors, resiliency, and developmental assets.[1] The work of researchers such as Hawkins, Catalano, and Miller (1992) has identified various risk factors in the individual, peer, family, school, and community contexts; exposure to multiple risk factors increases the likelihood that young people will engage in behaviors such as substance abuse and delinquency. In addition to risk factors, they have also identified individual and community protective factors such as positive social orientation, positive relationships, and clear expectations, which can balance or buffer against risk factors (Hawkins et al., 1992).

Resiliency research, which draws on risk/protective factor theory, reminds us that many youth who grow up in high-risk conditions do in fact develop social competence and lead successful lives. Studies point to common characteristics of resilient youth (such as social competence, problem-solving skills, autonomy, and a sense of purpose) and of environmental factors that support resiliency (such as caring relationships, high expectations, and opportunities to contribute) (Bernard, 1991). The Search Institute's asset framework is becoming an increasingly popular tool for helping programs and communities identify the strengths and needs of youth. Their research provides another useful lens through which national trends and priorities can be observed and shaped. This framework can be particularly helpful to youth professionals who find themselves in advocacy roles within communities, as they engage in trend analysis and priority setting and planning. The explicit relationship between assets and risk behaviors— the more assets youth have, the fewer risk behaviors they will engage in (Benson et al., 1999)—is a compelling illustration of the need for preventive or positive youth development programs rather than remedial or problem-focused interventions.

Most organizational efforts to identify competencies for youth workers include a theoretical background in child and adolescent development. However, they often fail to address the need for exposure to practice-oriented research about topics such as engaging children and youth in learning through nonformal experiences. One exception is the framework set forth by the High/Scope Educational Research Foundation in their approach to working with adolescents. High/Scope provides a research-grounded approach to effective youth-adult interactions that can guide program development and implementation as well as staff training (Wilson, 2000) in a range of youth-serving settings. Their emphasis on active learning, cooperative learning, engaging youth in planning and reflection, and youth leadership development has been translated into training modules that help professionals understand and apply relevant research in those areas, regardless of their particular program setting.

In addition to an understanding of theory, youth development professionals need to maintain an ongoing awareness of the current cultural trends and needs affecting the populations of youth with whom they work. For example, an adult who is developing a program to engage young people living in a residential juvenile facility would benefit from being familiar with current research briefs available through the Office of Juvenile Justice and Delinquency Prevention (http://ojjdp.ncjrs.org) that address trends among juvenile offenders, innovative practices within residential programs, and challenges facing the overall system. Similarly, a youth worker involved in a program targeting the children of migrant farm workers should become familiar with recent literature related to that population. Demographic realities in most parts of the United States mean that most youth workers must be knowledgeable of the cultural realities of youth from different racial or ethnic backgrounds than their own. Awareness of the cultural contexts of the young people we work with increases our ability to develop positive relationships, create safe learning environments, and plan relevant activities.

The Ability to Create and Maintain Positive, Safe Learning Environments in Which Youth Have Meaningful Roles and Responsibilities

Although positive relationships with adults who understand relevant theory and trends are critically important, supportive relationships are not enough. Youth need experiences and opportunities that build on their existing strengths and challenge them to try new things and develop new skills. Youth development professionals are in a unique position to provide such challenges, if they have the tools and skills to do so.

The ability to create positive, safe learning environments relies heavily on the first two skill areas explored—youth workers must be able to use existing resources to plan opportunities and experiences that reflect the needs and interests of youth. Whether the environment in question is a club meeting in a church basement, an after-school art program, or a residential summer camp, it requires the constant watchful eye of adults who are tuned into group dynamics and peer relations, physical safety, and the need to provide participants with meaningful roles and responsibilities.

In order for young people to become responsible adults, they need opportunities to take on genuine responsibilities in the various contexts in which they grow and develop, including youth programs. The same is true for the development of decision-making skills—we expect that as teens become adults their ability to make decisions will improve, but unless we provide them with real opportunities to practice making decisions and reflect on the consequences, we may be disappointed. Providing youth with choices (within a clear structure) is equally important in order to increase ownership and motivation. Effective youth workers understand the importance of offering young people choices and providing leadership roles, and they also have the skills to do so successfully. Choices and roles must be framed so that youth will experience success, and skilled youth workers are able to balance teens' need for increased independence with the need for group accountability and safety (both physical and psychological). They not only provide meaningful roles for youth; skilled workers support youth as they take on those roles, at the same time monitoring the overall climate of the entire group as well as the progress of the specific activity or experience underway.

Also implied in the ability to create and maintain positive, safe learning environments is a range of organizational skills that youth development professionals need in order to manage the logistics and maintain the flow of programs and activities. In addition to familiarity with teaching techniques, planning and creating positive program environments requires efficient management of resources, communication skills, time and priority management, creativity, and problem-solving skills. Depending on their role in an organization, youth development professionals may find themselves interacting with a group of youth one minute and planning upcoming programs the next. Being able to switch modes—to relate comfortably with teens as well as with colleagues, parents, or those who represent potential funding sources—is another important quality of effective youth professionals; it requires being perceptive, flexible, and having good social skills. A key challenge for youth development professionals is being able to enter the world of children and youth in an authentic way while maintaining an awareness of the bigger picture—other interactions occurring within the group, the program environment as a whole, and the perspectives of families, administrators, and community members.

❖ CHARACTERISTICS AND BELIEFS

When the Center for Youth Development and Policy Research interviewed youth workers about how they perceived their own professional needs, they tended to emphasize the importance of personal attitudes or beliefs over that of specific skills (Zeldin, 1993). In their book *Urban Sanctuaries*, McLaughlin, Irby, and Langman (1994) point out that effective youth program leaders have what they term a "wizardry," which, although it is not magic, is almost as difficult to describe because it is so highly personal. The following three categories attempt to synthesize the characteristics and beliefs that describe successful youth workers.

Optimistic: Seeing Youth as Positive, Productive Contributors (or Potential Ones) Rather Than Problems or Liabilities

A commitment to community youth development begins with a genuine belief that young people are capable, competent members of society whose voices and opinions are valuable. Successful youth development professionals see adolescence not as a stage to be survived but as a time filled with promise, creativity, enthusiasm, and curiosity waiting to be channeled into positive activities and opportunities. Genuine belief in the potential of young people leads to meaningful and authentic relationships that involve mutual give-and-take between adults and young people. A basic belief in or disposition toward youth as positive resources leads to high expectations on the part of the adults working with youth, and high expectations are a critical ingredient of successful youth programs (Pittman & Irby, 1996). A Center for Youth Development and Policy Research survey found that almost all youth workers interviewed stressed that their "positive orientation toward youth" was key in allowing them to be effective (Zeldin, 1993). Specifically, 47% attributed their effectiveness to the fact that they felt respect and appreciation for youth.

Successful youth development professionals see "potential and not pathology" when looking at the youth they serve (McLaughlin et al., 1994). When youth are viewed in this way, as positive potential resources, youth programs necessarily become places where these valuable resources can be developed rather than places that simply keep kids out of trouble. Successful youth development professionals tend to locate the "problems" of disadvantaged and high-risk youth primarily in the broader society and in the failure of different support systems to care for these youth, as opposed to blaming individuals themselves (McLaughlin et al., 1994). Youth workers who aim to direct and control will not be successful in gaining the trust and respect of the young people participating in their programs, who often arrive at them already marked by harmful labels that are rooted in negative stereotypes or misguided interventions.

Consistent, Yet Flexible

Young people deserve to have adults in their lives who are consistent, who mean what they say and who follow through on promises. Being consistent means a lot more than showing up for work on time; it means having consistently high expectations, consistently well-planned activities, and programs with a consistent structure or routine with which youth can become familiar themselves with and rely on.

Effective youth workers are intentional in the activities they plan, the decisions they make, and the feedback they provide. Serendipity and surprise will always be elements of youth work, but haphazard or poorly planned programs are potentially harmful to participating youth and will also weigh on staff and volunteers. Again, this is not just relevant at the program development level; the importance of planning and acting with intention is true on both the macro- and microlevels. Certainly, successful youth programs tend to evolve from clear goals and thorough plans that involve youth input. On a day-to-day, moment-to-moment basis, however, effective youth workers consider the potential impact of their every phrase and action, during everything from casual conversation to programmatic decision making.

By being aware that young people are keen observers, effective youth development professionals consistently model healthy attitudes and choices. Youth workers can have an enormous impact on the youth around them, in ways that are completely peripheral to the program or activity at hand. For example, by demonstrating an effective problem-solving strategy, having a constructive interaction with a colleague or spouse, showing the group how they struggle with decisions, or sharing their opinions about discussion topics, youth workers are in a constant state of modeling life skills and positive attitudes and behaviors.

However, though having plans and a consistent approach are extremely important, anyone who works with children and youth understands that *flexibility* is of great importance, too. The logistical realities of teens' lives today can include everything from balancing work, school, extracurricular activities, and sports to babysitting for siblings or parenting themselves. Planning programs that are accessible to a wide range of youth requires flexibility on the part of service providers and agencies. When surveyed by the Center for Youth Development and Policy Research, 41% of youth workers attributed their success in the field to their ability to be flexible, open-minded, and nonjudgmental in their interactions with youth (Zeldin, 1993).

And, just when you think you know how a group of teens is going to respond to an activity or question, prepare to be surprised. Effective youth workers must bring a plan or a vision of what they want to accomplish in an activity, but they must also remain perceptive enough and flexible enough to be comfortable moving in a new direction presented by the youth. This is easier said than done—building on youth input and allowing their voices to truly be heard requires that adults give up control over the final outcome without sacrificing what we know about making the process meaningful. So, although we must do our best to remain open, the best youth development professionals are constantly looking to strike a comfortable balance between structure and flexibility.

Passionate About Their Work and Committed to Young People

Teenagers have an acute ability to weed out phony adults, and it doesn't take them long. They sense when an adult is truly interested in their opinion about something, and conversely they sense when adults they are interacting with are distracted and would rather be somewhere else. Adults who are successful in working with youth tend to be those who feel driven toward the work by a true passion for what they do and who possess a strong commitment to influencing the lives of youth. The six youth development professionals or "wizards" described by McLaughlin and colleagues (1994) share a common "love for and commitment to youth, a mission and a vision to serve others, and a passion for a particular set of activities (p. 38)."

Many are drawn to the work because of their own experiences growing up in a specific community and a desire to give back, yet others overcome the challenge of being outsiders and are successful in working with youth from ethnic backgrounds and social classes that differ from their own (McLaughlin et al., 1994). Our notion of expertise must be broad enough when it comes to youth development to include key local community members whose backgrounds and experiences, in addition to the other important skills and characteristics discussed, are recognized as important qualifications (McLaughlin, 2000). Regardless of their origins and the types of programs with which they are involved, successful youth workers share a strong appreciation for the unique skills and interests young people bring to the table, as well as a strong belief in their own ability to make a difference. These beliefs are what allow them to approach this emotionally taxing and challenging work with an energy and authenticity that keeps them and their programs going, often in the context of scarce resources, relatively low pay, and limited upward mobility.

❖   IMPLICATIONS FOR PRACTICE,
      POLICY AND RESEARCH

To support the development of the skills and characteristics that have been described, youth-serving organizations need to offer or have access to consistent professional development opportunities designed to train and support staff entering the field at various levels of competence. The challenge extends beyond professional development, however. As youth development emerges as a field or profession in and of itself, the issue of staffing requires attention not only in the area of professional training, but also in terms of recruitment, compensation, and turnover (Hahn & Raley, 1998).

    As we address the issues of staff development and professionalization of the field, there must be continued emphasis on clarifying and articulating the key principles of the youth development approach as well as best practices for programs. As consensus continues to be built around the importance of emphasizing positive development rather than deterrence or problem-focused intervention, the need for highly qualified youth development professionals will become increasingly clear. Adults who enter the youth work profession do so out of a firm commitment to young people. Without adequate training, support, and compensation, however, we can only anticipate that an exceptional few will develop and maintain the necessary skills and characteristics to sustain a successful career working with young people.

    The development of agreed-on program quality standards, accreditation processes, professional core competency frameworks, and certification or endorsement opportunities for practitioners are important strategies that are currently receiving considerable attention in the field. Programs designed to provide professional, specialized learning opportunities in youth development should be innovative and accessible to undergraduate and graduate students as well as to practitioners already working in community-based settings. While meeting a critical unmet need in the workforce, university-based certification efforts can also foster and support critical dialogue between research and practice, bringing scholarship to bear on pressing contemporary youth issues.

The current convergence of interest on behalf of a wide range of stakeholders in the importance of the youth development approach, and specifically, the critical need to engage youth during the out-of-school hours, represents a unique opportunity. It is crucial that current knowledge (about the nature of effective programs, the importance of qualified staff and high-quality training, and youth worker competencies) is brought to bear on policy decisions and philanthropic trends in order for communities to successfully develop high-quality, comprehensive systems that are capable of meeting the needs of children and youth.

❖ NOTE

1.   This chapter was written prior to the release of the National Research Council's comprehensive report, *Community Programs to Promote Youth Development* (Eccles & Gootman, 2002). This volume provides a broad and rigorous synthesis of research and theory supporting the youth development approach and community-based youth programs.

❖ REFERENCES

Benson, P., Scales, P., Leffert, N., & Roehlkepartain, E. (1999). *A fragile foundation: The state of developmental assets among youth.* Minneapolis: Search Institute.

Bernard, B. (1991). *Fostering resiliency in kids: Protective factors in the family, school, and community.* Portland, OR: Northwest Regional Educational Laboratory, Western Regional Center for Drug-Free Schools and Communities, Far West Laboratory.

Center for Youth Development and Policy Research (1996). *Core competencies from national youth-serving agencies.* Washington, DC: Academy for Educational Development.

Eccles, J. S., & Gootman, J. A. (Eds.). (2002). *Community programs to promote youth development.* Report for the National Research Council and Institute of Medicine, Committee on Community-Level Youth Programs for Youth, Board on Children, Youth and Families. Washington, DC: National Academies Press.

Hahn, A. B., & Raley, G. A. (1998). Youth development: On the path toward professionalization. *Nonprofit Management & Leadership, 8*(4), 387-401.

Hawkins, J. D., Catalano, R. F., & Miller, J. Y. (1992). Risk and protective factors for alcohol and other drug problems in adolescence and early adulthood: Implications for substance abuse prevention. *Psychological Bulletin, 112,* 64-105.

Hersch, P. (1998). *A tribe apart: A journey into the heart of American adolescence.* New York: Ballantine Publishing.

Indiana Youth Institute. (2001). *Youth work: More than child's play.* Indianapolis: Indiana Youth Institute.

McLaughlin, M. (2000). *Community counts: How youth organizations matter for youth development.* Washington, DC: Public Education Network. Retrieved September 25, 2002, from www.publiceducation.org/cgi-bin/download-manager/publications/p72.asp

McLaughlin, M., Irby, M., & Langman, J. (1994). *Urban sanctuaries: Neighborhood organizations in the lives and futures of inner-city youth.* San Francisco: Jossey-Bass.

National 4-H Council. (1997). *Professional research and knowledge taxonomy for 4-H youth development.* Washington, DC: Author.

Pittman, K. J., & Fleming, W. E. (1991). A new vision: Promoting youth development. Washington, DC: Center for Youth Development and Policy Research.

Pittman, K. J., & Irby, M. (1996). *Preventing problems or promoting development: Competing priorities or inseparable goals?* Takoma Park, MD: International Youth Foundation.

Roehlkepartain, E. (1992, March). Why teens need adult relationships. *RespecTeen Newsletter.* Retrieved September 27, 2002, from www.search-institute.org/archives/wtnfa.htm

Wallace–Reader's Digest Fund (1996). *Progress and opportunities: Strengthening the youth work profession.* New York: Author.

Wilson, A. (2000). Timely intervention: Seizing an opportunity to tap teen potential. *High/Scope ReSource, 19*(3), 4-6.

Zeldin, S. (1993). *Professional development for youth workers: What is best practice?* Washington, DC: Center for Youth Development and Policy Research.

18

The Essential Youth Worker

*Supports and Opportunities
for Professional Success*

Joyce A. Walker

Youth workers are essential players in community efforts to promote positive youth development. They work in a vast array of agencies, organizations, and community settings. They typically bring passion to their work as well as a deep commitment to help young people. They seldom come to the work with a predictable set of educational experiences, a shared philosophy and language, a common understanding of human development, or a shared sense of youth work history and purpose. Calls to build the field of youth development work

AUTHOR'S NOTE: I would like to acknowledge the Youth Development Leadership graduate students who conducted the interview research cited in this article: Janet Madzey-Akale (project manager), Julie Austin, Robin Bell, Beth Kiene, Douglas Kress, Debra Sakry Lande, Bobby Lay, Jennifer Lick, Jaye McGruder, Winston Jackson Ray, and Lauree Williams.

acknowledge that the quality of programs and the outcomes for young people are directly related to the competence and capacity of the adults who guide them. This chapter explores ideas for systematic opportunities and comprehensive community-wide supports designed to strengthen the professional development and competence of community-based youth workers drawn from the practitioner perspective as well as academic, administrative, funding, and intermediary perspectives.

A report from the Carnegie Council on Adolescent Development (1992) called *A Matter of Time: Risk and Opportunity in the Nonschool Hours* focused attention on the significance of out-of-school time in the lives and development of young people. Approximately 6.9 million children 5 to 14 years old (18% of children in the age group) care for themselves after school on a regular basis, whereas 39% of grade-school-age children participate in enrichment activities such as sports, lessons, clubs, and programs before and after school (National Institute on Out-of-School Time, 2001). Young adolescents aged 9 to 14 spend 42% of their waking hours in discretionary activities such as watching television, playing sports, or pursuing hobbies, art, and outdoor activities (Carnegie Council, 1992). Children and adolescents have as many as 36 hours of discretionary time each week that are ripe for constructive learning, play, contribution, and exploration in safe, structured places under the influence of caring adults.

> Across all of the vast universe of community programs studied, *the quality of adult leadership was consistently named as both vitally important and inadequately addressed.* Youth-serving agencies, religious youth groups, sports programs, parks and recreation services, and libraries all report that the adults who work with young people in their systems, whether serving on a paid or voluntary basis, are the most critical factor in whether a program succeeds, but *do not receive adequate training, ongoing support and supervision, or public recognition.* (Carnegie Council, 1992, p. 87, emphasis added)

The call to improve the quality of adult leadership has been increasing (Larner, Zippiroli, & Behrman, 1999; McLaughlin, 2000). Youth workers are the front line of the programs, organizations, and systems that touch young people in the nonschool hours. They work at the intersection where the young person meets the system, and they define in large part the everyday experience a young person has with a program. They are paid employees and volunteers and sometimes a mix of both. Few could question their power to shape and influence the experiences young people have, for better or worse. The question remains: What is the best way to ensure that those adults trusted by the community to work with its children in the out-of-school hours get the supports and opportunities they need to succeed?

❖ ASKING THOSE WHO KNOW BEST

To understand the challenge of improving the equality of adult leadership in community youth development programs, youth workers were asked what they need to succeed in their work. Ten graduate students in the University of Minnesota's Youth Development Leadership (YDL) master's of education program conducted conversational interviews with 43 youth workers in Minneapolis and St. Paul. In order to have a balance of experience, culture, race, and gender as well as a cross-section of agencies in the interviews, those youth workers selected to be interviewed were recommended by other local practitioners. Interviews lasted approximately 2 hours and focused on five main areas of interest:

- Who are you? What do you do? How did you come to learn what you know?
- Think about the reality of what you do compared to the way you would really like to do it. What is the difference between the way you do your work and the way you would like to do your work?
- What ways of learning have worked for you? Not worked for you?
- What could a professional organization of youth workers offer to you?
- How and from whom would you like to get the training and education you need?

The interview data were collected and analyzed by the YDL graduate students, all youth work practitioners themselves. The graduate students transcribed 23 of their interviews and a clerical aid transcribed the other 20. Ethnograph computer-assisted text management software was used to code the interview text once the students determined the coding categories based on their reading of the interview manuscripts. The project manager (a YDL Program graduate) and the students worked together on the coding; the project manager entered the coding in the Ethnograph, wrote the draft papers that were circulated and critiqued by the students at their weekly meetings, and drafted the final report.

The 43 youth workers interviewed were older, experienced people representing a good cross-section of Minneapolis and St. Paul agencies and organizations. The majority were female (56% female and 44% male). Nearly two thirds were 26 to 40 years old (63%), with 16% over age 40 and 21% under age 25. Fifty-eight percent had been in the field between 5 and 15 years, 15% for 16 or more years, and 27% for less than 5 years. The ethnic/racial composition of the group was 44% European American, 37% African American, 9% Asian/Asian American/Pacific Islander, 5% multiracial, and 5% other. They worked for a wide variety of organizations involving young people in neighborhood, educational, sports and recreation, treatment, counseling, residential, corrections, cultural and religious, street/outreach, employment and training, and traditional youth-serving programs. Many examples in this chapter grow out of these interviews as well as from experiences of educators and youth workers in the Twin Cities over the past 10 years. Although the examples are local ones, they are representative of similar activity in communities across the country.

❖ THEY TOLD US WHAT IT TAKES TO SUCCEED

In 1999, with the interviews complete and the findings drafted, a round table was convened to make recommendations to address the training needs and professional development interests of youth workers in the St. Paul-Minneapolis metropolitan area. Thirty-two youth workers and three invited experts from Boston, Chicago, and Milwaukee gathered to share experiences and respond to ideas generated by the local interviews (Madzey-Akale & Walker, 2000). They created an action agenda to advance the youth development field and to strengthen the role of community-based youth workers, agreeing that youth workers must

1. have access to a range of training and education options;

2. be part of an ongoing system of professional development;

3. know that their work is legitimate, recognized, and valued;

4. work in supportive environments and climates that foster success;

5. understand the ways in which they are publicly accountable;

6. use a common language of positive youth development; and

7. be part of a system for advocacy and influence.

This agenda establishes a framework to discuss practical ways to support and strengthen youth workers, the agencies and organizations that employ them, and the communities whose children they engage on a daily basis.

Preparation: Education, Training, and Professional Development

Youth workers stressed the importance of sound preparation for the challenging work they do. They want access to a flexible range of education and training options as well as to a system of ongoing professional development. Unanimously, those interviewed wished to improve their knowledge and understand how to apply it to their work. They expressed a need to have time away from work to pursue training and education options, and they stated a preference for practical adult learning experiences grounded in their work and role.

Generally, youth workers have educational credentials, but they lack a common core of knowledge and experiences that integrate learning and work. The Twin Cities sample all had high school diplomas or equivalent degrees. Eighty-four percent had some postsecondary education: 58% had 2- or 4-year degrees. Two of the workers interviewed had completed master's degrees (in guidance and religious education), and six others had completed some graduate work. Areas of academic preparation included sociology, child psychology, education, social work, youth studies, anthropology, criminology, family social sciences, counseling psychology, international relations, business and finance, fine arts, and journalism. Similarly, the National Training Institute for Community Youth Work's (2002) evaluation study of national BEST (Building Exemplary Systems for Training Youth Workers) sites found that nearly 29% of youth workers surveyed had some college coursework and another 52% had college or graduate degrees.

Based on the interviews and analysis, youth workers learned what they know today primarily by hands-on practice and discovery on the job. They understand the importance of reflecting on their own successes and failures as well as learning from the experiences of others. They expressed a desire for education and training that is affordable, uses diverse methods, focuses on applied research, and has a place for young people to join the conversation. They expressed a desire to observe each other working and to intentionally blend the academic and practitioner perspectives.

Theory Versus Practice

In the interviews, youth workers voiced a general distrust of academic theory. Some expressed the belief that theories are often put forward to challenge or repudiate the wisdom of experience in unwarranted ways. Some felt that theory is only used by people who have never been in the trenches, making comments such as the following:

> You learn more in 40 hours on the job than you do in one hour of training.

> If you go strictly on book knowledge and what you read in textbooks, you will be lost in the world of young people.

> You can read articles or books, but you really don't have a clue until you are there with the kids.

Although theory is the antithesis of practice for some, others with some youth studies education admitted the excitement of connecting theory with reflective practice in seminars, internships, or training sessions:

> I think it's important to have a balance of books and real-life experiences. There has been a blend for me, in that the formal education I received has given me certain insights, and experience has given me other insights—and I think they have both worked well for me. So, I didn't always think like that. I thought that experience was the most important. But over time, I realize that it's a balance.

When asked to identify the critical elements in preparing a youth worker for work with young people, youth professionals who participated in these interviews said that (a) knowledge of self, (b) knowing how to be in relationship with others, and (c) competence in a basic youth worker skill set are essential elements to becoming successful youth professionals. That skill set emphasizes communication skills, setting boundaries and clear expectations, and methods of holding youth accountable. It includes basic group work skills, conflict resolution, knowledge of youth development, youth culture, cultural competence, referral resources, and skills for organizing and collaborating.

Youth workers require more than competency in a skill set to feel truly competent in their work. Baizerman (1995) speaks of youth work as a vocation; others speak of it as a calling. This language suggests that the larger field of asset-based work with young people in nonschool (usually voluntary) settings is an evolving career path that moves through periods of volunteer and paid full-time and part-time work in different agencies and organizational settings. Youth workers interviewed spoke earnestly about (a) the power of lived experience (personal life experiences and significant people in one's life) and (b) learning and critical reflection grounded in actual practice as central features of learning to be a youth worker (Madzey-Akale & Walker, 2000). They emphasized that being with youth provides some of their most important learning experiences.

Education and Training Model

The preferred education and training model that emerges is one blending academic study with on-the-job work experience, a model that weaves together theory, subject matter, methodology, and application. It is a model of the craftsperson or apprentice characterized by cycles of supervised experience, reflection, study, application, and more reflection. The teacher training model of preservice education (subject matter competency followed by student teaching and certification) is not congruent with the ways youth workers currently enter and advance in their work.

When asked about specific contributions a university or college might make to their education and training, youth workers emphasized exposure to applied research and knowledge, access to a range of courses that offer credibility and status, and a willingness to engage with them in meeting community needs. They suggested internships and field experiences in conjunction with coursework to provide hands-on experience and critical reflection. They prefer instructors who ask provocative questions, stimulate discussions, and clearly value the experience and perspectives of the youth workers. They prefer to learn from people working in the trenches. This calls for a partnering of community and university faculty to teach courses and bridge the gap between practitioners and academics. Those interviewed recommended that all training and educational programs be jointly planned and cotaught.

Perceived Role of the University

The youth workers communicated their respect for the university's capacity to collect and disseminate research, evaluations, best practices, vital statistics, and trends in youth development as well as to influence new directions in the field. A cohort model is popular because it builds connections with professional colleagues and creates a support group for returning adult students (Madzey-Akale, 1996). These workers stated their belief that a truly engaged university, more visible in the communities it is trying to serve, could be a significant networking force in the state, nation, and world. They see the advantage to university continuing education units or credit for training, noting that it is respected in the community and thus valuable to the youth worker. "I took tons of classes when I was going to the university, but I didn't have any hands-on experience. Now that I have the hands-on experience, taking classes will be really helpful."

Beneficial partnerships with institutions of higher education must overcome some inherent limitations. Many collegiate departments are poised to meet the professional needs of those in their discipline, but fewer are organized to respond to professionals who require knowledge, skills, and field experiences informed by multiple disciplines such as education, human development, social work, health, recreation, and administration. Some instructors lack firsthand experience working with youth, or they have not done it for many years. Faculty commonly do research and report in academic journals, but they may not know how to apply that research to the real-world issues facing young people and youth workers. University teaching tends to be expert based and presented in a top-down way that is perceived to undervalue the experience of practitioners. Access to busy professors can be limited, and the university may be isolated from what is really going on in the communities surrounding it. All of these points deserve serious attention for any university department that considers getting involved in a partnership to support education and training for community workers.

Ongoing professional development supports and opportunities are cited as key to youth worker retention and success. Youth workers voice enthusiasm for work-related training, a professional organization to bring youth workers together, and the opportunities for networking, training, policy discussion, and topical issue seminars such an organization could offer. In the BEST evaluation (National Training Institute for Community Youth Work, 2002), 61% indicated that they have participated in professional development opportunities related to youth development, and 19% said they always have opportunities to share what they have learned with other staff members. Youth workers agree that they benefit from ongoing training opportunities combined with chances to reflect critically on their practice with others in the field.

New practitioner journals such as the *Community Youth Development Journal* and *Afterschool Matters* and foundation resources such as "When School Is Out" (Larner et al., 1999) and "A Matter of Time" (Carnegie Council, 1992), provide valuable articles and examples of best practices. New resources are also appearing on the web. Like many others, Public/Private Venture has put its reports online for easy access and downloading (www.ppv.org). Web sites such as that of the National Youth Development Information Center (NYDIC; www.nydic.org/nydic) and the Children, Youth and Families Education and Research Network (CYFERnet; www.cyfernet.org) abstract research and connect youth workers to people doing like work. All of these resources open the door to knowledge, connection and a collective recognition of our common work. What is needed locally is a forum that promotes discussion and reflection about what it all means for the youth in the local community.

Support: Success, Recognition, and Accountability

Youth workers describe their work as undervalued—rich in relationships and poor in pay. It is rewarding work that is emotionally and physically demanding. It is part-time, summertime, weekdays, evenings, and weekends. It can be 40 hours, 9:00 to 5:00, or it can be 24 hours per day, 7 days per week, 52 weeks per year. Youth workers commonly consider moving up to administration, over to a parallel area of interest, or into another field when they have children, get older, need money, or feel that they cannot get the opportunities for professional support and development that they need to keep going. "People leave when they can't make a living at it. We're not supporting it. It's not a legitimized field so people don't even look at continuous development."

Passion brings people to youth work, but it takes more than passion to keep them there. Youth workers need a supportive work environment that provides clear measures of success, organizational and public recognition, and clear standards of accountability. One part of the answer is professionalization of the field. Another significant source of support must come from peers, supervisors, administrators, parents and the larger community.

Professionalization

Youth workers support building expertise in the field. Professionalization offers the possibility of financial and career incentives. A more professional field elevates the status of the youth worker in the eyes of the employer, and it brings an increased sense of accountability for program outcomes for young people. Those who oppose certification, licensure, and minimum preservice education requirements worry about expanding perceived power differentials between youth and youth workers by virtue of increased expert status. They express uncertainty about who would set the standards and control the profession as well as how to guard against system bias harmful to untraditional or marginalized youth worker populations.

The notion of a professional—an expert with "a monopoly of judgment over their clients based on knowledge and expertise" (Hahn & Raley, 1998, p. 391)—exists in tension with the reality of life and work grounded in program co-creation, youth-adult partnerships, and informal educational approaches. At present, youth workers do not come to the work to be experts but to work with others to pay back what someone did for them, to follow in the footsteps of a parent or role model, or to make a difference in the community. They stay in the field for (a) the joy of being with young people, learning from them, contributing to their success; (b) the opportunity to help young people be heard and to advocate for them; and (c) the opportunity to give back to the community that supported them as young people.

Support from Supervisors and Organizations

Youth workers are challenged to succeed in multiple roles in their daily work. Good supervision can profoundly affect their success. An effective, well-trained supervisor intervenes in respectful ways when a worker gets off track with a young person; such a supervisor also advocates for their work in the context of the larger organization. A capable supervisor is not afraid to deal with conflict in a timely and effective manner. Good interpersonal and communication skills enable trained supervisors to consult and reflect with staff in productive ways. A strong supervisor values training and is not threatened when youth workers gain skills and knowledge to improve their work.

Organizational clarity of mission and vision provides the direction a youth worker needs. Work environments that promote teamwork and create space and time for collegial debriefing provide critical support for workers. Although teamwork is a widely acclaimed goal, it can be a difficult reality. When staff turnover is high, agencies and workers are constantly rebuilding the team. In a climate of uncertainty, youth workers don't ask for assistance because they don't want to appear incompetent. The same factors influence interagency collaboration. The stated goals of the collaborative may appear to conflict with the understood goals of a particular agency. Agency agendas must be clear from the top down to avoid the trap of incompatible demands.

Local intermediary organizations are uniquely positioned to make a difference in the capacity and impact of youth-serving organizations (Wynn, 2000). They have demonstrated success at structuring and staffing networking opportunities among practitioners, policymakers, those who provide funds, and others. Intermediaries are helping to build a sense of identity for the field, an emerging consensus on mission and goals, program practice standards, staff competencies, and agreed-on youth outcomes. This may be precisely the kind of assistance community agencies and organizations need to strengthen their focus and intention concerning positive youth development work. Greater focus on mission and goals provides clarity of direction for youth workers who deliver on the front line with youth and families.

Accountability

Support for youth professionals on accountability issues is essential. A youth worker must understand what is expected and what the accountabilities are. "A youth worker has a much more dynamic role than to supervise recreational activities or to be doing community service activities. They're not coordinating something, but they're actually in the clutch with youth, engaged" (Madzey-Akale & Walker, 2000, p. 28). Youth workers expressed a deep sense of responsibility and accountability in ways not always acknowledged by their agency. This includes responsibility for safety, health, and risk management; for programs and activities based on current best practices; for judicious and ethical behavior in their relationships; for balancing their allegiance to the young person, the parents, the employer and the community.

The discrepancy frequently felt between the youth worker's understanding of the work and the employer's or public's view of the work complicates the accountability issue. Is the youth worker accountable to an emerging professional standard or responsible as an instrument of the employer? Those interviewed and those at the 1999 follow-up round table felt the weight of accountability to a larger public—the young person, the parents, the agency, and the community. Ongoing support, training, and professional growth are essential to maintain responsibility and accountability in these areas.

New models for community youth development (Connell, Gambone, & Smith, 2000) focus on the complex interactions between investors, planners, practitioners, and evaluators involved in community-based youth development initiatives. Community engagement deepens into a commitment to youth development when there are clear long-term outcomes that improve the lives of young people. The reciprocity between community commitment and positive youth outcomes is centered on the program of intentional supports and opportunities for young people. The "Community Counts" report (McLaughlin, 2000) summarizes the findings of a 12-year effort to understand the strengths and best practices in youth-based community organizations. A key short-term recommendation for youth organizations is to "document your successes with youth in terms that are meaningful to you as well as [funding sources], schools, and other potential collaborative partners" (p. 29). In the long term, organizations should document and share what they do specifically as it relates to learning outcomes. This kind of documentation relates directly to capturing the core contributions youth workers make to the success of the work. It places a clear and focused accountability on the shoulders of the youth worker as well as on the organization to provide the supports and opportunities the work and the young people need to achieve the targeted outcomes.

A Voice of Influence: Common Language, Advocacy, and Influence

Youth workers interviewed described themselves primarily by the role they play in the lives of young people. It is "a role like no other."

They used terms such as *friend, advocate, advisor, teacher, counselor, connector, resource,* and *role model* to describe their relationship with young people. They also described themselves as learners, teachers, change agents, visionaries, referral sources, assessors, promoters, listeners, problem solvers, and risk takers. Few, if any, used terms such as *youth developer, youth development worker,* or *professional youth development educator.* The array of terms to personally mirror what youth professionals do, and the implications inherent in these terms, reflect not only a challenge in building a common language of work, philosophy, and vision that brings youth workers together via an identity spanning boundaries of place, space, and agency, but also the challenge of developing models of training and support. Yet names and language are critically important in creating a professional identity. When extension youth workers in Minnesota became known as extension educators working in youth development programs instead of extension 4-H agents doing 4-H programs, the scope and nature of their work changed dramatically. Colleagues and the public began to see them as community-based educators rather than activity coordinators.

There is no single definition—let alone a common language—of youth work. From a positive youth development perspective, youth work is intentional, community-based educational work with young people (roughly 9 to 19 years old) with the aim of promoting their positive physical, spiritual, and intellectual development and strengthening their capacity for productive personal and social relationships. The terminology—the nouns and verbs—and the belief systems underlying those words originate in different academic disciplines and philosophical traditions. The work is called life skills education (Hendricks, 1996), social education (Marsland, 1993), informal education (Jeffs & Smith, 1996), character/values education, and citizenship education. The participating youth are given all sorts of titles: clients; participants; partners; at-risk, vulnerable, or disadvantaged youth; and members. The field cries out for a common language that bridges the divide of place, site, history, discipline, and organizational turf.

Community-based youth work has deep roots in nonformal education (LaBelle, 1986), recreation studies, and social group work. It does not usually include work labeled as care, treatment, control, or intervention. In the United States, the youth work we know today grew out of the settlement house, progressive education, and community-school movements (Lyons, 2000). Many of the largest national youth-serving organizations devoted to positive youth development today had their origins in the late 19th century with the blossoming of an eclectic mix of young adult organizations based on faith, national origin, and the sponsorship of fraternal organizations (Erickson, 1988).

Moves to promote a common language and philosophy of positive youth development, particularly the Wallace–Readers Digest Fund staff development grants to the large national youth-serving organizations, have stimulated interest and activity at the national and local level. The national BEST Initiative has advocated for youth worker training based on a common language and the common principles and philosophy of youth development put forward in the National Training Institute for Community Youth Work's evolving curriculum called Advancing Youth Development. Many national youth-serving organizations have adopted similar training models for staff and local site leadership.

The Twin Cities BEST Youth Worker Training Project is having success generating real enthusiasm among community youth workers from diverse agencies and neighborhood groups with its curriculum, Promoting Youth Development: A Community Approach (Wood, Walker, Stein, & Wurster, 2000), an expanded, community-focused adaptation of Advancing Youth Development. The Twin Cities YouthWork Coalition (TCYC) convenes youth workers from a variety of work places for professional networking and training events. It sponsors quarterly educational forums on policy and topical issues. TCYC does not have nonprofit status, but it is held together by a Steering Committee of volunteer youth workers. Its quarterly gatherings draw between 50 and 200 people, depending on the topic. This association has the potential to become a professional membership organization that influences the direction of the field.

Finally, although youth workers identified advocacy as one of their principal responsibilities, it was the one about which they felt most ambivalent. The uncertainties are related to the risk of being criticized for taking time away from direct work with youth, of not having credibility in their agencies to speak on youth matters, and of not having influence in communities that may view them as "activity supervisors." Nonetheless, they feel passionate about connecting young people to resources, advocating for their rights, battling negative community perceptions about youth, generating support for youth development programs, speaking out against injustices, and promoting partnerships and inclusion of young people in the spectrum of community affairs.

At its heart, youth work is educational. It is not neutral. It is invariably value laden and political by the very nature of what it chooses to teach and promote. It has traditionally been the purview of nonprofit organizations that select programs and activities to support their mission. There are important youth development issues around which youth workers can rally to advocate and influence. First, what youth do after school does matter. The work and learning in the nonschool hours is powerful and significant (Carnegie Council, 1992). Second, the great variety of activities, settings, and program foci offered during the nonschool hours is an advantage because the many choices available are responsive to the varied needs and interests of families and young people. Third, there is a long history of intentional community-based education and leisure time activity supported by both public and non-profit organizations. Fourth, the quality of programs will improve and the outcomes for young people will be strengthened when the intention and professionalism of youth workers is supported.

The United States has never had a coherent youth policy. The America's Promise initiative (see www.americaspromise.org) is as close as we have come in recent years to articulating and building support for a community moral compact spelling out the reciprocal commitments that adults and young people must make for youth to have the successful outcomes so beneficial to the larger community. Across the nation, communities are experimenting with alternate funding streams to support community youth work (often lumped under the category of out-of-school programming). Minnesota permits limited local taxing authority to support youth development and service learning through community education. Pineallas County, Florida, draws funding for youth development work from the Juvenile Welfare Board, a tax-supported public entity. Certainly there is a need and an opportunity for youth workers to take an active voice in advocacy and policy matters affecting young people.

❖ AN EVOLVING MODEL TO SUPPORT SUCCESS

How do we legitimize, recognize, and value positive youth development work and those who do it? Some possibilities include the following:

- Building a profession on the model of teachers, nurses, and social workers
- Building a credentialing system based on core education, training, and experience
- Building a field through recognition of mastery and demonstration of leadership

Discussions about creating a youth development profession become contentious when criteria for professional practice depend on "systematic theory" or "a monopoly of judgment" over clients (Hahn & Raley, 1998). The practitioner values of shared power, co-creation of programs with young people, and collaborative work with community are counterintuitive to an expert stance and licensed judgment. Other defining aspects of a profession generally include codified standards of ethical conduct, accreditation, licensing systems to regulate and control membership, and a professional association. It is appropriate to ask whether this kind of exclusive, expert model is even desirable in the field of youth development work.

Building local systems for credentialing is an important outgrowth of the National BEST Initiative, a 15-city youth workers training effort funded by the Wallace–Reader's Digest Fund and conducted under the guidance of the National Training Institute. By developing collaborative education and training programs with community colleges, YouthNet in Kansas City and the Chicago Youth Agency Partnership have moved forward in establishing a benchmark of competencies and experience that the community is encouraged to accept as the required bottom line for youth development workers. Fundamental to this strategy is a definition of standards and outcomes flexible enough to include and value experienced youth workers who may lack academic training.

The language of the Carnegie Council on Adolescent Development (1992) is the language of leadership. A model of field building based on leadership and mastery in action in the community—a craft model combining formal learning with apprenticeship—is being explored in Minnesota. It seeks to rally youth workers from diverse sectors to study and to demonstrate leadership in the field of positive youth development. This suggests a broad construct of advocacy, accountability, and action launched for, with, and on behalf of young people and their development. Leadership to build a field premised on a philosophy of strengths-based promotion and development invites individual and agency participation around a common challenge rather than the more elite model of the profession. The University of Minnesota's master's degree in the College of Education and Human Development is intentionally designed as an interdisciplinary study in Youth Development Leadership for those who openly profess and demonstrate a normative, asset-based way of working with and on behalf of young people. The question of how to build the field, strengthen adult leadership, and improve youth development outcomes for young people remains a challenge. It is critical that youth workers in the field join the discussion.

❖ A CHALLENGE FOR EVERY SECTOR

The voices of practitioners, administrators, those who contribute funds, academics, and interested community leaders lay out the challenge of mobilizing supports and opportunities for community youth workers to ensure that they can provide the quality leadership that our youth development efforts and programs merit. This is not the responsibility of the youth work professionals alone. It presents a challenge for every sector.

Youth workers are challenged to marshal the time and energy necessary to establish leadership for the field. To support themselves and ensure their success, youth workers need to move beyond passion for their work to peer-endorsed standards of competence and accountability. This suggests establishing a self-determined professional identity, most likely through a local association of youth development workers. The issues of common language and a clearly articulated guiding philosophy of youth development can be addressed through agreement under the auspices of a professional association. If youth workers themselves are to determine standards of best practice and public accountability, an association is a reasonable forum and sponsor for the discussion. It is also in the association that advocacy for the field and discussions of public policy are likely to happen.

Youth development organizations are challenged to create more supportive and focused workplaces. Community organizations and agencies will benefit from fully valuing an investment in positive youth development and the youth workers who make it possible. This means opening access to a range of education and training opportunities for staff, creating incentives and rewards for participation in training and professional improvement, and fostering a stimulating work climate that engenders commitment and success. A theme that runs through all these supports is the need for critical reflection on one's work in a safe environment among wise, experienced, and trusted colleagues.

Academic institutions are challenged to find creative ways to support the education and continuing professional development of youth development professionals. To ensure an ongoing selection of training and professional development opportunities, academic institutions can offer course work at the undergraduate and graduate levels. Coursework in youth studies or community youth development are best offered weekdays, evenings, and weekends. Practitioners recommend the inclusion of a community internship and a series of reflective seminars. Leadership is a reasonable focus for graduate programs in such colleges as education, human development, and social work, or in interdisciplinary centers or institutes. Graduate programs are ideally tailored to embrace a wide variety of undergraduate majors as well as a wide variety of professional experiences. The potential for outreach classes and continuing professional development cotaught by practitioners and faculty is great and can be woven into partnerships with organizations such as American Humanics (Ashcraft, 2000). Web-based learning and distance-learning approaches are gaining popularity for reasons of convenience and economy; however, youth workers benefit from cohort designs and practical, hands-on demonstrations and participation. These are more challenging additions to distance education, yet essential options for those with long histories of learning in traditional classrooms.

Intermediary organizations have a vital challenge to continue to build a base for the field and support for the community-based organizations that do the work. Youth workers embrace the fundamental tenets of positive youth development as a common basis for their work. Because they do not share common job descriptions or job titles, and because they work for such a variety of agencies, they find the growing body of youth development research and best practice literature helps legitimate their work in the eyes of supervisors, agency heads, parents, colleagues, and community decision makers. The philosophy and language bridges their differences and joins them with others in a spirit of professional purpose. Wynn (2000) has proposed that intermediary organizations are well poised to provide training, management assistance, accountability assistance, knowledge dissemination, and help in establishing standards.

Intermediaries such as Public/Private Ventures, Chapin Hall Center for Children, the Search Institute, and the Academy for Educational Development have taken the lead in disseminating position papers, research reports, evaluations, and best practice information to practitioners. Foundations such as the Wallace–Readers Digest Fund, Carnegie Council on Adolescent Development, and the Packard Foundation have published reports (of conferences, roundtables and task force work) that have done much to inform the field. Youth development research needs to be available in a consumer-friendly fashion to help youth workers, volunteers, administrators, and board members understand the complexity of the work and the importance of using an asset-based model in the work. Intermediaries have done an excellent job of making their reports and resources understandable. The role of convening, facilitating, capturing, and in other ways promoting connections and conversations among people interested in the field of youth development work is equally critical.

In the final analysis, the key to success is the commitment of communities to make youth development a priority for their time, resources, and policy initiatives. The community also has a role in supporting youth worker success. Neighborhood organizations, local governments, foundations and intermediary organizations are all stakeholders in the success of local youth development programs. They must resist a cookie-cutter approach to agency work and outcomes. These influential stakeholders can encourage agencies to reflect community values, hopes, and priorities in their missions and goals. They are in a position to demand accountability for mutually negotiated outcomes. And they can support youth workers and their work by regularizing the funding streams and tying funding to outcomes. Perhaps more than anything else, these stakeholders can articulate and reinforce the community's moral and social compact with its children, making clear what the community will do for youth and what children and young people are expected to give to their community.

❖ REFERENCES

Ashcraft, R. (2000). Where youth work preparation meets higher education: Perspectives from an American Humanics campus program. *Applied Developmental Science*, 4(Suppl. 1), 38-46.

Baizerman, M. (1995, May). *Youthwork with "street kids" as the praxis of a community's moral compact with its youth: An overview*. Unpublished manuscript, University of Minnesota at St. Paul.

Carnegie Council on Adolescent Development. (1992). *A matter of time: Risk and opportunity in the nonschool hours*. (Report of the Task Force on Youth Development and Community Programs). New York: Carnegie Corporation of New York.

Connell, J., Gambone, M. A., & Smith, T. (2000). Youth development in community settings: Challenges to our field and our approach. In *Youth development: Issues, challenges and directions.* Philadelphia: Public/Private Ventures.

Erickson, J. (1988). *Directory of American youth organizations.* Minneapolis: Free Spirit Publishing.

Hahn, A., & Raley, G. (1998). Youth development: On the path toward professionalization. *Nonprofit Management and Leadership, 8,* 387-401.

Hendricks, P. (1996). Targeting life skills model. Ames: Iowa State University.

Jeffs, T., & Smith, M. (1996). *Informal education—Conversation, democracy and learning.* Derby, UK: Education Now.

LaBelle, T. (1981). An introduction to the nonformal education of children and youth. *Comparative Education Review, 25*(3), 313-329.

Larner, M. B., Zippiroli, L., & Behrman, R. E. (1999). When school is out: Analysis and recommendations. *The Future of Children, 9,* 4-20.

Lyons, E. C. (2000, Summer). Creating an agency culture: A model for common humanity. *Afterschool Matters, 1*(1), 18-29.

Madzey-Akale, J. (1996, May). *Master of education youth development leadership program: Program evaluation.* Unpublished manuscript, University of Minnesota at St. Paul.

Madzey-Akale, J., & Walker, J. (2000). *Training needs and professional development interests of Twin Cities youth workers summary.* Minneapolis: University of Minnesota Extension Service, Center for 4-H Youth Development.

Marsland, D. (1993). *Understanding youth: Issues and methods in social education.* St. Albans, UK: Claridge Press.

McLaughlin, M. (2000). *Community counts: How youth organizations matter for youth development.* Washington, DC: Public Education Network. Retrieved September 25, 2002, from www.publiceducation.org/cgi-bin/download-manager/publications/p72.asp

National Collaboration for Youth. (1997, August). *Credentialing activities in the youth development field.* Washington, DC: National Assembly of National Voluntary Health and Social Welfare Organizations.

National Institute on Out-of-School Time. (2001, March). Fact sheet on school-age children's out-of-school time. Wellesley, MA: Wellesley College, Center for Research on Women. Retrieved October 3, 2002, from www.niost.org/factsheet.pdf

National Training Institute for Community Youth Work. (2002). *BEST strengthens youth worker practice: An evaluation of building exemplary systems for training youth workers (BEST): A summary report.* Washington DC: Academy for Educational Development.

Pittman, K. (2000). Balancing the equation: Communities supporting youth, youth supporting communities. *CYD Journal, 1*(1), 32-37.

Roth, J., Brooks-Gunn, J., Murray, L., & Foster, W. (1998). Promoting healthy adolescents: Synthesis of youth development program evaluations. *Journal of Research on Adolescence, 8*(4), 423-459.

Wallace–Reader's Digest Fund. (1996). *Progress and opportunities: Strengthening the youth work profession. An analysis of and lessons learned from grantmaking.* New York: Author.

Wood, E., Walker, J., Stein, J., & Wurster, P. (2000). *Promoting youth development: A community approach.* Minneapolis: Center for 4-H Youth Development.

Wynn, J. R. (2000). *The role of local intermediary organizations in the youth development field.* Chicago: Chapin Hall Center for Children.

Zeldin, S. (1993). *Professional development for youth workers: What is best practice?* Washington, DC: Center for Youth Development and Policy Research.

19

Community Youth Development: Youth Voice and Activism

Francisco A. Villarruel, Daniel F. Perkins,
Lynne M. Borden, and Joanne G. Keith

We began work on this volume prior to the September 11, 2001, attacks on the World Trade Center and the Pentagon. Since that time, bumper stickers and posters have been seen around the country stating, "We will never forget" or "8:48—the time the world changed." The terrorist acts have changed our nation's perception of safety, but they have also, in many ways, contributed to a redefinition of patriotism and national community. Virtually every corner of our nation mourned and has felt the impact of that September day. By the same token, much of our nation, we argue, remains unchanged.

Recently, for example, the middle-school daughter of one of the authors spoke, along with three other student council leaders, to her school board about a post–September 11 decision to cancel the annual eighth-grade field trip to an out-of-state amusement park. Excerpts from their presentation are offered here as a reflection on this volume, and, more important, as a statement by youth on the issues we discuss.

We understand that some parents and students applaud the decision made by the superintendent. They have doubts about the safety of an out-of-state activity. However, we represent the eighth-grade student body and parents who do not favor this decision. We believe that we represent the majority of the student body, and not just a few students. For many of us, this trip is something that we have been anxiously awaiting for the past 2 years. Some of our older brothers and sisters went on these trips, as well as some of our parents. We believe we should not be penalized for not sharing the same opinion as others. We do understand that, for some, this is an issue of concern and fear about safety. But as former President Franklin D. Roosevelt once stated, "The only thing we have to fear is fear itself." We are not trying to take away our friends' right to be fearful. We too have fears in our lives. In fact, as former Apollo Astronaut Neil Armstrong once stated, "Fear is not an unknown emotion to us." For us, this is a trip that celebrates our accomplishments, which celebrates our graduating from the eighth grade.

The students went on to say,

As you can see, what we are trying to suggest is something that Marie Curie once stated, "Nothing in life is to be feared, only to be understood." The September 11th issue should not cause us to stop living our normal lives, to throw away traditions that have meaning for students, but rather, it should help us to think together what we can do to understand and learn from these situations, not only to make sure that we can maintain our traditions, but also maintain our safety.

Immediately after the presentation of their views, the middle school students who spoke received a thunderous ovation from their parents and peers, as well as from school board members who were in attendance. In addition to thanking them, the school board president acknowledged how proud she was of the "articulate and well conceptualized arguments" that had been presented. She was proud, not only of how "bright" these students were, but also that they were taking time out of their daily lives to participate in the governance of their school.

However, as often happens, it ended there. The school board president reminded everyone that this was not a time for discourse, and that the school board would take the arguments put forth by these four middle school students under advisement. As the group, along with their peers and parents, exited to the hallway, there was a swell of exuberance, acknowledging these youth leaders for their presentation. But for these four individuals, there was something more noticeable—both a sense of relief (that their presentation was over) and a sense of disappointment (questioning whether they did make a difference; whether their ideas were really heard and whether this would lead to a reversal in the school policy). For the adults, too, who were in attendance, it raised the question (again) of whether community leaders really value the input of youth. For these adults, it would have been easier to stand before the school board themselves and question the decision and decision-making process. Instead, they provided support and encouragement to these young individuals to express their feelings in their own voice, only to witness a procedure that all but dismissed the content of what was offered. Four months later, the decision was reversed. The public notification of the policy reversal occurred in the print and radio/television media first. One week later, the superintendent met with only two of the students who participated in the school board meeting. According to one of the students, the superintended stated that their presentation was influential, insightful. Moreover, he shared with these two students that their comments were perhaps the "most effective" of any comments offered by students and parents in the school district. (It is unfortunate that this information was not made public!)

If, as a nation, we are to join with all humankind in achieving a more democratic world, we must harness the energy of our youth and provide them the necessary positive support to be heard and to contribute in meaningful ways to their communities. By engaging and providing youth with real opportunities to contribute to the communities in which they live, the clubs and organizations in which they participate, and the families in which they grow up, we believe that we are ensuring the successful development of youth now and in the future.

❖ ENGAGING WITH YOUTH

A closer inspection of the excerpt quoted above reveals two ideas that repeat themselves thematically in this volume: engagement and activism. First and foremost, these youth were asking, in part, that they be engaged in decisions that impact their lives. Undoubtedly, some might argue, the ones who came forward and spoke were considered to be the more articulate or the "leaders" of the students, but that is not relevant. The point is that they desired and believed that they had an obligation to be involved in the decision making. Obviously, the policy to ban out-of-state trips was made without talking with the student body, and clearly, these students wanted to be involved in the discussion and drafting of policies that affected their lives. We do not wish to imply that the school board, which is probably typical of any adult governing body at a community level, was insensitive to the ideas or arguments put forth by the students. However, we suggest that they failed to look beyond responding to the presentation. Rather than inviting the youth to collaborate with them or establishing some mechanism for formally involving the youth in drafting and implementation of the policy issue concerned, the school board only acknowledged the value of the youths' voice.

In any community, there are doubtless more youth than there are "seats" to consistently capture the voices of youth. But as Huber and her colleagues note in Chapter 14, there is no real systematic opportunity for youth input unless adults purposefully construct it. Youth as partners is not a new phenomenon in our nation, nor is it a practice that is widely accepted. What the scientific literature demonstrates is that it does work. More important, the literature reveals that youth tend to feel more connected to their communities and the processes of community development when they know that a peer represents them. Youth engagement in their community, or "mattering," fosters their own development. The importance of mattering is described in the National Research Council (2002) report entitled "Community Programs to Promote Youth Development":

> Positive development is not something adults do to young people, but rather something that young people do for themselves with a lot of help from parents and others. They are agents of their own development. To foster development, then, it follows that settings need to be youth centered, providing youth—both individually

and in groups—the opportunity to be efficacious and to make a difference in their social worlds—we refer to this opportunity as "mattering." (p. 103)

Ironically, the actions of the school board reinforced a marketing philosophy of our nation, which is that of a "disposable society." Although the eighth graders' verbal contribution was publicly valued for a few moments, no real effort was made to immediately involve them in a further process of negotiation. Their testimony was taken as passionate, articulate, and a reflection of the good job we are doing in educating our community's youth. These actions, unfortunately, parallel a continuing national trend that essentially dismisses the significance of youth and adolescents. Zero-tolerance policies in public schools, for example, recognize the mistakes of youth rather than their accomplishments. In other words, youth are noted for their transgressions (Drizin, 2001) and not for their potential to contribute to the systems and environments in which they live and that, ultimately, they will inherit. Coupled with the increased tendency to send youth to adult courts (and sentencing), these actions cause us to ask whether our nation has (either consciously or unconsciously) adopted a philosophy of seeing young people as "disposable youth" who cannot overcome their transgressions. Ironically, we seem to be at an impasse with respect to how this should or can occur. In the juvenile justice system, for example, communities appear to be waiting for directives from the courts, while the courts are seeking answers from communities. As Brown and his colleagues note in Chapter 11,

Communities and agencies that serve youth are expecting more from courts than decisions. The often-unstated expectation is that the orders entered as part of the courts' decisions will work for the positive development of youth. The second expectation is that adequate resources will be provided to implement programs to provide the education or services to the end result of developing capable youth.

It is not altogether surprising that Brown and his colleagues conclude their chapter by stating the following:

Despite (or perhaps because of) massive changes in the juvenile justice system over the past decade, the system too often failed to alter the trajectories of troubled youth or prepare them to assume productive adult roles. The combination of confinement, supervision, surveillance, and treatment commonly provided to youth in the system has not achieved the desired results. Nevertheless, many states continue to increase spending on juvenile corrections, with little result. This chapter suggests that state and local policymakers and the juvenile justice system promote initiatives that combine the principles of youth development and workforce development.

In both of these instances—the school board decision and the engagement of adjudicated youth—the voices of youth and their integration/engagement into communities appear to be lacking. In Chapter 15, Perkins and Borden highlight, as a critical element of success for youth programs, creating a sense of belonging for youth. These examples demonstrate how we all too often alienate youth instead of engaging them and providing them with the opportunity to establish a sense of belonging and ownership in youth programs they join and in the communities in which they live.

One critical factor that we view as essential in the effort to authentically engage youth in community initiatives lies in the underlying theme of the first section of this volume—that the developmental pathways of youth are not identical, and are, in fact, influenced by their contexts. Lerner (1995), an advocate of developmental contextualism, argues that the relationship between adults, youth, and the communities in which they live is interdependent and reciprocal, and that this relationship should be at the forefront of any effort to provide programs and policies that might ultimately increase the likelihood of contributing to an individual's growth and (positive) developmental outcomes. But, as Rodriguez, Morrobel, and Villarruel note in Chapter 3, all too often adult decision makers do not understand or have at their disposal information concerning the unique developmental challenges and strengths of the youth they are supposed to serve. Moreover, as discussed by Denner and Griffin (Chapter 6), as well as Russell and Andrews (Chapter 7), additional attention must focus on gender and sexual identity development, both within and across ethnic, cultural, and racial groups, if communities are to accurately respond to and meet the needs of youth in their respective communities.

❖ ACTIVISM

Over the past decades, or perhaps for even longer, professionals who work with youth have developed and dedicated themselves to a national movement: positive youth development. Grounded in establishing opportunities for all youth, the positive youth development framework has captured the interest of youth professionals, parents, civic leaders, policy professionals, researchers, and parents who collectively are interested in sustaining the quality of life and offering opportunities for community health for future generations. However, problems arise when we are trying to implement a philosophy in our programs and communities.

As the chapters in this volume illustrate, the strategies used to create youth-friendly environments should be related to issues of context and culture. Skills that adults need are not altogether different across communities, but how we engage with youth does vary across contexts. By the same token, these chapters underscore an approach for developing a systematic change in focus that ultimately leads to the sustainability of youth programs—a move toward community youth development as opposed to positive youth development. Although the concept of community youth development is not new, it does differ from the positive youth development framework in one major respect: It is concerned with raising the level of accountability, significance, and urgency for developing comprehensive opportunities for all community residents (Perkins, Borden, & Villarruel, 2001). Stated somewhat differently, the notion of community youth development rests on the philosophy that communities must develop comprehensive and seamless community-wide efforts that promote positive youth development for all young people, providing them with the opportunities to develop positive relationships, skills, competencies, and attitudes that will assist them in making positive choices for their lives. More importantly, the notion of community youth development raises the responsibility of adults, in collaboration with youth, to advocate for opportunities and structures that provide young people with sustained positive relationships with adults and opportunities to use newly acquired skills in the real-world experiences of their communities.

In the scenario that we introduced at the beginning of this chapter, youth felt that their rights and privileges had been violated, so they took it upon themselves, with support from a few teachers and parents, to go before the school board. As the parent of one of these youth, one of the authors was aware of the number of adults who were accessible to them as resources and from whom these youth had, on other occasions, sought guidance and assistance. When one student was asked why she sought the input and guidance of these adults, she responded that these adults listened to them, even when they did not agree with their views, and challenged them by asking clarifying questions to strengthen their arguments. But more important, she stated, was the fact that when the young people felt that their views were not being heard, these adults either helped them find their voices or became their spokespersons. In other words, these adults became advocates for the youth.

Another example of how youth and adults can (and should) work together in responding to issues that impact the developmental opportunities for youth can be noted in a recent policy report entitled "¿Dónde Está La Justicia?" (Villarruel & Walker, 2002). In this report, the authors provide data that illustrates that Latino communities, and their youth in particular, are increasingly singled out by the criminal justice system. Specifically, the report illustrates that harsh and disparate treatment at all stages of the justice system (including police stops, arrests, detentions, waivers to adult criminal court, and sentencings) is a grim reality for many Latinos. The authors note that these facts spell trouble for Latino youth, who are part of the largest and fastest-growing racial/ethnic group in the United States. To address these issues, the authors provide recommendations for how Latino communities, law enforcement professionals, youth, their parents, the justice system, advocates and grassroots organizers, public officials and policymakers, and researchers, both individually and collectively, must work together to provide positive developmental options for Latino youth.

As youth professionals, we might be wise to consider a similar approach to advancing the notion of community youth development both locally and nationally. Skills that effective adults need in working with youth in a positive developmental paradigm are discussed in Chapters 17 and 18. What is apparent, however, is that the role of the adult youth professional is somewhat indistinct. It shifts from educator to coach, from authority figure to an individual who provides opportunities for growth and development, and from keeper to advocate.

There is a disproportionate amount of focus and funding for community youth development initiatives compared to other life stages. This is not to argue that funding for other life stages (e.g., early childhood or senior citizens) is unimportant or even less important. It is, however, necessary to recognize that programs and opportunities that allow youth chances to become part of a community's leadership structure, let alone valued and recognized members of communities, are generally lacking and greatly needed.

Ironically, these two concepts—youth engagement and activism—suggest that the civic engagement of youth in our society is critical to changing our nation's recognition and development of skillful youth. In Chapter 13, Flanagan and Van Horn issue a strong challenge when they state,

> If the community youth development approach is to realize its full potential for nurturing the next generation of local and national leaders—of engaged, committed citizens—we need to take seriously the need for greater innovation in the development of new youth institutions that respond to and build on the wealth of assets of our increasingly diverse population of young people.

Perhaps the most succinct summary of the community youth development approach and the focus of this volume has been articulated by Karen Pittman (1999) of the Forum for Youth Investment: "Problem-free isn't fully prepared. And fully prepared isn't fully engaged." (para. 3). Being both fully prepared and fully engaged is necessary for youth and their development in their communities in order for them to become the future's effective leaders and involved world citizens.

❖ REFERENCES

Drizin, S. (2001). Arturo's case. In W. Ayers, B. Dohrn, & R. Ayers (Eds.), *Zero tolerance: Resisting the drive for punishment in our schools* (pp. 31-41). New York: New Press.

Lerner, R. M. (1995). *America's youth in crisis: Challenges and options for programs and policies.* Thousand Oaks, CA: Sage.

National Research Council. (2002). Community programs to promote youth development. Committee on community-level programs for youth. Board on Children, Youth, and Families, Division of Behavioral and Social Sciences and Education. Washington, DC: National Academy Press.

Perkins, D. F., Borden, L. M., & Villarruel, F. A. (2001). Community youth development: A plan for action. *School Community Journal, 11,* 39-56.

Pittman, K. (1999, September). The power of engagement. *Youth Today,* p. 63. Retrieved September 28, 2002, from www.forumforyouthinvestment. org/yt-powerengage.htm

Villarruel, F. A., & Walker, N. E. (2002). ¿Dónde Está La Justicia? A call to action on behalf of Latino and Latina youth in the U.S. Justice system. Washington, DC: Building Blocks for Youth. Retrieved September 28, 2002, from www.buildingblocksforyouth.org

Author Index

Subject Index

About the Contributors

Nicole Sigler Andrews is an independent consultant in Minnesota. She previously worked with the University of Minnesota Extension Service, Center for 4-H Youth Development, focusing on adolescent health issues. In that capacity, she worked with a USDA Cooperative Extension network—the Bridge for Adolescent Pregnancy, Parenting, and Sexuality (BAPPS)—that provides research-based resources to support community programs for youth and their families. She received her master's degree in family education at the University of Minnesota.

Cheryl K. Baldwin is Assistant Professor of Recreation Management in the School of Hotel, Restaurant, and Recreation Management at Penn State University. She earned her Ph.D. at the University of Illinois at Urbana-Champaign and an M.A. in recreation, park, and leisure studies at the University of Minnesota. Her research interests focus on adolescents' use of free time, adolescent motivation for leisure (art, sports, hobbies, and community activities), and the evaluation of community youth development programs. Ongoing research includes the examination of parent influences on adolescent leisure and program-theory-based evaluations of nonformal education settings.

Lynne M. Borden is Extension Specialist and Associate Professor for children, youth, and families in the School of Family Consumer Sciences at the University of Arizona. Her research relates to a young person's development, with a specific focus on community youth development, participation in out-of-school time, community programs that promote the positive development of young people, and public policy. Her work includes working with communities to strengthen their community-based programs through evaluation and training. Specifically, her research is focused on assessing the influence of youth programs on the developmental trajectory of young people.

She currently cochairs the Research on Adolescence's Special Interest Group on Out-of-School Time as a Context for Development.

David Brown is Executive Director of the National Youth Employment Coalition (NYEC). His current work includes spearheading NYEC's policy work, tracking implementation of the Workforce Investment Act across the nation, and leading an effort to connect youth employment and juvenile justice. Prior to joining NYEC, he was a senior policy analyst with the National Governors' Association, where he focused on youth-related state policy issues. Over the past 22 years, he has benefited from a range of youth policy and program experiences within both public and nonprofit youth-serving organizations at the national, state, and local levels.

Linda L. Caldwell is Professor of Recreation and Park Management and Professor in Charge of Research for the School of Hotel, Restaurant, and Recreation Management at Pennsylvania State University. Much of her research has centered on adolescents, leisure, and health; she is particularly interested in leisure education, prevention research, and the developmental aspects of leisure. Currently, she is the lead investigator on an NIDA-funded substance use prevention program that helps middle school youth learn to use their leisure time wisely. She also is involved with several international projects that focus on developing youth competencies and healthy lifestyles through leisure.

Marsha Carolan is Associate Professor of Family Studies and Program Director of marriage and family therapy in the Department of Family and Child Ecology, Michigan State University. She received her doctoral degree from Virginia Tech and her master's degree from the University of Connecticut. Her current research interests are in areas related to families and health, including diabetes risk and prevalence in children and adolescents and prevention of eating disorders in youth. In 2001, she received a distinguished Teacher-Scholar Award from Michigan State University.

Tamara C. Cheshire is Adjunct Faculty in the Department of Anthropology at Sacramento City College. Her interests lie in American Indian education and tribal sovereignty issues as well as in developing online courses. She is currently teaching a course called "Native Peoples of California" and two courses on the Native American experience.

Edward DeJesus serves as a consultant on youth issues for the U.S. Department of Labor, the Annie E. Casey Foundation, the National Youth Employment Coalition, the New York Association of Training and Employment Professionals, YouthBuild USA, and *The Source* magazine. He has addressed more than 700 youth service organizations and community groups, as well as more than 75,000 young adults. He has worked with the National Youth Employment Coalition to conduct research on effective programs that help youth acquire and maintain jobs. As a member of the Sar Levitan Center for Youth Policies at John Hopkins University and while serving on the Task Force on Employment Opportunities for young offenders for the U.S. Office of Juvenile Justice and Delinquency Prevention, he increased awareness among policymakers of the needs of out-of-school youth. He is the President and Founder of the Youth Development and Research Fund, Inc. (YDRF), a leading authority on urban youth employment and educational issues.

Jill Denner is Senior Research Associate at Education, Training, and Research Associates (ETR), a nonprofit health education agency. She uses research-based knowledge to inform the design and evaluation of school and community-based interventions for adolescents, and to evaluate and build the evaluation capacity of community-based agencies. Her current research interests are in gender roles, HIV prevention, and the role of youth in increasing educational equity. She received her Ph.D. in developmental psychology from Columbia University.

Theresa M. Ferrari is Assistant Professor and Extension Specialist with Ohio State University Extension 4-H Youth Development. Her 22-year career in extension has included both county- and state-level positions in Maine, Michigan, and Florida. The current focus of her work is expanding 4-H programs through after-school delivery models and conducting research on positive youth development in out-of-school time. She serves on the National 4-H Afterschool Leadership Team and Ohio State's P-12 Initiative. In addition, she teaches courses on youth programs in the Department of Human and Community Resource Development and advises graduate students in extension education. She received her Ph.D. in family and child ecology from Michigan State University in 1998.

Constance Flanagan is Professor of Youth Civic Development at Penn State University. She completed her Ph.D. in developmental psychology at the University of Michigan. Her work in the area of adolescents and the social contract concerns the factors in families, schools, and communities that promote civic values and competencies in young people. She directed a seven-nation study on this topic as well as a study of intergroup relations and beliefs about justice among youth from different racial/ethnic backgrounds in the United States. Two new projects include a longitudinal study of peer loyalty and social responsibility as it relates to teens' views about health as a public or private issue and to their inclinations to intervene to prevent harm to one another, and a study of the developmental correlates of social trust. She cochairs the Society for Research in Child Development's Committee on Public Policy and Public Information. She is a William T. Grant Faculty Scholar and a member of the MacArthur Foundation's Network on the Transition to Adulthood and Public Policy. She is on the advisory boards of Health Rocks!, Student Voices, and CIRCLE (the Center for Information and Research on Civic Learning and Engagement).

Jeff Frommeyer is a social worker for Hospice of Holland Home in Grand Rapids, Michigan. He received his joint master's degree in administrative social work and urban studies from Michigan State University in 2001. He has worked in a variety of intergenerational community settings that promote community, youth, and family well-being, including serving as Coordinator of the Mayor's Youth Advisory Committee in a large metropolitan area. He coordinated community development policy initiatives including the Kent County Homeless Study and served as the first editor of the *Journal of Community Exploration* sponsored by the Michigan State University Urban Affairs Student Association.

Amy Griffin is a doctoral student in the Department of Family and Child Ecology at Michigan State University. Her research interests include youth and community asset development, program evaluation, and measurement of youth development concepts. She also works as a program evaluation consultant for nonprofit organizations concerning youth development. She has an M.A. in Interpersonal Communication from Michigan State University.

Tianna L. Hoppe-Rooney is a doctoral candidate at Michigan State University in the Marriage and Family Therapy Program. She is interested in the area of disordered eating and body image disturbances among adolescents through a family systems and ecological paradigm. She is working with the City of East Lansing to develop and implement an after-school counseling program to offer strengths-based life enhancement groups for adolescents, targeting the transition through puberty and self-image. In addition, she is researching the effectiveness of an innovative prevention program for disordered eating among preteen girls.

Melissa S. Quon Huber is Research Associate at Michigan State University, jointly appointed in the Community and Youth Development Program in the Department of Family and Child Ecology, the Community and Economic Development Program, and the Department of Psychology. She received her Ph.D. in ecological/community psychology at Michigan State University. Her research has focused on youth advocacy in community and school-based initiatives. She has been a volunteer for various community youth leadership groups and has 10 years of experience in evaluating community and educational initiatives that affect families and their children. She recently received a University/Community Partnership award from the Michigan Neighborhood Partnership for research conducted in Detroit. Her research has been published in the *Journal of Community, Work, and Family* and in the *Academy of Management Executive.*

Angela J. Huebner is Assistant Professor and Extension Specialist in the Department of Human Development at Virginia Tech, housed at the Northern Virginia Center in Falls Church. She is a community-based action researcher; her work focuses on helping communities to understand and assess the risk and protective factors found in their local youth and in designing programs to meet specific needs for adolescents. She completed her undergraduate degree in psychology at the University of Nebraska at Lincoln and her master's and doctoral degrees in family studies at the University of Arizona in Tucson.

Walter T. Kawamoto is Assistant Professor in the Family and Consumer Sciences Department at California State University, Sacramento. His graduate work included an NIMH-sponsored study conducted with the assistance of the Confederated Tribes of Siletz Indians of Oregon. He also teaches a course at CSUS focusing on indigenous families. He was a member of the American Indian–Alaska Native Head Start Research and Outcomes Assessment Advisory Panel.

Joanne G. Keith is Professor and Extension Specialist in the Department of Family and Child Ecology, Michigan State University. Her scholarship includes integration of research, teaching, and outreach related to community youth development. Current research includes an assets-based approach to positive youth development from elementary school age through college; demographic trends related to children, youth, and families; and community collaborations on behalf of children, youth, and their families. She works with graduate students, faculty, and communities on approaches to community youth development. She is the faculty cochair of a committee to develop an online graduate degree and certificates in youth development in collaboration with the Great Plains Idea, a consortium of 10 land grant universities. The youth development degree and certificates are scheduled to go online in the fall of 2003.

Cathryn Maddalena is an outreach specialist for Michigan State University's Projects for Community Inclusion, a position that she has held for 15 years. She assisted in the development of the Employment Training Specialist Certification curriculum used in Michigan and Indiana to train and certify supported employment personnel. She has collaborated on a variety of research and demonstration projects with the Developmental Disabilities Institute at Wayne State University and the Institute for Disability and Community at Indiana University. She currently provides training and technical assistance to community rehabilitation organizations, mental health agencies, and schools concerned with the transition of students from school to community life across Michigan. She is also a researcher involved in collecting data related to psychosocial rehabilitation for individuals with mental illness.

Sarah Maxwell is a Ph.D. candidate in the School of Public Policy at George Mason University (GMU). She has taught courses in the Administration of Justice Program, Department of Public and International Affairs, at GMU. Before entering the doctoral program, she received a number of federal and state grants that provide funds for youth employment programs. She was instrumental in organizing a federal task force on employment and training for court-involved youth and also serves as a consultant for the National Youth Employment Coalition.

Diana Morrobel is a staff psychologist at the Rafael Tavares Hispanic Mental Health Clinic at Columbia-Presbyterian Medical Center in New York City. She received her Ph.D. in clinical psychology from Michigan

State University in 2001. Her research interests focus on Latinos in the United States, with a particular interest in HIV antibody testing and other health-promoting behaviors among Latinas, Latino youth development, attitudes toward mental illness, and acculturation. Her clinical work involves performing clinical assessments and providing psychotherapy to monolingual Spanish-speaking adults and families in a predominantly Latino community in New York City. Most recently, her clinical experiences have led her to pursue research that explores the clinical manifestations and treatment of anxiety and depression among Dominicans. She has lectured on performing research with Latinos and has also consulted on cultural issues pertinent to counseling and treatment.

Edna Olive is Founder and Executive Director of ROCKET, Inc. (Reaching Our Children with Knowledge, Expertise, and Teaching), which provides consultation, training, and advocacy to organizations and professionals serving children and youth. In 1994, she received an Ed.D. in special education, with a focus on emotional and behavioral disorders, from George Washington University. As an educator with over 20 years of experience, she has served in a number of professional capacities including teacher, state education officer, principal, director, curriculum developer, and adjunct professor. She has developed and managed therapeutic treatment and educational programs for troubled youth and adolescents throughout the Washington, D.C., and Greater Metropolitan areas. She is a certified national senior trainer in Life Space Crisis Intervention (LSCI) and serves on the Board of Directors for Reclaiming Youth International in Sioux Falls, South Dakota.

Esther Onaga is Associate Professor in the Department of Family and Child Ecology at Michigan State University. She is currently Chair of the Disability Interest Group of the Society for Community Research and Action. She is Principal Investigator for a project on inclusive recreation for children and youth with disabilities. Her work in the community includes being a parent trainer for the Parent Training Information Center for Michigan and a member of the Parent Advisory Committee at the local school level.

Karen L. Pace is a program leader for Diversity and Multicultural Education with Michigan State University Extension's Children, Youth, and Family Programs. She has created educational programs and curricula for nearly 20 years for people who work with and care about young people. She teaches and facilitates workshops and training programs in communities across Michigan and across the country on issues of character education, diversity and multiculturalism, bullying prevention and social justice education. She is also part of the national faculty for CHARACTER COUNTS! (a nonpartisan, community-driven effort that brings diverse people and organizations together on issues of character education). She holds a master's degree in family and child ecology from Michigan State University and has completed extensive learning in social justice education through the Institute for Intercultural Communications; Cultural Bridges; VISIONS, Inc.; the Leaven Center; and the Healing Racism Institute.

Daniel F. Perkins is Associate Professor and Extension Specialist of Family and Youth Resiliency and Policy in the Department of Agricultural and Extension Education at Pennsylvania State University. He received a Ph.D. in family and child ecology in 1995 from Michigan State University. His research examines factors and assets related to a young person's development, including youth engagement in positive opportunities during out-of-school time, strengths-based programming, and family and youth resiliency. His work also includes the evaluation of community-based programs, and he is currently evaluating several violence prevention programs. He provides leadership to the Statewide Children, Youth and Families at Risk Program and travels extensively around the state working with Family and Consumer Sciences and 4-H Youth Development agents on issues related to children, youth, and families.

Jean E. Rhodes is Professor of Psychology at the University of Massachusetts in Boston. She received her Ph.D. in clinical/community psychology from DePaul University. For over a decade, she has conducted research on the mentoring of children and adolescents, including an extensive analysis of the Big Brothers Big Sisters national impact study. In addition, she has explored the influence that natural and assigned mentors have on adolescent mothers. She is a Fellow in the American Psychological Association and a member of the MacArthur Foundation Research Network on the Transition to Adulthood. She has published a book and many articles and chapters on the topic of youth mentoring.

Michael C. Rodriguez is Assistant Professor of Measurement, Evaluation, and Statistics in the Educational Psychology Department at the University of Minnesota. He received his Ph.D. in measurement and quantitative methods at Michigan State University and an M.A. in public affairs at the Humphrey Institute of Public Affairs, University of Minnesota. His current research addresses large-scale test design, item writing, and reliability theory. He also has substantive research interests in Latino youth development and conducts methodological research in the evaluation of youth development programs. He is currently validating several youth development program evaluation instruments with Spanish-speaking immigrant youth.

Jennifer G. Roffman is a postdoctoral research fellow in the Department of Psychology at the University of Massachusetts, Boston. She received a Ph.D. in human development and social policy from Northwestern University in 2000. Her work focuses on the impact of mentors and other significant nonparental adults on youth well-being.

Stephen T. Russell is Director of the 4-H Center for Youth Development at the University of California, Davis, in the Department of Human and Community Development. He completed his Ph.D. in sociology at Duke University in 1994 and is a William T. Grant Foundation Scholar (2001-2006). His research focuses on adolescent sexuality development and the health and well-being of sexual minority youth. He leads a national USDA Cooperative Extension network—the Bridge for Adolescent Pregnancy, Parenting, and Sexuality (BAPPS)—that provides research-based resources to support community programs for youth and their families.

Jennifer Sazama is Codirector of Youth on Board. Since the age of 11, she has led hundreds of workshops on youth voice, youth power, and improving relationships between young people and adults, both nationally and as far away as South Africa. Prior to joining Youth on Board, she established and directed Youth in Action (a program designed to organize and empower teens to take leadership in their neighborhoods) at the Villa Victoria youth center in Boston's South End. In 1993, she founded the Resource Center for Youth and Their Allies, a nonprofit organization that coordinates ongoing support groups for youth workers, disabled young people, teen mothers, and other groups. She has also authored or coauthored 10 publications pertaining to youth involvement. She currently serves as vice president of the Re-evaluation Foundation and as a foundation board member for the Church Home Society.

Vincent Schiraldi is Founder and President of the Justice Policy Institute (JPI) and former President of the Center on Juvenile and

Criminal Justice (CJCJ). He has conducted cutting-edge criminal justice research and media advocacy. He has authored numerous studies on topics including race and incarceration, the tradeoff between prison and university spending, and school violence and media coverage of juvenile crime, among others. He has also been featured on national television, radio, and in print media discussing and debating emerging justice issues and has published numerous commentaries on adult and juvenile justice.

Carola Suárez-Orozco is Executive Director of the David Rockefeller Center for Latin American Studies at Harvard. She is also Coprincipal Investigator of a longitudinal, interdisciplinary study at the Harvard Graduate School of Education, examining the adaptation of Central American, Chinese, Dominican, Haitian, and Mexican youth. Her research focus in recent years has been on the intersection of cultural and psychological factors in the adaptation of immigrant and ethnic minority children, with particular focus on Latino youth. She has conducted research in the United States as well as in Mexico and Argentina.

Beth Van Horn is an educator for Penn State Cooperative Extension. She completed her Ph.D. in the Department of Agricultural and Extension Education at Pennsylvania State University. Her research focuses on youth civic involvement in community groups.

Francisco A. Villarruel is Associate Professor in the Department of Family and Child Ecology and a research associate in the Institute for Children, Youth, and Families (ICYF) at Michigan State University. He is also affiliated with the Julian Samora Research Institute (JSRI), which is committed to the generation, transmission, and application of knowledge to serve the needs of Latino communities in the Midwest. He earned his Ph.D. in human development at the University of Wisconsin—Madison. His research interests focus on Latino youth and families, community youth development, and policies that promote the well-being of youth. He is the recipient of several awards, including the W. K. Kellogg National Fellowship, an ETS-HACU Policy Fellowship, and the CIC-ALP Fellowship. He is also coauthor of *¿Dónde está la justicia? A call to action on behalf of Latino and Latina youth in the U.S. justice system* (July, 2002), the first national analysis of Latino and Latina youth in the juvenile justice system.

Joyce A. Walker is Professor and Youth Development Educator at the Center for 4-H Youth Development, University of Minnesota. She coordinates the Youth Development Leadership M.Ed., a professional studies program in the College of Education and Human Development, and is Project Director for the Minnesota Youth Work Institute. Her work on organizational approaches to youth development, community youth policy, and youth worker professional development reflect her priorities for substantive bridging of research and practice. Her Ph.D. in adult education is from the University of Minnesota.

Amy Weisenbach is an M.B.A. student at Harvard Business School. A long-time advocate for youth participation, she founded the At the Table initiative at the Innovation Center for Community and Youth Development. (At the Table is a collaborative effort that aims to increase youth participation and hosts the online clearinghouse www.AtTheTable.org.) While in college, she served on the boards of a number of nonprofit organizations, including the National 4-H Council, where she helped to increase the number of youth members on the board.

Nicole Yohalem is Manager of Learning and Research of the Forum for Youth Investment. Previously, she served as Youth Development Specialist at Michigan State University, where she developed, implemented, supported, and evaluated community-based youth programs in the Cooperative Extension Service. She also served as Extension Educator at MSU, developing 4-H programs that serve urban youth. From 1990 to 1995, she worked in the adolescent division of the High/Scope Educational Research Foundation, where she staffed and later directed the foundation's residential programs for teens while developing training materials for use in a wide range of youth programs. She received her M.Ed. from the Harvard Graduate School of Education in its multidisciplinary risk and prevention program.